September in the Rain

The Life of Nelson Riddle

September in the Rain

The Life of Nelson Riddle

Peter J. Levinson

Taylor Trade Publishing

Lanham • Boulder • New York • Toronto • Oxford

Published by Taylor Trade Publishing
An imprint of The Rowman & Littlefield Publishing Group, Inc.
4501 Forbes Boulevard, Suite 200, Lanham, Maryland 20706

Distributed by NATIONAL BOOK NETWORK

Library of Congress Cataloging-in-Publication Data
1-58979-163-0

∞^TM The paper used in this publication meets the minimum requirements of American National Standard for Information Sciences—Permanence of Paper for Printed Library Materials, ANSI/NISO Z39.48-1992.

Manufactured in the United States of America.

This book is dedicated to the peerless musicianship of Nelson Riddle's "regulars," and to all those who recorded with him.

Contents

Acknowledgments

RESEARCHING THE LIFE OF NELSON RIDDLE was not an easy task. Except for several books on Frank Sinatra in which Nelson prominently figured, there had been practically nothing published regarding Nelson's work with other major singers, much less anything concerning his musical background or his life.

Early on in this process, however, I received a phone call from Rosemary Acerra, the oldest of Nelson's four daughters. We first met at the Frank Sinatra Conference at Hofstra University in November 1998. Without her consistently intelligent suggestions and kind and forthright assistance, I simply would not have been able to write this book.

I must also thank Chris Riddle, Nelson's second-oldest son, who leads the Nelson Riddle Orchestra. His enthusiasm, his pride in his father's work, and his willingness to share so many reminiscences were of tremendous importance to my book.

I would be lax if I did not also acknowledge the help of Nelson's other children: Skip Riddle, Tina Bellini, Cecily Finnegan, and Dr. Maureen Riddle. They were always completely candid and happy to be of help.

I want to especially thank Charlie Briggs and the eminent arranger Bill Finegan. These two gentlemen first recognized Nelson Riddle's talent back in 1937 in Rumson, New Jersey. Charlie's diligence enabled me to get in touch with various musicians who had played with Nelson in "kid bands" during this period. Going back even further, retired *Milwaukee Journal* editor Dick Leonard was able to describe the childhood he shared with Nelson, while Nelson's first cousin, Bob Runyon, provided the anecdotes and insight that revealed the kind of home and parenting that molded Nelson's personality.

The contributions of Nelson's "regulars"—the musicians who worked with him for decades in the recording studios—provided the color surrounding the enduring recordings he made. Foremost among them are Bob Bain and George Roberts. They are not only superb musicians but also Nelson's very close friends. I cannot forget, however, the generosity of Don Raffell, Emil Richards, Vince De Rosa, Milt Bernhart, Buddy Collette, George Werth, Champ Webb, Lloyd Ulyate, and Rick Baptist.

Sid Cooper and Buddy DeFranco were especially helpful in describing the very fulfilling year Nelson spent with Tommy Dorsey's band. The brilliant composer and arranger

Johnny Mandel described the impact of Dorsey's band. Both Mandel and Bill Finegan explained how Dorsey's ace arranger Sy Oliver influenced Nelson's writing career.

Frank Sinatra, Jr.'s comments and recollections were especially valuable. He not only was of great assistance in providing me with information about his father's work with Nelson, but the tremendous respect and love that he had for Nelson was also evident.

Music publisher Ivan Mogull was helpful in several ways. He brought many great songs to Nat Cole and witnessed many of the immortal recordings that Nat and Nelson made together. I must also thank Ivan's cousin, Artie Mogull, as well as Dominic Mumolo and especially André Previn, for giving me, among other things, an understanding of Nelson's problems with Les Baxter during his initial recordings with Nat. The generous help given by Nat Cole's widow, Maria, as well as their daughters Natalie and Carol, cannot be overlooked.

I would be remiss if I failed to mention the aid provided by other music publishers Jeff Sultanof and Frank Military. Along with Rosemary Acerra and Chris Riddle, it was Military who helped open the window to the discovery of the comeback album Frank Sinatra and Nelson Riddle planned, which came too late, as Nelson unfortunately passed away before it could be recorded.

I want to also especially thank author Jon Burlingame for the countless ways he helped me discover much about Nelson's television and film-scoring work. He and the composers Elmer Bernstein and Walter Scharf made it possible for me to evaluate Nelson's work in this field. Eddie Forsyth contributed a clear picture of Nelson's first excursions into weekly television on *Naked City* and *Route 66.*

Ira Koslow provided me a total understanding and appreciation of the challenges involved when Linda Ronstadt first wanted to record an album of standards with Nelson. Ira also facilitated my interview with Linda as well as those with other people who were important participants in these recordings.

My thanks go also to Keith Pawlak, Dr. Rob Cutietta, Gary Cook, Jim Taylor, Joe Swinson, and Mia Schnaible at the University of Arizona School of Music and Dance, where the Nelson Riddle Archives is now located. I appreciate their cooperation as well as the various courtesies they extended to me.

I would also like to acknowledge the tremendous assistance given me by Alan Wright, who a few years ago in England started *Nelson's Notes,* a regularly published magazine that continues to chronicle Nelson's many musical contributions. Alan was always available, cheerful, and willing to help. I must also thank Alan's good friend Vic Lewis, Nelson's longtime English business representative, who provided valuable information.

Others I would like to thank are Paul Atkinson, Judi Bain, Richy Barz, Lou Brown, Trish Deaton, Digby Diehl, Alan Eichler, Ed Ezor, Carmen Fanzone, Chris Farnon, Hal Gaba, Madeleine Gabriel, Rosemarie Gawelko, Gregg Geller, Todd Gold, April Gow, Fred Grimes, Terry Gross, Joe Harnell, David Horowitz, Chuck Hurewitz, Wayne Hutchison, Kat Johl, Audree Kenton, Ann King, Mauri Lathower,

Merri Lieberthal, Tom Morgan, Dan Morgenstern, Stephanie Murray, Sujata Murthy, Maria Niemela, Ryan Null, Jordan Ramin, Dr. Michael Reynard, Ric Ross, Robert Scott, Jerry Sharell, Paul Shefrin, Gwen Shepard, Mike Swanson, Judy Tanen, Dolly Vannelli, Ridge Walker, Judy West, Mike Wilpezewski, Dick Winters, Bob Woods, and Shelly Wright.

Once again, I can never repay the invaluable help provided by my two assistants, Anita Coolidge and Julie Compton. Anita's unique patience and dedication as well as her keen literary judgment were of constant help during the writing of *September in the Rain*. Julie's intelligence and nonstop good humor—even via e-mail from London—while preparing the transcripts were extremely important. My thanks also go to Sasha Goodman, my very capable agent, and to Bob Nirkind and Sarah Fass at Billboard Books, who I found to be extremely helpful and focused editors; they were always conscious of what was best for my book. Eric Levin at *People* magazine introduced me to the noted author Joan Peyser, who, in turn, arranged my introduction to Bob Nirkind. I thank both of them for that. My apologies to anyone I have inadvertently overlooked.

The love and sense of humor of Grace Diekhaus, my wife for the last eighteen years, helped me throughout the writing of this book. She remains the high point of my life. My gratitude extends to my late parents, who, each in their own way, instilled in me the love of the arts and the strong sense of purpose that remain within me.

I interviewed the following people in researching and writing *September in the Rain: The Life of Nelson Riddle*: Rosemary Acerra, Berle Adams, Richard Adler, Anna Maria Alberghetti, Van Alexander, Ray Anthony, Julie Andrews, Peter Asher, Sid Avery, Eddie Bailey, Bob Bain, Buddy Baker, Rick Baptist, Louise Baranger, Tino Barzie, Bettina Bellini, Louie Bellson, Max Bennett, the late Fred Benson, Alan Bergman, Mike Berkowitz, Milt Bernhart, Elmer Bernstein, Edna Mae Blind, Ray Briem, Charlie Briggs, Alan Broadbent, Laurie Brooks, the late Les Brown, Lou Brown, Ray Brown, Ralph Burns, Artie Butler, Marvin Cane, Pauline Canny, the late Frankie Carle, Ralph Carmichael, Benny Carter, Ernie Chambers, Mahlon Clark, Maria Cole, Natalie Cole, Buddy Collette, John Collins, Sid Cooper, Don Comstock, Jack Costanzo, Warren Cowan, Buddy DeFranco, Vince De Rosa, Donfeld, Jane Dorsey, Dennis Dragon, the late George Duning, Lois Duning, Larry Elgart, Herb Ellis, Barbara Ernest, Ed Ezor, Carol Faith, Sy Feldman, Manuel Felix, Rob Fentress, Gregg Field, Bill Finegan, Cecily Finnegan, Bob Flanagan, Frank Flynn, Salvatore "Tuttie" Fontana, Eddie Forsyth, Ian Fraser, Johnny Fresco, Al Gallico, Nat Garrantano, Sid Garris, Terry Gibbs, Hershel Gilbert, April Gow, Fred Grimes, Marilyn Gripenwaldt, John Guerin, Earle Hagen, Corky Hale, Marie Hammond, Bill Harbach, Jack Hayes, Walt Heebner, Mitch Holder, Bill Holman, Paul Horn, Saul Ilson, Sue and Bob Iwasaki, Norm Jeffries, Carol Kaye, Bob Keane, Paul Keyes, the late Howard W. Koch, Ira Koslow, Sandy Krinski, Mike Lang, Ronny Lang, Mauri Lathower, Elliot Lawrence, Steve Lawrence, Dick Leonard, Al Lerner, the late Lou Levy, Stan Levey, Mark Lewis, Vic Lewis, Berwyn Linton, Jay

Livingston, Alan Livingston, Ray "Butch" Long, Sid Luft, Gisele Mackenzie, Bob Magnusson, Laura Mako, Ginny Mancini, Monica Mancini, Johnny Mandel, Barry Manilow, Bob Mann, Delbert Mann, Paul Mantee, Dick Martin, Al Martino, George Massenburg, Johnny Mathis, Billy May, Mike Melvoin, the late Tommy Mercer, Wilfred Middlebrooke, Frank Military, Bill Miller, Mitch Miller, Ivan Mogull, Artie Mogull, Tom Morgan, Jack Mozzaroppi, Dick Nash, Ted Nash, Bob Newhart, Dominic Mumolo, Larry O'Brien, Father James O'Callaghan, Anita O'Day, Stephen Paley, John Palladino, Jane Powell, André Previn, Gene Puerling, Donald Quimby, David Raksin, Don Raffell, Sue Raney, Uan Rasey, Helen Reddy, Emil Richards, Bill Richmond, Chris Riddle, Maureen Riddle, Skip Riddle, George Roberts, Linda Ronstadt, Betty Rose, the late Arnold Ross, Ric Ross, Johnny Rotella, the late Mickey Rudin, Pete Rugolo, Bob Runyon, George Russell, Eva Marie Saint, Tommy Sands, Walter Scharf, Al Schmidt, Kenny Schroyer, Peggy Schwartz, F. M. Scott, Nick Sevano, Bud Shank, Artie Shaw, George Shearing, Tom Sheils, Sandi Shoemake, Allen Sides, Ray Sims, Frank Sinatra, Jr., Joe Smith, Paul Smith, Tommy Smothers, Gary Stevens, Jeff Sultanof, Tony Terran, Ed Thigpen, Alphonso "Funzy" Tomaino, Ed Townsend, Lloyd Ulyate, Bob Van Etten, Danny Vannelli, Gerry Vinci, Al Viola, Ivins Voorhees, Bill Watrous, Champ Webb, Sheila Wells, Chauncey Welsch, George Werth, Terry Woodson, Margaret Whiting, Andy Williams, John Williams, Gerald Wilson, John Wisniewski, Allan Wright, Lee Young, and Bud Yorkin.

Preface

Hey kids, dig the first takes,
Ain't that some interpretation?
When Sinatra sings against Nelson Riddle strings
Then takes a vacation.
　　　　　　　—Van Morrison, "Hard Nose the Highway"

WHEN I BEGAN MY CAREER in the music business in November 1958, my two foremost musical heroes were Frank Sinatra and Nelson Riddle. Over the next few years, as I got to know these supremely gifted artists personally, I sensed that one of the things that seemed to connect them was loneliness; it was certainly one of the prime ingredients in the nonpareil mournful ballads created by the two North Jerseyites. In time, I discovered that many of the most talented artists were also the loneliest. It was they who often contributed the most enduring music.

During the the 1991 PBS special *The Voice of Our Time,* the late Mel Tormé observed, "Frank Sinatra was singing to us and about us." As the musical architect of the singer's amazing Lazarus-like comeback in 1953, the unflappable Riddle created the musical backgrounds and helped set the moods for Sinatra during the 1950s—his most artistically successful recording period—and for much of the following two decades. Riddle's association with "The Voice" deservedly earned him a sterling reputation and afforded him the opportunity to pursue what became a thriving career as a film and television composer.

Shortly after Sinatra died on May 14, 1998, it occurred to me that there was a worthwhile book in Nelson's life. As I began researching the project, I found that this biography would not only be the story of an important musical craftsman, but would also show how Nelson's talent helped to shape an era of music which virtually ended in the early 1960s.

The zeitgeist of the period from the mid-1930s to the 1950s dictated that many young musicians and singers spend an exacting apprenticeship playing in big bands on an endless skein of one-nighters. Stars weren't born, but as a result of this difficult apprenticeship, those with innate ability and dedication often developed lasting careers.

As it happened, both Frank Sinatra and Nelson Riddle emerged from this vaunted era of the great dance bands. Both of them honed their musical careers while working for the same demanding bandleader, Tommy Dorsey, their tenures separated by less than two years. Riddle adapted Dorsey's brand of swing and brought it into a more modern context, utilizing combinations of such instruments as muted trumpets, the bass trombone, flutes, French horns, and strings to create his unmistakable sound.

This era ended abruptly with the first appearance of the Beatles on the *Ed Sullivan Show* on February 9, 1964. A new music was suddenly at hand, reflecting the convictions as well as the frustrations of a new generation and propelled by an insistent, pounding rhythm. Then, magically, in the early 1980s, Riddle's arrangements for Linda Ronstadt, contained in the three highly successful albums on which they collaborated, revived his career.

Today, many fail to remember that it was Nelson's work with Nat "King" Cole that provided Cole with his initial acclaim within the music industry. His series of beautifully written ballad arrangements for the singer began with such epic records as "Mona Lisa," "Too Young," and "Unforgettable." Surprising to some, their association encompassed thirty-eight more records than Nelson arranged for Sinatra.

Following his first records with Cole, Nelson became Capitol Records's "house arranger," writing for the emerging label's stars—Peggy Lee, Margaret Whiting, Ella Mae Morse, Judy Garland, Dean Martin, and seventeen others. Inevitably, he began an association with Ella Fitzgerald. The meaningful collaboration started auspiciously with their definitive five-volume George Gershwin "songbook." Six other albums followed.

There is absolutely no doubt that Nelson Riddle was endowed with true musical genius. Unfortunately, however, so many people I interviewed observed that he was a failure at life, making one mistake after another.

Nelson grew up emotionally malnourished, the only child of a deeply troubled marriage between his mother, Albertine, who had been raised in a European aristocratic atmosphere, and his father, the amiable but unmotivated Nelson Smock Riddle, who she treated like a football—someone to kick around. The sadness that permeated Nelson's childhood stayed with him and caused him to develop a sardonic outlook on life. This was one reason I titled my book *September in the Rain*. The title also refers to one of the foremost arrangements Nelson wrote for Frank Sinatra.

Nelson's first marriage to Doreen Moran resulted in seven children, one of whom died in infancy. His frequent philandering, coupled with Doreen's excessive drinking, caused insoluble problems in the first decade of their marriage. When he became the musical director of the television show hosted by Rosemary Clooney, another important pop singer, he began a serious affair with her, which led to a catastrophic marital situation that ultimately ended in his 1969 divorce. Three months later he married Naomi Tenen, his dedicated secretary, because, as he described it, "I owe it to her."

Tenen had herself endured a deprived childhood as one of two daughters of a selfish and distant stage and film actor. After entering into marriage for the first time at the age of forty-nine, she expressed her disdain for Nelson's children and barred them from their household. She did not want them to enjoy advantages she had never had. Reliving his own home life as a child and afraid to "rock the boat," Nelson reluctantly went along with Naomi's wishes.

In the way that life often influences art, these depressing life experiences had a profound effect on the moving arrangements he wrote for Frank Sinatra in their *In the Wee Small Hours* and *Only the Lonely* masterpieces.

I first met Nelson Riddle in the winter of 1962 when I interviewed him for a profile in *Los Angeles Magazine*. Weeks later, when I was offered a job by a Hollywood public relations firm, I tried to convince him to hire a publicist (namely me). After meeting a few times to discuss the situation, he decided not to go along with my proposal. Ultimately, this decision to not hire me or any other publicist proved to be detrimental to the furtherance of his career. But making wrong career decisions plagued him throughout his life; as one musician noted, "He never realized he was NELSON RIDDLE."

Nelson finally emerged from two decades of relative anonymity when Linda Ronstadt recognized the importance of his musical heritage and chose him to help her revisit some of the most enduring pop music standards. She brought him out of the limited scope of his recording studio existence and onto the concert stage to work with her in the United States, Australia, and Japan, giving him exposure before a young audience who had barely known his work, or, if it had, had dismissed it as being part of "older people's music." His revival proved to be short-lived, however, as Nelson died before the third Ronstadt album was completed, while starting work on an (until now) completely unknown new project with Frank Sinatra.

★ ★ ★

America has once again adopted the music of its young African Americans, this time with the hip-hop rage. But Messrs. Armstrong, Ellington, and Parker, and Ms. Smith and Ms. Holiday, helped to change the face of popular music forever with jazz, which emphasized improvisation working off the sometimes melodic base of the blues. Today, melody is almost nonexistent in the predominant genres of pop music. During the late 1960s and '70s, when rock reigned supreme, Nelson often suffered from a lack of work. Now, in the age of Eminem, there would be absolutely no place for him.

It is certainly true that in the last few decades, as a country we have lost all sense of history and its importance. In addition, we have always been guilty of building up our gifted artists, then systematically tearing them down and dispensing with them as their music is swept aside by the music of the emerging generation. Perhaps all of this indicates that America is still a new land with little regard for its musical heritage.

I can only hope that *September in the Rain* will create a new appreciation for the music and contributions of Nelson Riddle. If it leads to his gaining some of the stature he deserved but never managed to attain during his lifetime, I shall have succeeded.

PETER J. LEVINSON
Malibu, California, May 2001

Photo courtesy of the Nelson Riddle Memorial Library at the University of Arizona School of Music and Dance, Tucson, Arizona, and the Naomi Riddle Estate.

CHAPTER 1

The Jersey Years

Ya know, all those years I never saw Nelson smile or laugh," remarked Emil Richards, a vibraharpist and percussionist who recorded frequently under Nelson's leadership for two decades. "He just seemed to be an unhappy kind of guy." Richards was not alone in feeling this way; his sentiment is shared by many others who recall the gloom and unhappiness that characterized Nelson Riddle's life.

Nelson's somber outlook flew in the face of the fact that he had established an impeccable reputation for the consistency of the sophisticated and impressionistic musical arrangements he wrote for the foremost pop and jazz singers of the twentieth century—Frank Sinatra, Ella Fitzgerald, and Nat "King" Cole—during his almost fifty-year career. He maintained his negative attitude despite the fact that he had written brilliant arrangements for over two dozen other important vocalists, including Judy Garland, Peggy Lee, Johnny Mathis, Rosemary Clooney, Steve Lawrence, rock star Linda Ronstadt, and opera star Kiri Te Kanawa. (With his help, Ronstadt and Te Kanawa successfully crossed over into classic popular music.) This was even stranger given the Oscar he received in 1975 for *The Great Gatsby* (a gold album), his four other Academy Award nominations (for *Li'l Abner, Can-Can, Robin and the Seven Hoods,* and *Paint Your Wagon*—also a gold album), and the total of forty films he scored overall. Among Nelson's other achievements were two hit instrumental records of his own, "Lisbon Antigua" (#1 on the *Billboard* pop chart and a gold record) and "Route 66," the theme of one of several television series he scored, beginning with *Naked City,* including *The Smothers Brothers Comedy Hour* and *The Julie Andrews Hour,* and ending with the third Bob Newhart show. This was in addition to his seven Emmy Award nominations, which included one for his score for the first miniseries, *The Blue Knight* starring William Holden. And it was notwithstanding the three Grammys that Nelson won (out of eleven nominations) for his composition *Cross Country Suite*, written for clarinetist Buddy DeFranco in 1958, and his arrangements for *What's New* (1983) and *Lush Life*

Preceding page: Nelson appears overwhelmed by his trombone in a 1920s photograph outside his family's New Jersey home. This was the instrument that he was to play in the bands of Charlie Spivak, Tommy Dorsey, and others, and which became the centerpiece of his famous arrangements in the decades that followed.

(1985) for Linda Ronstadt.[1] His star on the Hollywood Walk of Fame on Hollywood Boulevard symbolizes Nelson Riddle's career—one of both achievement and substance.[2]

★ ★ ★

Nelson Smock Riddle, Jr., was born on June 21, 1921, in the small town of Oradell, New Jersey, a bedroom community across the Hudson River and ten miles west of New York City. He was baptized at the Dutch Reform Church in Oradell. Smock was an old Dutch family name.

Nelson's outgoing, fun-loving father, for whom he was named, was of both English-Irish and Dutch parentage. Fundamentally a sign painter, a craftsman, a sometime commercial artist, and an amateur cartoonist who enjoyed creating new characters, unfortunately he seemed to have very little interest in making a profit for his efforts. Nelson, Sr., also had a love of popular music; he played trombone and ragtime piano, the latter an instrument which his son adopted at the age of eight.[3]

Nelson's mother, Marie Albertine Riddle, passed on to her son a deep and abiding appreciation of classical music. He remembered her singing French folk songs to him when he was a little boy, one of which, "Frère Jacques," was later adapted and became the basis for his swinging arrangement of "Brother John." Marie Albertine, better known simply as Albertine, was a small woman—five foot three or four—rather dwarfed by her husband, who was slightly over six feet tall. She was born in 1888 in Mulhouse, France, a town in Alsace-Lorraine, a province near the German border that had been a subject of bitter contention between the two countries on and off for hundreds of years. It was the West Bank of that time. Her father was Spanish and of noble lineage; he claimed that his family had been part of the Spanish monarchy that had once ruled Holland. As a child, Albertine was raised in a convent.

Albertine had been married once previously, and her divorce led her to leave the Catholic church. Because of her alleged upper-class European heritage, she always projected an aristocratic demeanor which gave her an air of superiority. When she married Nelson, Sr., she believed she had married beneath her and never hesitated to make it clear to her second husband that he should, indeed, feel fortunate to have a wife from such a noble background. The fact that her husband was a weak and unambitious man, as well as a poor businessman who constantly struggled to make a living, was the source of ongoing problems between them. Without question, Albertine was the dominant force in the Riddle household.

A few years before Nelson, Jr., was born, Albertine had given birth to a stillborn son. In all, she withstood six miscarriages during her life, and these losses added a further undercurrent of grief to her already troubled marriage. Bob Runyon, Nelson's first cousin, who had firsthand access to the inner workings of the Riddle household, observed, "I believe that the death of the first child was a major step in the evolution of Albertine's self-perception as some kind of a martyr and victim in a life which failed her expectations. I also think it's likely that Albertine's loss occurred at a time when

Nelson's parents, Marie Albertine Riddle and Nelson Smock Riddle, are shown in portraits taken in 1956, shortly after Nelson brought them to California to live.

Photo courtesy of the Nelson Riddle Memorial Library at the University of Arizona School of Music and Dance, Tucson, Arizona, and the Naomi Riddle Estate.

frustrations, and perhaps some regrets, were starting to have a negative impact on her life. This tragedy significantly added to her developing attitude toward Nelson, Sr., and later Nelson, Jr., and what she saw as her life going sour. It's also possible that, in times of conflict and stress, Albertine would reflect back on the death of her infant son and somehow transfer all or most of the blame onto Nelson, Sr., for allowing it to happen, and retroactively justify her negative perceptions as his fault and not hers."

Nelson often referred to the "strait-laced and stodgy" environment in which he grew up.[4] This went along with the obvious coldness and the lack of a nurturing atmosphere in the household. Albertine exerted a fierce control over her only child from the beginning.

Still, she doted over her young son and took pride in the crocheted knit caps she made for him. As he grew up, she could often be very loving toward him. The sentiment expressed in Gil Scott-Heron's piercing song "Home Is Where the Hatred Is" seems to clearly describe the climate in the Riddle household. These factors were central to the aura of sadness that surrounded Nelson later in life.

Albertine was a housewife at a time when most married women were housewives, but it was a role that she felt was not very fulfilling. In the United States of the 1930s, only one mother in ten worked outside the home. As Nelson pointed out, his mother "had many other interests" (which may have been conscious or unconscious efforts to avoid housewifery): "She was very bright, having studied at Columbia. One of her passions was dietetics. She was one of the very early protagonists of healthful eating. [It] got to the point that she would only bake bread and cakes made up of whole wheat flour."[5]

An important aspect of young Nelson's home life was his father's principal hobby—music. There were weekly rehearsals with his four- or five-piece band in the front room of the house. Nelson, Sr., could play "Maple Leaf Rag" on the piano exclusively on the black keys—no mean feat. According to Nelson, during these rehearsals there was usually a trombone—an instrument his father also played—placed on top of the piano.

Nelson began taking piano lessons at the age of eight and studied with three different teachers, hoping to emulate his father's talent on the instrument. Although he never became adept as a piano soloist, learning to play the piano helped instill in him the rudiments of harmony. The piano later became the instrument he played while composing and writing arrangements.

Beginning in the seventh grade, Dick Leonard was Nelson's closest friend at Benjamin Franklin Junior High School in Ridgewood, New Jersey. At that point, Nelson was playing piano and Leonard was struggling to learn the violin. "He used to walk by our house on the way to school. He lived out quite a ways, but he walked every day, usually leaving about the same time as I did. We were in the same history class. I thought he was an impressive guy—he had a deep voice. We had a good teacher, Mary Egan, who used to like to dramatize the news. You might remember the 'Time Marches On' short subjects on radio and in movie theaters. She needed somebody with a deep voice to say, 'Time marches on,' so she picked Nelson. She would say, 'Okay, Nelson, speak deeper!' And Nelson would say, 'I'm speaking as deep as I can, and stop bellowing at me.' . . . I remember that so well. That distinguished Nelson as someone who would tell the teacher to stop bellowing—not everybody would do that."

Ridgewood is another of the upper-middle-class bedroom communities of New York. The west side of the tracks, up on the hill, was where the money was. You could see the Empire State Building from there. Nelson and Leonard lived on the east side of town. They both became interested in journalism, and Nelson began seriously thinking of making a career of it. Dick Leonard eventually became the editor-in-chief of the *Milwaukee Journal.* During the period when Leonard ran the newspaper, from 1967 until 1985, it was considered one of the foremost dailies in the country.

Nelson brought attention to Leonard with an article entitled "Assembly Review" that he wrote for *The Key,* the Benjamin Franklin Junior High School paper: "It has been my duty during the past year to report on assembly programs. . . . A few of those which to my mind were outstanding were: Room 317's presentation, written and directed by Dick Leonard. Though the play itself was worthy of favorable comment, Dick's pinch-hitting [sic] when the play was found to be too short was the incident that 'immortalized' the show."

He continued, "I believe that the assembly schedule could be improved by having more lectures and less plays, but, of course, this would mean considerable extra expenditure and would cut down the amount of student talent utilized." This pronouncement would seem to be still another example of Nelson's serious demeanor, even at this age.

Leonard's friendship with Nelson continued at Ridgewood High School. Nelson was the piano player in the Willow Club, a dance band composed of about a dozen student musicians from the high school orchestra that would play for concerts in the town and occasional dance jobs.

Nelson began taking trombone lessons in Paterson, New Jersey, at age fourteen. After only eight visits, however, the lessons came to an abrupt end; the music teacher told Nelson not to return because he had not been paid his fee of one dollar per lesson.[6] Looking back on this incident years later, Nelson said, "Anybody worth his salt would have gone out and sold some papers. I don't know why that didn't occur to me. I guess I was a spoiled brat."[7] For the next several years Nelson learned to play the instrument through the combination of studious practicing and rehearsing with various bands.

The non-payment of the miniscule cost of Nelson's music lessons was indicative of the nature of the Riddles' blue-collar existence in 1935—the middle of the Great Depression. Nelson remembered, "We didn't feel the Depression at all. My father made his own Depression. It was all the same to us because we were already in a depressed state by the time the Depression got there."[8] Despite Nelson's assertion, the hovering bleakness of this period obviously made an indelible impression on him.

Dick Leonard remembered one particular Christmas when the Riddle family was broke. Nelson was unhappy because there wasn't any Christmas for him. Leonard recalled, "The next time I saw him he was all smiles, and I asked, 'What happened?' He said, 'I went out and bought myself two suits for Christmas.' That raised his morale. They weren't expensive suits, but they were a change and that brightened his picture."

Things were so desperate that the family moved to wherever his father's company, Ridgewood Signs, could find work. Despite Nelson, Sr.'s talents as an artist, sign painters were in little demand at a time when most businesses were struggling merely to keep themselves solvent.

For a while, Albertine departed from her role as a housewife to take care of her husband's business. Dick Leonard remembered, "They had a studio upstairs on one of the main streets of Ridgewood. She wore a smock, and she was up there doing art work and that type of stuff. They were partners in the studio. They would do signs or billboard-type things or illustrations.

"His mother was terse and business-like. I would describe her as sarcastic and not too affectionate. She would be smiling at times, or even laughing, but it was not a warm laugh! More like 'I'm [smiling] because it's the thing to do.' His father, on the other hand, was a warm, easygoing, and friendly guy."

Leonard remembered the time that he and Nelson were in a writing contest and were the two finalists. Leonard ended up winning the contest. The prize was a book, and Albertine was given the assignment of illustrating the dedication by hand on the front page. "She embellished it quite a bit," said Leonard. "Nelson was a little bit disturbed about that—his mother having to do the book which I had 'taken away' from him. It wasn't jealousy. He was kind of amused by it—the irony of it got to him."

One night, Leonard and Nelson were sitting on the front steps of the Leonard home. Leonard informed his friend that he had been accepted at the University of Wisconsin, which prompted Nelson to express concern about what was going to happen to him because he didn't have enough money to go to college.

In these terrible times, Nelson, Sr., would often work for barter. For instance, in Metuchen, New Jersey, where the Riddles lived for a time, he worked for a Mr. Meyers at his tavern. In exchange, the tavern owner would invite the Riddles and their young son over for a meal.

The Riddle family learned that renting a new place often meant that the first month's rent was free. If Nelson, Sr., couldn't find a way to make the second month's rent, they would simply move.

★ ★ ★

Bob Runyon recalls Nelson, Sr., as being "a kook—and I use that in a nice way . . . he was a character, but very affable, a lot more happy-go-lucky than Nelson, Jr." He remembered the two Riddle men playing trombone duets on tunes like "Harbor Lights" and "Red Sails in the Sunset," which led to sing-alongs during the four or five times the two families got together each year.

Bob and Nelson were related on his mother's side; he was one of Nelson's five cousins who also lived in Metuchen. "Nelson had a good rapport with his father," Runyon added, "but I thought Albertine was terribly spoiled. . . . At family gatherings all the women helped prepare the meals—except Albertine. [By her actions] she gave the impression 'I'm above this—they are my servants.' She would sit in a chair and hold court. She was always well dressed, very neat—a French kind of chic. She had thick gray hair and was always well coifed, wore glasses, and had a very determined stride as she walked. When she spoke, she had an accent and was snippy, with no sense of humor and very little warmth. She expected both Nelsons—and everybody else, too, for that matter—to cater to her. Uncle Nel was doing the 'Yes, dear' bit. If they had a little tiff going, he would fade away. He'd retreat.

"As I recall, they did not get along very well. . . . They'd live apart for a period of time, then they'd get back together. As a boy, Nelson watched his father get swatted like a fly. It was a hopeless situation."

Dick Leonard vividly recalled one night when he and Nelson were double-dating. Since neither of them could drive yet, one of their parents had to drive them around. "On this night, Nelson said to his father, 'How are you feeling, Pop?' Nelson's father said, 'Like I've been goosed with a pineapple!' which was his way of describing life with Albertine."

It's the contention of "Skip" Riddle—actually Nelson Smock Riddle III, the oldest of Nelson, Jr.'s six children and the older of his two sons—that "[Nelson's] relationship with his mother was horrible, and he got no support from his father. His father was a lovely man, but he was not available either. He didn't make a connection with my dad. They had this triangle situation going on and everybody was competing with everyone else. Everyone became quite manipulative in order to get what they wanted in order to keep the peace."

Leonard remarked, "My mental picture of Nelson is he's walking past the house with his trombone . . . with a slouch, looking a bit out of this world. It wasn't so much dour. It was more dreamy."

He feels that Donald Cook, the director of the Ridgewood High School Orchestra and the school's music teacher, was important in Nelson's musical education: "Whenever somebody screwed up, like in the violin section, he'd stop the music and come over and have a conference about what you did wrong. But you could always hear Nelson the minute this happened. He was at the piano, and you could always hear the piano start tinkling. He had his own little world over there. He didn't need anybody else.

"I used to sit near him in both history and mechanical drawing. We were supposed to be sketching things, like you do in mechanical drawing, but he'd be drawing something far away thinking about a musical arrangement or something."

At Ridgewood High School, Nelson couldn't get along with another student named Stewart Moore. Moore used to ridicule Nelson for playing music; he thought it wasn't a worthy occupation. Dick Leonard recalled that they even threw a couple of punches on one occasion. "One of the things that Nelson would bring up [years later], and he did it more than once, 'God, he's sneering at me for becoming a musician, and what did he do later on? He became the head of a playing card company!'"

Nelson and Donald Quimby, a classmate of his at Ridgewood High and a member of the high school band in which Nelson played first trombone, got a chance to hear Ravel's famous *Boléro* at a Carnegie Hall concert with Serge Koussevitzky conducting the Boston Symphony Orchestra. Nelson said, "I've never forgotten it. It's almost as if the orchestra leaped from the stage and smacked you in the face. . . . The only thing wrong with the 'Boléro' was that it was overplayed. [Even so] it's the most absolutely tantalizing slow addition of instruments to this long, long crescendo, which is really the message of the 'Boléro.' . . .'"[9]

Quimby also recalled attending a performance of the Brahms Second Symphony with Nelson and two other schoolmates at Newark's Mosque Theater. On a third occasion, they attended a performance of one of the three segments of Wagner's Ring cycle at the Metropolitan Opera in New York. Nelson realized that listening to classical music on records and on the radio was simply not the same as witnessing live performances of such important works. These performances made an indelible impression on him.

By his teenage years, Nelson had grown to almost his full height. He was six foot two and slim, with dark, curly hair he combed straight back; all of this gave him an imposing and handsome presence. He was a good student with a reported IQ of 138, but due to his family's financial situation, there was never any thought of his attending college when he graduated from high school in June 1939.

He was dead set on becoming a professional musician. In those years, most young musicians joined dance bands rather than going to college to pursue their careers. As

Nelson recalled, "I wanted to be a jazz trombone player, but I didn't have the coordination. I only had the ideas."

In 1938, his last year in high school, Nelson persuaded his parents to allow him to move to Rumson, then a small village on the North Jersey shore of the Shrewsbury River, but today a prosperous small town that is home to many Wall Street executives. The Riddle family had previously rented rooms there during the summer.

The purpose of his yearlong stay in Rumson was to allow Nelson to work with various "kid bands" composed of fellow high school students. These bands had plenty of opportunities to play for dances throughout the area, thus allowing Nelson to expand his experience as a working musician and also enabling him to help out his family financially. Albertine rented rooms for herself and her son in a tiny old house that had gas but no electricity in neighboring Fair Haven. Nelson, Sr., came down from his studio in Ridgewood on weekends.[10]

Nelson wanted Dick Leonard to come down and spend the summer of 1938 with him. He had plans for the two of them to build a sailboat together—pursuing his thoughts of becoming a marine architect—but Leonard had no interest in boats. With his new friend from Rumson, Sven Rolfsen, Nelson wound up building a fourteen-foot sailboat that could cut through the ice for use in the winter. He often went kayaking during the summer.

Bob Runyon recalled that one afternoon, when he and Nelson were sailing in Nelson's boat on the Shrewsbury, they were caught in the wake of a speeding motorboat, which threatened to engulf them. In an attempt to alleviate their panic, Nelson asked his cousin, "What are the important bands up in North Jersey?"

It was during that summer that trumpeter Charlie Briggs, who led a quintet at a roadhouse called the Log Cabin in neighboring Highlands, met the fledgling trombonist. Briggs's band was called the Briggadiers. "We had only ten tunes that we could play. They were stock arrangements," he recalled.

"I still remember it as though it happened yesterday. One day there was a knock on the door. Whoever it was kept knocking. It was an incessant knock. I stopped the band, and said, 'Okay, fellas, take a couple of minutes, and I'll answer the door. . . .' This young man with a trombone in his hand comes in. I shook his hand, and he says, 'My name is Nelson Riddle, and I want to play in your band.' That's exactly how it happened. I said, 'Well, we don't need anybody now, and I don't think we've got any second trombone parts.' And so he walked in the house, and he said, 'Well, I'll transpose one of the sax parts.' I said, 'That can't be done.' He said, 'Well, let's give it a chance.' I said, 'Okay, but we've got to get on with the rehearsal. . . .'

"On that particular day we were playing 'September in the Rain.' [The arranger] Bill Finegan had put this together, little parts of it, and Nelson said 'Can I take it?' I said, 'Go ahead. Let's try it with the band,' fairly certain that we were not going to do anything."

Nelson's first band gig, which was with Charlie Briggs and the Briggadiers at the Garfield Grant Hotel in Long Branch, New Jersey, in 1939. Nelson is at the far left in the second row.

The "September in the Rain" chart had originally been written by Finegan for Glenn Miller, who was then struggling with his first band and soon would be opening at the Paradise Restaurant in New York. Briggs said to Finegan, "How did you think of something so beautiful?" The accomplished arranger replied, "Well, it was raining. I stayed up 'til four o'clock in the morning. I cranked out most of it that night."

Just before the band started playing Finegan's arrangement, Charlie Briggs introduced Nelson by saying, "Nelson would like to play some trombone for us." "Everybody was kind of frown-faced," Briggs recalled, "'cause in those days four bucks was what they paid a man in the band and, for high school kids, that was big dollars, and they didn't want to have to share it."

Discussing when the Briggadiers tried out the chart with the transposed part written by their new second trombonist, Charlie Briggs recalled, "I don't know to this day what he really transposed or played, but we went from a 60-percent band to a 100-percent band with just his insertion into the brass section. I think Nelson came in as a fairly fundamentally trained young trombone player because to do something like that indicated he knew more than a lot of guys did. We knew we sounded better so we wanted to take him into the band. After that Nelson started writing some things.

"We didn't have enough money. Everybody pitched in and said, 'Look, we'll take half a buck off every one of us.' Nelson's first gig with the Briggadiers was at the Garfield Grant Hotel in Long Branch. Then we got to playing more local dance dates and proms."

As a result of the Briggadiers' sudden gain in popularity, more money was available, and Charlie was soon able to pay Nelson his four bucks.

One night, the Briggadiers were playing at the Rumson Fireman's Fair. The bandstand wasn't big enough to include Nelson, so two cinder blocks were stacked on top of each other and covered with a drape, and Nelson sat on them. "I forget what the tunes were, but something real fast, and with Nelson we had the two trombones, two trumpets," Charlie Briggs reflected. "We stood up to play a couple of bars and when he went to sit down after a few choruses, he stumbled and fell backwards off the bandstand. Now, the bandstand was about three and one-half feet high. When he was falling he never removed the trombone and kept playing his part while lying on the ground! His obligation or his desire was to make sure that this part was played correctly. But that was Nelson; he expected everybody to do the same."

According to Briggs, shortly afterwards, it was he who casually introduced Nelson to Bill Finegan. He explained, "Bill lived in a place right across from the old Rumson Hotel. Although he was only about twenty-two, he taught most of us in high school." Finegan, however, recalls his introduction to Nelson differently, explaining that Nelson, Sr., approached him first, saying, "I know you're the guy who can teach my son arranging." This meeting led to the most meaningful relationship of Nelson Riddle's young musical life.

As Nelson remembered it, "He showed me how to write some simple things for dance orchestras. I remember one of the first assignments he gave me was to write a chorus of 'Swanee River' for five saxes (two altos, two tenors, and one baritone)." In addition, Finegan urged Nelson to experiment. For example, he showed his pupil how a gentle sound could be created in an arrangement by mixing two clarinets and two cup-muted trumpets.[11]

Despite being only four years older than Nelson, Bill (or "Billy" as he was called in those days) Finegan was considerably more musically sophisticated than his student. A few years before that, he had played trumpet and piano, with a musical group that had won the competition hosted by the famous Major Bowes's *Original Amateur Hour* radio program. He then went on an extensive one-nighter bus tour cross-country for $35 a week. Ultimately, Finegan wound up writing a total of over three hundred arrangements for Glenn Miller over a four-year period (1938–42), which included Miller's classic "Little Brown Jug" as well as "Sunrise Serenade" and "Song of the Volga Boatmen." He also shared the arranging chores with Jerry Gray on the 20th Century Fox musicals *Sun Valley Serenade* and *Orchestra Wives,* in which the Miller Band appeared. Finegan later moved on to Tommy Dorsey. Today, he refers to Miller as "a martinet" but is proud of the fact that "The Sentimental Gentleman of Swing" once said, "I'll buy anything Bill writes."

In the early 1950s, a brief neo–Glenn Miller craze emerged when RCA Victor successfully launched the Ralph Flanagan Orchestra with the hit record "Hot Toddy." Spurred on by this success in 1952, RCA approached Finegan and his partner, the equally talented Eddie Sauter, who had reinvigorated the Benny Goodman Orchestra in the early 1940s with his modern arrangements. Together they founded the Sauter-Finegan Orchestra. The renowned record producer Dave Kapp, then head of A&R (Artists & Repertoire) for RCA said, "I don't know what kind of band they're going to have, but I respect both of them so much so we're going to sign them."

The varied instrumentation of the Sauter-Finegan Orchestra—additional percussion, English horn, piccolo, bass clarinet, etc.—playing unusual contemporary arrangements featuring miraculous tone colors eventually proved to be too progressive for 1950s America. It was years ahead of its time and ultimately disbanded in 1957.

Even today Bill Finegan feels a strong kinship with Nelson Riddle. The two of them kept in close touch for the next several years. Nelson continued to value Finegan's counsel and was never lax about acknowledging the significance of the time he spent under Finegan's tutelage; for many years he absolutely idolized Finegan.

As Nelson noted, "Bill's arrangements for Glenn [Miller]demonstrated that great originality and inventiveness are possible even within the restrictive confines of a highly stylized band, which the Miller Orchestra certainly was."[12] During the course of their listening to classical music, which Finegan also admired, he brought to Nelson's attention Shostakovitch's First Symphony in F Minor, which had premiered in 1937 and brought the young Russian composer his initial recognition. Finegan further instilled in Nelson the realization that the entire process of arranging involved listening to the musical contributions of many varied types of composers, starting with classical music, plus a concentrated program of trial and error.

Nelson recalled, "I showed up for a lesson one afternoon and [was] confronted by a very exhausted Finegan, up all the previous night—unshaven, red-eyed, and standing in the midst of a small pile of score pages reprinting no less than twenty-six possible introductions for the same arrangement, as yet unfinished."[13]

"He wanted to learn how to play jazz trombone," Bill Finegan remembered. "He claimed he didn't know anything about it, and yet he was quick to grasp whatever I gave him to play on the trombone. I felt he was talented because he could read well, and he had ideas. He could write them on paper, but he couldn't get them out fast enough so I started writing out jazz choruses for him to play."

At that time Finegan was working on an arrangement of "Lonesome Road" for Tommy Dorsey. (Ironically, Dorsey played it for Glenn Miller, who liked it so much that he offered Finegan a job in 1938.) This arrangement was to become an important addition to Dorsey's library.

Bill Finegan conducting
the Sauter-Finegan Orchestra
at a rehearsal for a 1990
reunion concert. The brilliant
arranger was Nelson's first
and most important mentor.

Finegan said, "I showed Nelson what I had written. I played it on the piano for him, and he was very intrigued with it. That's when the idea popped up for him to become a writer. That was the key thing. We put it on the rack of the piano, and I scribbled the title on the top of the manuscript. I misspelled it, which I never do. What was really important was that, in looking over the arrangement, he could convert what he heard me play on the piano into instruments.

"I told him not to stay up all night writing, but most writers that I knew would do that last minute thing all the time," (including Nelson), Finegan continued. "We'd sit up all day and night for two days discussing the ins and outs of writing. I mean, how positive is a writer? We're always unsure. We have those ups and downs of unsureness about everything. Unfortunately, he had that down way of looking at things when I first met him. I used to give him holy hell about this all the time. I used to say to him, 'C'mon, man, how about being upbeat for a change?' He was a worrier, and he was also very negative. He would never show his best side to people. [Years later] I still thought of him as a kid. I cared a lot about what I did, and I think I transferred that to Nelson. I once saw a documentary on the artist Chagall. In it, Chagall said, 'Never say "That's good enough."' That's what I think I taught him."

Bill sent Nelson to study privately with Rudolf Winthrop, who was the bandmaster at Rumson High School. Bill had studied counterpoint, classical harmony, and theory with Winthrop, an Austrian who had been a student of Engelbert Humperdinck, the important classical composer. Emigrating to America, Winthrop brought with him a thick Viennese accent, the kind often depicted in film biographies of young would-be musicians, singers, and composers.

As Finegan explained it, "Winthrop taught classical harmony, which is a very strict discipline. One thing I know Nelson learned from him is how to write bass parts—bass lines. That was very important to him, which certainly showed up later in his arrangements." Nat Garratano, the president of Local 399 in Asbury Park, said that Winthrop held Bill Finegan and Nelson up as role models when he taught. As Nat remembered, "He used to say, 'If you students will listen to me, maybe you'll become important in music the way Bill and Nelson did.'"

After several months, the duo of Riddle and Finegan ended their once or twice weekly sessions in 1939 when Finegan's commitment to Glenn Miller became a priority. That same year, Nelson wrote his first arrangement; the tune was "I See Your Face Before Me," written by Arthur Schwartz and Howard Dietz.[14] His mentor had laid the groundwork—now it was up to Nelson to continue working with bands writing arrangements and playing trombone.

★ ★ ★

During one of his father's summer weekend visits to Rumson, Nelson listened on the Motorola radio in Nelson, Sr.'s 1936 Dodge to a concert emanating from the Robin Hood Dell in Philadelphia. He marveled at the brilliance of Leopold Stokowski and the Philadelphia Orchestra—the texture of the music and its precision and dynamics. Listening to other classical music programs with the car door half open, he drained the battery in his father's car on more than one occasion.

His interest in classical music had intensified less than a year earlier and was partially due to his Uncle Luther's new wife, Dorothy Dixon. Her brother had died suddenly and had left her an old wind-up portable Victrola, which she offered to Nelson along with several 78-rpm records. One of the records was a Victor Red Seal disc. On one side was "Reflets dans L'eau" ("Reflections in the Water") and on the other side was "La Cathédrale Engloutie" ("The Engulfed Cathedral"), both by Debussy and both performed by the famous pianist Jan Paderewski. The ever musically conscious teenager wore out many cactus needles listening to this records. After that he began enjoying the Impressionist composers—Ravel, more Debussy, and later on Delius. And as a result of this exposure, Nelson became attracted to Impressionist visual artists as well.[16]

In 1939 Nelson took a respite from his dance band activities by venturing further south to Atlantic City to play third trombone in the New Jersey State Orchestra under conductor Eric DeLamarter. Nelson recalled, "At least I made State Orchestra, and there were only three trombonists picked from all the high school bands in the state."[15] Such compositions as the Rienzi Overture by Wagner and Dvořák's familiar *New World* Symphony were featured in the repertoire of the Orchestra. Learning and continuously playing compositions of this kind also proved to be important in his later development as an arranger.

In June of that year Nels, as he was called, graduated from Rumson High School. The school's yearbook, *The Tower,* included this thumbnail description of him: "With his learned dissertations, he sets our heads awhirl."

The Briggadiers folded that same spring. However, with Nelson's growing interest in classical music, his increasing proficiency on the trombone, and his developing technique in writing dance band arrangements, he was ready to branch out anyway. For a time, he and Charlie Briggs played with Jake Mazzaroppi's twelve-piece band.

Saxophonist Ivins Voorhees, a member of Mazzaroppi's band, remembered an incident at an Italian wedding when Nelson's usual ultra-serious manner suddenly turned playful. "There was a fellow named Art Terranova who played tenor saxophone with me in Jake's band. We, of course, sat in the front row in front of the brass section. Things were getting very loose at the wedding. Nelson joined in by soaking a hamburger roll in beer and slapping it on the back of Art's bald head when he [Art] sat down after playing a solo."

For the next two years, Nelson and Charlie were members of Peter Galatro's band in neighboring Red Bank, and then Bruce Cobb's band in Long Branch. When venue buyers couldn't afford the price of a big band, he and Charlie would work as part of three-, four-, or five-piece groups—a prime example of supply and demand.

The Asbury Park Casino was then an important summertime venue for big bands. Peter Galatro's band was booked as the relief band opposite a parade of important names. This was during the summer of 1939, when Nelson was writing most of the arrangements for Galatro's band.

Alto saxophonist John Wisniewski, another bandmate of Nelson's with the Galatro band, recalled Nelson's up-tempo arrangement of "South of the Border," coincidentally a tune he arranged again fourteen years later for his first recording session with Frank Sinatra: " 'South of the Border' was a kick number, and, man, that was as modern as something you would hear today—maybe even more so. Nelson was fantastic as a writer."

During that season, one of the major bands playing at the Casino was that of Louis Prima. Charlie Briggs remembered with decided glee, "There were about four thousand in the Casino that night. We almost tore the place apart with Galatro's fourteen-piece band. This was something nobody had ever heard before—Nelson's special arrangements that you just didn't hear local bands do. They weren't expecting anything like that. The crowd didn't want to get off the dance floor. Prima got so furious he demanded to know who the hell were we trying to show him up. It got to the point where he was in such a fit of rage that all the guys had to take their arrangement books off the music stands when we took an intermission because he was ready to kill us!"

Bob Van Etten played bass with Galatro when Nelson was writing arrangements and playing trombone for the band. Before a dance date in nearby Lakewood, Van Etten remembered how Nelson demonstrated 13th chords on the piano, something he had learned from Bill Finegan, which was extremely musically advanced for a teenage musician. "He was far above us as a student of music," Van Etten noted.

In the next several years, Van Etten saw Nelson play with Charlie Spivak and

Tommy Dorsey and made a key observation about Nelson's behavior: "Nelson was not a snob. He never forgot where he came from."

Clarinetist Alphonso "Funzy" Tomaino was a member of Bruce Cobb's dance band and had been a member of the Briggadiers. He was very impressed by Nelson's ability as an arranger even then. "Having later graduated from music school [Juilliard] I learned a lot, and it reminded me of what he used to do. I used to think, 'What the hell is he doing?' I'd walk into a room and there he was plunking intervals and listening to intervals. These were the rudiments of arranging. He was working on any material that was advantageous to his arranging. We were the guinea pigs. He was the doctor and we would play his arrangements. This was a time for him to gain experience, to take out his mistakes and see if his voicings were correct. He was very intuitive in [creating] the sound of his music. He stopped when he knew a mistake had to be corrected. At the time we were talking about Glenn Miller's sound, a sound we had never heard before. Here was a fella duplicating that same sound at an early age. We were really impressed."

Tomaino also recalled Nelson as being "a very unostentatious guy. He was all music. He was an inward sort of person. I wouldn't say introverted entirely, but along those lines."

It's Tomaino's opinion that Rudolf Winthrop had a greater influence on Nelson as an arranger than Bill Finegan did: "Nelson had a different kind of a beat, particularly around a vocalist, and, of course, his dance music was completely different from Bill's."

Looking back over those years, Charlie Briggs remarked, "Even at the early stages when we were young kids in high school, Nelson was writing stuff that was a little tough to handle, but he'd take the section, he'd hold the band, and he'd rehearse the band. We'd go through the brass section parts with him, and some of us couldn't cut it. In those days if you were a trumpet player and hit high C or D above high C—well, you were some kind of special. Now they whistle two octaves higher! But he did other things that were very majestic. He wrote the harmonics of all the instrumentals so beautifully that even the third trumpet guy felt like he was a first trumpet player."

Like many of Nelson's close boyhood friends, Briggs's friendship with him endured. He was privy to some of Nelson's recording sessions years later with Nat "King" Cole and Frank Sinatra. Charlie speculates that "Nelson Riddle would have been a success if he'd turned to the banking business or wanted to be the CEO of a company because he was smart, he was honest, and could do everything in a very forthright manner. I really think he could have been a success at anything."

CHAPTER 2

The Apprenticeship
Continues

Bill Finegan was no longer providing weekly arranging lessons for Nelson, but he kept in constant touch with his former pupil and continued to supervise his writing. He pointed out that initially it was Nelson's intelligence, not his arrangements, which drew him to Nelson.

In the fall of 1939, Finegan managed to get Nelson a job playing trombone and arranging with a band led by clarinetist Tommy Reynolds. Chet Arthur, then the President of Local 399 in Asbury Park, New Jersey, and a friend of Finegan, recommended Nelson, telling Reynolds, "New fella came to town, plays pretty good, and writes very good arrangements."[1]

Reynolds had the distinction of not only sounding like clarinetist Artie Shaw but also resembling him physically. His band was essentially a territory band that worked in the New York/North Jersey environs, and Nelson had already left it by the time it began recording for Vocalion and Okeh in late 1939 and early 1940. Although he was never credited, presumably a few of the thirty-three tracks the band recorded contained arrangements written by Nelson Riddle.[2]

It was while he was a member of Reynolds's band that Nelson first encountered Conrad Gozzo, who was later to achieve near legendary status as a lead trumpet player with Woody Herman, Stan Kenton, Billy May, and Ray Anthony, among others. The gregarious trumpeter, who hailed from New Britain, Connecticut, and the shy, diffident trombonist became friends instantly. Years later, Gozzo's powerful and penetrating sound—"bigger than a schoolyard," as several musicians described it—was one of the trademarks of the Nelson Riddle Orchestra on its Capitol recordings during the 1950s and early '60s.

In 1940, on his nineteenth birthday, Nelson moved on to another dance band after only a few months with Reynolds. This one was led by clarinetist and saxophonist Jerry Wald. Wald, too, styled the sound of his band after that of Artie Shaw and even added strings just as Shaw had done when he returned from his self-imposed hiatus on the

Preceding page: Merchant Marine Apprentice Seaman Nelson Riddle poses in New York's Riverside Park in a 1943 photo.

Mexican Riviera earlier that year. Since Benny Goodman and Shaw led the two bands that made significant breakthroughs in the second half of the 1930s, these bands served as models for several new bands that were starting out at this time. By including strings in his band, Wald led Nelson to the realization that they could be used as a luxurious cushion in an arrangement, while providing strong rhythmic support.

Unfortunately, however, the fact that Nelson didn't have an 802 union card prevented him from playing in New York, where the band had a location engagement, so Wald couldn't use him as a trombonist. Nelson and Albertine moved into an apartment on East 18th Street, which he used as a base to write arrangements for Wald and applied for his new union card, which required a six-month residency. Nelson was essentially supporting Albertine, who was then separated from Nelson, Sr.

Ivins Voorhees remembered seeing Nelson at his first date with Charlie Spivak's band at the Capitol Theatre in Passaic, New Jersey, in late 1940. Once again it was Bill Finegan who got the job for his protégé. For weeks beforehand, Spivak had approached Finegan when the Spivak Band was working at the Café Rouge at the Hotel Pennsylvania in New York. "Spivak practically cried to me," recalled Finegan, "'When are you going to find me a writer?'"

"When the band came on at the Capitol Theatre," said Voorhees, "we were sitting in the first row. Nelson gave us a big wave. Backstage he introduced us to the Three Stooges who were appearing on the bill with Spivak. We all went to a diner where one of the guys got a pie thrown in his face by one of the other Stooges. Months later, having played Nelson's arrangements with Bruce Cobb, I could recognize which of Spivak's arrangements were his—it was the voicings, the way he phrased for the saxes."

Charlie Spivak had been a formidable lead trumpeter who displayed a sweet tone and had a wide range and, like Harry James and Tommy Dorsey, he had no need to warm up before a gig. Although Spivak had played lead for the Dorsey Brothers Orchestra, Ray Noble, Ben Pollack, Bob Crosby, Tommy Dorsey, and Glenn Miller's first band, he was never renowned as a jazz soloist.[3] Artie Shaw referred to him as "a nice guy but not much of a leader. He was well known for taking good care of the drunks on the bands he worked on when he was a sideman." Spivak also had the unusual distinction of being the only lead trumpeter-turned-bandleader in the big band era to hail from Kiev, Russia.

In 1940, Glenn Miller, who had gained national prominence with his breakthrough engagement at the Glen Island Casino the previous summer, financed Spivak when he took over Bill Downer's band, a territory band that regularly worked at a Richmond, Virginia, roadhouse called the Nightingale. From the start, Spivak was unhappy with the band, except for the superb bassist Jimmy Middleton. He began rebuilding it, and Nelson Riddle was a part of the process. Spivak acquired Willie Smith on lead alto, Dave Tough on drums, Les Elgart on lead trumpet (who years later led his own successful band), and the vocal quartet the Stardusters (which included lead singer June

Hutton, sister of the flamboyant and sexy Ina Ray Hutton, who was the foremost female bandleader of the time.

Later, Spivak added Jimmy Priddy, Paul Tanner, and Frank D'Annolfo, who had comprised the trombone section with Glenn Miller before Miller received a commission to join the Army Air Force and disbanded his civilian orchestra in September 1942. For a time, Glenn's brother Herb was part of the Spivak trumpet section. Other members of the band were saxophonists Don Raffell and Harry Klee, drummer Alvin Stoller (who replaced Dave Tough), and pianist and arranger Dave Mann. Its chief arranger, Sonny Burke, who began with Les Brown's original band at Duke University, wrote the band's theme, "Star Dreams," but normally didn't travel with the band. Don Raffell said of Sonny, "He was the nicest man I ever worked for in the music business. He was a pleasure to be around at all times. He never had a bad word to say about anybody." Raffell, Klee, Stoller, and Burke were to become colleagues and close friends of Nelson Riddle in Hollywood a decade later.

In evaluating Charlie Spivak, the distinguished composer, French horn player, educator, and writer Gunther Schuller contended, "One of his major career miscalculations, in a burst of modesty and reticence, was to virtually abandon for awhile his brilliant open horn playing—in which Harry James was garnering all the laurels at the time—and resort to a delicate, intimate, always muted styling that was, alas, too subtle for the average dance-band fan."[4]

Toward the end of his life, Nelson Riddle reflected on Spivak in these terms: "They used to call him cheery, chubby Charlie Spivak. He was very pleasant and an excellent trumpet player. Charlie's control of the instrument and his tone were magnificent. He had the breathing apparatus on the trumpet that Tommy Dorsey had on the trombone. Tommy became one of the great legends of all time; Charlie didn't."[5] Nelson added, "Charlie wasn't equipped to be a bandleader—he didn't have the flair, he didn't have the color, the veracity."[6]

When asked how it was to work for Spivak, Don Raffell observed, "Everybody got along with Charlie until you asked him for a raise, and then he'd start to cry. I remember one day we were at the Strand Theatre in New York, and he drove up. He's got a nice new car—it was a Cadillac, I think, and he had a whole stack of alligator luggage. I said to him, 'Which of these are mine, Charlie?' He didn't like that very much!"

Actually, Charlie Spivak and his Orchestra became established as a bona fide attraction during that March 1941 engagement at the Strand Theatre. Within months of being financially backed by Glenn Miller, Spivak was able to pay Miller back. Nelson Riddle noted, "At the time I was making $109 a week, which was then a lot of money. Of course, we had to do five shows a day for me to make that. We started at eleven o'clock in the morning and finished at eleven o'clock at night."

Don Raffell remembered, "There was a wonderful feeling in the band. Everybody got along. Before the band played a tune, Charlie would stand there and beat the tempo off and sing the chart to himself. He wouldn't care if it took three hours to find the right tempo.

"I must say, Nelson's charts always used each section well, and he never got junky or messy. His arrangements weren't complicated. That's one of the secrets of any arranger. When he brought in an arrangement for Charlie to check out, he would walk around in circles while the band ran it down for the first time. He felt belittled if Charlie made any changes."

The saxophonist recalled his first impression of Nelson when the two worked together on the Spivak band: "He was a nice guy, very humble. It seemed as though he felt intimidated at all times. His mother was the cause. She practically told him what time to go to the bathroom. She told him what to do, how to do, and when to do.

"His parents visited with him shortly after he joined the band when we played at the Glen Island Casino and then after that when we were at the Hotel Pennsylvania. His father was a very nice, meek person, but his mother ruled the family with an iron fist. I saw a lot of his mother—enough to make you throw up. Nelson was what you'd call, I guess, a mama's boy." (Ironically, Bob Runyon remembers Nelson writing the arrangement of "Dear Mom" for Spivak.)

Since Spivak's band during the 1940–42 period toured mostly in the northeast corridor, Albertine made frequent visits to see her son. On occasion, she traveled by car with June Hutton's mother. Bob Runyon remarked, "She decided that if she wasn't going to have much influence on developing the career of her husband—a sign painter—she could still control the life of her son, who might make something of himself as a musician or as an arranger."

Dave Mann, who was Nelson's roommate at the time, described Albertine as constantly applying pressure on her son: "She influenced everything he did. I never heard him even refer to his father. He was a small-town kid who had no knowledge of the music business, baseball, politics, or girls. He had no girlfriends. One night I got a hooker for myself and another for him. He was extremely reluctant about the whole thing."

I asked Mann if he or any other members of the band ever questioned Nelson as to why his mother came to see him so often. "No. I certainly never asked him, and I don't remember any of the other guys asking him. Right away, I saw that he was a namby-pamby, very sheltered kid. I felt I would have hurt him if I'd asked him that.

"I also remember that Albertine was a disciple of George Fox, a French mystic, similar to Edgar Cayce. She turned Nelson into a health food nut. He always drank rosehips tea and carried around wheat germ in powder form in a bottle."

Don Raffell also remembered, "He used to practice every day on his trombone. You could describe him as being merely an adequate player. He was never really good. In fact, there was one night at the Glen Island Casino when the slide on his trombone slid off and hit one of the dancers on the dance floor." Similarly, Dave Mann recalled one afternoon when Nelson was rehearsing in front of an open window in their room at the Mayflower Hotel in Akron, Ohio. He was playing a series of E-flats which required going from the first to the seventh position on the trombone. The latch on his trombone slide loosened and the slide flew out the window—narrowly missing a pedestrian—and was dented beyond repair.

Raffell recalled one of several incidents that led to Nelson's being regarded as flaky, or at best preoccupied: "The band comes up out of the pit one day in 1942 at the Strand Theater in New York. You hear a clankety-clank, bang bang! I turned around and saw Nelson's chair go off the back of the bandstand. He had fallen over. He could do things like that because he was not thinking about anything except what *he* was thinking about. Who knows—an arrangement no doubt!"

Trumpeter Danny Vannelli met Nelson on November 10, 1942, at the Empire Theater in Fall River, Massachusetts, when Vannelli left Les Brown's band to join Spivak. He remembers the date because he recalls Nelson's complete astonishment over his ability to play three shows without any rehearsal. Danny liked Nelson from the start and soon became Nelson's new roommate. He referred to him as a "very quiet and unassuming fellow and a real gentleman. You had to start any conversation with him. He was often morose, but he made his point when he spoke.

"I also noticed that when he wrote arrangements to feature Charlie he always saw to it that the backgrounds didn't interfere with presenting Charlie correctly. He wanted him to sound good. I also saw that he was very versatile in his writing. He quickly learned about the different styles of each of the soloists and then wrote arrangements that really featured them. You might say he formed an opinion about a musician early on."

From getting to know Nelson, Vannelli also discovered that early in his career Nelson figured "there wasn't much to do for piano players because there was only one in each group. He decided to take up the trombone because there were three and four in a group, and he had a better chance of making a dollar. That's why he switched to playing trombone. Both his heart and mind, however, were really on arranging."

Unfortunately, Spivak was at first slow to make use of Nelson Riddle as an arranger. And when he did, he offered him the princely sum of $5.00 an arrangement—$7.50 when he copied all the parts.

In the first months, when the Spivak band played a New York location date, right after opening night Nelson would consult with Bill Finegan. Finegan said, "He had no confidence in his writing at this time, so I'd go over his charts and say 'This is great.' Or if there was anything radically wrong, which never happened really—but if it was glaring—I'd fix it for him. By then he was pretty much on his own—he was doing great. He was finding his own voice. He was highly influenced by me, and I kept telling him, 'Listen, find your own way, man,' and he worked on it."

Listening recently to Nelson's arrangement of Josef Myrow's "Autumn Nocturne" (written for Spivak), the Oscar-, Tony-, and Emmy-winning arranger and composer Ralph Burns remarked, "There's a standard dance band arrangement of the time, very clean and very white-bread. It's written in the Glenn Miller style. Charlie obviously tried to make his band sound as much like Glenn Miller as possible. But Nelson really knew how to voice for instruments. Even then he knew how to write."

In 1942, Bing Crosby had a stupendous hit record with Irving Berlin's "White Christmas," which he introduced in the Paramount movie *Holiday Inn*. (Since this recording continues to sell briskly, it is believed to be the biggest-selling single record of all time.) Freddy Martin's band also recorded the song, but it was Charlie Spivak's recording with Garry Stevens on the vocal that became the popular dance band hit version of the tune and a highly popular selection on jukeboxes. As a result, it sold over a million copies. The chart was by Nelson Riddle, whose salary had increased by the summer of 1942 to $15 an arrangement and was writing one or two charts a week. Stevens was paid a measly $10 for recording the song.

Always thinking like a true artist, Nelson was considerably more proud of his work on "Autumn Nocturne" than on "White Christmas." He wrote, "Claude Thornhill had a great record on that song, but Myrow said he liked our arrangement."[7]

Stevens pointed out, "If you listen to Nelson's arrangement of 'White Christmas,' it starts out with Spivak's trumpet solo, then the band, and ends up with a vocal, and finally goes back to the band again. That doesn't work on a stage show when you're trying to feature the band singer doing 'White Christmas.' So Nelson wrote a second arrangement that featured the vocal."

Originally both a vocalist and trumpeter, Garry Stevens had come to Spivak's attention after saxophonist Harry Klee told him that Stevens would be an able replacement for the band's singer, Bill Howard. Stevens auditioned for the job and was hired. Almost immediately he noticed the band's third trombonist, Nelson Riddle.

"He was writing a lot of arrangements and showed a lot of talent," Stevens recalled. Contrary to Don Raffell's opinion about Nelson's writing, Stevens felt, "As a new, aspiring arranger, he used to write too busy. And sometimes, when the band would segue out of an instrumental passage into the vocal, he'd write an eight-bar interlude. You'd wonder where the heck it went! I'd wonder 'Where do I come in?' You know, a band singer has to sing in tempo because people dance to our music.

"After a year of working together, one day I said, 'Nelson, why don't you start writing some 'footballs' [whole notes] so I can sing what I'd like to sing.' Nelson took it well, actually. He was always interested in learning to improve himself. I liked his attitude and admired his sense of humor."

Shortly thereafter, Nelson wrote a chart on "Dark of the Moon," which the Spivak Band was recording for Okeh, the Columbia Records subsidiary label. Apparently the backgrounds behind Stevens's vocal were too obtrusive. Spivak decided to cut out the vocal and record the tune as an instrumental. Stevens affirms, "That background was so busy you wouldn't realize that it was written as a vocal arrangement."

Dave Mann called Nelson "an instant, intuitive arranger. From learning to write with Billy Finegan, he brought a different dimension to his work. The French impressionists like Debussy and Ravel really influenced him. They helped broaden his outlook, which made him different from most dance band arrangers."

Mann, before becoming a dance band pianist and arranger, obtained a degree from Curtis Institute in Philadelphia, where among other music courses he studied conducting. He tried to instill the rudiments of conducting in both Spivak and Riddle. It would have been beneficial to Nelson to be able to demonstrate to the band exactly what he wanted to accomplish in his arrangements. According to Mann's recollection, neither succeeded in developing any pronounced talent in that area.

Dr. Paul Tanner recalled the day in 1942 when, as part of Glenn Miller's three-man trombone section, he joined the Spivak band. "It was at Shea's Theatre in Buffalo. Charlie decided to put the trombones in the third row behind the trumpets so that he could hear the trumpets easier and also so he could contribute to the section. As a result of our arrival, Nelson moved over to fourth trombone. This didn't seem to bother him at all. After the next set, on my suggestion, Charlie agreed to move the trombones forward to the second row where they belonged. I then realized that Charlie's trumpet section was ragged compared to Glenn's, which was so precise.

"Nelson and I became instant friends. In Nelson's arrangements for Charlie he always wrote them so that the backgrounds were full and could stand alone. He used lots of sustained notes in order to achieve a full sound. That made it hard for us brass players to play them. I also felt that he thought his job was to fill up the room with sound. As a trombonist, I always felt he knew his chords, but he never really had any solo opportunities. He was fundamentally a section player."

Reflecting on these years as an itinerant dance band musician, Nelson said, "When I was a kid playing with dance orchestras, I was one of the lucky ones who could sleep on the bus. In those days they didn't have that rule that the bandleader could only take you 750 miles each day in any direction. You'd climb on the bus after a job at 1:00 in the morning and you might still be traveling at 10:00 the next morning. Check in the hotel, all these people are nice and shiny going to work, and they're looking at this bunch of ruffians who climbed off the bus and are sitting around in various attitudes of dejection in the lobby, waiting for the rooms to be ready.

"I used to do my sleeping on the bus, so that when I would go upstairs, I'd shower, put clean clothes on, and walk around town. I saw a lot of little towns and some big ones that way. The other guys were exhausted; they'd stumble out of bed at five o'clock, just in time to shave, dress and eat."[8]

The Spivak band was constantly on tour, working theaters, college proms, military bases, and the usual spate of one-nighter dance dates. It played many of the prestige dance locations such as the Café Rouge and Frank Dailey's Meadowbrook on the Pompton Turnpike in Edison, New Jersey. In theater engagements the band occasionally backed singers like Mildred Bailey, Connee Boswell, Pearl Bailey, and Dennis Morgan, the

Warner Bros. film star. Through these many months on the road, working in such a variety of venues and settings, Nelson was beginning to perfect his craft as an arranger.

Harry Klee recalled, "When we had a rehearsal of the band, Nelson would pass out little slips of paper with maybe six, eight, or ten bars of music on them, where he was trying a new kind of voicing—you know, for new sounds. He did this all the time back then, cataloguing what he thought was good and discarding what wasn't."[9] Nelson later acknowledged, "I learned quite a bit in that band."[10]

A key learning experience for Nelson while working movie theater engagements with Spivak was sitting backstage on the bandstand between shows behind the screen, concentrating on the musical score in the film being shown. As an example, he recalled what an impression Warner's 1941 epic *The Sea Wolf* (based on the novel by Jack London) made on him. "I was fascinated. That first got me interested in picture scoring."

Faust Canino, who played lead alto saxophone for the Peter Galatro band (which included Nelson) during the summer of 1939 in Asbury Park, New Jersey, heard Charlie Spivak as a guest on an after midnight call-in radio show in Miami one night in 1961. He decided to call the station to speak to the bandleader. When he reached Spivak, he asked him what he thought of Nelson, based on the time Nelson had worked for him. Spivak condescendingly replied, "Oh, yes, he did a fine job." When asked if he ever saw any spark of genius in his young arranger, Spivak replied, "No, at the time he was [just] an average arranger."

★ ★ ★

By 1943, Nelson Riddle and every other twenty-two-year-old American male was a prime candidate to be drafted into military service. The nation's war machine was working on a twenty-four-hour basis and more military personnel were desperately needed for the island-hopping campaigns in the Pacific Theater and the impending landings in North Africa. By this time, the Allies had broken the Axis code and the invention of radar had seriously affected the domination of the North Atlantic sea lanes by German submarines. Still, the frightful number of losses of merchant seamen on convoys such as those making the long trip from eastern seaboard ports to Murmansk in northernmost Russia, beset by constant strafing and bombing by German planes based in Norway, was astounding.

Being less than a true patriot, Nelson found that going to war simply didn't jibe with his ambitions. He discovered a way of circumventing the draft by joining the Merchant Marine at Sheepshead Bay in Brooklyn, where he could become a member of the orchestra and also write arrangements. This suited his purpose considerably more than joining the war effort. Thus, when he joined the Merchant Marine in January 1943, he was assured of staying on land in one place and playing music at the same time.[11]

Lieutenant Junior Grade Jack Lawrence of the U.S. Navy, then known primarily as the lyricist on Harry James's hit records "Ciribiribin" and "All or Nothing at All," was originally stationed at the Coast Guard base at Manhattan Beach in Brooklyn, where he put together a dance band for the base. In one of those "here today, gone tomorrow" turn of events that frequently occurred in military and naval circles, Lawrence suddenly reemerged as the Morale Officer at the Merchant Marine base in neighboring Sheepshead Bay. (Lawrence recently quipped, "At the time, somebody said, 'It happened faster than you could say Jack Lawrence!'")

Speaking of Harry James, at this time, Nelson was also trying to find other outlets for his arrangements with major dance bands. He approached Frank "Pee Wee" Monte, Harry James's manager, in the winter of 1943, just as James was beginning to reach the peak of his popularity. He wanted Monte to buy his arrangement of "A Wing and a Prayer," a popular patriotic song of the mid-war period that had been introduced in the Army Air Force show *Winged Victory*. In his accompanying letter to Monte, Nelson explained that the composer Alec Wilder had given him a lead sheet on the tune, which precipitated his writing an arrangement of it. Nelson was paid $50 for his arrangement, but James never recorded it.

In addition to Nelson Riddle, Lawrence recruited such musicians as bassist "Doc" Goldberg from the Glenn Miller Band; clarinetist Willie Schwartz, whom Miller had first utilized to achieve his famous patented sound by having Schwartz play an octave above the tenor saxophone playing in the lower register; trumpeter Lyman Vunk from Charlie Barnet's Band; trombonist George Arus, formerly with Tommy Dorsey and Artie Shaw; and pianist Cy Walter, one of the premier New York cocktail pianists. Other musicians in the Merchant Marine orchestra were violinists Freddy Buldrini, from the Metropolitan Opera Orchestra, and Zelly Smirnoff, formerly the concertmaster of the NBC Symphony. The drummer was Nat Polen, who years later became a major soap opera star on ABC's *One Life to Live* playing the role of Dr. James Craig. The band singer was Tommy Mercer, who later was featured with Charlie Spivak, Ray Anthony, and the Dorsey Brothers.

The leader of the dance orchestra, which often played at the USO centers in Brooklyn and Manhattan as well as at the Stage Door Canteen in New York, was Dave Terry, who had arranged for large orchestras such as that of André Kostelanetz. Its principal arranger was former Glenn Miller arranger George Williams, along with former Sammy Kaye arranger Ralph Flanagan (né Fleniken), then a trumpeter but later a pianist when he led his own band. Nelson and the virtuoso cellist Alan Shulman, formerly of the NBC Symphony, whose conductor was the towering figure Arturo Toscanini, shared the remainder of the writing duties for this exceptional twenty-eight-piece orchestra.

Saxophonist and composer Johnny Rotella was a member of the band at Fort Monmouth in 1943. Years later he worked with Nelson on various gigs in Los Angeles. He remembered, "The officer in charge of the band at Fort Monmouth in 1943 tried hard to recruit Nelson for our band there; then he found out that Nelson was a member of the Merchant Marine band."

In looking back over this period in the Merchant Marine, Nelson facetiously recalled that the orchestra was greatly assisted by "the fair maidens of Brooklyn who arrived in busloads to help the boys keep their minds off their troubles by contributing other troubles affecting the heart and other unprotected places."[12]

In addition to dance music, the Maritime Service Orchestra also played concert music. In order to form a marching band that could parade in front of a viewing stand, it was expanded to 40 musicians, and, on occasion, it was further augmented to 110 pieces, making use of Naval Reserve musicians. The marching band was under the direction of former Morton Gould arranger Phil Lang. Trumpeter Eddie Bailey, a member of the band who became Nelson's close friend, proudly exclaimed, "It was a great orchestra. There was absolutely nothing like it when it marched down the street."

The Maritime Service Orchestra was put together by Lawrence primarily for recruiting prospective seamen into the Merchant Marine. Seemingly, the all-star Orchestra's formation was also a way to create competition for Glenn Miller's Army Air Force Band, which was then forming. Through his infinite connections, Lawrence was also able to secure stars of the magnitude of Jack Benny, Danny Kaye, comedienne Billie Burke, and film actresses Carole Landis and Madeleine Carroll as guests on the half-hour recruiting show heard on the CBS and NBC radio networks as well as on local stations WOR and WNEW in New York.

One day, immediately after rehearsing Nelson Riddle's arrangement of one of Lawrence's tunes, "Whispering Pines," Terry exclaimed, "What an arrangement! He's never written for strings before and look what he came up with!" According to Eddie Bailey, Terry wasn't aware that Nelson had consulted with Alan Shulman before he wrote it.

Lawrence added, "Nelson was a sweet, quiet, hardworking guy. In a thousand years, you would never have thought he'd become NELSON RIDDLE! Years later, fortunately for me, he arranged a lot of my songs." (Lawrence must have been especially pleased with Frank Sinatra's second and considerably more exhilarating version of "All or Nothing at All," which Nelson arranged at a much faster tempo than the classic Harry James/Sinatra rendition.)

Nelson's immediate acceptance by Dan Terry led to his arrangements for Tommy Mercer to sing such pop standards as "All the Things You Are," "Begin the Beguine," and "Night and Day" for the dance band. Mercer later headed Ft. Lauderdale's tourism bureau for many years and later led his own band in South Florida. He often featured Nelson's arrangement of "Night and Day." "It almost sounds like the arrangement he wrote for Sinatra later on—incredible. I remember saying to him, 'Please don't forget me when you get out of the service,'" the late singer recalled.

Essentially, this stellar group of musicians considered themselves civilian musicians who deigned to allot the Merchant Marine nine and one-quarter hours of each day Monday through Friday starting at 7:45 A.M. and ending at 5:00 P.M. Jack Lawrence saw to it that their evenings were free. Their only real hardship was having to take the subway to Brooklyn from Manhattan at 6:00 A.M.

Violinist and music contractor for the orchestra Gene Orloff explained, "After playing for the raising of the flag, most of the time, unless we had to rehearse, there was really nothing to do until the flag was lowered at the end of the day. We spent most of the time playing cards."

In addition to his responsibilities with the orchestra, each musician was busy working every night in New York. Orloff played on several radio shows. Among his various recording dates, Alan Shulman was frequently part of Axel Stordahl's orchestra backing Frank Sinatra; Stordahl's beautifully crafted ballad arrangements were central to establishing "The Voice" as the biggest figure in popular music in wartime America.

At this time, Nelson was living in an apartment at 11 West 87th Street in Manhattan with Albertine while playing with Willie Schwartz in various bands at the Park Avenue Armory and trying out his latest charts. Since his father was still struggling with his business, Nelson's income from arranging helped support Albertine.

★ ★ ★

Pianist Lou Brown and the late brilliant jazz drummer Shelly Manne were two Brooklynites who were based at the Coast Guard station in Manhattan Beach and played in the band. The Coast Guard station shared the use of the canteen for recreational purposes with the Merchant Marine base. This is where Brown and Manne got to know Apprentice Seaman Nelson Riddle.

Brown said, "Nelson was so serious. He never talked about girls the way we did. He and Eddie Bailey were always together discussing music. I must say, though, that Nelson took full advantage of having this wonderful group of musicians to work with, which had a big effect on him later on. He met Alan Shulman there, who was a real talent. He became very important to him."

Having as much free time as he had, and realizing the depth of Alan Shulman's talents, Nelson spent hours listening to Shulman's suggestions on how to write for a large orchestra. Despite his earlier experience with Tommy Reynolds, Jerry Wald, and Charlie Spivak, it was here that he learned the secrets inherent in juxtaposing woodwinds and brass with strings. Seeking sources of discussion, they frequently listened to various classical and pop albums as well as to Broadway show albums. The work of Robert Russell Bennett, the dean of Broadway orchestrators, had been Shulman's original inspiration.

Alan Shulman became, next to Bill Finegan, Nelson's most important teacher in his early years as an arranger. Currently incapacitated by a series of strokes, Shulman recently referred justifiably to Nelson as "my student for orchestrations." He called him a "so-so trombonist," but when asked if, when he initially met him, he thought of Riddle as being a true talent, he replied emphatically, "Yes!"

Through the assistance of his cellist son Jay, I was able to grasp the depth and versatility of Alan Shulman's arranging talents by listening to a tape of recorded works that began with a compelling chamber jazz piece from May 24, 1940, performed by the New Friends of Rhythm. The piece featured the clarinetist Buster Bailey, and showed the sensuous nature of Shulman's writing. An unusual treatment of Stephen Foster's "Oh, Susannah!" with Arthur Fiedler and the Boston Pops found Shulman quickly transforming the song from a familiar folk song into alternately a classical chamber piece and then a symphony. A pair of Jerome Kern standards ("Can't Help Loving That Man" and "All the Things You Are") as sung by Metropolitan Opera diva Rise Stevens revealed how deftly Shulman voiced woodwinds and illustrated how he used strings as a background for woodwinds and brass. The latter charts gave me reason to conclude that, less than a decade later, Nelson was influenced by Shulman in making use of this precise kind of writing for a large orchestra while providing the settings for Nat Cole, Frank Sinatra, and other singers.

Eddie Bailey perhaps best summed up the uniqueness of Alan Shulman when he said, "Alan had the greatest ear of any musician I ever came across. He had better than perfect pitch. I've simply never met anybody like him."

★ ★ ★

As had been his habit all along, Nelson practiced his trombone every day. He would go into a room where folding chairs were kept at the Merchant Marine base and practice by himself. He often asked Eddie Bailey, "How come you don't have to practice?" Having spent almost four years as lead trumpeter for Les Brown, Bailey had developed a firm lip, which meant that constant practice wasn't necessary.

Bailey said of Nelson, "He was like a brother to me. He was such a kind person—he wasn't the kind of guy who rapped other people. He wasn't a loud guy. He was the type of guy you could trust."

He also laughingly remembered how clumsy Nelson was in those days. "He would buy a pair of new shoes and then right away he'd walk right through a puddle. If he bought a suit with two pairs of pants [as was the custom in those days] he would automatically tear the suit jacket." One could perhaps speculate that this was another indication of how Albertine's overbearing presence stifled Nelson's emotional growth.

"He certainly wasn't clumsy when he wrote music," Bailey continued. "He knew what he was doing. I can remember how he took big band hits like 'Poinciana,' which had been so successful for Glenn Miller, and wrote a far different interpretation of the song."

In observing the slowly but steadily developing career of Nelson Riddle, it is easy to recognize his complete dedication to music. He was not the typical carefree young musician or sailor of the period who spent his free time drinking with the guys or pursuing women. Music was everything to him.

As a perfect example, the Maritime Service Orchestra included a large number of Jewish musicians. In October 1943 they petitioned to be allowed to take the day off for Yom Kippur, the day of atonement for all Jews. At first there was official opposition to

PFC Nelson Riddle and his bride, Doreen Moran, in their wedding photograph, taken at Camp Croft, South Carolina, on October 10, 1945.

their wishes. In order to demonstrate the seriousness of their beliefs, all of the Jewish musicians stayed away from a subsequent rehearsal, as did most of the non-Jewish members of the orchestra. This did not include Nelson Riddle, however. He believed he had too much to learn and too much to accomplish to take the day off!

During the spring of 1944, Alan Shulman was taken ill with the measles while composing his "Suite Based on American Folksongs for Violin and Piano." He desperately needed score paper to start work on his commission, which was due to be premiered on April 24, 1944, at Carnegie Hall. Nelson Riddle, his faithful student, gathered up a ream of score paper and arranged to have it delivered to him. The accompanying message revealed his dedication to his new mentor. He stated how sorry he was that Shulman was ill, but ultimately indicated his eagerness for Shulman to be well again so that he could continue learning from him.

By this time, Nelson had gained valuable musical experience, first by spending two years on the road, playing and writing for a name dance band, then as a result of his seventeen-month-long association with an orchestra of first-rate professionals. Most importantly, during the latter period, he was working under the personal tutelage of a true master in Alan Shulman. But the best was still to come, in the person of Tommy Dorsey—"T.D."—once dubbed the "General Motors of the Band Business" by none other than his former band singer, Frank Sinatra.

CHAPTER 3

The Sentimental
Gentleman of Swing

Drummer Buddy Rich once referred to Tommy Dorsey as "the most beautiful and melodic trombone player who ever lived." This remark masked the incendiary personal feelings between the drummer and the bandleader. Bill Finegan recalled a band rehearsal in Hollywood during which Rich objected to a directive from Dorsey and responded with an untoward remark. Dorsey immediately went after Rich, chasing him off the bandstand, out of the theater, and down Vine Street. On another occasion, it was reported that the volatile Dorsey struck the arrogant drummer "upside the head" with his trombone.

Buddy DeFranco, who played second alto and clarinet and who singlehandedly brought the clarinet out of the swing era and into bebop, spent almost six years working for Tommy Dorsey. "If you could put up with him and he could put up with you, you could learn a lot from him," DeFranco stated. "The whole band learned from him. Not only the trombone players—everybody. Frank Sinatra would have attested to that. . . . His leadership was obvious. He was a born leader. He was also a stormy perfectionist with a short fuse. His use of bad language was unlimited. When he quit drinking, which he did for about a year when I was with him, it got worse. Everybody used to wish he'd go back to drinking again. Buddy Rich's whole living countenance—he lifted it directly from Tommy Dorsey. So did Frank Sinatra."

According to Jane Dorsey, Tommy's widow, the larger-than-life personality of Jackie Gleason was also derived from Tommy Dorsey. Gleason did a number of dates with the Dorsey Orchestra when he was practically an unknown and paid Dorsey back years later by giving him and his brother Jimmy their own CBS-TV show, *Stage Show,* immediately preceding his own show.

The five-time Oscar-winning film composer John Williams offered, "There is a sensibility that begins with one of the most important trombone players [Dorsey] who hailed from the Pennsylvania coal mining country that affected a singer from North Jersey [Frank Sinatra] and a young arranger also from North Jersey [Nelson Riddle]. There was a sarcasm that Nelson had that I really think originated with Tommy Dorsey."

Johnny Mandel, the highly esteemed composer and arranger perhaps best known as the composer of "The Shadow of Your Smile" and "Theme from *M.A.S.H.* (Suicide is

Painless)" recalled, "Tommy Dorsey was a very complicated guy, but he knew precisely what he wanted—like Lyndon Johnson. Nelson was fortunate to work for him because Dorsey may have been the best bandleader of them all. Like Frank Sinatra, Tommy Dorsey was many people—and like Lyndon Johnson he had all kinds of sides to him. He also knew how to put on a show like nobody else."

Berle Adams, the prominent former MCA agent, noted, "Dorsey couldn't stand in front of a bad band. If he didn't have the right musicians, he would go out and steal them from anybody. 'I don't care about friendships,' he said."

This was Thomas Francis Dorsey, "The Sentimental Gentleman of Swing." Dorsey, whose familiar theme song was "I'm Getting Sentimental over You," and who was unquestionably one of the most vital and influential bandleaders in the history of American music. As Artie Shaw, who first knew Dorsey when they worked together as radio musicians, observed, "I was in awe of his leadership. He was a fine editor. He demanded discipline and commanded respect. He made the trombone into a singing instrument. I think Tommy's overall importance has been downplayed over the years—Glenn Miller gets all the attention." Further expressing his disdain for Miller's place in big band history, Shaw then added, "Glenn's death turned out to be a good career move."

As soon as his seventeen-month enlistment in the Merchant Marine expired, Nelson left New York for Chicago by train to join Tommy Dorsey and his Orchestra on May 11, 1944. He replaced trombonist Charlie Small during an engagement at the Panther Room of the Hotel Sherman in Chicago. He spent the next eleven months with Dorsey in the third trombone chair and served as one of Tommy's arrangers. The bandleader was well aware that his own talents didn't extend to arranging, which is one good reason why he always hired a staff of skilled arrangers.

In gauging the overall development of an artist, it is not always "How long did he spend with so-and-so?" It's "What did he learn from that experience?" In addition to furthering his arranging technique, Nelson learned more from working for Tommy Dorsey than from his association with any other musical organization up to that time. As Nelson described it, "It was worth its weight in gold, even at the unsensational rates of those days."[1]

Bill Finegan, who was still writing arrangements for Dorsey, most likely got Nelson the job, although Finegan can't remember for sure. Alto saxophonist Sid Cooper, who had joined the Dorsey band two months before Nelson, speculates that a music publisher who had hired Nelson to write some arrangements might have initially recommended him to Dorsey.

Despite the fact that Dorsey often approached new band members by pointedly asking in his often grating, nasal-toned voice, "Well, shitheel, are you going to give me trouble or are we going to be okay, or what?" the soft-spoken Riddle adapted himself rather easily to this new and highly charged musical setting and its forceful leader. In the words of Buddy DeFranco, Dorsey was "defensive and offensive right from the beginning." (In a strange way, for Nelson it must have been almost like dealing with Albertine!)

As DeFranco recalled, "Nelson didn't complain about anything. I think he really liked Tommy's direction at the time."

Milt Bernhart, one of Nelson's "regulars" (the core of musicians he hired frequently for recording from the 1950s to the 1980s), once asked him if he developed his writing while doing one-nighters with Dorsey. Nelson replied with a characteristically sarcastic retort: "No, I spent most of my time getting my laundry done and seeing to it that I didn't get poisoned eating in dingy restaurants."

Being on the road enabled him to become close to several musicians such as DeFranco and guitarist Bob Bain, who he was later to work with and who became life-long friends. His roommate during his time with Tommy Dorsey was trumpeter Mickey Mangano, who he also later often hired for Hollywood recording sessions.

When Nelson first joined Tommy Dorsey's orchestra, Gene Krupa was the drummer. He was replaced by Buddy Rich, fresh from his dishonorable discharge from the Marine Corps, back for his second stint with Dorsey. Nelson recalled, "Buddy's drumming improved the band's sound. I remember one occasion—the Air Force flew us from California to a big airfield in Phoenix, Arizona. Then we had to take a bus to where we were going to play the concert. As we went along on this bus, Buddy kept seeing these telephone poles with placards on them, saying 'Tommy Dorsey and his Orchestra featuring Gene Krupa.' Buddy was getting madder and madder. We got on the field, started the rehearsal, and halfway through it Buddy slammed down the sticks—'I'm walking off. I'm not going to sit here and play notes for another drummer.' Tommy just turned and looked at him, and said, 'You better stick around. Because, if you don't, you're not going to get off this field alive!' He meant it."[2]

I asked Sid Cooper how Tommy Dorsey might have approached Nelson Riddle to begin writing arrangements for the band. Did he say, "Okay, You're here—start writing?" "Right, Tommy was that way," Sid replied. "He would like to hear things you did, but he would never hit you on the head and press you. We were practicing our horns during the day and perfecting our musicianship and also writing at the same time, which eighteen other guys in the band weren't. He never pushed me that hard, and I'm sure he didn't push Nelson. I think he was very aware of what Nelson did right from the beginning or he wouldn't have recorded [the arrangements he wrote]. I think there's the Finegan thing, too, because Tommy was very fond of Finegan, and Finegan liked Nelson—that was in Nelson's favor. Tommy never said that to anybody, but I think that's the way he thought."

Sid Cooper remembered the circumstances surrounding the time Tommy first asked Nelson to write for the band. "There was a radio show the band appeared on during the summer of 1944 called *The All-Time Hit Parade,* that featured a well-known singer as a guest each week. Every Sunday, the show featured an arrangement of a song that had been on the *Hit Parade* earlier. Tommy gave me one to write on a Friday night to be ready to rehearse on Saturday. When he hit me with this one, it was 'Top Hat, White Tie, and Tails,' the Fred Astaire tune, to feature the Sentimentalists [the singing group that replaced the Pied Pipers with Dorsey]. He said, 'Go over to the other fellow, Nelson, and work it out together.'

"Nelson and I went to one of the studios that was being rented by music publishers across the street from NBC, which used to be at Sunset and Vine in Hollywood. Nelson would go over there every morning that we weren't busy with something else and study and write. That was his very existence at the time.

"It was just a chorus and a half. We went up to the publisher's office when nobody was there and immediately got to work on it. Nelson looked at me, and I looked at him. Nelson was not much with words. I said to him, 'Where do you want to start and where shall I . . . ?' He said, 'Well, you start it, and I'll pick it up at the seventeenth bar . . .' and that's the way we went. Within an hour and a half or so, we were through the arrangement and gave it to the copyist.

"There was a noticeable difference in style between us," Cooper continued, "but it seemed to work out. It was quite simple: I was trying to write a Modernaires [Glenn Miller's singing group] type of arrangement. When Nelson wrote the bridge, he threw a bit of a fugue in there, and it was quite different from anything I would have written. I wrote it as a typical swing arrangement, the fastest I knew how to do it to get out of the studio. That was always my style. Nelson wanted to sit there and linger with it and suffer with it."

Sid Cooper recognized the results of Finegan's teaching on the first two charts Riddle wrote alone for Dorsey, "Like Someone in Love" and "Sleigh Ride in July." Others included cover versions of hits like "There's No You," "Out of This World," and "I Should Care." Two charts that Dorsey never recorded but continued to play were Nelson's perfect showcase for his ballad style, "You're Mine You," as well as "Laura."

Regarding the latter arrangement, Buddy DeFranco said, "What was amazing about Nelson was that he had enough sense to leave the chord progressions that David Raksin wrote. You don't have to add any extraneous chords. 'Laura''s that kind of thing. Even though he kept the basic 'Laura' structure, and the basic harmonic, he chose in some areas to throw in a few altered chords. It gave an ethereal effect to the song and to the arrangements. The guys in the band loved it, but Tommy said, 'Get that out of here. That's not the 'Laura' I know.' He then trimmed it down pretty good. I think that's when he began calling Nelson 'The Cloud,' and sometimes 'Cloud 9.'"

Working for Dorsey gave Nelson easy access to strings, since Dorsey's band had an even larger string section than the Maritime Service Orchestra. It even included a harp. Dorsey had hired most of Artie Shaw's string players when Shaw entered the navy in

1942. By then, Nelson had recognized the depth of his preference in arranging; he later recalled, "I loved to write for strings. I incorporated in my arrangements large areas that were primarily devoted to strings. I had enough time to try out different string voicings and thus was able to add to my 'tool box' proportionately."[3]

It's probably no accident that Nelson Riddle felt himself immediately drawn to writing for strings. It has long been recognized that string instruments, especially the violin, emit frequencies that particularly touch the heart. One could also speculate that his string arrangements musically expressed the underlying sadness that was already so much a part of him.

During my first interview with Nelson, which took place in March 1962 for a piece in *Los Angeles Magazine,* I remember him telling me, "Tommy Dorsey referred to the strings as 'the mice.' After I wrote my first few arrangements for him, one night he invited me to have dinner with him. He told me, 'I like your writing, but you're relying too heavily on 'the mice.' You're making them too important. I'm thinking of getting rid of them soon. They're basically a tax deduction so I want to keep that flexibility, but when I get rid of them I want to have arrangements that the band can still play.'

"I was crushed by that news," Nelson continued, "but I revised my plans so that I started writing without leaning on the strings. It was just as well. I then learned to write both ways."

Actually, within months eight more strings were added to the section—a vivid example of Dorsey's ever-changing ideas. From December 1944 until June 1945 Dorsey led his "Big Bertha Band," which was comprised of forty-six men.[4]

DeFranco described Nelson's writing for Dorsey as "very modern. It was sort of a Ravel derivative, which everybody studied at the time. There used to be the adage, 'If you want to learn about orchestration, take a look at Ravel's scores.' And combined with what he gleaned from Bill Finegan . . . he did, well, all of us did . . . we took what we wanted from the giants and for our own purpose made our own voice out of them. That's exactly what Nelson did.

"Tommy used to scream at almost all of the arrangers for writing too much and trying to get too far out. Nelson and Finegan were the guys who wrote what they wanted to write, and it was way ahead of its time. Tommy would say, 'No, take that out . . . and trim it down.' Bill and Nelson would get bent out of shape because they were proud of what they had written. But Tommy, like most bandleaders, knew what the public wanted, and he tailored those arrangements to the public. Tommy's idea of a good arrangement was more like Sy Oliver—ya know, blood-and-guts-type arrangements."

★ ★ ★

Who was Melvin James (Sy) Oliver and why was he so important to Tommy Dorsey—and to the subsequent development of Nelson Riddle? To answer that question, one must turn again to Bill Finegan, whose first arrangement for Tommy Dorsey—the chart for "Lonesome Road I and II" (a two-sided record)—was highly influenced by Sy

Oliver's writing style for Jimmie Lunceford. Finegan said proudly, "I like to think that this arrangement led to Tommy's wanting to incorporate Lunceford's kind of music into his band, and it's what caused Tommy to hire Sy in the first place."

The musical image of Jimmie Lunceford and his Orchestra, termed by no less than the late, renowned big band expert George T. Simon as "without a doubt the most exciting big band of all time," was markedly shaped by the compositions and particularly by the arrangements of Sy Oliver.[5] The completely self-taught arranger, nicknamed Sy because he had studied psychology, joined Lunceford in 1933 as a trumpeter. Oliver's well-remembered arrangements included "Dream of You," "Four or Five Times," "Swanee River," "My Blue Heaven," "Organ Grinder's Swing," "For Dancers Only" (which became Lunceford's theme song), "Margie," "By the River Sainte Marie," "'Tain't What You Do," "Cheatin' on Me," and "Ain't She Sweet." Regarding his arranging prowess, the renowned jazz immortal Benny Carter said, "Sy was the master of economy."

The Lunceford band, composed entirely of black musicians, was so popular that it sometimes had two or three hit records on the pop chart at the same time. In the late 1930s, it was a bigger draw than either the Basie or Ellington bands. Bill Finegan described the Lunceford band as having "a down-home kind of swing, Basie's band was loose-jointed, Duke's band strutted."

James Melvin (Jimmie) Lunceford was a former saxophonist and flutist, as well as music teacher, who graduated from Fisk University in Nashville and later studied at City College of New York (CCNY). He taught at Manassas High School in Memphis, where he organized a student band. From there he started his own orchestra and began recording for Columbia Records, moving to New York in 1933.

Instead of playing an instrument, like Paul Whiteman, Lunceford led his truly legendary orchestra by waving a baton. His musicians were immaculate in their dress, and like Duke Ellington, Lunceford wanted his musicians to present themselves as gentlemen of jazz. When working theater engagements they carried six different uniforms. Their uniforms were changed before every show, as were their music stands. There was even a special curtain used specifically for theater dates that was carried on the band bus. While playing ensemble passages on certain "flag-waving" numbers, the brass section of the band would turn to the left while the reeds would simultaneously veer to the right, always maintaining the tempo. The entire trumpet section would wave its derby hats in front of its horns to alternately muffle and open up the sound of the section. Such practices were later copied by many other bands. The musical precision and theatricality of the Lunceford Orchestra was maintained through a deep-rooted sense of pride and *esprit de corps*.

Tommy Dorsey admired discipline, showmanship, and most importantly first-rate musicianship, which is exactly what the Lunceford Orchestra displayed. The best way to duplicate that, Dorsey felt, was to hire away Sy Oliver, which he did in July 1939, agreeing to pay him $5,000 a year more than Lunceford was paying him.

In June 1935, right in the middle of playing "I'll Never Say 'Never' Again" during an engagement of the Dorsey Brothers Orchestra at the Glen Island Casino, Tommy had a serious dispute with his older brother, alto saxophone and clarinet player Jimmy (who he always referred to as "Lad" or "The Brother"), over the tempo the band was playing the tune. Tommy abruptly left the stand and immediately decided to form his own band.

Within two years, Tommy Dorsey and his Orchestra became established as a popular dance band as a result of such hugely successful recordings as "Marie," "Song of India," "Who" and "Boogie Woogie." Although they were essentially dance bands, a strong preponderance of jazz was the element that caused Goodman, Shaw, and Charlie Barnet's groups to become the leading bands of the time. The jazz quotient of Tommy Dorsey's band, on the other hand, despite having such talented soloists as trumpeter Bunny Berigan, tenor saxophonist Bud Freeman, and drummer Dave Tough, was lacking—except for the Dixieland group within the band called "The Clambake Seven," for which Deane Kincaide arranged. Dorsey, while an adequate Dixieland trombonist, was forever envious of Jack Teagarden, the premier jazz and blues trombonist of the time.

Tenor saxophonist Babe Russin left Benny Goodman in the fall of 1938 to join Dorsey. Over a several month period, he and other band members encouraged Dorsey to phase out "The Clambake Seven" and to embark upon a new direction to become more of a swing band. In a *Billboard* article dated December 31, 1938, under the title of "Swing It, Sweetly!," Tommy Dorsey made it clear where his sympathies lay: "Swing is smooth, easy to listen to, and calm enough for the most conservative dancer—there are no extraneous flourishes or 'out-of-the-world' take-offs by individual instrumentalists. . . ."

Once he agreed to change the musical outlook of his band, who was better equipped to make that transformation happen than Sy Oliver? Essentially, Dorsey wanted to bring Jimmie Lunceford's music to a white audience and to depart from leading a middle-of-the-road dance band that depended on featuring danceable versions of the popular songs of the day.

It's certainly no accident that a key factor in the success not only of Tommy Dorsey but of Benny Goodman and later Harry James was due to the extraordinary writing talents of the African American arrangers Fletcher and Horace Henderson, Edgar Sampson (Goodman), and Jimmy Mundy (Goodman and James). These white bandleaders fully realized that when it came to crafting highly individual jazz charts, with decided style and brio, such writers could consistently deliver "the real thing."

In Johnny Mandel's view, "Before Sy Oliver came to work for Dorsey, Tommy had a pretty good band, but when it swung it really didn't swing. It was like Glenn Miller's band trying to swing. When Sy joined Dorsey, Sy and Buddy Rich were the motors

Tommy Dorsey and his Orchestra in a 1944 MGM publicity photo taken on the set of *Thrill of a Romance,* which starred Esther Williams and Van Johnson. Nelson Riddle is seen at the end of the trombone section with Buddy Rich on drums and Bob Bain on guitar. Sid Cooper and Buddy DeFranco on tenor saxophone and clarinet are next to Dorsey. The vocalists Bonnie Lou Williams and Bob Allen are in the foreground along with the Clark Sisters.

behind the "new" Dorsey band. Joe Bushkin on piano and Sid Weiss were also helpful. With [trumpeter] Ziggy Elman and Frank Sinatra's help, the band became a monster. But it really became a monster because of Sy."

Oliver's arrangements for Dorsey of tunes like "Easy Does It," "Deep River," and "Hallelujah!" were designed to highlight the bandleader and his three trombones. His arrangement for "Well, Git It" featured trumpeter Chuck Peterson and Ziggy Elman; "Quiet, Please" featured Buddy Rich, who had been convinced to leave Artie Shaw by the news that Sy Oliver was to become Dorsey's principal arranger. "For You" was a song that featured Jo Stafford, who had emerged from the Pied Pipers and became one of the most pure pop singers who ever lived. Sy showcased his own singing with the duet he shared with Stafford on the sublime "Exactly Like You." This was not to mention such tunes as "The One I Love," "It's Always You," "Imagination," "Polka Dots and Moonbeams," "Without a Song," "Dolores," "Blue Skies," "It Started All over Again," and others, all of which he arranged after Frank Sinatra joined Dorsey's band in February 1940.

Gerald Wilson had replaced Sy Oliver in the Lunceford trumpet section and soon after became Sy's lifetime friend. A long-established arranger and bandleader in his own right, Wilson described the effect Sy Oliver had on the Dorsey band, "When you bring in a guy who can really do jazz well [suddenly] your harmonics change. The rhythmic patterns that you use are jazz. The jazz is coming. And don't forget, Tommy Dorsey had good men who could play this music."

Sy Oliver was drafted into the Army in 1942; by 1944 he had been promoted to sergeant. Nevertheless, he continued to write for Dorsey on a part-time basis, and his vast library of arrangements was still a mainstay of Dorsey's presentation.

From August 1, 1942, until November 1944, however, no records were produced that featured musicians because of an edict laid down by the head of the American Federation of Musicians (A.F. of M.), James C. Petrillo. The pompous Petrillo foolishly believed that his ban on recordings using musicians would result in more work through personal appearances for his union members. Petrillo's unfortunate decision led to the practice by major labels of recording singers with choral backgrounds that took the place of musicians. This was best exemplified by the beautiful *a cappella* ballad recordings made by Frank Sinatra on Columbia during this period. The success of these records was a key factor in singers becoming increasingly more important than big bands.

As soon as the recording ban was finally lifted, Dorsey brought his band into the RCA Victor studio on Sycamore in Hollywood on November 14, 20, and 22, 1944. From these first three recording sessions came two highly successful big band standards. The first was Sy Oliver's arrangement of his own composition "Opus #1," with memorable solos by Buddy DeFranco on clarinet and Bruce Branson on baritone saxophone. The second record was Sy's version of Jimmy McHugh's "On the Sunny Side of the Street," which featured the Sentimentalists and Branson.

At the bridge of the arrangement of "Sunny Side of the Street," there is a memorable muted trombone chorus—played by the entire Dorsey trombone section—which restates the theme. One of the members of that trombone section was Nelson Riddle. "Opus #1" became extremely popular; for years afterwards it seemed as though Dorsey's record of the tune and Billy May's spirited arrangement of "Cherokee" for Charlie Barnet's band were the theme songs of choice for many important disc jockey radio shows.

The two-beat arranging style of Sy Oliver featured the repetition of certain underlying rhythmic patterns that were prevalent in many of his arrangements. This was not lost on the eager and dedicated Riddle. He couldn't help but notice the inherent charm in Oliver's writing—his strong sense of the beat, the basic swinging effects, staccato phrases with an element of humor, a brilliant sense of continuity and climax—which was combined with his superlative use of dynamics.[6] (As Oliver once told Dorsey's close friend Eddie Collins, "Dynamics, that's the secret.")

Playing the multitude of Oliver-arranged instrumentals and vocals—often two and three times a night each—with the Dorsey band made a vivid and indelible impression on the musical matrix of Nelson Riddle. And from the viewpoint of an arranger, he could see precisely how well they worked.

As Bill Finegan, with great profundity, pointed out, "There is a straight line between Nelson's sitting in that Dorsey trombone chair playing those Sy Oliver charts, which had real identity, and the up-tempo arrangements that he started writing for Frank Sinatra nearly ten years later." This highly significant statement was echoed by such qualified arrangers as Johnny Mandel, Gerald Wilson, Sid Cooper, and the late Les Brown, who started as an arranger with his first band in 1938.

Ralph Burns went even further in agreeing with Finegan on this point when he said, "That's absolutely right. Nelson used the kind of figures that Sy used to write. Beethoven built on Mozart—don't ever forget that! Every composer and arranger builds on somebody else. You're not born [as an arranger] and you don't put earmuffs over your ears."

All told, Sid Cooper believes Nelson wrote about a dozen charts for Dorsey in the eleven months he was a member of the band—roughly one arrangement a month, starting at $20 an arrangement. One of these arrangements was for a tune called "Tomfoolery." But in addition to Finegan, Cooper, and Nelson, Dorsey also employed arrangers Hugo Winterhalter (later known for his sometimes overly dramatic string arrangements for Eddie Fisher in the 1950s), and Freddie Norman, both of whom were very different in their musical approaches.

★ ★ ★

Bob Bain, who was the guitarist in the Dorsey band during Nelson's tenure there and later played the memorable guitar solo on Nelson's famous *Route 66* theme, agrees that Tommy's nickname for Nelson, "The Cloud," was perfectly apt. "Everybody thought of him as this foggy guy." (Coincidentally, Nelson had written the arrangement for a song called "Cloud Nine" for Charlie Spivak.) As we have seen, Nelson's complete absorption in improving his trombone playing and arranging technique was the reason Dorsey and most of his fellow musicians had this impression of him.

Sid Cooper related an incident that reflected on the kind of person Nelson Riddle really was: "The guys in the band were all staying at the Halifax Hotel in Hollywood. It was inexpensive and it was near the place where we were rehearsing. Nelson would get up early every morning even though we worked late the night before. I would sleep in. My wife was in her early twenties, my daughter was three years old. He would sit there and talk with Ethel and Carol beside the fishpond in the courtyard of the hotel. Then he would walk to a coffee shop before going over to a publisher's office. There he would listen to his records—mostly the hot classical records of the day: Delius, and of course, Debussy, Ravel—all very romantic music with beautiful chord structures. He was able to make use of them in arranging popular music.

"One day, after talking with Ethel and Carol, he left to start his usual routine. Ethel suddenly realized he had left his portfolio in the courtyard, which contained his records and score paper. She and Carol walked over to the coffee shop to find him. Nelson was extremely surprised to see them, and when he saw the portfolio in Ethel's hand, he said, 'Oh, my gosh! That's all my music!'"

Cooper concluded that Nelson's apparent absentmindedness was most likely due to his being lost in thought, "thinking of what he heard the night before or where he was going to use it in the next thing he wrote and how he was going to interpret it."

Yet, in 1974, thirty years later, Nelson came into the Empire Room of the Waldorf-Astoria, where Cooper was leading a small dance band following singer Sergio Franchi's nightclub act. After the set, Cooper went over and greeted Nelson, who immediately asked, "How's that little dark-haired girl?" In the intervening years, Carol Cooper had become (and still is) Vice President of N.S. Bienstock. With her husband, Richard Liebner, who heads up the agency, they represent several major TV news personalities such as Mike Wallace, Dan Rather, and Diane Sawyer. Nelson may have illustrated various instances of vagueness during his days with Tommy Dorsey, but he was not out of touch with what was going on around him.

The anger in Nelson Riddle, which was often just below the surface, was revealed by an incident that took place in 1944 at the 400 Club in New York, where the Dorsey band was playing an engagement. On the bandstand Nelson sat on the end of the second row, right behind Buddy Rich's left shoulder. The dance floor was full, and the show was a big success. Unfortunately, the maitre d' and the waiters didn't appreciate the band. They glared at the musicians with disdain. Nelson was so irritated by their contemptuous attitude that purely out of spite he would put out his cigarette on a tray full of food as it went by.

★ ★ ★

In recalling Dorsey days, Bob Bain said, "I was interested in writing so I enjoyed talking to Sid and Nelson about writing for a band. We'd get together and maybe listen to a classical record once in a while, if we could. I remember Nelson liked to listen to *La Mer* by Debussy. He loved that orchestration. I think he, with Finegan, kind of took that apart. They took the score and saw what Debussy did. It was like a music lesson.

"I don't know if he got it directly from Debussy, but Nelson was the first one that I knew of that really used triads [three-tone chords, the harmonic basis of tonal music] in a pop arrangement. He always heard those passing triads that became his signature line right off the bat. He used them all his life. Triads had the same basic structure as Debussy's music. Now everybody does it. It's a standard thing to do."

What is also important to realize is that playing a myriad of popular songs on a regular basis, not only those of the time but also established pop standards, gave Nelson the knowledge and understanding of a great many important and diversified composers. In addition, the respect that Nelson gained from Dorsey for his writing also eventually extended to his trombone playing. When the bandleader was otherwise involved or decided to leave midway in the last set, on occasion he delegated Nelson to play his solos.

"Concerning his trombone playing, I thought he was very good," Sid Cooper said. "He was very confident in what he was doing. The other fellows were scared, afraid to tackle it. Dorsey would start off on a high B, and it would be like somebody else playing a low F-sharp. I'm sure Nelson was concerned with it, but when he played it . . . it didn't sound like Tommy at all. The high B was there. . . . There was a confident kind of sound in the solo. Today the guys who are playing high Bs can play that same B an octave higher. But the way it was then, that was a high note. It was really one of *the* high notes."

Bob Bain recalled things slightly differently: "Nelson didn't want to play high. Nobody wanted to stand up and have to hit that C-sharp, where Tommy liked to play, and then have Tommy out there waiting for him to miss it."

In an August 1967 bylined story in *Crescendo International,* Nelson said of his playing during his sojourn with Dorsey: "I don't think I would have been any great flash as a trombone player. I got a good sound, but I recall Tommy saying that I held my jaw too rigidly, whatever that means."

While arranging for the Four Freshmen during the 1950s, Nelson complimented Bob Flanigan, the leader of the group, for his trombone playing technique. He admitted to Flanigan, "I had to warm up for forty-five minutes when I was playing for Dorsey." Ann Clark, one of the Sentimentalists, recalled that after seeing Nelson play a long passage on the trombone, his lips would be swollen and he would turn pinkish around the mouth.

★ ★ ★

In the late spring and summer of 1944, Tommy Dorsey and his Orchestra played an extended engagement at the Casino Gardens, a large dance pavilion in Santa Monica that Tommy jointly owned with his brother Jimmy and Harry James. The booking coincided with the band's appearance in the Esther Williams-Van Johnson MGM romantic extravaganza *Thrill of a Romance.* (Williams related in her autobiography that this was the movie that established her as a full-fledged star.)[7] This trip to southern California, the first of Nelson Riddle's life, was to have great significance.

The Dorsey band was featured in several scenes in the movie and played songs including Nelson's arrangement of "I Should Care." If you look carefully when the film plays on AMC (American Movie Classics) or TCM (Turner Classic Movies), you might catch a quick glimpse of Nelson in the trombone section as the band plays "Song of India." Somehow, Nelson was also given the opportunity to write a little background music—two or three vignettes that were part of the musical background of the film.

Sid Cooper recalled that one was an interlude that required writing for strings. Small and insignificant though this kind of writing might have been, it had a major effect on Nelson. This experience caused him to solidify his desire to become a film composer, following up on his initial thoughts while working movie theater dates with Charlie Spivak.

Nelson reveled in the glamour attendant to the making of films—the pretty girls, the costumes, and the fantasy of it all. This was the opposite of everything he had ever known. And what opportunities the film industry offered for arrangers and composers to create music for large orchestras that played the scores! Twelve years later he would return to MGM, the supreme dream factory, to write arrangements for one of its last epic musicals, *High Society*.

While working by day on *Thrill of a Romance* and by night at the Casino Gardens in 1944, Nelson often ate dinner at a small French restaurant in the Lido Hotel in Hollywood. He noticed the attractive cashier, Barbara Moran, and began to talk to her one night. When he learned, however, that she was still in high school he lost interest in her. On looking back at the incident fifty-six years later, Barbara (Moran) Ernest recalled, "I thought he was very nice, so I decided to introduce him to my big sister. For years afterwards, Nelson would tease me by saying, 'You're the one I was interested in first.'"

One night that summer, Nelson met Don Raffell, his old friend from the Charlie Spivak band, for dinner at the Lido. Don had left the Spivak band in Los Angeles right after its appearance in the film *Pin Up Girl* with Betty Grable at 20th Century Fox. He enthusiastically told Nelson about all the work for musicians in the new American paradise.

Raffell, who knew their waitress, Doreen Moran (Barbara's sister), contends that it was he, and not Barbara, who actually introduced Nelson to her. Don remembered, "During the meal I said, 'Nelson's been watching you walk around'—I was kidding her—'and he's very intrigued.' She blushed, of course. She was very shy."

Doreen and Nelson started dating immediately. In the course of getting acquainted, she explained to Nelson that she had never worked as a waitress before—she was merely trying to help out the owners, who were personal friends who had encountered great difficulties getting help during the war.

Born in 1922, Doreen had graduated—as the class valedictorian—from Fremont High School in Southwest Los Angeles in 1941. She briefly attended Woodbury College, but she was intent on helping in the war effort. She left college to become a "Rosie, the Riveter," building bombers for North American Aircraft Corporation. (At the same time, Norma Jean Mortenson, later to become known as Marilyn Monroe, was doing similar work for Radioplane in Burbank, California.) In keeping with Doreen's patriotic spirit, she danced with G.I.s to the music of the big bands at the Hollywood Canteen. Later, she worked as a photographer and cigarette girl at plush Hollywood supper clubs.

Nelson was attracted to Doreen's looks. She was five feet six inches tall with light brown hair, hazel eyes, deep dimples, and a trim figure. He felt comfortable with her warm and friendly manner, which was just the opposite of his.

Doreen was of Irish descent and one of eight children, three of whom had died in infancy. Her father, Henry Meryl Moran, was a former member of the cavalry, stationed on the Mexican border. He wound up as a recruiting sergeant based at Fort MacArthur in San Pedro, California, where the Moran family lived on the Army post. Henry died of septic poisoning at forty-one, leaving Doreen's mother, Annah Moran, with little money and five children to raise. Barbara Ernest recently remarked, "Mama was one of the first women's libbers."

Bob Bain remembered meeting Doreen one night when he picked up Nelson at the Halifax Hotel to go to work. They drove out to the Casino Gardens with Doreen sitting in the middle. Bain recalled, "When we got to the gig, I left them to get out of my tuxedo because I discovered I had leg makeup all down my leg. In those days, women's stockings were rationed, and because of that all the girls wore leg makeup instead of stockings! Doreen was very embarrassed."

Buddy DeFranco remembered, "Nelson had a funny way of saying things. He'd say, 'You remember Doreen. She's the one with the big legs.' But he married her, and he thought she was great. Once in a while, to be cute, if a good-looking girl went by, he'd look at her and he'd start, with a silly grin on his face, to dribble. It was idiotic . . . drooling. It was the silliest thing. We called him 'Nelson Dribble!'"

DeFranco went on to describe Nelson's normally elegant appearance, "I think maybe the influence of his mother, who said she came from royalty, gave him that kind of regal outlook, except when he would wear a tuxedo. At first glance he would look great . . . on top of the world, and then the tuxedo shirt would be sticking out under his jacket. That was Nelson as far back as I can remember. But even up close his personality was elegant. He had a regal bearing, a distinctive personality, a great [deep] voice, and a good sense of humor."

★ ★ ★

Nelson and Doreen's courtship was interrupted shortly after it began when the Dorsey band moved on to San Francisco before proceeding east to Chicago. Dorsey was away from the bandstand for several weeks following a brawl involving himself, the actor Jon Hall, and Tommy's bodyguard, Allan Smiley. The fight began when Hall came on to Tommy's wife, Pat Dane, and resulted in serious injuries and eventually, a jury trial.

In the intervening months, Nelson corresponded with Doreen on almost a daily basis and called her constantly from the road. Nelson missed her so much that he talked her into moving to New York in the late fall of '44. By then the Dorsey band was playing an extended hotel engagement at the Café Rouge of the Hotel Pennsylvania.

Doreen rented a tiny one-room apartment on Park Avenue and at first worked as a department store perfume salesperson. As a result of her ability to sell beauty products, she received several raises in salary in a short period of time.

At a company called Parfum L'Orle, Doreen met Edna Mae Blind, who was to become her close friend. Shortly afterwards, the two young women began working as models for *Parade* magazine, then in its infancy. Edna Mae referred to Doreen as "the most outgoing individual you've ever met in your life! She was fun, and she was very well liked. As a matter of fact, she used to talk to [total strangers] in Times Square, and I used to say, 'Doreen, you just can't do that!' And she'd look at me and say, 'I don't know why not!'

"She really got Nelson's career off the ground. He was a very kind, good guy—not flamboyant at all—extremely low key. He was never front and center—you noticed that in any of the television shows that showed him conducting. He never was a hot dog."

Inevitably, Doreen would have to endure the scrutiny of Albertine, which was, of course, no trivial matter. Nelson, Nelson, Sr., and Albertine were living at the time in an apartment on West 72nd Street in New York, which Doreen told Edna Mae was "the gloomiest, darkest place I have ever been in in my life! It gave me the shudders."

Upon meeting Nelson's parents, Doreen noticed that Albertine kept referring to her husband as "Ennis." She finally figured out that she was calling him N.S.—the initials of his first and middle names (Nelson Smock). Albertine made constant requests, such as "N.S., please get me my brandy. I'm having palpitations." Doreen could scarcely miss Albertine's autocratic demeanor, and yet, there was no money to support it; it was a completely hollow aristocracy. Needless to say, Doreen's first meeting with Albertine didn't go well.

As Barbara Ernest, now the only remaining member of the Moran family, rightly surmised, "I don't think she [Albertine] ever thought any girl, including Doreen, was good enough for her son. I know that she had been very negative about any girls Nelson had brought around in the past. But that didn't deter Doreen, and it certainly didn't deter Nelson."

Their relationship wasn't affected by Nelson's draft notice, either. It was rather a miracle that he had been deferred this long. Upon leaving the Merchant Marine, he had almost immediately been asked to report for a physical and was classified 1A. Finally, on April 9, 1945, Nelson left the Tommy Dorsey band and entered the Army in New York.

Shortly before Nelson gave Dorsey his notice, Bill Finegan offered what he thought was the most important musical advice he ever gave him: "I think I spent three days and nights with Nelson almost without sleep. I told him to put his trombone in the case. By this time he had gotten to the point where he was a good writer. He could solo a little on trombone—he just was nothing special. I told him, 'When you play in the band and write, the leader treats your writing like it's a hobby. He'll play the stuff, but you won't get paid much for it. . . . Sy Oliver had told me that Jimmie Lunceford used to give him two bucks a chart. I told him, 'Be a writer and they will take you more seriously.' After much agonizing, Nelson finally agreed to give up [his trombone playing]."

Years later, Nelson described his association with Tommy Dorsey as follows: "I had become a good trombone player in the Merchant Marine band. [Therefore,] I was good enough to play in the Dorsey band. And Tommy wasn't easy on trombones, either. He was stern, but he was very good to me, and he was quite supportive of my budding career as an arranger."

Nelson was immediately sent to Fort Dix, New Jersey, for processing. His only contact with music was hearing Bing Crosby's record of "The Anniversary Waltz" being played over the loudspeaker at 6:00 A.M. as the recruits were summoned to fall out of bed and report for formation.

After a few days at Fort Dix, Nelson described being "piled into Civil War–era railroad cars and puffed down to Camp Croft, South Carolina. We were immediately marched to a wide, flat area carpeted by warm green grass, and told to sit down. A second lieutenant stepped out on the balcony of a nearby building and instructed us to file away whatever skills we had acquired in civilian life and that, from this day, we were all foot soldiers.

"The man next to me began to cry very softly. Later he told me that he had been a civil engineer and that, up 'til the moment the 'shavetail' made his fateful announcement, he had been certain the Army would use him in some engineering capacity. I told him that I was a music arranger and trombone player. I couldn't tell if he felt better or worse after that."[8]

Luck seemed to be with Nelson even then, as, contrary to the young officer's pronouncement, he was transferred to the band at Camp Croft after completing basic training. Now that WWII had ended, the majority of the battalion went to Nagasaki, Japan, as the vanguard of the first occupation troops.

Nelson and Doreen discussed getting married after he finished basic training. Albertine, however, was dead set against it. Fortunately, Nelson consulted again with Bill Finegan. This time the subject wasn't arranging, it was marriage. Bill recalled, "He and Doreen came out to my house in Tenafly, New Jersey. They stayed overnight. Everything took a couple of days with him. It wasn't that he was dense . . . but it would take a long time for something to get through to him. He was very upset over his mother's opposition to their getting married."

"I screamed at him, 'If this is the girl you want to marry, do it. It's your decision, not your mother's, about whom you want to marry. Get on with it!' My ex-wife and I helped him with some of the technicalities to set up getting married—the license and so forth."

As he had in the past, Nelson took Finegan's advice. With good reason, Sy Oliver once referred to Finegan as "the human tranquilizer." Nelson and Doreen were married on October 10, 1945, at Camp Croft.

When Nelson was making final preparations for their wedding, he called Albertine requesting that she send him the close to $5,000 he had saved while working for Charlie Spivak, the Merchant Marine Band, and Tommy Dorsey. She wound up giving him half of the money. She figured the rest was hers.

CHAPTER 4

Hollywood Calling

After their marriage, the Riddles settled at Camp Croft, near Spartanburg, South Carolina, to begin married life. However, they were soon forced to relocate when Nelson was transferred to Fort Knox, Kentucky. There he led the band at the officers' club. This was still another example of Nelson's luck in beating the system by being allowed to play music instead of having to deal with the rigors of soldiering.

At Fort Knox, he met Norm Jeffries, the drummer in the band. They worked together for slightly over a year. When Nelson left Fort Knox, Jeffries remembers him advising him to learn to play some mallet instruments so that he could double on percussion. As Jeffries recalled, "He said to me, 'You can come out to Hollywood, and I can put you to work.' I guess that's where he figured he was gonna end up."

During his stint at Fort Knox, Nelson had an accident in which a garage door came down on him and knocked out his front teeth. A senior officer who had taken a liking to Nelson's band at the officers' club directed him to the officers' dentist rather than the enlisted man's dentist for immediate dental surgery. "For the rest of his life he had pivots for front teeth. You couldn't tell the difference," Chris Riddle, Nelson's son, said, "but he didn't play very much after that."[1] This unexpected development served to support Bill Finegan's caveat concerning the uselessness of Nelson's continuing to play the trombone when his principal ambition was to arrange and compose. Finegan's advice was heeded—at least for several years.

In order to provide for Doreen and himself, Nelson once again solicited arranging gigs from various civilian dance bands. One assignment was from Les Elgart, whose brother, Larry, arranged for the band and played lead alto while trumpeter Les was the leader. Les, Nelson, and Larry had been fellow members of the Charlie Spivak band only a few years before.

Larry Elgart, perhaps best remembered for his instrumental album successes *Hooked on Swing* and *Hooked on Classics* during the disco era, recalled how he first knew Nelson Riddle: "Nelson had a few favorite voicings that were typical Bill Finegan which became typical Nelson Riddle—the fourths . . . intervals of fourths. It was very characteristic, especially in the woodwinds or in the strings, and it was very beautiful, with nice open spaces.

"Bill Finegan liked this boy, young as he was, and he had a lot of talent. That's how Bill talked about Nelson," said Elgart. "All the time when [Nelson] was in the Army he was sending arrangements to us. I think we paid him about $50 an arrangement. And the kind of tunes that we played were pretty crummy tunes. They were the tunes that the song pluggers were trying to make happen because we had radio air time while we were working at the Palladium on Broadway."

On June 26, 1946, Nelson Riddle was discharged from the Army at Camp Atterbury, Indiana, after serving only fifteen months on active duty. Tommy Dorsey wanted Nelson to return to his band, but Doreen realized that if he did that he was going to sit in the trombone section and write arrangements and he was never going to gain any respect. According to Chris, she told Nelson, "You've got to make up your mind. You've got to either put down the trombone and pick up the pencil, or put down the pencil and pick up the trombone," which was similar to the advice Bill Finegan had given him. He and Doreen therefore decided to head back to New York, because that's where the work was.

Nelson immediately contacted the Elgarts, looking to pick up with them where he had left off. "When Nelson got out of the army he had established a sound, but it was not a swingy sound," Larry Elgart noted. "I never thought of him writing swinging arrangements. That was the furthest thing from his talent. He was writing ballad arrangements then.

"He was a lot more prolific than Bill Finegan was. [Finegan was then the Elgarts' principal writer.] All told, I think Nelson wrote twenty-five to thirty arrangements for us. I remember one of his favorite things to listen to was 'Ports of Call' by Ibert. That's where he got a lot of inspiration for his writing."

Larry Elgart pointed out the difference between Finegan and Riddle, and the reason for Nelson's eventual success: "While Bill was still a genius, Nelson wrote with a lot more abandon. He wrote more freely."[2]

Nelson's relationship with the Elgarts eventually came to an abrupt end after a recording session, when Nelson strenuously objected to the way Les played a particular trumpet solo. "This is impossible," he admonished Larry. "You've got so many good guys . . . why do you keep featuring your brother?" Nelson's outspoken behavior would be duplicated countless times in the decades ahead in Hollywood recording studios.

Larry Elgart referred to Nelson as "a time bomb." He recalled taking a hansom cab ride from Central Park South to 72nd Street with Nelson and Doreen, who were having a serious row over religion, centering on birth control. "It was horrible. He was the kind of guy that always appeared to be very cool, but he also seemed depressed and about ready to explode.

"He also had a real problem transposing a score [the process of taking the notes on a manuscript page and transferring them to the individual instrumental parts]. You have to have somewhat of a mathematical mind to do that well. When he went to a record date he was so nervous. I know that because it happened when he was with me a few times."

While he was in the army, Nelson had corresponded with the bandleader Elliot Lawrence after having seen Lawrence's band perform in New York. After his interlude with the Elgarts ended on a discordant note, Nelson began writing arrangements for Elliot Lawrence and his Orchestra in the summer of 1946.

"Some of the guys in the band told me that he was a very good writer. That's how I started with him," recalled Lawrence. It's interesting to note that Lawrence, who in the last five decades has built an excellent reputation for himself, including being the musical director for the Tony Awards for the last thirty-three years and the Kennedy Center Honors for the last nine years, has long had good taste in hiring arrangers. He employed such well-regarded jazz arrangers as Gerry Mulligan, Al Cohn, Tiny Kahn, and Johnny Mandel to arrange for his band when it was in its infancy.

"There are some arrangers whose work you put on the music stand, the band plays it right down, and it sounds great," Lawrence pointed out. "I will give you three examples of that: Ralph Burns, Neal Hefti, and Torrie Zito. Their arrangements are exciting. They never get better, they're always great. They don't need much fixing. It's the way somebody writes for the instrument, knows the band, and knows the right feeling. Three of the great orchestrators whose work was entirely different from that were Eddie Sauter, our friend Nelson Riddle, and Al Cohn. In other words, their arrangements didn't play down gracefully with the band. The way they wrote for instruments, they were always trying something new. Eddie Sauter was in the Stravinsky mood.

"By the time Nelson got to me he was experimenting harmonically, writing charts in two keys at the same time. . . . With Nelson you had to dig it out. Second of all, he was trying a lot of things that maybe weren't in the best register for the horns, and it was unusual, just like Eddie, and you'd have to work on it, and finally when you get it, it would be great. That's something that people don't really mention."

Lawrence described Nelson Riddle as "a very gentle man and sort of laid back, so I began to give him a lot of things to write. I would think he wrote at least twenty-five scores for me. At that time we were doing four or five shows a day in theaters, and the theater owners would ask, 'Don't you have anything that really shows off the piano [Lawrence's instrument] or shows off the band?' Nelson wrote a lot of those kinds of things for me."

For a dance band of the period, it was very unusual for Lawrence's band to include a French horn, oboe, and bassoon in its lineup. These were instruments that Nelson relished writing for but previously had never been given commercial opportunities to do so. After Lawrence gave him an assignment to write a piece for oboe, Nelson admitted to Doreen, "I don't know how to write for oboe." Doreen pointed toward the 42nd Street Library and said, "Go down there and pick up some books. You're going to learn to write for oboe!"

As vehicles for these specialized instruments, he wrote arrangements of "Rhapsody

Albertine Riddle in an uncharacteristically smiling pose, with Doreen Riddle holding her new son, Christopher. Nelson is flanked by his oldest son, Skip, and his oldest daughter, Rosemary. Notice how uncomfortable Nelson seems in a family setting.

in Blue" and "Malagueña" for Lawrence, which were perfect for presentation in movie theater engagements. In effect, these marked the debut of Nelson's writing of concert arrangements.

In line with that, Nelson also wrote a symphonic kind of arrangement of "Stardust," which featured strings and the French horn player John Graas, for Tex Beneke, who had taken over the leadership of the Glenn Miller Orchestra. Trombonist Milt Bernhart remembered being quite taken with Nelson's arrangement of the Hoagy Carmichael classic when he heard it in Chicago at the Oriental Theater in 1946. He also recalled that Tex Beneke announced that "Stardust" had been arranged by "Nelson Riddle, Jr." "That was the first time I had ever heard his name," said Bernhart. Henry Mancini and Milt Bernhart's two friends, Conrad Gozzo (whom Nelson had first met on the Tommy Reynolds band) and Pete Candoli, were members of the Beneke band. "I remember they seemed impressed with Nelson's work, and they weren't usually that outgoing about anything," Bernhart added.

★ ★ ★

In working with him, Lawrence said he often found Nelson down, but always thought that was because Riddle was having a financial struggle. Doreen volunteered to help him with his career, so Nelson taught her how to copy his arrangements—not an easy chore. This saved him the cost of having to hire a copyist, but created new problems.

Lawrence said, "If the copying is done by someone who isn't a musician, it's difficult, and it looks awkward. Here we have Nelson's very tricky, hard things for the band to play, copied in Doreen's hand, which made it really terrible. The guys would say 'Can't you get another copyist?' And I'd say, 'No.' Then they'd say, 'I can't read it. Is that a sharp? Is that a natural?' She must have been sitting up half the night trying to copy those hard scores of his, and then we'd get the results!"

At that time, the bands of Les Elgart and Elliot Lawrence weren't as established as they would become in the next few years, while Bob Crosby, Bing's younger brother, had been leading a name band for over a decade. His singing style was decidedly influenced by his older brother, especially in the lower register.[3] His major contribution, however, was in successfully presenting orchestrated Dixieland,[4] featuring such stalwart practitioners as trumpeters Yank Lawson and Billy Butterfield, tenor saxophonist Eddie Miller, clarinetists Matty Matlock and Irving Fazola, guitarist Nappy Lamare, pianists Bob Zurke and Jess Stacy, bassist Bob Haggart, and drummer Ray Bauduc. Despite giving up his band during World War II, Bob Crosby's hit records, such as "South Rampart Street Parade," "The March of the Bob Cats," and "Big Noise from Winnetka" had long since made his orchestra and his small band within the orchestra, the Bob Cats, a significant attraction.

In the fall of 1946, Bob Crosby was in the midst of a several-week-long engagement at the Strand Theatre, then located at 48th Street and Broadway in New York. Bob Bain had left Tommy Dorsey to settle in Hollywood and subsequently joined the Crosby band. Gil Rodin, who managed the Crosby band and had been instrumental in its success, had promised Bain, "If you go on the road for three months with us, we'll have a real good network radio show that you can play on when we come off the road."

Unfortunately, the three-month tour was extended, whereupon Rodin, to placate the musicians, told them, "Well, it's going to be a much longer tour, but you will have the radio show when you get back home. Ford is going to be the sponsor of the show. Everybody's going to get a new Ford." (In the fall of '46, a new car was indeed a luxury. The Detroit factories hadn't converted themselves to start mass-producing new automobiles after four years of turning out military vehicles. Rodin had made the kind of offer no musician could refuse!)

One day Bain was walking down Broadway between stage shows and came upon his old friend Nelson Riddle. After exchanging pleasantries, Bain asked Nelson what he was doing. "Looking for work," he replied. "Well, do you want to write for Bob Crosby?" Bain asked him. "I'll write for anybody," said Nelson. "Come up and meet Bob," Bain offered. "I know he's up in his dressing room right now."

After Crosby was introduced to Nelson, the bandleader asked him what tune he would like to arrange for the band. Nelson said he would like to try to write a new version of the ballad "I'll Never Be the Same." When he brought it in, Crosby admired his interpretation. Nelson then arranged "Night and Day." Soon, he was writing three charts a week for the Crosby band. Crosby paid him $75 per arrangement.

Within a few weeks, Crosby asked Nelson, "Would you like to come out to California with the band? I've got a new radio show coming up." He told Nelson that he could count on writing at least two arrangements a week for the show. Nelson, in his by now patented downbeat, understated manner answered, "Sure. Nothing's happening here. I'd like to go back to California."

Nelson and Doreen arrived in Southern California on December 5, 1946, looking forward to a new musical start. They took up residence with Doreen's mother, Annah, at her home on 59th Place between Normandie and Vermont in South Central Los Angeles. They had very little furniture, but eventually they purchased a grand piano, which Nelson needed for his writing. As a family car, they bought a black 1939 Buick convertible.

What happened next is something symptomatic of the music business, wherein promises made in 1946 or 2001 mean little and often nothing. This was a flagrant example of the famous quote from the renowned Hollywood producer Sam Goldwyn, who reportedly once said, "An oral contract isn't worth the paper it's written on."

True, the fifteen-minute radio show *Club 15* was sponsored by Ford, it was on the NBC radio network, and Bob Crosby was eventually the host of the show, which aired Monday through Friday. It also starred on different days Margaret Whiting, the Andrews Sisters, and the Modernaires. But after three weeks of minimal work for Nelson, who contributed arrangements for Jerry Gray, the brilliant former Artie Shaw and Glenn Miller arranger, it was decided that Gray would write all the arrangements for the show and conduct his own orchestra. Bob Crosby had to suddenly go back on the road with his band in order to pay off an IRS debt.

And although the advertising slogan for Ford in 1946 was "There's a Ford in your future," it never applied to Bob Crosby's musicians. This was the first of several unfulfilled promises that led to Nelson Riddle's eventual complete disillusionment, which turned into hatred, concerning the manner in which business was conducted in the higher echelons of the music industry.

Hiring Jerry Gray meant saving the cost of having to pay the sixteen musicians that comprised Bob Crosby's band. Gray was given a budget to hire only eleven musicians. Although Nelson may have left *Club 15* before Jerry Gray took over, he probably heard this band perform. It was an all-star group of choice big band musicians consisting of, among others, trumpeter Conrad Gozzo; tenor saxophonist Ted Nash; his old friend, alto saxophonist Willie Schwartz; pianist Jimmy Rowles; and drummer Alvin Stoller, all of whom would begin recording with Nelson on a steady basis only a few years later.

In discussing Nelson and the strange and obtuse ways of the music business, André

Previn, the distinguished conductor, composer, and musician, said, "Well, sure, but that goes all the way back. A marvelous quote of the nineteenth-century composer Bizet was, 'Music, what a wonderful profession, and what a horrible business.'"

In Los Angeles, Nelson now found himself a stranger in an essentially new and completely different musical environment. Once again he had to sit out the six-month residency requirement in order to obtain a Local 47 Musicians' Union card so he could work a steady location job—that is, if he needed to start playing trombone again. There were few immediate job prospects for him as a writer. To add to the pressure, Doreen was seven months pregnant with their first child.

Tommy Mercer, Nelson's old friend from the Merchant Marine band who was then the band singer for Charlie Spivak, remembered running into Nelson in front of Sy Devore's then well-known men's store on Vine Street in Hollywood. Nelson later went to see the Spivak band at the Hollywood Palladium during its engagement there. He wound up writing several arrangements for the band, among them a version of Nat "King" Cole's "Nature Boy" for Mercer to sing with the band.

Seeking more work, Nelson also contacted Elliot Lawrence. He began sending him arrangements, still copied by Doreen. "You could tell, of course," remarked Lawrence. "I still have some of them somewhere. In fact, I gave a lot of them to the University of Wyoming to its study library and you can still see her writing. It looks like someone who is copying in a mirror—you know, the stems don't always go the way they're supposed to go! Nelson continued writing for me for awhile. Some of them were used on our album for Columbia Records."

Nelson also approached Frankie Carle, whose band was playing an engagement at the Hollywood Palladium. The late bandleader described the experience of having Nelson write for his band by saying, "It was like a dream come true." Carle recalled, "A young man came up to me and said, 'I'd like to arrange for you.' I said, 'I have an arranger, Al Avola,' who was on salary and who stayed with me until I gave up my band in 1975. He arranged my composition 'Sunrise Serenade'—that made me. I told Nelson, 'I know your reputation . . . sure, give me a couple of songs, and I'll think about it.'"

The first arrangement Nelson wrote for Carle's band was "Let a Smile Be Your Umbrella." "He wrote a lot for us after that," Carle remembered. "He stayed with me 'til about 1953. Every two weeks or so he'd come up with a new arrangement, and I'd pay him good and that was it. He was a great guy to work with. We called him Nelly. He wrote instrumental arrangements and stuff for vocalists as well. He was one of the greatest arrangers I've ever known. Outside of Al Avola, to me he was the best. Everything he wrote I recorded. I think he must have written easily seventy-five arrangements for me. I was lucky to have him."

In a departure from writing for big bands, the accomplished accordionist Ernie Felice, who could play bebop on his instrument and recorded with the Benny Goodman sextet, hired Nelson to write for his small group consisting of accordion, clarinet, bass, and guitar. Felice had a steady gig at the popular Tail of the Cock restaurant in Los Angeles on La Cienega Boulevard and thought using Nelson's arrangements would help showcase his group. By now, Nelson had graduated to receiving fees of $100 to $150 per arrangement.

★ ★ ★

The ultimate downfall of the big bands had begun during the summer of 1946. Attendance at ballrooms, nightclubs, and one-nighters declined sharply. The wartime prosperity that was a boon to the band business was suddenly over. Returning veterans, who had been zealous followers of the big bands, spent their money on homes, education, new cars, and their families instead of going out to dance. There were other factors that entered into the decline of the band business as well. Fundamentally, however, it was the emergence of the singers, which began with Frank Sinatra's rise to stardom in 1943, that was the most important reason for the decline.[5]

In December 1946 the following orchestras disbanded: Benny Goodman, Harry James, Tommy Dorsey, Woody Herman, Stan Kenton, Les Brown, Benny Carter, Jack Teagarden, and Ina Ray Hutton. There were still plenty of bands touring, but intelligent, forward-looking musicians realized the road was a dead end and certainly no place to exist if they were interested in raising a family. As Champ Webb, big band saxophonist and later one of Nelson Riddle's "regulars," described the experience of being on the road: "It only takes about a year and a half and you've had it." Gerry Mulligan was once quoted as saying, "Life on the road is murder. It's as though life begins and ends when you have your horn in your mouth. It's like the loneliness of the long-distance runner."[6]

Suddenly, a large corps of young and talented musicians who could easily read and play many kinds of music and could also solo—prerequisites for becoming successful studio musicians—settled in Los Angeles. Among the many opportunities there were records, radio, and movie work in profusion.

In the decade before this infusion of new musicians, there had been an influx of European refugees, musicians who had emigrated to Southern California after fleeing from Nazi persecution. They found work in the symphony orchestras, on radio programs, and in film work. This was during the heart of the era of epic film scores written by Bernard Herrmann, Erich Korngold, Max Steiner, Franz Waxman, Miklos Rozsa, the Newmans (Lionel and Alfred), and others who had large orchestras at their disposal in the major movie studios—MGM, 20th Century Fox, Paramount, and Warner Bros.

Although there was plenty of work, the highly qualified European refugee musicians had the choice of assignments in both motion pictures and radio. Local 47 eventually passed a quota law that established that if a musician did movie studio work he or she was prevented from performing on radio shows. This law also forbade work for either group in the Hollywood Bowl Orchestra, for instance, but recordings and jingles (then called "transcriptions") were not affected.

At first, the by now firmly ensconced group of film studio musicians with lucrative commitments resisted the arrival on the scene of the upstart big band musicians. They scoffed at the abilities of such musicians, many of whom came with significant jazz credentials, including work for such modern big bands as those led by Woody Herman and Stan Kenton. They emphasized to film studio music executives that these musicians weren't reliable and couldn't combine the versatility and discipline needed for studio work.[7] This new group of upstart musicians, however, was not to be denied. Film studio music conductors knew full well the true value of these "carpetbaggers."

Bob Bain was one of the first to make the transition to movie studio work. He had been working with André Previn's jazz quartet. Previn recommended him to Johnny Green, who conducted the MGM Studio Orchestra.

Saxophonist Ronnie Lang, who later worked frequently in the studios with Henry Mancini and on occasion for Nelson as well, looked back on this important time for studio musicians: "From the standpoint of money, any time you played music that was recorded, whether it was a record, radio or television show, or motion picture, it paid better than working in a band playing dance music. The scales for musicians were higher for recorded music than live music—that is, unless you were a star and had your own band. I was still on the road with Les Brown, but when I came home from the road there were a lot of avenues in those days. There were a lot of recordings going on, there were commercial jingles, and there was shortly to be live television."

James C. Petrillo, took good care of union members by hammering out a beneficial contract for network radio musicians. The scale for a musician was $125 a week—a good wage for the time—and he or she was paid fifty-two weeks a year for a maximum of twenty hours of work a week. Anything over that was considered overtime. Saxophonist Dom Mumolo, who was on staff at NBC for twenty-four years beginning in 1947, put it in the best perspective by stating, "I was able to buy my house, pay for it, and send my kids to college."

NBC was where Nelson Riddle found steady work as a staff arranger beginning in April 1947. He was referred to the network by fellow arranger Gus Levine.

The NBC West Coast Orchestra, which consisted of twenty-two musicians, was under the direction of Henry Russell, himself a skilled pianist, arranger, composer, and conductor. Russell intended to modernize the way music was featured on radio programs. When he began conducting a show called *Hollywood Calling,* he hired Levine, Riddle, and others, including Billy May, the former trumpeter and arranger for Charlie Barnet and Glenn Miller.

Russell wanted to develop a new library of cues (a cue is a musical bridge that goes under a piece of dialogue or action)—for instance, a thirty-second cue for a chase sequence, a fifteen-second cue for the ending of a scene, or a twenty-second cue that just faded away if the scene changed. The new staff composers and arrangers would build up a cue library that could be used for different shows—brief musical studies in menace, nostalgia, romance, and many other moods. Such work was important in the development of these musical artisans, who would eventually start writing for films and dramatic television shows in the years ahead. It also allowed them to hear exactly what they had written and make immediate changes with the good-sized orchestra at their command. This was their fundamental job—arrangements were written only when they were assigned, while there were anywhere from two to as many as twenty cues a week for the staff to write.

John Williams remembered that his father, John Williams, Sr., who played drums and percussion in Mark Warnow's orchestra on *Your Hit Parade* on NBC, had marveled at Nelson's ability to write cues, and especially the arrangements that he wrote for the show. Another musician said that on one particular *Hit Parade* show Nelson wrote some forty-seven cues! Working on *Your Hit Parade* gave John, Sr., the opportunity to introduce his young son to Nelson.

One of the principal radio programs Nelson contributed to was the then local (but later network) weekly dramatic show, *Halls of Ivy,* for which Russell had composed the theme. The show, which ran from 1950 to 1952, concerned the life of a college dean and his wife and featured the film star Ronald Colman and his wife, Benita Hume. Other shows Riddle wrote for were *The Dean Martin and Jerry Lewis Show, Hollywood Calling, The University of the Air, Bekins Music Hall,* and *Time to Dream.* The latter, a local KNBC show, was broadcast from 11:30 to midnight Monday through Friday and had a format calling for soft, easy listening music.

Another arranger and composer Nelson met at the time was Buddy Baker, who at eighty-three is still very active, teaching at USC. Baker recalled how upset Nelson became one night after a Martin and Lewis show. "Dean had said on the air, 'Here's an arrangement written by our bandleader, Dick Stabile,' before singing a song Nelson had arranged. I said to him, 'Nelson, they're always saying, "This is Tommy Dorsey's arrangement," when Tommy never wrote it.' He figured other people were taking credit for his work." Within a few years, this same grievance would prominently surface again in Nelson's life.

He attracted the attention of Henry Russell as well as members of the staff orchestra for the high caliber of his work. Russell kept a close watch on Riddle's rate of development. He started him working on local shows and then assigned him to the more important national shows, which required more precise and involved writing.

Trombonist Lloyd Ulyate recalled that Henry Russell hired him for an NBC radio show for which Nelson arranged the music. "He wanted me to play bass trombone on the date," said Lloyd, "so I borrowed one, even though I had never played it before. Nelson wanted fuller chords, which he could get with the much lower register of the bass trombone."

Nelson's first opportunity to write for an important singer occurred in early 1947, just before he started to work at NBC. It was for none other than Bing Crosby. Sonny

Burke, Nelson's old friend from the Charlie Spivak band and his one solid contact in Los Angeles at the time, brought him to Bing's attention. Burke, the well-regarded and likeable former arranger, had become head of A&R on the West Coast for Decca Records, then one of the four major recording labels. Crosby was then the company's most important artist.

An unsubstantiated story revealed that in 1944 Crosby did a date with the Tommy Dorsey band, which was probably a joint radio appearance. At a rehearsal, after running down a particular tune, Bing wanted to know who had written the chart. Tommy told him it was Nelson Riddle. Bing was introduced to Nelson and gave him a business card with his arranger John Scott Trotter's phone number and told him to contact him if he ever would be interested in writing arrangements for him.

At first, Nelson served as a ghostwriter for Trotter. Over a three-year period, he wrote about two dozen charts for Crosby, one of which, "That's How Much I Love You," reached #17 on the *Billboard* pop chart in April 1947.

Finally, Nelson got his chance to actually conduct a recording date with Bing. Bob Bain, who played on the date, recalled calling Doreen as soon as they had finished recording. "Nelson wasn't nervous but Doreen sure was," Bain recalled. "I had promised her that I would call her to let her know that everything went okay, which it did."

Paul C. Shure, one of the premier violinists of the time in Los Angeles, first worked with Nelson on these Crosby recording dates. It was Shure's opinion that, "In the beginning he was not a great string writer. I mean he was relatively inexperienced at string writing. He wrote, of course, for brass from the beginning. He was rather shy and he was not pushy with the musicians. Even as a young person I had this undercurrent feeling that this guy was always trying to rise above some unhappiness. He loved a good story and when he really let himself go he could laugh, but he was pretty dour normally. I think it was part of his work nature. He felt that everybody should work as hard as he did."

Nelson's arranging for Crosby's recording dates provided a natural segue for him to begin writing for Trotter on Bing's weekly NBC radio show during the period from 1947 to 1950. Nelson's musical association with Bing would last for almost two decades.

Trumpeter Uan Rasey, a member of John Scott Trotter's orchestra, first began working under Nelson's direction at that time. "He wrote a couple of arrangements for us at the beginning," he related. "I told him that he wrote too hard and to ease off. He was a trombone player and he wrote with very few rests. He did have good chord structures, good thoughts, and good harmonies. After that, the next one was a little easier. I would say he wrote somewhere between twelve and fifteen arrangements for Bing's hour-long show." Rasey went on to say that Trotter would pass on some of Nelson's arrangements, as they were "too strong at times. Nelson didn't realize how hard it was for the trumpets."

★ ★ ★

In 1947, when he had time off from his principal employer (NBC), Nelson used the G.I. Bill of Rights at first to study the creative and spiritual aspects of music with Wesley LaViolette, who also taught the arrangers and composers "Shorty" Rogers, André Previn, Stan Kenton, Bill Holman, and Jimmy Giuffre. Milt Bernhart remembers that Rogers told him, "Nelson had no pretensions about anything. He wasn't sure the world was going to treat him well."

At Doreen's suggestion, he used the G.I. Bill again to pay for weekly lessons in composing and classical orchestration from Mario Castelnuovo-Tedesco, a classical composer who had written the guitar Concerto in D for Andrés Segovia, the world-renowned guitarist. Like so many classical musicians who had come to southern California from Europe, Tedesco was Jewish. Mussolini's edict in July 1938 that "Jews don't belong to the Italian race" marked the beginning of the dictator's anti-Semitic campaign.[8] As a result, Tedesco left Florence for America in early 1939. He was held in such high esteem in classical music circles that Arturo Toscanini and Jascha Heifetz agreed to act as his co-sponsors in America.

According to Jack Hayes, once the dean of film studio arrangers along with his partner, the late Leo Shuken: "It seemed like everybody was studying with Mario—Previn, [Henry] Mancini, and a lot of others. Mario never had any great things happen [for himself], but everybody realized his importance. It was because of his compositions . . . he really was an unbelievably saintly man."

Tedesco's method of teaching orchestration was to have his pupils study a piece written for piano and assign the lines in the piano solo to various sections or solo instruments in the orchestra. Many of his pianistic examples were works by such brilliant and diverse composers as Albeniz, Schubert, Brahms, and Debussy.[9]

Nelson referred to Tedesco as "my foremost instructor. [He] was always there, ready to help." He regretted that he had not met Tedesco earlier. Their association lasted almost two and one-half years, until a sudden onrush of writing assignments forced Nelson to end his studies with Tedesco. As Nelson wrote, "The skills I would have acquired from him would have given me the tools to transcend the title 'arranger' and perhaps would have given me an earlier and firmer footing in the composition of film scores, which were my first love."[10]

Former trombonist Dr. Paul Tanner summed up Tedesco's influence when he said, "He caused Nelson to write more pretty things. More importantly, he enabled Nelson to write anything he wanted." "Without him," Nelson declared, "I would not have achieved the skill and fluency I later developed in handling large groups of instruments."[11]

In 1949, Nelson found work as a ghostwriter of arrangements for the popular CBS radio show *The Carnation Hour*, which initially starred Buddy Clark (who was killed in a plane crash), then Tony Martin, and finally Dick Haymes and Jo Stafford. Haymes's accompanist, former Harry James pianist Al Lerner, acknowledged, "When Nelson's stuff came in—wow! There was a world of difference between what he wrote and what the other guys had written, so he became a regular contributor to the show."

During this same period, Lerner wrote a jazz ballet for the Columbia film *All Ashore,* which was used as background for a dream sequence involving Mickey Rooney, who co-starred with Dick Haymes. "Nelson arranged it using a big orchestra, and it turned out very, very well," according to Lerner. This was one of several Columbia movies that Nelson worked on, thanks to the composer George Duning, who had originally introduced him to Morris Stoloff, the director of music at Columbia.

It was Victor Young, the musical director of *The Carnation Hour,* who originally asked Nelson to contribute an instrumental arrangement to feature the orchestra on the show. Once again it was word of mouth that led to this assignment; Young had been unhappy with some of the other arrangements that he had been given to conduct.

Young was as beloved for his warm and amusing personality as for his formidable talent as the composer of such standards as "Sweet Sue," "When I Fall in Love," "Street of Dreams," "Ghost of a Chance," "Love Letters," "My Foolish Heart," and two tunes that became favorites of jazz musicians, "A Hundred Years from Today" and "Stella by Starlight." During the mid-1920s, he had played violin in Ben Pollack's band when it included Benny Goodman and Glenn Miller. Among the many important films the small, cigar-chewing composer and ace casino player scored were *For Whom the Bell Tolls, Golden Earrings, Samson and Delilah, The Quiet Man, The Greatest Show on Earth,* and *Around the World in 80 Days,* the latter memorable for its beautiful and majestic theme.

Young recognized the very real talent that Nelson Riddle possessed. He asked Nelson to accompany him to the soundstages when he conducted large orchestras playing his film scores, which were awash with strings. Having recently started to write cues at NBC, Nelson was now getting first-rate schooling in screen composing by watching a true master working at his craft.

But perhaps even more importantly, Nelson learned from Victor how to get along with a singer. "Victor just refused to let a singer bug him," Bob Bain observed. "If a singer said, 'That's too busy behind me,' he'd say, 'Fine.' Then he'd say to the string section, 'Lay out strings. Lay out from bar so-and-so to bar so-and-so.' Then the singer would say, 'Well, gee, there's nothing there. Victor, I need a little more.' Then he'd bring it right back. And then the singer would be happy. But he knew how to do it. He didn't fight with them."

Victor Bay, the former Philadelphia Orchestra violinist and staff conductor for the CBS Radio Orchestra in New York, taught Nelson musicology and conducting in 1950 and '51.[12] In the years ahead, Nelson would often use Bay in his string section for large orchestra dates. Considering that Nelson's lack of ability as a conductor was legendary among musicians, I asked Jack Hayes how much Bay had succeeded in teaching Nelson the art of conducting. Hayes replied, "I could never fault Nelson for that because a conductor is a conductor. As far as I'm concerned, if he gets the job done, he's a good conductor."

On February 19, 1947, Nelson and Doreen's first child was born. They named him Nelson Smock Riddle III, despite the fact that Nelson abhorred his middle name; this seems like an example of his sardonic sense of humor.[13] Nelson III was soon nicknamed "Skip."

Skip completed high school but failed to complete his education as a music major at USC, although he demonstrated an interest in becoming a jazz pianist and singer after studying with the highly respected Jimmy Rowles. "I felt I needed to get out from under the shadow and try to figure out what my life was supposed to be," Skip related.

He later entered the advertising business, first in Los Angeles, then in Honolulu, New York, and Tokyo. Skip now runs Riddle, Inc., a successful advertising consultancy business based in London, along with a joint venture in Tokyo. Skip attributes part of his love for London to his father, himself a dedicated Anglophile.

Having an attractive, outgoing wife and a new son should have provided Nelson Riddle with some semblance of happiness and stability. Instead, his never-ending struggle for employment continued to contribute to his prevailing disconsolate mood. He began to find solace in the bottom of a martini glass. He also found young and pretty women, attracted by the glamour and power inherent in the entertainment business, who were more than willing to have brief flings with him.

While devoting herself to her new son, Doreen continued her mission to further Nelson's career. She was driven to seeing the fulfillment of his potential. Sadly, in her quest on his behalf, she never developed anything of her own. Her existence centered on helping Nelson.

Nelson spent most weekdays in Hollywood seeking writing assignments, delivering them to recording studios, and making new contacts. He wrote at home because he couldn't afford an office, but he wasn't much of a participant in family life, despite the fact that he had spent his youth looking for someone who would adore him and take care of him.

When he got home from work, arguments often ensued and in time became more pronounced and vituperative. Given Doreen's deep connection with Catholicism and all it entailed, birth control continued to be one of their big issues, according to the Riddle children. After awhile, Nelson studiously avoided confrontation, always trying to keep the peace instead of dealing directly with his very real problems with Doreen. He merely blocked them out and focused on his career. For Nelson, as Yogi Berra once remarked, "It was *déjà vu* all over again." He was reliving Nelson, Sr.'s reactions to Albertine's tirades of years before.

At the time, the late arranger George Siravo's reputation for writing challenging charts for Frank Sinatra was growing. He met Nelson one day at the Columbia Records studios on Sunset Boulevard in Hollywood. "The first time I ever laid my eyes on Nelson, he was on crutches and was so bandaged, he looked like a mummy," the arranger said. "He looked like somebody in a war hospital scene. He told me he was driving while he was bombed, and hit a tree while driving through Beverly Hills. He had been laid up in the hospital. He said, 'If you're overladen with work, if you have any crumbs, if you could throw me a bone, I would greatly appreciate it.'"[14]

Years later, Nelson showed his son Chris the precise spot where the accident took place. He exclaimed, "That's my tree. I took that tree out." Among other injuries, he broke his ribs and wrecked his car in the accident.

Nelson's career problems and the difficulties he and Doreen were having, however, failed to have an effect on their sex life. Less than fourteen months after Skip's birth, on April 2, 1948, Rosemary Riddle arrived. She was named for her mother's sister, who had died of Hodgkin's disease at the age of nine. Today, Rosemary and her husband Joey are retired schoolteachers with two grown children. They live in Tinton Falls, New Jersey, close to the Rumson-Asbury Park area where Rosemary's father first started working in local dance bands sixty-three years ago.

The year 1950 proved to be a milestone in Nelson Riddle's career. Early that year, Henry Russell was let go by NBC and was replaced by Robert Armbruster. Russell's entire arranging staff was also fired, which, of course, meant that Nelson was unemployed once again.[15] Armbruster gave him several writing assignments, but, as Nelson discovered, radio was suddenly an anachronism. That year television finally replaced radio in the eyes and ears of the general public as the most important form of media communication.

Nelson continued to be busy in the recording studio following his significant initial work with Bing Crosby. This led to his arranging some single records for Dorothy Lamour, Bing's old "Road" movie sidekick, and for such other recording stars as Carmen Cavallero, Polly Bergen, Fran Warren, and Patty Andrews. In addition, in November 1951, he arranged "Where or When?," "Neapolitan," and "Ciribiribin" for Mario Lanza, who during this period had singlehandedly made opera popular to the masses through his starring roles in film musicals. And although he had left *Club 15* just after its inception, he was still ghostwriting for both Bob Crosby and Jerry Gray on the show.

★ ★ ★

One afternoon before Nelson left NBC, Dom Mumulo, Champ Webb, and Jim Williamson, a tenor saxophonist and flutist, were sitting in folding chairs in the hall at NBC taking a break. Les Baxter, one of four background singers on *Halls of Ivy*, wandered by. Baxter's varied musical experience had included stints as a tenor saxophonist with Freddie Slack's band, a member of Mel Tormé's hip singing group, the Mel-Tones, as well as a record session contractor. Baxter told the musicians, "I just signed with Capitol Records. I'm going to need some help. Do you know a good arranger who could assist me?" According to Mumulo, "The three of us all popped up at the same time: 'We've got one right here—Nelson Riddle.'"

Les Baxter was tall, blond, very personable, and a born salesman. These were the impressions I got from the afternoon I spent meeting with him during the winter of 1962, before writing liner notes for his album *The Primitive and the Passionate* for Reprise Records. By then, Baxter had gained a solid reputation for writing compositions and arrangements of exotic music as a result of his success on Capitol with the memorable Yma Sumac album *Voice of the Xtabay* and Martin Denny's composition, "Quiet Village."

While he claimed to have genuine talent as an arranger, several other arrangers and musicians vehemently declared that Baxter's real talent rested on making excellent use of the talents of others who ghostwrote arrangements for him. Their byword was, "The less Baxter, the better."

André Previn related an amusing and apocryphal story that revealed exactly what Les Baxter was all about. When Baxter grasped the fact that Mario Tedesco was teaching all the formidable new arrangers on the scene, he decided to get in on the action by becoming one of Mario's students. As Previn recalled, "We all thought, 'Well, that's admirable.' A couple of months later I asked Tedesco how Les was doing. In his sweetest way, he said, 'It was pointless.' I asked why. He said, 'I would give him assignments, and he'd hire somebody to do them!' Isn't that beautiful? To go and take lessons and then have your homework done by a professional! It just broke me up, and I asked, 'But maestro, how did you figure that one out?' And he said, 'I knew the handwriting of the man who was doing it!'" (Bob Bain related that Dr. Albert Harris, then a guitarist, was Baxter's ghostwriter. Milt Bernhart noted that apparently Baxter maintained his relationship with Harris, since he was the ghostwriter for much of Baxter's exotic music during the next several years.)

Lee Gillette produced Nat Cole, the brilliant jazz pianist and singer, whose Trio's records were a mainstay of Capitol Records. Cole was also recording with a large orchestra. For his next recording session, Gillette decided to produce him using a new and different format. Since Cole came from a religious background, Gillette wanted to present him in a gospel setting, backed by a choir, on a quasi-religious song called "The Greatest Inventor of Them All," seemingly inspired by the success of the song "The Old Master Painter." Peggy Lee and Mel Tormé had recorded the song as a duet, which was then on its way to becoming a Top 10 single record for Capitol.

Gillette hired Baxter to conduct the orchestra and chorus on the "Greatest Inventor" session, most likely because of his background as a group singer. In turn, Baxter sub-contracted Nelson Riddle (this was the first time Nelson had worked for the Hollywood-based label) to arrange one of the non-choral tunes on the record date.[16] The song was "Mona Lisa," and it was recorded on the afternoon of Saturday, March 11, 1950. Since the label had very little faith in the commercial potential of the song, Capitol planned to release it as the B-side of "The Greatest Inventor of Them All."

The song that ultimately became "Mona Lisa" was written by Jay Livingston and Ray Evans and introduced in the unsuccessful Paramount film, *Captain Carey, U.S.A.,* starring Alan Ladd. Originally, *Captain Carey, U.S.A.* was filmed under the title *O.S.S.* "Mona Lisa" was specifically written for use in a scene in which Ladd's character, who was fighting the Germans alongside the Italian Partisans, was operating a clandestine radio. A singer-accordionist was supposed to sing a code song to warn Ladd of the Germans' imminent arrival. The song was then entitled "Prima Donna, Prima Donna." Paramount, however, changed the title of the film to *After Midnight,* and the songwriters were instructed to rewrite the lyrics of the song to fit the new title. The opening phrase became "After midnight, after midnight."

Lyricist Ray Evans's wife, Wyn, who was an art connoisseur, had another idea. She felt strongly that the song should concern itself with Leonardo da Vinci's masterpiece, a particular favorite of hers. As a result, in an attempt to humor her, her husband wrote a new set of lyrics. At Paramount, the production singer hired to sing the song on the demo record for the soundtrack did one take with the new "Mona Lisa" lyrics as well as another of the "After Midnight" version.

As Jay Livingston remembered, ". . . So now it was a fairly simple matter to convince [Louis] Lipstone [the head of Paramount's music department] to use the more graceful 'Mona Lisa' lyrics for the Italian song. The studio sent it to all the big-name Italian singers: Sinatra, Como, Damone. All of them turned it down."[17]

Since Livingston's brother Alan was then head of A&R for Capitol, Jay was reluctant to have Alan present the song to Nat Cole. He didn't want Cole to think there was any collusion between the brothers. Eventually, Carlos Gastel, Cole's manager, brought the song to Cole.

At the time, the singer was going through severe problems with the Internal Revenue Service and his second wife, Maria, was expecting the birth of their first child (who turned out to be Natalie Cole). Further, Nat was understandably nervous about recording new material that didn't sound anything like a surefire hit.

Cole's first reaction to the song was decidedly negative: "What kind of a title is that for a song?" he asked. Louis Lipstone beseeched Gastel to get Cole to reconsider. Finally, Jay Livingston went to Cole's home and played the song for him. While listening to it, Maria Cole, who was a central figure in many of Cole's career decisions, made a face at songwriter Marvin Fischer, who was visiting the Coles at the time, and asked pointedly, "Why do an Italian song?"[18] However, after hearing Livingston's rendition, Nat, while not enthusiastic, was at least convinced enough to record it.

★ ★ ★

In late February 1950, Bob Bain was invited to dinner at Nelson and Doreen Riddle's first home of their own on Walavista Road, right next to the railroad tracks in the Palms section of Los Angeles. He arrived at approximately 5:00 P.M., directly from a recording session, carrying his guitar in its case. Nelson informed Bain that he had just been given an assignment to write an arrangement of a new song for Nat Cole entitled "Mona Lisa." He proceeded to show Bob the lead sheet of the song. On looking at it closely, Bob noticed that the song was written in thirds. As he recalled, "It laid out real well that way."

Bain immediately opened his case, pulled out his guitar, and began playing the opening chords to the song. Nelson liked what he heard so much that these chords were recorded by guitarist Irving Ashby as the introduction of Nelson's arrangement, just preceding the beautiful swell of strings leading into Cole's memorable vocal. In hindsight, Nelson's skillful use of strings in the "Mona Lisa" arrangement portended his career as a film composer.

A few weeks later, the King Cole Trio and the Lionel Hampton band were co-headlining the bill at the Earle Theater in Philadelphia. Backstage, Cole played a dub of the record that had been sent to him for Hampton and Jack Costanzo, who had just been added to Cole's group on bongos. Costanzo predicted that the record would be a major hit for Nat, and Hampton heartily agreed. Still somewhat doubtful about the quality of his recording of "Mona Lisa," Cole said, "If it's a hit it will only be because of the arrangement!"

Around the same time, Livingston and Evans were part of a Paramount contingent traveling first class in a private railway car. They and other contract players (including actors John Payne and William Bendix) were on a two-week publicity tour for the soon-to-open film *The Eagle and the Hawk*. As part of the tour, Livingston and Evans were interviewed by pop music disc jockeys in Baltimore, Indianapolis, Pittsburgh, Philadelphia, Washington, Atlanta, New Orleans, Beaumont, Dallas, and Houston. Livingston remembered, "They wanted to interview us because we were Hollywood songwriters, so we gave them the record. I think we really made the record happen. When the record came out in Harlem, the radio station WLIB started playing 'Mona Lisa' right away. When we came back, it was a hit."

"Mona Lisa" became the #1 record on the *Billboard* pop chart on June 10, 1950. It sold 1,000,000 copies that year and remained on the chart well into 1951. In 1950, the song also won an Academy Award for Best Original Song from a Motion Picture. It turned out to be the most important single record in Nat Cole's long and hit-filled recording career, with the possible exception of his final hit, "Ramblin' Rose." "Mona Lisa" had at last made Cole a major star.

The billing on the record of "Mona Lisa" was, in large print, "Nat 'King' Cole"; it also read "Les Baxter and his Orchestra." Baxter took full credit as the arranger of the tune. Both Duke Ellington and his superlative aide-de-camp, arranger Billy Strayhorn, who were Cole's foremost musical idols, told Nat that "Mona Lisa" contained the best background arrangement for any song of his that they had ever heard, and also said it was one of his finest performances.[19]

This was Nelson Riddle's first major success, yet it did nothing to further his career. He was still fundamentally a ghostwriter getting little or no credit for his work. This rankled him considerably. The axiom, "When hard work meets opportunity, success often happens" wasn't yet true for Nelson.

CHAPTER 5

Nat "King" Cole Was
a Merry Old Soul

On June 12, 1942, at a time when the Axis powers were at their zenith in terms of territorial expansion—and, accordingly, American morale was at its nadir—Capitol Records, an upstart record company based in Hollywood, California, released its first single record. The artist was Paul Whiteman, the popular bandleader who, during the 1920s, had amazingly been dubbed "The King of Jazz" (although he rightly considered it a misnomer). The tunes he recorded were "The General Jumped at Dawn," backed with "I Found a New Baby." Neither side elicited any significant reaction from the public.

On that same Whiteman recording date, Billie Holiday, then under contract to Columbia Records (and therefore thinly disguised as "Lady Day" on the record label), recorded one of her signature tunes, "Travelin' Light." It was arranged by Jimmy Mundy and featured a trombone solo by Skip Layton. Jazz musicians including Holiday's close friend Lester Young (tenor saxophone), former Lunceford mainstay Trummy Young (trombone), Alvy West (alto saxophone), Artie Shapiro (bass), and Willie Rodriguez (drums) were included in order to instill more of a jazz feeling into Whiteman's orchestra.

"Travelin' Light" was significant for another reason. Although its melody was written by Trummy Young, its clever lyrics were by Johnny Mercer, one of the three founding fathers of Capitol Records and its first president. The other two were Buddy De Sylva, a well-established songwriter and head of film production at Paramount Pictures, and Glenn Wallichs, creator of Music City, the first important modern self-service record store. It was in the back room of Music City, located at Sunset and Vine Streets in Hollywood, that the Capitol label was born. Wallichs ran the company and set up its record distribution system, while De Sylva supervised A&R.

Capitol's next single record releases, Mercer's "Strip Polka" and "G.I. Jive," and Freddie Slack's "Cow Cow Boogie"—a boogie-woogie novelty number featuring a stirring vocal by eighteen-year-old Ella Mae Morse—proved to be breakthrough hits. These successes caused the company suddenly to be viewed as a promising entity in the record business.

Nonetheless, despite the shortage of shellac, which was not only vitally needed for the war effort, but also the main ingredient used to manufacture 78-rpm records, and the musicians' strike in the summer of 1942, Capitol continued on its path to becoming a leading record company. Glenn Wallichs instilled a true family atmosphere among the label's executives, staff, record producers, and artists. The late Fred Benson, a personal manager at the time, recalled, "Glenn and Dorothy Wallichs were like your aunt and uncle." The belief that the impossible simply didn't exist added to the genuine spirit of creativity that pervaded both the company's choice of recordings and its business practices.

In 1942, Capitol Records grossed $195,000; in 1943, $750,000. By 1944, the company's revenues had made a sizable jump to $2,250,000. This was the result of signing and launching the recording careers of such talents as Margaret Whiting, Andy Russell, Jo Stafford, Paul Weston, Peggy Lee, and Betty Hutton. In 1945, Mercer provided the company with its first #1 hit with his version of the Harry Warren/Mercer song "On the Atchison, Topeka, and the Santa Fe" from the MGM musical *The Harvey Girls*; the song also won an Academy Award the following year as Best Original Song from a Motion Picture.

In 1945, the arranger and conductor Paul Weston's chart of Johnny Mercer's "Dream" (one of the few songs for which Mercer wrote both music and lyrics) for the Pied Pipers, with its yearning sentimentality, became one of the definitive ballad recordings of the war years. It was Capitol's second #1 hit. Shortly thereafter, Weston became the company's first musical director. "There wasn't any rush of artists from other companies trying to get on Capitol," Weston recalled. "I remember a lot of people said, 'This'll last a couple of months.'"

As exemplified early on by the release of "Travelin' Light" and by the signing of Benny Carter in 1943 and Stan Kenton and Coleman Hawkins in 1945, there was an avid interest in jazz at Capitol. This originated with Johnny Mercer, the gap-toothed Savannah, Georgia, native, who was dedicated to the music. Originally a singer and a lyricist, Mercer had worked during the 1930s as a band vocalist with Paul Whiteman and Benny Goodman, both of whom he eventually signed to Capitol. But Mercer's most valuable signing of a jazz musician occurred in the fall of 1943, when he signed the King Cole Trio, led by the pianist and singer Nat Cole, to the label.

The King Cole Trio's first recording, "Straighten Up and Fly Right," was recorded on November 2, 1943, and reached the Top 20 on the pop chart. The Trio, with Nat again singing, followed that with a cluster of hits over the next few years, including "Gee, Baby, Ain't I Good to You?" (the flip side of "Straighten Up and Fly Right"), "Sweet Lorraine," "It's Only a Paper Moon," "Frim Fram Sauce," and "Route 66." "The Christmas Song" (Nat's first #1 hit) and "Nature Boy" (also a #1 hit) found Nat being accompanied by a big orchestra that incorporated his bassist and guitarist.

After hearing Cole's first vocal records with the Trio, Buddy De Sylva said, "If Nat Cole was white, he'd be the biggest thing in the country." A&R head Alan Livingston and his staff of Capitol producers readily concurred. Henceforth, in order to reach a mass white audience, Nat Cole was recorded as a standup ballad singer.

This, then, was the supreme talent whom Nelson Riddle had aided in making a resounding hit of the poignant ballad "Mona Lisa." By 1952 Cole's record sales had totalled a staggering 15,000,000. This led to Capitol Records joining RCA Victor, Columbia, and Decca as one of the four leading recording companies.

★ ★ ★

Nathaniel Adams Coles was born in Montgomery, Alabama, on St. Patrick's Day, March 17, 1919, the youngest of four children born to Edward Coles, a grocer, and his wife Perlina. Like so many African American families living in the Deep South during this period, the Coles family emigrated to Chicago in search of a better life in 1923. By this point, Edward, who had been a deacon of the Beulah Baptist Church, was a full-fledged reverend.

Nathaniel's older brother Eddie, a pianist, bassist, and tuba player, began sneaking into jazz joints on the south side of town. Among those he saw perform was Louis Armstrong, who had created an absolute sensation in 1922 playing second cornet with his musical father, Joe "King" Oliver, as part of the fabled Creole Jazz Band, after which he had moved on to New York and then returned to Chicago to become the principal soloist with the Carroll Dickinson Orchestra. Other musicians whom Eddie greatly admired were pianist Earl "Fatha" Hines, clarinetist Jimmie Noone, and trombonist "Kid" Ory. He shared his enthusiasm for the new music with Nathaniel, who took to playing piano.

In August 1931, Nathaniel had the opportunity to catch one of his first musical heroes, Edward Kennedy "Duke" Ellington, play in a Chicago park with his "Famous Orchestra" (as it was billed). This led him to aspire to become a pianist and bandleader. With Ellington as his first inspiration, Nathaniel soon developed a keen appreciation of Earl Hines's "horn-like" approach to jazz piano.

He started his own group, the Solid Swingers, which developed a solid reputation around Chicago. When Eddie returned from playing an engagement in Madrid with Vernie Robinson's Syncopators, he arranged what turned out to be a disastrous tour of the South for his younger brother's group.

On November 13, 1936, Nat (as he began to be called) took a job playing piano in Noble Sissle and Eubie Blake's revue, *Shuffle Along*. It was also during this time that he met and married a dancer named Nadine Robinson (who later wrote such tunes for her husband as "Jumpin' at Capitol" and "Easy Listening Blues"). After the show closed, the newlyweds went on a tour that eventually brought them to Southern California.

Nat Cole, who had by now dropped the "s" from his last name, later explained, "I played every beer joint from San Diego to Bakersfield." Although he worked principally as a solo pianist, he also occasionally led various small combos.

The year 1937 was an important one in Cole's career. It was the year he formed the first King Cole Trio with bassist Wesley Prince and guitarist Oscar Moore. The initial

A young and determined-looking Nelson Riddle makes a point as Nat Cole looks on during a 1950s Capitol recording session.

recognition given the Trio was during its six-month-long engagement at the Swanee Inn, Jim Otto's club in Los Angeles. A year later, Johnny Mercer, as well as personal manager Carlos Gastel, who always had a nose for discovering major talent, first saw the group perform at the Swanee Inn.

The cohesion of the King Cole Trio, which exhibited its own musical language, led to fantastic interplay between the three instrumentalists. It was also a brilliant study in swinging small-group jazz. Following the inspiration of Earl Hines, Nat had mastered a fluid, melodic right-hand style along with a spare, harmonically advanced left-hand comping attack.[1]

Cole became such an adept and inventive jazz pianist that Art Tatum, generally considered the most astonishing jazz pianist in history, came to see him perform. Oscar Peterson, another titan of the jazz piano, was quick to admit that Nat Cole's piano playing was his main inspiration. Cole's influence is also easy to discern on Peterson's few vocal recordings.

Cole began singing with his Trio in May 1939, when he first recorded "Sweet Lorraine" (which had been clarinetist and bandleader Jimmie Noone's theme song) for the Standard Transcription Company. The record was played on the radio but wasn't available in record stores. It received considerable airplay on black radio stations, and in 1941 the group signed with Decca Records. The King Cole Trio's recording contract led to its becoming nationally known.

Continuing his jazz heritage, Cole recorded well-remembered versions of "I Can't Get Started," "Indiana," "Body and Soul," and "Tea for Two" with Lester Young. He also appeared and recorded as part of Norman Granz's first "Jazz at the Philharmonic" (JATP) concert on July 2, 1944, in downtown Los Angeles. This concert featured all-star sidemen like trombonist J.J. Johnson, tenor saxophonist Illinois Jacquet, guitarist Les Paul, bassist Red Callender, and drummer Lee Young (Lester's brother), who later became Cole's drummer.

In the interim, Nat Cole became the first male singer with jazz roots since Louis Armstrong to be an overwhelming pop success.[2] Moreover, the tall, elegant singer/pianist had developed a totally unique and intimate vocal sound that did wonders to raise the level of even the most trivial pop material. With the advent of his commercial success as a singer, the inevitable tug-of-war between the singer and the jazz critics began. Nat tempered the situation slightly when, in 1952, he promised, "My heart is still with jazz."

The King Cole Trio format was eventually dissolved, and Nat began to both record and perform in person in front of a large orchestra, although sometimes he devoted a portion of his program in nightclubs and concerts to include a trio segment. Jazz's loss became the public's gain.

Nat Cole's unique artistry made him a major star. As Maria Cole, his second wife, succinctly described it, "[His] polish and creativity made a mark that won't be equalled."

It also didn't hurt that Nat Cole was warm, friendly, and dignified—characteristics that 1950s white America expected from black performers it had deemed worthy of acceptance. Early in his career he became known within the music business, and later by the public, for being a superstar who also managed to be a human being. Retired music publisher and Cole confidant Marvin Cane described Cole's personality and charisma when he referred to him as "Mr. Cream."

Cole wasn't an Uncle Tom, although then-attorney Thurgood Marshall, who had just won the landmark *Brown v. Board of Education* trial and later became the first African American Supreme Court justice, accused him of being one. By the same token, like most black performers of that time, he didn't believe in making waves. As Maria Cole related (referring to his black critics), "They didn't think he was angry enough."

Cole's anger would have been justified. Shortly after his family moved into a house at 201 South Muirfield Road in Hancock Park—the bastion of old-moneyed Los Angeles—a burning cross was placed on his lawn. After the incident, the Hancock Park Property Owners Association informed him they didn't want any undesirables moving into the neighborhood. Nat characteristically replied, "Neither do I. And if I see anybody undesirable coming in here, I'll be the first to complain."

On April 10, 1956, at the Municipal Auditorium in Birmingham, Alabama, a contingent of White Knights, a racist organization from neighboring Anniston, physically attacked Cole onstage in the middle of a concert. Before the rednecks were arrested, he was knocked across the piano bench—which broke in half—and slammed onto the floor. He limped off the stage, touching his swollen lip. Backstage, he seemed stunned: "Man, I love show business, but I don't want to die for it!"[3]

(As an ironic postscript, John Collins, a Montgomery, Alabama, native and Cole's guitarist at the time of this terrible incident, returned to Birmingham in 1995 for the first time since that awful night to be presented with the keys to the city. No doubt as an expression of deeply felt guilt, the Birmingham Civil Rights Institute also presented him with a plaque inscribed "Inspired by the past, a vision for the future.")

★ ★ ★

During the remaining months of 1950, Cole recorded a spate of songs with one of his regular arrangers, the redoubtable Pete Rugolo. In spite of the huge success of "Les Baxter's" arrangement of "Mona Lisa," Baxter did not ask Nelson to ghostwrite anything else for Nat Cole until February 2, 1951, eleven months after their first success together. The tune was "Too Young," a beautiful love song written by Sylvia Dee with a plaintive lyric by Sidney Lippman. It had been brought to Cole by one of his closest friends, music publisher Ivan Mogull. Mogull arranged for Lippman to play the tune for Cole at the Zanzibar in New York, where he was playing one of his last trio dates.

Dee's lyrics incorporated the phrase, "They tried to tell us we're too young," which was indicative of the fact that lyricists were beginning to pander to the emerging youth culture.[4] On April 14, 1951, slightly over two months after it was recorded, "Too Young" became a smash hit with enduring popularity and signified Nat Cole's second successive #1 hit record arranged by Nelson Riddle.

Cole told *Time* that the song was successful because he sang words rather than notes. As he explained it, "When I perform it's like I'm just sitting down at my piano and telling fairy stories." To another writer he said, "Well, I guess I just get to the heart of people's feelings, that's all."[5]

An incident took place during the "Too Young" recording session that was to have important repercussions on the career of Nelson Riddle. Artie Mogull, Ivan Mogull's cousin, attended this session. (Years later, as a music publisher, Artie was instrumental in Bob Dylan's rise to stardom, and as president of Tetragramatton Records, he was also responsible for John Lennon and Yoko Ono's infamous nude album cover for *Unfinished Music #1: Two Virgins*.) Lee Gillette, Cole's longtime record producer, was Artie's closest friend.

"Right in the middle of one of the first takes of the tune there was something wrong in the arrangement," Artie remembered. "Over the intercom, Gillette asked Les Baxter to correct it. Baxter walked over to a guy [Nelson] who was sitting along the wall, who corrected the mistake. Lee turned to me with, 'Who the hell is that?' I said, 'I don't know.' Lee said, 'Well, after the session, let's find out.'" The truth finally was beginning to emerge.

I heard related stories from Billy May, Pete Rugolo, and Chris Riddle. All of them are of considerable significance.

May had first learned about Nelson when Nelson was with the Charlie Spivak band. It was Bill Finegan who told him what a promising arranger Nelson was. When he first heard Nat Cole's recording of "Haji Baba," which contained Nelson's chart, he sent Nelson a wire congratulating him on it.

"I didn't really know Nelson too well at that time," recalled May. "I ran into him at a bar, where he started telling me he got pissed off at Les Baxter 'cause Les had put his name on his arrangements for Nat Cole, and they were great arrangements. I told him to speak up to Nat. I said, 'Make sure he knows *you* wrote the charts. Tell him what you want.'"

Shortly thereafter, Pete Rugolo, who was a close friend of Carlos Gastel, was in Gastel's outer office waiting to go out to lunch with him at the then-popular Sunset Strip restaurant, The Cock and Bull. "The door of Gastel's office was open, so I couldn't help but overhear the conversation that was taking place inside," recalled the arranger. "I heard Nelson Riddle explaining to Carlos that he had written the charts for 'Mona Lisa' and 'Too Young' and that Les Baxter was taking all the credit. When I heard that, I knocked on the open door and went in and said, 'Carlos, that's true. I know that Nelson wrote those things because I ghosted for Les Baxter, too.' [Rugolo had contributed significantly to the amazingly successful Yma Sumac debut album, *Voice of the Xtabay,* whose arrangements were attributed to Baxter.] I told Carlos to please use him on the next Nat Cole date because he would find out that Nelson really wrote the arrangements. Carlos said all right, he would. The rest is history. . . . I knew about Nelson. I wasn't a close friend, but I wanted Carlos to know that he wrote those arrangements." Even in the music business, on rare occasions, honor is displayed among competing craftsmen.

Chris Riddle, who was born on May 8, 1950, just at the time "Mona Lisa" was emerging as a major hit, told this story about how his father first gained important recognition: "My mother said that when those two records took off—'Mona Lisa' and 'Too Young'—she told my father, 'Listen, Nat and the Trio are playing at the Windsor [a restaurant/nightclub behind the Ambassador Hotel on 8th Street in downtown Los Angeles].' She told me they went there at the time they were completely broke, and that she said to Dad, 'You're going to go and tell him that you wrote those arrangements.' Now, that's what my mother told me, and she told me that a bunch of times. After that, when Nat Cole finally began working with Dad, Nat said, 'I thought you were the copyist because you were always running around fixing notes in the fiddle section.'"

The overall significance is clear: these incidents led to the discovery by Nat Cole of the true identity of the writer of the two glorious arrangements of his two hit songs. This information was paramount to the future recording careers of both Nat Cole and Nelson Riddle.

As Marvin Cane pointed out, "When Nat made up his mind about something, nothing could budge him." Cole recognized Nelson Riddle's genuine talent and realized that the musical backgrounds that Nelson had created for him fit in perfectly with his approach to ballad singing. Besides that, Nelson's two charts had suddenly catapulted Cole into a position as one of the industry's biggest record-sellers.

Rhythm guitarist Al Viola said, "Musicians were talking about how Nelson wasn't getting credit for some of the arrangements he had written for Nat Cole. I had been working with Harry Klee, and he, too, was talking about Nelson. He talked about the unusual harmonic structures Nelson used in his writing." Clearly, the buzz around Hollywood among studio musicians was that Nelson Riddle was someone whose talent was deserving of genuine respect.

★ ★ ★

For a long time afterwards, Nelson simply couldn't forget Les Baxter and how he had usurped credit for being the arranger of two such unqualified recording hits. The shock of it was even more of a blow to him than the Bob Crosby fiasco had been. Even now, after he had arranged for the biggest male singer of the day, he was still struggling to get the recognition due him.

"Les Baxter loomed over everything," recalled Bill Finegan. "I could never understand it. . . . Nelson never told me why he hated him, he just hated him. I said to Nelson, 'You're obsessed with this guy. Why don't you drop him?' When somebody would do me wrong, I would pull down the shade, and he would cease to exist. His name never came up. He became a non-person to me. I said, 'Why don't you try that?,' but nothing worked."

English radio personality Stan Britt interviewed Nelson in Hollywood in July 1977, at which time the spectre of Les Baxter was still with him. Still deeply affected by the "Mona Lisa" incident, he said, "That was my first lesson. That is, in order to get credit for an arrangement in those days you also had to conduct the orchestra, so I saw to it that I was [henceforth] conducting the orchestra. That was a major step. It's really amazing what the difference was between arranging somebody else's recording date and then doing your own."

Nat Cole and Nelson Riddle conferring in Nelson's dressing room preceding the July 17, 1957, *Nat King Cole Show* that aired on NBC-TV.

Another arranger and composer who had already created an outstanding reputation for himself, and who genuinely admired Nelson, was André Previn. "Not many people know that I used to be a jobbing arranger," Previn revealed. "I was working on the *Dinah Shore Show* writing arrangements. I wasn't the only arranger by any remote means. I was on the show as a guest once in awhile, but from time to time they'd get stuck, and I'd write a couple of arrangements.

"One night at around nine o'clock I was at NBC in Burbank. I walked out into one of those dimly lit corridors, and there was Nelson. He was writing for the *Nat King Cole Show* [which debuted in 1956]. We decided to have some coffee just to keep our eyes open 'til we got home. . . . As we walked down the hall, we saw Les Baxter. Nelson suddenly grabbed me by the wrist, and he said, 'I can't stand that man. He always takes credit for things he didn't do.' I had already been through that myself, and I said, 'Nelson, so what? He's unimportant.'"

After exchanging pleasantries, Baxter informed Nelson and Previn that he had to turn out an arrangement overnight on a deadline. Suddenly, Nelson nudged Previn and said, "Les, what are friends for? I tell you what. Let's the three of us go into that empty studio over there. I've got a lot of [score] paper. Now, it's easy. I'll do the first third, André'll do the second third, and you do the shout chorus, and we'll be finished in an hour."

Baxter thanked his two colleagues but begged off, saying, "I can't let you do that."

Nelson overruled him, however, and asked for the name of the tune and the key. As Previn remembered, "I was beginning to be amused by it, and also kind of horrified."

Previn and Riddle completed their respective parts of the arrangement. After about five minutes, according to Previn, Baxter said, "Oh listen, this is crazy! I mean I'm really grateful to you guys, but I'm just going to go home and do my part." "Nelson wheeled on him and said, 'You do it right now!' So I said, 'Well, let's see what you've got.' He'd written one bar in the woodwinds, and I know this sounds crazy but the first note was a note for the oboe that doesn't exist on the instrument."

Previn brought this fact to his attention, whereupon Baxter said, "Oh, how silly. I meant that to be in the clarinets." Nelson proceeded to throw down the manuscript paper and say, "Oh, fuck off!" He and Previn then headed for the parking lot.

"When we got there, I asked Nelson, 'What happened to you?' He said, 'I can take anything but I can't take a real fraud who steals credit.' And never, never again did I see Nelson get angry about anything," Previn concluded.

This incident not only shows how musical arrangers seem unable to tolerate shams within their profession, but it also shows the deep respect they have for their colleagues, which extends to their looking out for one another. Ivan Mogull's conclusion was: "To me, they are the nicest part of the music world. They're very low-key, placid people. I find them to be introverts, and they express themselves in their music. They are to me the star behind the star."

★ ★ ★

Over the next nine years, Nat Cole and Nelson Riddle collaborated on the staggering total of 251 more recordings. Throughout his career, Cole made use of Nelson more than any other arranger or conductor. Their association led to such major hits as "Unforgettable," "Somewhere Along the Way," "Strange," "Because You're Mine," "Pretend," "That's All," "Blue Gardenia," "I Am in Love," "Return to Paradise," "Darling Je Vous Aime Beaucoup," "Answer Me, My Love," "Haji Baba," "Smile," "The Sand and the Sea," "A Blossom Fell," "I'm Gonna Laugh You Right Out of My Life," "Love Is a Many Splendored Thing," "Night Lights," "To the Ends of the Earth," "Ballerina," "Send for Me," "An Affair to Remember," "Non Dimenticar," "You're My Thrill," "Autumn Leaves," and "Wild Is Love." Nelson's "Mona Lisa" and "Too Young" arranging credits were finally given him by Capitol, but not until the 1960s.

Nelson's first credited arrangement for Nat Cole, "Unforgettable," owes much of its popularity to his use of one of the most familiar and commercial jazz instrumental sounds of the era. This was the sound of the George Shearing Quintet, a group that first emerged from the bebop period of the early 1950s, and whose familiar sound is still heard in films and television shows today.

Shearing described his highly original musical trademark by explaining, "If the sound of the Glenn Miller saxophone section was scored for piano, playing all five voices, with vibes playing the top, guitar playing an octave lower than the vibes, that's the whole secret. The only thing remaining is to put it in a key which is mellow enough." He acknowledged that he had been profoundly influenced by the Glenn Miller Air Force Band, which he heard in Great Britain during World War II.

Nelson made use of the Shearing sound as a background for the introduction of "Unforgettable." He realized that Nat's jazz-influenced voice was a perfect fit with the Shearing sound, to which he added strings.

"Imitation is the greatest form of flattery," Shearing said. He added that when the record was released, a lot of people asked him, "When did you record with Nat Cole?" "I said, 'Never.'" (Eventually, Nat and George recorded an album together for Capitol, *Nat King Cole Sings/George Shearing Plays*, released in 1961.)

Following the release of "Unforgettable," Shearing and Nelson finally met at Capitol Records, and a long-lasting friendship ensued. "He used to come and hear me all the time," Shearing recalled. "I think Nelson and I have been somewhat of an influence on each other, really. I heard the chords he used. He heard the chords I used, and when I wanted to make him feel his own presence in the room, I'd use a certain kind of harmony. I admired the man so much as a gentle, harmless individual and a wonderful writer who also had a great, original sound," Shearing added. "I can always tell a Nelson Riddle chart when I hear it. Always, always."

★ ★ ★

When I asked his view on the legacy of the musical association of Nat Cole and Nelson Riddle, Alan Livingston's succinct reply was: "Together they created the first major black romantic singer who reached the white audience." He went on to say, "I think that's a classic contribution, and I think quite possibly it was important to race relations as well—the acceptance of somebody that you're listening to in a romantic mood who happened to be black. In those days they had what they called 'race records.' They were black records, made for the black market, and you didn't find black records made for the pop market. Nat was the one who made that move first."

In addition to their close musical rapport, a genuine affection developed between the singer and the arranger. Nelson also told Stan Britt, "Nat Cole was the easiest person I ever worked with." The many recording sessions they did together were never marred by serious problems. "With Nat it was easy," said Billy May, who also wrote extensively for him. "If there were mistakes made, they were easily corrected."

A genuine respect for both Riddle and Cole also prevailed among the musicians. Saxophonist and oboe player Champ Webb recalled these recording sessions: "Nelson wrote magnificent changes. His backgrounds were lyrical. He would back them with a counter melody. . . . His mind was so organized. He said to me once, 'When I write you a solo, I can hear you playing it.'"

Violinist Paul C. Shure, who had first worked for Nelson Riddle when Nelson began ghostwriting for John Scott Trotter in 1947, recalled, "We had ten, maybe twelve fiddles on those sessions with Nat, plus six violas and four celli. Nat was so easygoing.

He didn't like to make a lot of takes. He had a lot of concentration, and he'd sing a song through and either like it or not. But I was always impressed with Nat because he didn't say, 'Well, let's do another one because maybe it'll be better'—that unprofessional type of thing. When he liked it, that was it. If he was happy with something, he knew right away: 'Let's go to the next tune.' He was very pleasant to the band always. I had very little hint of any prima donna. . . ."

Asked whether he had witnessed any gradual change in Nelson's writing for Cole, Shure answered, "Nelson made great strides in a comparatively short period of two years or so. I always felt that he was learning his craft all the time. He was a very industrious guy, not the type that instantly did something. He was not the kind that had flashes of incredible genius; he worked at it, and he got better and better. . . . That also enabled him to demand a bigger string section. He got to the point where he could do something on a session to refine and to change and so forth. He also learned the art of balancing, because in the beginning he had no idea of that—balancing the sections with the woodwinds and the saxes and the strings.

"When he wrote for strings alone, he really listened, and he probably learned a lot about mixing from the guys in the booth. He was able to put in his two cents as he learned. He didn't accept his successes. . . . He had to be prodded, but he had an open mind about it. I felt he was always open to a good suggestion from somebody he respected."

John Collins, whose fourteen-year tenure with Cole coincided with the beginning of the singer's association with Nelson Riddle, recalled, "Other arrangers had a whole big story going on behind Nat, but Nelson was subtle. He'd have a whole thing going on under Nat, but it complemented Nat. His harmonies were immaculate, and he had marvelous taste. He was never flamboyant. It was just natural. Riddle understood each singer he wrote for; he really understood what Nat was about. He was a champ."

Collins explained that on the big orchestra recording dates with Nelson and others, Cole refrained from playing piano. Buddy Cole, Jimmy Rowles, Ray Sherman, and during the late 1950s, Frank Sinatra's pianist, Bill Miller, who could play like Nat, were some of the pianists who worked on these recording dates. The guitarist stressed the fact that since Cole had perfect pitch, the entire orchestra could tune up to him as when, for instance, he sang the opening of the song "Funny" *a cappella*.

In spite of the fact that Nat Cole's success was due to his exemplary ballad singing, in 1955 Lee Gillette produced *The Piano Style of Nat "King" Cole* with the orchestra conducted by Nelson Riddle. This album of romantic standards highlighted Cole's melodic piano style and allowed him also to display his obvious jazz credentials. At the time of its release, Cole remarked, "This is the first real piano work I've done in a long time."[6]

Although Cole didn't sing on the album, Nelson's arrangements were written as if he were accompanying him as a singer. The seventeen selections were split almost evenly between up-tempo arrangements using a big band and slower numbers with an orchestra that included a full string section. Even though this was a very accomplished album musically, it was not a commercial success, in part because Cole didn't sing on it.

Singer Margaret Whiting attended several of the Cole/Riddle recording sessions. She recalled them with great fondness: "Nat Cole was a heavenly guy—so funny and cute and such a gentleman. There was nothing rough about the sessions. Everything was calm. The guys didn't swear; they didn't do anything out of their way that they shouldn't have. Nelson was marvelous with Nat Cole—very different, very instinctive—he wrote beautiful, wonderful things for him."

The highly regarded and versatile reed player Buddy Collette, who worked with Nelson consistently for over thirty years, noted, "Nelson didn't have to write flashy for Nat. He realized that early on." In Nelson's years with Cole, Collette noticed how Nelson would devise a certain new writing pattern that he liked to use, but he wouldn't necessarily try it with Nat. "He saw that if he wrote the right chords and the right notes—a G7 and whatever—that would work fine because Nat was such a total musician and such a versatile singer. He didn't need a rhythmic boost in the arrangements behind him." Drummer Louis Bellson pointed out, "Nat was a little looser than Frank Sinatra in the way that he sang and the way he worked with the rhythm section."

Lee Young was not only Cole's drummer, but was also in charge of his musical presentation on the road. After returning from a tour with Cole, Young would meet with Nelson about preparing further recording sessions. Nelson remembered Young asking him one day, "How come you don't write the same for Nat as you do for Frank?" "It was hard for me to explain to Lee, but if you'd written the same for Nat as you did for Frank, it wouldn't have been appreciated. You had to write simpler for Nat—he was a simpler person. He was a wonderful man, and a fine, instinctive musician."[7]

The second African American ballad singer to appeal in a major way to young white audiences was Johnny Mathis, who came on the scene in 1956. His favorite male singer has long been Nat Cole. "The thing that made Nat special to me, and to probably anybody who makes music, is that he utilized every aspect of whatever it is that made up that total musical package," Mathis remarked. "His jazz piano playing was, of course, overshadowed very much the way that 'Fats' Waller's piano playing, which was also brilliant, was overshadowed by his compositions and personal appearances.

"The fact that he had a small [vocal] range didn't limit him because he sang within that, and he could sing absolutely anything because he was such a good musician. He sang the blues, jazz, Christmas music, sacred music, and he sang popular music better than anyone else did. Over the years Nat proved that practicing, studying, diligence, and your pursuit of whatever you're doing in music, is the thing that sets one apart from mediocre people. And until he died he was still experimenting and still reaping the rewards of a great, great career—a very short career, mind you, but a very great career."

Nelson also pointed out, "Nat had absolute pitch—he could go from one number into another, and no introduction was needed. He would do that quite often in a concert. You never had to worry about Nat—he knew the note before you played it. He could come in cold."

"When you're talking about Nat Cole and Nelson Riddle, you're talking about two smooth-as-silk people," Ivan Mogull declared. "They suited each other. They were both very low-key people. They went to the studio. There was no B.S. There was a job to be done, and they both did it beautifully."

Due to the heavy touring schedule Cole maintained, it was occasionally necessary for Nelson to record with him in the midst of his engagements at the Chez Paree in Chicago or the Copacabana in New York. On one such Saturday afternoon recording session, there was a sound that continued to leak into the control room as Nelson and the orchestra began running down the songs that were to be recorded. Considerable recording time had been lost trying to track down the source. Finally, someone realized that the sound was emanating from a radio Nat Cole was listening to; he was tuned into a broadcast of a Milwaukee Braves game, as he was a fervent admirer of Henry Aaron, who years later became the all-time home run king.[8]

Whenever Cole recorded with Nelson in New York, Nelson was sure to hire his old Merchant Marine sidekick, trumpeter Eddie Bailey. On one such occasion in 1953, instead of calling him on the telephone, Nelson merely rang the doorbell of Bailey's midtown apartment, telling him he needed him on a Nat Cole recording date a few days later.

Cole saw to it that Paramount hired Nelson to score *St. Louis Blues* (1958) in which he portrayed W.C. Handy, the so-called "Father of the Blues." For that film score, Nelson contributed one of the definitive arrangements of the famous title song.

On November 5 of that same year, *The Nat King Cole Show* debuted on NBC-TV, marking the first network variety show hosted by an African American musical personality. The first episodes were fifteen minutes long; later, the show was expanded to thirty minutes. Nelson worked as musical director of the show during most of its year-long run. This included conducting the orchestra for nine "live" broadcasts, five from Los Angeles and four from New York. On one particular show there was a panic because it was discovered after the dress rehearsal that the entire show ran about twenty seconds long. Cole quelled the production staff's panic by saying, "Don't worry, Nelson will know what to do. He'll just change the tempo a bit and everything will be fine."

From the beginning, sponsors were reluctant to back the show, which forced NBC to discount the cost of sponsorship. "Madison Avenue is afraid of the dark," Cole quipped pointedly. It was much easier to sell advertising time for the shows hosted by Eddie Fisher and George Gobel—two mediocre, nonthreatening performers. As a result, Nat Cole's final NBC show aired on December 17, 1957.[9]

It is important to realize that the musical success of Nat Cole's collaboration with Nelson Riddle fit the context of 1950s America. The Eisenhower era saw the effects of the return of the veterans of World War II—how they helped to develop a civilian economy that prospered. It was the decade of the suburban house, the six o'clock cocktail shaker, and the regulation gray flannel suit.[10] "Conformity, conservatism, and consensus" was how longtime *Christian Science Monitor* film critic David Sterritt characterized the period.[11] Beautiful love songs served up with lush string backgrounds perfectly reflected the quiet and serenity of the decade. At the time, however, only the music critics were aware of the greatness inherent in what Cole and Riddle had created.

Not many people would have speculated that fifty years later the recordings made by Nat Cole and Nelson Riddle would have survived the test of time and would continue to be praised for their artistic excellence. In 1992 and 2000, respectively, their recordings of "Mona Lisa" and "Unforgettable" were elected to the NARAS (National Academy of Recording Arts and Sciences) Hall of Fame as records of "lasting or historical significance." In the thirty-six years since his death, Cole's record royalties from Capitol Records have reportedly been a minimum of $1,000,000 annually, and some years considerably more than that.

During the mid-fifties, when Nelson was enjoying this successful period working for Nat Cole, the Riddles lived in Santa Monica on 7th Street between Margarita and Montana Streets. Chris and Rosemary remember this brief period as being the happiest days for the family. In later years, Nelson would often drive the children by the house, pointing out to the younger ones, "This is where we lived." As Maureen Riddle, the youngest of the Riddle children, recalled, "There was a tremendous amount of sadness about Dad's having lost whatever the family had in those days." She said that one day her father began to cry as he lamented, "I'm sorry I was never able to create that for you and [his youngest daughter] Cecily."

★ ★ ★

Chris Riddle first met Nat Cole at the age of five, when he was taken by his father to one of their recording sessions. "Nat and Dad were very close friends. In fact, I think my father loved Nat Cole as a man would love another man. Not in today's context. He was such a magnetic person . . . such a sweetheart of a guy. He was always upbeat.

"I think another reason why Dad loved Nat so much was that Nat showed him something that was very different. I remember going to Nat's house over in Hancock Park one Sunday afternoon with my father. Nat had a new 1960 black Fleetwood Cadillac. We heard a crash and went outside. Someone had sideswiped his car deliberately. Nat had no reaction. . . ."

During their nearly ten years of working closely with one another, Nelson would meet frequently with Nat at his home to plan the concept for each particular album. Nelson remembered, "He would sit at the piano and play a very pianistic jazz fill as a guide to the mood he expected in the arrangement we were discussing. It was my task to try to translate this mood to orchestral terms, and many times it worked out well. . . ."[12]

Nat always picked out his own songs first, listening to material brought to him by Ivan Mogull, Marvin Cane, Al Gallico and others. Out of the close working relationship between Nat and Nelson evolved the close friendship that led to Nat and Maria driving out to Malibu for dinner when Nelson moved his family to 3853 Carbon Canyon. The Riddles, in turn, attended parties at the Cole home.

Asked whether the practice of an African American entertainer and his wife visiting with a white business associate's family was considered out of place in Hollywood during the 1950s, Maria Cole replied, "No, no, that had been going on for years. That was normal. The only thing, as I said, was we became close. They had four kids and they were a very close-knit family. I don't know what Nelson and Nat would discuss— probably music or sports, particularly baseball. Doreen and I had fun. We would talk about kids or dogs or something. The children were small—my two older ones, the adopted girl, Carol, the oldest girl, was my sister's child. Then I had Natalie. My son was adopted when he was five months old. Then I had the twins. That's how we had five children!"

In the course of their friendship with the Riddles, Maria observed Nelson and Doreen's relationship. "In those years it was wonderful. Doreen was a very, very moral woman. She was raised by the [Catholic] church and lived by the church. She was kind of old-fashioned. She was pretty—long hair, Irish—well, we just got along like peas in a pod. I adored her."

Maria agreed with Rosemary Riddle Acerra's assessment that it was unfortunate that Doreen had absolutely no hobbies or interests other than Nelson and his career and her children. "I don't remember her ever being at an opening or anything. She was a homemaker."

Regarding Nelson, Maria remarked, "He was a very sweet, but a little insecure, unassuming man. He had that kind of bland exterior, although he'd say something dry once in awhile. He wasn't comfortable, period. But he really was a very good person. Nelson had no show business crap about him."

★ ★ ★

In 1959, Nat Cole and Connie Francis embarked on a concert tour of the Northwest and western Canada, backed by Hal McIntyre and his Orchestra. Nelson conducted the orchestra during Cole's portion of the program, which closed the show. Berwyn Linton was a trombonist in McIntyre's orchestra and recalled how Nelson made one of his very rare appearances playing trombone in these years. As the concert began, "Nelson was seated in the trombone section before he stood up as part of the section when it played a solo passage. After that, he walked off the bandstand and acted as emcee to get the show started.

"I remember one particular night Nelson tripped when he jumped off the riser on his way to the microphone at center stage. He bumped into the mike and apologized. He said he hoped he didn't embarrass anybody in the audience. I thought that was classy of him."

Based on Linton's comments, it seems that Nelson was unusually comfortable on stage during this tour. Usually, when compelled to speak to the audience during personal appearances, his discomfort was apparent; he would mumble his introductions to the songs and often failed even to smile.

★ ★ ★

Looking back on her father's association with Nelson Riddle, Natalie Cole called him "my father's musical alter ego. I thought Nelson was a supersensitive, fragile, and vulnerable man. I think that Dad was much the same. I really think they saw those qualities in each other. Nelson spent time giving my dad what was required for him musically."

The first time Natalie actually worked with Nelson was in the summer of 1960 in Los Angeles. She was brought onstage at the Greek Theatre by her father to perform as a special guest in the touring production show *I'm with You,* which costarred singer Barbara McNair. (The show's title was later changed to *Wild Is Love.*)

In 1962, when Natalie was twelve years old, she sang two or three times with the Malibu Music Men Plus One, the quintet that performed at Nelson's and her father's parties. The group, which featured two horns (alto saxophone and trumpet), included Skip Riddle on piano and Dennis Dragon (son of the conductor Carmen Dragon and older brother of Daryl Dragon, the Captain of the 1970s pop duo Captain and Tenille) on drums. Dennis Dragon facetiously remarked, "I don't even know why this group existed—probably for political reasons. The hot tune that Natalie sang was 'A Tisket, a Tasket' [originally made famous by Ella Fitzgerald with the Chick Webb band]. We played a few get-togethers at Nat's home and also a few socials. We were young; it was a groove."

Nelson worked closely with Natalie when he was musical director on her first television special for CBS-TV, which aired on February 12, 1978. The guests were Johnny Mathis; Earth, Wind & Fire; and Stephen Bishop. Nelson wrote a new arrangement of "Mona Lisa" specifically for her to perform on the show. He recalled, "Apparently the magic of that song still persisted, for as she and I rehearsed the number in preparation for the show, she stopped singing at one point, put her arms around me, and burst into tears. I guess her Daddy, never far from her thoughts, seemed even closer at that moment. I know he was for me."[13]

★ ★ ★

In March 1960, Nelson and Nat collaborated on the "concept" album *Wild Is Love.* The twelve original tunes, written by Dotty Wayne and Ray Rasch, were recorded in a matter of days. Linked together, they told the story of a love affair. Nat referred to it as "the biggest thrill of my career. . . . The scope of a musical had been conceived for a record with a new kind of simplicity. . . ." It was both an artistic and a commercial success (it made the Top 10), although some Cole associates felt it was a wayward departure from his usual love song formula, and it hasn't stood the test of time.

Nelson's arrangements were more varied than usual—by turns brassy, erotic, and enchanting. By the very nature of its subject matter, *Wild Is Love* proved to be very timely. Its 1960 release coincided with the availability of the birth control pill and the resulting sexual revolution.[14]

Despite this success and their close personal friendship, as often happens with longtime musical associations, the combination of Nat Cole and Nelson Riddle gradually began to cool off. Soon the hits stopped coming. In addition, Nelson was spending considerable time writing for Frank Sinatra's frequent recording sessions and was writing for other Capitol artists as well.

Nat started using Ralph Carmichael, another one of Les Baxter's former ghostwriters, to write for him. The warm and affable arranger remembered, "I observed a kind of cooling in their relationship because it was a period of time when Nat and Sinatra were kind of vying for supremacy. Nat thought that Nelson was giving the good stuff to Sinatra. It just seemed to me like Nelson kind of pledged his allegiance to Frank and that bothered Nat, but not to the point where it showed in their personae when they were in the same room. . . . I never heard any disparaging remarks, none at all, but I observed that as the weeks went by I was spending more time with Nat talking about projects. I would go over to Las Vegas with Lee Gillette, and we would talk about the next album.

"Nelson had just done a magnificent job on *Wild Is Love*—wonderful writing and very creative. All of the tunes had been cut, but they wanted an overture, and they also wanted a string background for Nat's narration. For some reason, they let me finish it off."

In the next few years, Carmichael arranged such hits for Nat Cole as "That Sunday, That Summer," "The Lazy-Hazy-Crazy Days of Summer," and "L-O-V-E." He, as well as Billy May and Gordon Jenkins, who had worked with Nat earlier when Nelson was unavailable (i.e., working for Frank Sinatra), joined Belford Hendricks (who arranged "Ramblin' Rose") to arrange the remainder of Nat Cole's recordings. Nelson's friendship with Nat continued, but their musical association had ended.

During two different periods in 1961, Carmichael conducted *The Nat King Cole Story* for Capitol, which was essentially a rerecording of Nat's most significant hit records with the original arrangements in stereophonic sound. Working on this project gave Carmichael the opportunity to survey the extent of Nelson's work with Cole. "The thing that is amazing with Nelson is that you take the tremendous breadth, the scope of all those wonderful tunes—what you're looking at is the work of one of *the* most versatile arrangers. I'd put him in a class with only two or three others. . . . The voicings and the chords and his figures with strings were just beautiful. Nelson made a motion picture score out of each one of his charts."

When I asked Carmichael his impression of Nelson Riddle as a person, he replied, "When you're young, you always have somebody you'd like to be like. Well, I always wanted to be like Nelson Riddle. It's that simple."

★ ★ ★

In August 1964, the singer Jack Jones and I spent the better part of a day at the Fairmont Hotel in San Francisco with Nat and Maria Cole during Jones's engagement there. I can still remember Nat's unpretentious manner and dry sense of humor. He seemed to be a born storyteller. Nat was in San Francisco to co-headline with Frank Sinatra at a benefit performance at the Cow Palace to raise money to back the proposition on the ballot to ensure open housing in California. He said he had undergone some major dental work that day which prevented his appearance at the benefit. John Collins informed me that in reality a doctor in San Francisco had just diagnosed a cancerous tumor in one of Nat's lungs.

Nat had been a heavy smoker for years. He knew the hazards of his habit, but rationalized about how smoking gave a certain timbre to his voice. He claimed that smoking actually enhanced the intimate sound he had developed. "Otherwise," he said, "I'd be out of a job." His eventual use of a cigarette holder with a filter, given him by Carlos Gastel, was an unfortunate example of "too little, too late."

Cole continued working that fall before finally entering St. John's Hospital in Santa Monica to prepare for treatment of his serious condition. He died there on February 15, 1965, at 5:30 A.M., a month short of his forty-sixth birthday. Chris Riddle recalled that his father cried uncontrollably upon hearing the terrible news.

Comedian Jack Benny gave the eulogy at Nat's funeral at St. James Episcopal Church on Wilshire Boulevard in Los Angeles two days later. Nelson joined more than sixty active and honorary pallbearers, including Bobby Kennedy, Frank Sinatra, Count Basie, Sammy Davis, Jr., George Burns, Johnny Mathis, Jimmy Durante, Eddie "Rochester" Anderson, Danny Thomas, Steve Allen, Ivan Mogull, Frankie Laine, California Governor Pat Brown, Alan Livingston, Billy May, Gordon Jenkins, John Collins, Carlos Gastel, Glenn Wallichs, and others.[15]

Wallichs framed a meaningful corporate statement as chairman of the board of Capitol Records, Inc., which said in part: "Nat Cole's fame rested not on hit records or stage performances but in his conduct as a human being. . . . It is comforting to know that the human race is still capable of producing a Nat Cole. . . . No artist has ever meant so much to me before; none can ever mean so much to me again. . . ."[16]

A year later, Nelson arranged a Reprise Records tribute album entitled *NAT—An Orchestral Portrait*. He had lost one of his closest friends and the man who had given him a golden opportunity to display his talent. As Nelson described it, "Nat was my wedge." Without Nat having taken a stand on his behalf, one can only speculate on the ultimate fate of Nelson's career. This essential fact is too often overlooked in evaluating Nelson Riddle's career.

★ ★ ★

Beginning on October 10, 1951, another noted African American singer, Billy Eckstine, known as "Mr. B," began to use Nelson as the arranger for his MGM ballad recordings.

Like Nelson, Eckstine was a sometime trombonist (although a valve trombonist) and had previously been the leader of the first bebop big band from 1944 to 1947. Their musical association lasted until early 1954 and encompassed some fifty recorded tracks. This output included a choice Rodgers and Hammerstein album called *Enchantment.*

Also included in this output were four singles that reached the top 30 on the *Billboard* pop chart: "Kiss of Fire," "Coquette," "Send My Baby Back to Me," and "Lost in Loveliness." "No One But You" reached #3 in Great Britain in September 1954. The Eckstine recordings were popular, but Nelson's records with Nat Cole made a far greater impact on the American public. And while the Cole records helped Nelson gain a solid reputation within the music business, his arrangements for Billy had a minimal effect on his career. It is important to note, however, that Nelson recorded more often with only three other vocal artists—Frank Sinatra, Nat Cole, and Ella Fitzgerald.

But the greater gain for Nelson was that Capitol Records assigned him to write arrangements for some twenty-two Capitol artists during the period from 1950 to 1961. He assumed the mantle of Capitol's "house arranger." Right after starting to write for Cole on a regular basis, Nelson wrote charts for Jerry Lewis, Mel Tormé, Bob Manning, Kate Smith, Dick Haymes, Margaret Whiting, and Al Martino. Martino observed, "When he wrote for me, the tunes were nowhere as good as his charts."

With the exception of Jerry Lewis's novelty and children's records, the other charts Nelson wrote for these singers were geared toward trying to duplicate his success with Nat Cole by writing romantic string backgrounds. As with Eckstine, these records found Nelson receiving credit as an arranger and sometimes as a conductor as well. Unfortunately, according to Alan Livingston, he was merely paid scale for his arrangements.

Margaret Whiting was one of the singers Nelson wrote for most frequently during this period. Their collaboration encompassed twenty-two tracks. Among them was "My Own True Love," the vocal version written by Mack David of Max Steiner's famous "Tara" theme from *Gone with the Wind.* Whiting was particularly proud of that record. "People bought it," she recalled. "They said, 'What a gorgeous arrangement.'" The enduring singer also recognized the fact that Nelson "could be very tough with anybody he worked with [except Frank Sinatra and Nat Cole]. He wanted it letter perfect."

Another pop singer in the tradition of Jo Stafford and Dinah Shore was Giselle Mackensie. The Canadian-born singer saw another side of Nelson in the studio—something that Emil Richards and the other Riddle regulars rarely if ever saw—laughter. Of course, it helped that Mackensie was also blessed with an excellent sense of humor herself, perhaps best shown when she quipped easily while playing violin duets with Jack Benny. "A lot of musicians, especially serious musicians, they're terribly serious about themselves," Mackensie related. "Nelson wasn't like that. He was living in this world while writing stuff that came from out of this world. . . . Nelson got a kick out of that and he'd laugh about that and we'd make jokes. I admired his down-to-earthiness with such a good talent. . . . He did a lot of talking to himself when he was conducting, but he gave complete attention to people. If something happened, he'd start laughing."

Mackensie not only recorded a few Capitol single records with Nelson, but also did several personal appearances with him. At the rehearsal for a Denver date shortly before his death, Nelson rushed to her defense when a vocal group was encroaching upon her allotted time. He became angry and blurted out, "Miss Mackensie's a star, and I want you guys to get your music and put it over there or wherever you want to put it to get it out of the way." "He was really very thoughtful of human beings. Modesty is extremely attractive in a big talent," she recalled.

In 1952, during a period when Billy May was extremely busy getting his big band established and writing for other people as well, he contacted Nelson to write for Ella Mae Morse. Their first endeavor together was "Oakie Boogie,"[17] which turned out to be a minor hit. They next collaborated on a tune called "Blacksmith Blues." In writing the arrangement, Nelson indicated that he wanted some kind of a "ting" sound that would simulate the sound of a blacksmith striking an anvil.

Lee Gillette was the producer on this recording session. A former drummer, Gillette was very adept at coming up with ideas to solve problems pertaining to sound. Once again, Bob Bain proved helpful to Nelson. Rather than playing guitar on the recording date, Bain was pressed into service to "play" an ashtray with a triangle beater (similar in appearance to a brass pencil).

"We had trouble achieving the right sound," Bain recalled. "At Gillette's suggestion, John Palladino, the mixer [today he would be considered an engineer] directed me to hold the ashtray in my hand with a handkerchief. Then when I hit the ashtray with the triangle beater, the sound was deadened a bit and given a muffled effect. We went though quite a few ashtrays [reportedly six] on that date."

"Blacksmith Blues," written by Jack Holmes, turned out to be a startling #3 hit on the *Billboard* pop chart and sold 1,000,000 copies after its release on January 7, 1952. It had been recorded on December 12, 1951, in the lively Capitol studio on Melrose Avenue in Hollywood, which provided a delayed echo in its sound. One might describe this recording as an unusual example of "special effects."

Nelson later gifted Morse with a photograph on which he wrote, "My ashtray runneth over!" After their success with two hit singles, Nelson and Morse recorded ten more singles in just over two years, but none of these recordings were successful.

"Nelson was very talented, but he never said, 'Look at me, I'm so great. You like my work? Good. Hire me,'" was the way Sid Feller, who ran A&R in New York for Capitol during this period, described Nelson. "He was a pretty good businessman, 'cause he got himself an office and was able to get over-scale money for his arrangements as time went on. Each arrangement that he wrote created something that had never existed before. That, to me, is brilliant. Ninety percent of his stuff was really creative."

As part of his work at Capitol, Nelson was obliged to write arrangements for artists other than singers. Walt Heebner had left RCA Victor, where he had headed the A&R department on the West Coast, to head the custom recording department at Capitol. This meant producing transcriptions, among other things. These recordings were serviced to non-network radio stations.

"I came up with an idea of taking classic themes on which we would not have to pay copyrights, using public domain songs and classical material," Walt explained. "I got to know Nelson when he was working for Nat Cole in 1951. I didn't want him to use violins on these dates, just violas and celli. I wanted him to get the warmth and the depth of the low strings and how the high strings on cello or on viola sound different than they do on violins.

"The transcription service was on its way out. It took all my remaining budget to enable Nelson to record ten selections with brass, woodwinds, and strings using twenty-five or twenty-six men. We could do five in a one-hour session; we wound up doing ten tunes in two hours—things like 'None But the Lonely Heart,' which is taken from Tchaikovsky, and 'My Reverie,' from Debussy. The object of recording these transcriptions was for Nelson to take them to the A&R department to show that he could do something album-wise on his own. Unfortunately, they were turned down by the A&R committee—'the Florsheim Club,' the toe-tappers. When Nelson told me that, I felt bad about it so I finagled fifty pressings to be made up to send to Nelson to do what he wanted with them."

Listening to these transcriptions almost fifty years later, one can immediately recognize certain musical figures Nelson utilized in his transcription writing that he was soon to adapt in his writing for Nat Cole later in the decade. Some examples of this are his frequent use of the celeste, various trombone choruses, well-placed French horn and muted trumpet voicings, pizzicato strings, and occasional harp flourishes. The accomplished harpist Corky Hale remarked, "He was one of the best writers for harp, and there are a lot of guys who can't write for it. Maybe the reason he wrote so well for the instrument was because he admired Ravel and Debussy who were great writers for the harp."

★ ★ ★

Capitol Records was far from Nelson's only employer in the early 1950s, however. In October 1951, he wrote an arrangement for Ray Sinatra, Frank's cousin, of "London Bridge." Their association continued the following month, when he served as Sinatra's ghostwriter for arrangements of "Where or When?," "Ciribiribin" (Harry James's famous theme song), and "Neapolitan Love Song" for Mario Lanza.

In a big band format the following year, Nelson contributed an arrangement of "Begin the Beguine" for clarinetist Bob Keane, an Artie Shaw sound-alike, on his Del-Fi Records album, *Big Band Bash*. Keane noted accurately, "It was typical Nelson Riddle." He was referring to the way in which Nelson made use of repeating patterns with the trombones, his familiar trademark in the years ahead.

The musician-turned-record-company-owner added, "Nelson came up with a great idea for the vocal group he had assembled for the date. Two girls and two guys laid down the total vocal, then Nelson had them sing it a second time over their first rendition. This gave the group somewhat of a choral-group sound. This is a common practice today—it's called 'double-tracking,' but I believe this was a first in the recording industry in those days. Today, this effect is achieved with a piece of electronic equipment."

In 1952, Nelson had two arranging jobs that were far afield from the kinds of things he had been doing. The first was for Louis Jordan, who recorded for Decca Records and was then best known in the jazz and R&B realm. The most successful of the tracks he arranged for Jordan was the single "I Didn't Know What It Was." This was not rhythm and blues, but instead Nelson's use of strings and woodwinds, the combination which had been successful for him with Nat Cole.

The other job, recorded on December 11, 1952, for RCA Victor, was the novelty song, "The Choo Bug Song," which he arranged for Phil Harris. At that time, Harris was enjoying success with records like "That's What I Like About the South" and "Smoke, Smoke, Smoke That Cigarette." At this particular session, Nelson also arranged a version of Hoagy Carmichael's "Love Will Soon Be Here" that was never released.

That same year, Nelson reestablished his musical association and friendship with Bill Finegan in Hollywood when he helped Bill out, instead of the other way around. Finegan had been commissioned by Victor Young to write a symphonic-type arrangement of Tommy Dorsey's theme song, "I'm Getting Sentimental over You" for a Decca album featuring Dorsey's band plus strings, which Young would conduct.

Dorsey's manager, Tino Barzie, recalled, "I was living with Bill at the Blackburn Apartments on Franklin in Hollywood. Tommy knew that when Bill went to sleep you couldn't get him up. And now it was getting closer and closer to the recording session."

"I was in a bind," Finegan recalled. "My mind had gone blank. I had a chunk of it done, but I would sometimes get in a complete funk where everything would stop. I was at a total loss. I called Nelson, and he said, 'I'll come around and help you out.' In the meantime, one of the string players from Tommy's band was copying what I had written page by page."

Barzie added, "When Nelson arrived, he and Bill started discussing the arrangement, and then they got to work. The next thing I knew, Bill couldn't write because Nelson was using the piano and this threw Bill off. So one or the other went out to the convertible I had parked at the curb under a streetlight. And there is Nelson filling in the chords under the streetlight finishing the arrangement. I looked out and didn't believe it—I'll never forget it."

In 1953, Nelson arranged two single records for singer Lorry Rain on the now-defunct Kem label, a Capitol subsidiary. They were "A-Wooin' We Will Go" and "There's Nothing Left to Do But Cry" which reached #22 and #21, respectively, on the pop chart. With a voice that was reminiscent of the plaintive, rather soothing style of many other 1950s female vocalists, Rain lacked a musical identity of her own and never achieved any measure of stardom.

In Nelson's original logbook, where he listed all of his arranging jobs from 1948 to about 1958, there is a notation that in May 1955 he wrote fourteen pages of arrangements for the Billy Wilder–directed comedy, *The Seven-Year Itch,* starring Marilyn Monroe, and seventeen pages for the film *Love is a Many Splendored Thing,* the well-remembered Jennifer Jones/Bill Holden romantic vehicle. These arrangements for the scores of both 20th Century Fox films were under the supervision of the famous conductor Alfred Newman. These movies provided Nelson with his first experience in writing for films, working with a large orchestra.

★ ★ ★

Bass trombonist George Roberts grew up in Des Moines, Iowa. His openness and basic kindness reflect his Midwestern upbringing. Roberts had been an important soloist with the Stan Kenton band for three years, during which time he was featured on Johnny Richards's arrangements of "Alone Together" and "Stella by Starlight," as well as on Bill Russo's composition "23°N, 82°W." Through these and other Kenton charts, the bass trombone had at last begun to come into prominence.

When Roberts decided to leave the road shortly before his wife was about to give birth to their first child, he decided to settle in Los Angeles. He went to see Lee Gillette, who was also Kenton's longtime producer, seeking studio work. It was in Gillette's office at Capitol that Roberts first met Nelson Riddle. Nelson said to him, "I've always wanted to use the bass trombone. I just haven't heard anybody that I really wanted to write for." The two men became instant friends.

Almost immediately, Nelson began to make use of Roberts's unique sound on Nat Cole recording dates. As Paul Tanner observed, "George played delicately and pretty on a clumsy instrument. He really opened up the bass trombone business."

One night, when Roberts was visiting with Nelson at the Riddle home, Nelson said, "I have to have an identity!" "You already have one," Roberts countered. "Nobody writes for bass trombone, Harmon mute trumpet, flute, and strings except you. That's your identity!"

The Nelson Riddle sound, which incorporated the influences of Bill Finegan's harmonies, Sy Oliver's arrangements, and Maurice Ravel's compositions—plus the important addition of George Roberts's bass trombone, muted trumpet solos by Carroll "Cappy" Lewis or "Sweets" Edison, Harry Klee's flute, and Joe Comfort's leaping bass lines—was soon to become familiar to popular music fans. It proved to be central in providing the setting for the comeback of Nelson's next collaborator—Frank Sinatra.

CHAPTER 6

"The Voice" Becomes a Cello

By the early 1950s, the luster was gone from Frank Sinatra's career. Columbia Records had released him when his record sales dwindled; CBS had canceled his weekly television variety show after two dismal seasons; MGM had dropped him after a succession of box office failures; MCA, the talent agency that represented him, had given him his release because he became difficult to sell and he was often a problem; if that wasn't enough, he owed the government over $100,000 in back taxes. By April 1953, about the only thing about Frank Sinatra that still sparkled was the superb cap job done on his teeth ten years earlier when he was attempting to look more Hollywood than Hasbrouck Heights.

Frank's family-man image, brilliantly constructed by publicist George Evans, wasn't helped, either, when he crossed continents on a moment's notice to pursue Ava Gardner, one of the most devastatingly beautiful women of the last century, while still married to Nancy Barbato, his wife of over a decade and the mother of his three children. Although deeply conservative 1950s America took little notice of career reversals, leaving home to run after Gardner was something entirely different.

Sinatra's surly response to questions from reporters concerning *l'affaire* Gardner, plus his mercurial behavior with just about anyone he worked with, caused the *New York Daily News* to ask, "Anyone know of a bigger bore just now than Frank Sinatra?"[1] The nightclub and music business entrepreneurs who lunched at Lindy's in New York, as well as the film and television decision-makers who dined at Chasen's in Beverly Hills concurred: "Frankie is finished."

But in early 1953, contrary to the myth perpetuated by Mario Puzo in *The Godfather*, it wasn't the placement of a horse's head on a Hollywood mogul's bedspread that caused the apparently washed-up crooner to be considered for the role of Pvt. Angelo Maggio in Columbia Pictures's film version of James Jones's novel of between-the-wars soldiering, *From Here to Eternity*. Rather, it was the combined efforts of Ava Gardner, Sinatra's new William Morris agents Bert Allenberg, Sam Weisbord, and George Wood, and even a few of the more prominent Mafia dons who worked on Columbia president Harry Cohn ("I don't get ulcers—I give them"). Despite the lack of enthusiasm that Cohn and director Fred Zinnemann initially exhibited toward this suggestion, Cohn finally relented and agreed to give Sinatra a screen test.[2]

Drummer Louis Bellson remembered playing an engagement with Duke Ellington at Storyville in Boston. Sinatra was booked at the Latin Quarter in Boston (owned by Lou Walters, Barbara Walters's father) and was drawing few patrons. Bellson's wife, Pearl Bailey, brought him in to see the members of the Ellington band. "Frank looked real good, sunburned," said Bellson. "He had been in Africa with Ava Gardner where she was shooting a movie [*Mogambo*]. He said, 'Pearl, I'm getting ready . . . they've offered me a movie called *From Here to Eternity*. They're paying me $1,000 a week, which is nothing.' You know what Pearl told him? 'Take it and don't look back.' That's exactly what she said, and that's exactly what happened."

Securing this role (for which Eli Wallach had been considered) and spending eight weeks shooting on location at Schofield Barracks, near Honolulu, turned Sinatra's career completely around—although no one realized it at the time.

Only a few months earlier, Sam Weisbord had called Alan Livingston to inquire whether there would be any interest in signing his new client to Capitol Records. Surprisingly, after considering Weisbord's proposal for a moment, Livingston replied, "Yes, I would be interested." Weisbord was so taken aback that he said, "You would?"

"Those were his exact words," recalled Livingston. "I added, 'Yeah, I'll sign him. Bring him in.' Weisbord brought Frank in, and he was a pussycat. He was delighted to be there. I must say that in those days he was 'not much to look at, nothing to see.'"

The deal was hardly an industry-shattering one. In fact, it was a mere pittance—a union scale advance plus a five-percent royalty for seven years with yearly options ("About $145 a recording session," Livingston recalled). If it didn't work out in a year, the company would merely fail to pick up his option. Sinatra signed the contract at Lucy's Restaurant in Hollywood with his manager, Hank Sanicola; Livingston; and Livingston's wife, actress Betty Hutton, as witnesses.

Livingston had already set a precedent by signing diversified performers and projects that at first resembled anything but sure things—for instance, Billy May, Bugs Bunny, Kay Starr, Al Martino, the Beach Boys, Bozo the Clown (and, years later, the Beatles, The Band, and Steve Miller). He described the company's annual sales meeting in Estes Park, Colorado, in 1952: "I used to get up at these meetings and play records for the guys—update them on new artists, and tell them what we were doing. That year I announced, 'We've signed Frank Sinatra,' and the whole place groaned, 'Oohhh.' I said, 'Look, I only know one way to deal and that's with talent, and Frank is the most talented singer I know.' I cut it right there."

Well aware of the impact Nelson Riddle had made with his arrangements for Nat Cole, Livingston felt strongly that having Sinatra work with Nelson could be of vital importance in getting his recording career back on track. "After that I met again with Frank and said, 'I'd like you to work with Nelson Riddle.' He said, 'Oh Alan, I've been with Axel Stordahl for so long.'"

"Actually, Axel was a good friend of mine," Livingston explained. "Nelson had been recording with Nat Cole and a few other people. He was marvelous. We were so impressed with his accompaniment. He had a feel for how to back up a singer—not how to write an arrangement where *he* sounded good, but how to make the singer sound good.

"But Frank said, 'I can't. I can't leave Axel.' I said, 'Well, okay.' So we made his first record with Axel—'I'm Walking Behind You.'"

The song, arranged and conducted by Stordahl, was a "turntable hit" (a record that received considerable airplay but had mediocre sales.) At the same time, however, Eddie Fisher's version of it became a resounding #1 hit during the period when Fisher could do no wrong on records. (Years later Frank Sinatra described Eddie Fisher to Reprise Records president Mo Ostin as, "the only singer I've ever known who tunes up with a snare drum," alluding to Fisher's anything-but-impeccable sense of time.)

"Lean Baby" (the theme song of Capitol's newly launched Billy May band) was the flip side of "I'm Walking Behind You," although it had been recorded first. The arrangement was ghostwritten for Stordahl by Heinie Beau. The title of Sinatra and Stordahl's second single record, "Don't Make a Beggar of Me," was prophetic considering the singer's sad state of affairs at the time. It, too, proved to be unsuccessful.

Once it was apparent even to Sinatra that the Stordahl-arranged records weren't making much of an impression, Livingston's plan to pair Frank Sinatra with Nelson Riddle suddenly became a reality. Little did Livingston realize he had put Frank in the hands of the best musical caretaker he would ever encounter.

Nelson's first recording session with Sinatra took place on April 30, 1953. For this session, he conducted seventeen musicians at the KHJ radio studio at 5515 Melrose in Hollywood. When Sinatra walked into the studio, he saw a strange figure standing on the podium and asked the visiting Capitol record producer Alan Dell, "Who's that?" "He's just conducting the band. We've got the Billy May arrangements," Dell explained. The first two tunes they recorded were "South of the Border" and "I Love You," both arranged by Nelson but written in the "slurping saxes" style Billy May had designed for his new band. (Initially, May was to have arranged the tunes, but he was on tour with his band.) Since he was well versed as a ghostwriter, Nelson had no trouble handling this assignment. When the two sides were released, they were labeled "Frank Sinatra with Billy May and his Orchestra."[3]

Looking back on this recording session thirty-seven years later, Billy May observed, "It wasn't difficult for Nelson because, ya know, there's only so many things you can do with eight brass and five saxes. Nelson knew it, and I knew it. Nelson and I had become good friends. It was a quick thing for Nelson. Anyway, he had started working for Sinatra, and it turned into a hell of a deal for him."

The other two tunes recorded during the session were "I've Got the World on a String" (which Sinatra later often used as his concert opener) and "Don't Worry 'Bout

Me," both of which became hit singles, the latter when it was released over a year later. Dell recalled Sinatra asking him, "Who wrote that arrangement?" after completing the final take on "I've Got the World on a String." Dell replied, "This guy—Nelson Riddle." Frank said, "Beautiful."[4]

Veteran photographer Sid Avery, who photographed this and many other Sinatra/Riddle recording sessions for Capitol, remarked, "When Frank listened to the playback of the recording, he was really excited about it and said, 'Jesus Christ, I'm back. I'm back, baby, I'm back!' It was an upbeat style that Sinatra wasn't used to. I mean, all those melancholy recordings that he had done with Stordahl at Columbia. This was a totally new sound, and I said, 'God, this is great!' Everybody seemed to really sense it."

Milt Bernhart recalled the April 30 recording session. "When Nelson Riddle got up on the dais and the recording date started," Bernhart said, "he was in charge, but he was probably plenty nervous, I can guess. But I wouldn't have recognized the music as Nelson Riddle's. What I had heard of Nelson was based on what he had written for Bob Keane. I had worked on that date. I was just getting acquainted with him. 'I've Got the World on a String' was kind of a generic big band swing arrangement that I had heard from others—not many others, but there were others."

Voyle Gilmore, the designated producer for this recording session, was one of several producers for the Sinatra/Riddle sessions in the years ahead. But make no mistake: Frank Sinatra was at all times in complete control of everything he recorded.

Frank and Nelson had actually worked together in Hollywood almost nine years earlier. This was when Nelson was a member of the Tommy Dorsey band, which backed Sinatra on the *All-Time Hit Parade* radio show on September 17, 1944.

★ ★ ★

The word "control" is central to attempting to understand the highly complex and enigmatic personality of Frank Sinatra. Even when he first started working on New York radio stations and in North Jersey roadhouses in the late 1930s, he knew he possessed an undeniable talent for singing popular music.

In pursuing his quest, Francis Albert Sinatra (named after St. Francis of Assisi!) first saw America out of a bus window while on tour with the Dick Jurgens Orchestra for thirty-nine weeks. At that time, he was the lead singer of the Hoboken Four, winners on the Major Bowes radio program at New York's Capitol Theatre in New York on September 8, 1935.[5]

When Harry James asked Sinatra to join his struggling band in June 1939 and wanted to change his name to "Frankie Satin," he balked at the name change. James wanted Frank to change his name because he thought the name Sinatra was too Italian. He liked the name Satin because he felt it would suggest the smoothness of the singer's earnest, albeit tentative, singing style. Years later, Sinatra observed, "If I'd done that, I'd be working cruise ships today."[6] His edict at the time was, "You want the voice, you take the name."[7] From this moment on, no one would ever consider Frank Sinatra reticent or afraid to speak his mind.

The seven months he spent with James gave him an understanding of what big band singing was all about before he went on to join Tommy Dorsey's band in early 1940. It was here that he learned, among other things, how to be exacting in his musical presentation. This included learning to sing both up-tempo tunes and ballads, as well as developing a certain swagger and an unmistakable presence on stage. He later perpetuated the legend that he had given Dorsey a year's notice before he ventured out on his own on September 3, 1942.[8] It was very important to him to start to establish his own solo career before Bob Eberly, then the leading band singer, left Jimmy Dorsey.

Sinatra also knew it was his time. He was gaining a strong following singing the kind of melancholy love songs that perfectly fit the years of 1940–42—a time when young men were headed for military service and perhaps combat from which they might never return. At the dance pavilions where the Dorsey band appeared, young women listened attentively, entranced by the way Sinatra interpreted these songs. Perhaps the best example of his plaintive ballad delivery is the hit rendition of "I'll Never Smile Again," that featured him backed by Dorsey and the Pied Pipers.

Most importantly, it was in those years that Sinatra's singing style was perfected—his diction, his ability to convey the innate meaning of lyrics—to go along with his crooning bedroom baritone. Another key ingredient was his ability to sing long phrases without taking a breath—emulating Tommy Dorsey's uncanny ability to play lengthy passages on the trombone—thereby heightening the drama in his interpretation of lyrics. From watching Billie Holiday perform he had learned to project an aura of sexuality into the lyrics as well as how to bend a note. He sang of both virility and vulnerability. And always there was the sense of intimacy that caused women to feel he was singing to them alone.

When Sinatra left Dorsey, after playing a few break-in dates such as a Hartford, Connecticut, theater engagement with Duke Ellington, it was on to the Paramount in New York. He knew that making an impression in the "Big Apple" was vital to his career. Nick Sevano, who was his valet on the James band and band boy on the Dorsey band, and who was later associated with him again for several years, said, "He had a drive that I've never seen in anybody. . . . Nothing meant anything to him but his career."

Billed as "Extra Added Attraction" and backed by Benny Goodman's band during an eight-week engagement at the Paramount that began on December 30, 1942, the young singer was met with screams, ecstatic moans, and, yes, swoons by teenage girls dressed in almost identical blouses, skirts, and bobby socks, who tore up the seats and the aisles of the theater. This engagement launched "Moonlight Sinatra" (as Jimmy Durante dubbed him), who then became the biggest thing around, which is exactly what he always believed was his destiny.

All of that, however, could have come to an abrupt end if his draft board in Newark, New Jersey, had not, on December 27, 1943, rejected him for military service. The reasons cited were that he suffered from a punctured eardrum and a chronic mastoid condition that had been discovered during his physical examination. Additionally, at that same physical, Sinatra was cited as "suffering from psychoneurosis," but this was not given as a reason for his being designated 4F. At that time he was also measured as being five feet seven and one-half inches tall, not five feet nine inches tall as he claimed, much less five feet eleven inches tall as his souvenir program during the latter years of his concert tours stated.[9]

Size does matter. It was a key ingredient in Sinatra's behavior throughout his life. He felt he must always assert himself like the big guys did or he would be buried. (Years later, Sammy Cahn knowingly wrote a song for him (part of the *Robin and the Seven Hoods* score) entitled "I Like to Lead When I Dance.")

It's really no surprise that early in his career he was drawn to the "Men of Respect," who were often Sicilian like himself, and whom he first encountered in his native Hoboken/Jersey City environs. Early in his singing career, he discovered that they owned the nightclubs and other venues that presented the kind of entertainment in which he was involved. These men were tough, successful, and had unquestioned power. That appealed to the undersized singer with the skinny frame. He wanted success and power, and he wanted them badly.

Throughout his life, Sinatra relished being in the company of "wise guys," enjoying having their aura of power rub off on him. Similarly, they were extremely loyal to him, and over the years he continued to maintain his obligations to them. When things turned especially bad for him in 1951 and 1952, these powerful men kept his career alive.

After World War II, popular music changed. Frivolity was in. This was no time for beautiful ballads like Cahn and Styne's "I Fall in Love Too Easily." By the end of the 1940s, Frank Sinatra had considerable trouble finding a hit.

Mitch Miller and Sinatra couldn't agree on much of anything when Mitch took over pop A&R at Columbia in February 1950. Miller had become successful at picking out unusual novelty tunes and pairing them with various singers in Columbia's pop stable. When he coupled Frank with '50s mammary sensation Dagmar to record an ungodly song called "Mama Will Bark," it marked the end of their tenuous relationship. Miller insisted to me that, contrary to common belief, Sinatra's contract stipulated that he had final right of approval on his Columbia Records releases. Despite that, his records were increasingly unpopular. On his last Columbia single record, "Birth of the Blues" backed with "Why Try to Change Me Now?," he showed the beginning of a much freer way of handling an up-tempo arrangement; on the latter track he expressed a new sense of maturity in his approach to ballad singing.

Film appearances in less-than-stellar movies like *The Kissing Bandit,* in which he played a daring nineteenth-century Spanish adventurer; *The Miracle of the Bells,* in which he was a ludicrous choice as a pious young Catholic priest; and *Double Dynamite* with Jane Russell and Groucho Marx, in which he portrayed a nondescript bank clerk, coupled with the failure of his CBS-TV television show, indicated that the career of "The Voice" was slipping badly.

However, Sinatra's career troubles had no effect on his womanizing. After years of trifling with the likes of Lana Turner, Marilyn Maxwell, and most of the MGM female contract players, he started dating the studio's newly emerging star, Ava Gardner. "This time it was serious. The Barefoot Venus of Smithfield, North Carolina, was in some respects a perfect match for the Little Lord Fauntleroy of Hoboken. They had both come from well below the salt, and they loved the high life at the end of the table" was the way *Time* writer Ezra Goodman described their attraction to one another in his August 29, 1955, cover story.[10]

Up to this point, his affair with Ava Gardner was the only serious female relationship of Frank Sinatra's life in which he was not the dominant figure. He couldn't bear the fact that he couldn't control her. Throughout her life, Ava did what she wanted, when she wanted, and with whom she wanted. Sinatra's March 27, 1951, rendition of "I'm a Fool to Want You" remains the single most autobiographical record of his entire career.

No less an authority than Mark Twain once said, "Man will risk his life, his career for sex." Frank Sinatra, however, was willing to pay the price. The old Spanish proverb that warns, "God says, 'Take what you want . . . and pay for it,'" a favorite of Gardner's second husband, Artie Shaw, provides an apt analysis of Sinatra's winning and eventually marrying Ava Gardner. He divorced Nancy Barbato and soon afterwards he and Gardner married in Germantown, Pennsylvania, on November 7, 1951.

Months later, Gardner was quoted as saying, "I was asked 'How does it feel to be a home wrecker?' Now they ask, 'How does it feel to be married to a has-been?'" In the fall of 1953, MGM announced that Ava Gardner's marriage to Frank Sinatra was officially over. Their song may have ended, but the melody lingered on with Sinatra for more than a decade. As a result of the breakup, his singing took on an entirely new depth of meaning.

★ ★ ★

Based on his disillusioning experience with Les Baxter, one might assume Nelson Riddle would have been paranoid about having the first two of the four tunes he arranged for Frank Sinatra being credited to Billy May. But he also knew he had a second Sinatra recording session scheduled two days later. From the four sides recorded that day came Bob Wells and Freddie Karger's title song for *From Here to Eternity*. When the film had its world premiere in Atlantic City on August 17, 1953—during Sinatra's standing-room-only one-week engagement at the 500 Club in the beach resort—the record hit the *Billboard* pop chart.

After having recorded eight tracks with Nelson in less than a week's time, Frank Sinatra recognized the ability of this new arranger that Alan Livingston had foisted upon him, but he still wasn't totally sold. Conversely, Bill Miller, Sinatra's longtime pianist (who he called "Sunshine Charlie" because of his pasty complexion), had been duly impressed from the start by Nelson's uncanny, sophisticated sense of harmonies.

That fall, Milt Bernhart worked on another Sinatra-Riddle session, from which nothing was ever released. "Nelson had a free hand on this date," he remembered, "but he didn't write the right kind of arrangements. We rehearsed four numbers before Frank got there. The first tune was 'Wrap Your Troubles in Dreams,' and I thought it was just great. Frank sang about eight bars of it and then said, 'Take a break,' to the contractor, Dave Klein.

"Something was wrong. Nobody in the band picked up on it, however. It's my nature to be nosy. Frank beckoned Nelson by crooking his index finger, opened the door, and walked down the hall. Nelson followed him.

"I waited and counted to five and then followed them. It was dark. I stood in the shadows and listened. Nelson was standing with his arms pasted to his sides, pretty frightened. Frank was moving his arms all around describing things. Not mad. If he had been unhappy that would have been the end of Nelson Riddle, but he took the trouble. . . . He was describing the arrangement and what was wrong with it. Nelson had written so much music that the tunes could have stood alone as instrumentals. Frank couldn't sing through these arrangements, and he must have said to him, 'Nelson, look, there's a singer here.' You can just hear it. . . . He's creating a career for him by giving him a couple of pointers on how to write for singers. That was it. When we went back [after the break] Dave Klein said, 'The date is over.'"

The first album Sinatra recorded with Nelson Riddle was *Songs for Young Lovers,* released in 1953. Nelson conducted all of the tracks using eleven men, but only contributed the "Like Someone in Love" chart, which featured a flute solo, soon to be one of his trademarks. George Siravo had written the other seven notable arrangements, among them "A Foggy Day," "I Get a Kick out of You," and "They Can't Take That Away from Me," which Sinatra had been featuring in his nightclub engagements. The album credit read, "Accompanied by Nelson Riddle"; strangely enough, Siravo's name was absent.[11]

Flutist Paul Horn, who later worked for Nelson on various kinds of recording dates, remarked, "The flute has always been used in film scoring with a symphony orchestra. But for pop arrangements to use woodwinds like he used was unique, and the flutes played a major part in it. . . . The sounds of woodwinds, the colors—he was really a painter of sound. He used colors of musical instruments as a painter would use colors on a canvas. One of the primary colors is the flute."

At this juncture, Alan Livingston signed Nelson to a Capitol contract of his own, with a guarantee and a royalty agreement. This was the first recording contract of his career. Before that he had always been paid scale by Capitol for his arrangements and had received no royalties.

Shortly thereafter, Nelson came up with a swinging big band treatment of the familiar French song "Frère Jacques," a song he remembered Albertine singing to him in her native French when he was a little boy. He called it "Brother John," and it became a minor hit for Capitol. It was a perfect example of his still-developing big band sound and featured trumpeter Pete Candoli.

Next, Sinatra and Riddle recorded Carolyn Leigh and Johnny Richards's "Young at Heart," brought to Sinatra by Hank Sanicola, who in addition to being his manager was also his partner with Ben Barton in Barton Music, the music publishing firm. Having two such astute music men, along with Sol Parker (with whom Sinatra wrote "This Love of Mine"), Jack Bonanti, and Frank Military working for Barton Music gave Sinatra access to the best pop songs of the day. And the supreme classic pop songwriting team of the 1950s and early '60s, Sammy Cahn and Jimmy Van Heusen, writers of such future Sinatra staples as "All the Way," "Come Fly with Me," "Only the Lonely," and "My Kind of Town," were at his constant disposal.

Nelson provided Sinatra with a lush string background on the "Young at Heart" record. In early 1954 it became a #1 hit, his first in six years, and, perhaps even more important, it marked the first million-selling record of his career. Their musical association was now sealed.

With Nelson's increased workload he now could afford his own copyist. Doreen also was able to hire household help. She continued to encourage Nelson in his career while she stayed home with the children.

The second Riddle daughter and fourth child, now Bettina Bellini, was born on September 10, 1954. She, her husband Henry, and their two children live on a twenty-six-acre ranch near Escondido, California, north of San Diego. The Bellinis are proprietors of a successful car repair business. The "dynamo" aspect of Bettina's personality, according to her sisters Rosemary and Maureen, is directly traceable to their mother.

★ ★ ★

After close to a year of working with him, Nelson realized that the smoothness of the vintage Sinatra had been forever altered. His voice had deepened, no doubt partly from the effects of the combination of Lucky Strikes and Jack Daniels consumed during the long nights with and without Gardner. In one of Nelson's first interviews, he was asked to describe Sinatra's voice during this period. "It's like a cello," he said, adding, "Ava taught him the hard way."

Another time, Nelson admitted, "I didn't care for his original voice. I thought it was far too syrupy. I prefer to hear the rather angular person come through in his voice. I'm used to hearing it that way. . . . To me his voice only became interesting during the time when I started to work with him. . . . He became a fascinating interpreter of lyrics, and actually he could practically have talked the thing for me and it would have been all right. . . ."[12]

In 1954, the jazz element that had always been part of Sinatra's musical legacy was brought to the forefront in the concept album *Swing Easy*. It was a successful attempt to bring back the sound of the late 1930s band led by Red Norvo and Mildred Bailey ("Mr. and Mrs. Swing"). Arranged by Nelson for Sinatra and ten musicians, such tunes as "All of Me," "Just One of Those Things," "Wrap Your Troubles in Dreams" (obviously a new and improved version), and "I'm Gonna Sit Right Down and Write Myself a Letter" were punctuated by splendid solos by clarinetist Mahlon Clark, the late trumpeter Harry "Sweets" Edison, the late trombonist Ray Sims, tenor saxophonist Ted Nash, and vibraphonist Frank Flynn. ("He'd just write the chords and let you go," remarked Flynn.) Sinatra felt so secure in this new jazz context that he began the practice of altering lyrics while playing with the beat.

The album cover of *Swing Easy,* and especially the music, were important in introducing the new singing image Sinatra had created—that of the confident, carefree, big-city hipster gliding atop a swinging jazz beat, his Windsor-knotted tie pulled away from his collar and the proper lid on his head—a Stetson felt hat. (Sinatra was then often photographed in a hat in an attempt to disguise the fact that he was rapidly losing his hair.)

Years later Nelson reflected on Sinatra the swinger in comparison to his prowess as a ballad singer when he said, "I have a feeling that one of the two came naturally to him and one was manufactured. . . . He really wove dreams and spells and told stories with his voice."

During the latter part of '54 and into the spring of '55, Sinatra and Riddle concentrated on recording new material, constantly in search of hit record material. Among the songs they recorded were "The Gal That Got Away," Harold Arlen and Ira Gershwin's poignant ballad from Judy Garland's film version of *A Star Is Born,* and "Learnin' the Blues." The latter became their next #1 record and remained on the *Billboard* pop chart for twenty-one weeks. After this seemingly endless skein of successful singles and albums, Alan Livingston signed Sinatra to a new Capitol contract calling for a $200,000 yearly guarantee plus royalties.

★ ★ ★

In a story that could perhaps only have taken place in the music business, one afternoon in the fall of 1954, Dave Mann, Nelson Riddle's former roommate and pianist for the Charlie Spivak band, was walking down Broadway. Mann was feeling rather pleased with himself as only a songwriter can after finishing a song that he was particularly proud of writing. When he reached 55th Street, he encountered Frank Sinatra and Nelson Riddle getting out of a taxicab. They were headed for the Capitol Records office on the ground floor of the building.

Mann immediately approached Sinatra, whom he had accompanied on many Axel Stordahl record dates and with whom he had often spent time at Toots Shor's restaurant. He told Frank about his new song and then greeted Nelson, whom he had run into only a few times in the decade since they had been on the road together. As Mann recalled, "Nelson was carrying a briefcase with manuscript paper falling out of it, looking disheveled as ever."

Sinatra motioned to Mann to come inside with them. That was the signal for him to sit down and play his new creation, "In the Wee Small Hours of the Morning," which contained an almost perfect lyric written by Bob Hilliard. When Mann finished the song, Sinatra remarked enthusiastically, "That's my kinda song."

Sinatra and Nelson had gone over to the Capitol office specifically to set the keys for the arrangements Nelson was going to write for an album of torch songs (one might even label them "ballads of desperation") that Sinatra planned to record. This fortuitous meeting supplied the perfect title song for the album. It was the first tune elected to the Songwriters' Hall of Fame established in New York shortly thereafter.

On its release, *In the Wee Small Hours* received astounding critical praise. This album served to separate Frank Sinatra from his contemporaries for all time. He was at last accepted by the leading music critics as a truly formidable musical artist. The natural link between the choice of material and the way he got inside such songs as "When Your Lover Has Gone," "Ill Wind," "Mood Indigo," "What Is This Thing Called Love?" (after its final take, Sinatra blurted out, "Nelson, you're a gas!"), and "Last Night When We Were Young" showed exactly how he had lived his music. John Rockwell of the *New York Times* noted, "A public that had at first been titillated, then offended, by the Gardner-Sinatra relationship was now ready to recognize its validity once they heard it expressed as poignantly and painfully as this."[13]

In a 1982 radio interview with Jonathan Schwartz on the late lamented WNEW in New York, Nelson recalled, "On 'Last Night When We Were Young,' we went through it thirty times." (This was very different from the situation a few years later, when the lethal combination of ego and impatience would prevent Sinatra from extending himself that much in recording, much less in film acting.) "I was still very much in the learning process then," Nelson admitted. "He was extremely patient with me then—not all my fault, but at least half. In those days he had voice to burn, obviously."

On the *In the Wee Small Hours* album, Nelson's strings revealed no trace of the slick romantic feeling that had been so much a part of his arrangements for Nat Cole. These were maudlin-sounding charts written without any brass, but rather for a concentration of woodwinds, celli, and violins. As Nelson once observed, "Bill Finegan taught me to enjoy and appreciate the classics as the primary source of musical richness."[14] Listening now to the arrangements from *In the Wee Small Hours,* one is struck by the symphonic quality of Nelson's backgrounds. The truth inherent in his statement that "Mario Castelnuovo-Tedesco gave me a degree of assurance with larger, more symphonic groups of instruments," is highly visible in his writing throughout this classic album.[15]

Pianist Al Lerner said of Nelson's string writing, "You could recognize it immediately. It wasn't like Axel Stordahl, who was bland compared to Nelson. He used a lot of auxiliary chords and harmonic structures for the strings, which, to my knowledge, hadn't been heard before." Johnny Mandel remarked, "All of us [arrangers] were really taken by his work on that album. I think it was Nelson's masterpiece."

Years later, Frank Sinatra, Jr., opined, "Nelson Riddle's ability to build a song to its rightful peak coupled with my father's innate understanding of lyrics was heaven-sent for the long-playing record. Storytelling was no longer limited to the three-and-a-half minute song."[16]

Nelson mentioned the trick he had borrowed from Sy Oliver of having the band romping along and then suddenly cutting off the brass while the rhythm kept going and the strings just laid there. "The strings were always a nice, soft cushion—and I think it enriched the orchestra immeasurably. These ingredients combined to form my sound. As far as I'm concerned, the sound that I got behind Sinatra is *my* sound. He brought his voice to the picture; I brought my orchestra. And if he wanted to sing with Gordon Jenkins, then Gordon brought *his* sound over."[17]

Through his close musical association with Sinatra, it seemed only natural that Nelson would soon be working with him on television shows and in films. And so it was that in 1955 that Nelson wrote Frank's arrangements for *Guys and Dolls* and for the title song of the MGM comedy *The Tender Trap*.

One afternoon, while Nelson was recording the songs from the *Guys and Dolls* score with Frank on the soundstage at Goldwyn Studios during the fall of 1955, Doreen called in a panic. She was terrified that their Carbon Canyon hillside home in Malibu was being threatened by one of the almost yearly autumn wildfires that was roaring out of control. In an example of Sinatra's well-known concern for the welfare of his friends, when Frank was informed about what was taking place he offered to dispense as many studio trucks as needed in order to move the Riddle family's belongings to a safe place. Fortunately, the fire veered in another direction, and the emergency was averted. "But the offer was there when it was needed most," Riddle recalled.[18]

Another indication of how Frank Sinatra did things his way, and how it benefited Nelson, took place during the 1955 ninety-minute live NBC-TV production of the musical version of Thornton Wilder's *Our Town*. This was one of the first shows telecast in color and the fourth Producers Showcase of that year directed by Delbert Mann. The producer was Fred Coe, who hired Sammy Cahn and Jimmy Van Heusen to write the songs. Mann assisted in the casting of the two romantic leads, rising stars Paul Newman and Eva Marie Saint. Newman had to audition for the role and won it based on his rendition of a raucous blues. Saint had sung only once previously, in a Provincetown Playhouse production of Kurt Weill's *Down in the Valley*.

The lead in the television version, which concerned life in a small New Hampshire town, was the stage manager—played by Frank Sinatra, who sounded more North Jersey than New England. (As an actor, Sinatra never bothered to alter his accent to hide his Hoboken roots.) He was nevertheless convincing, smoking a pipe while moving in and out of the play as the interlocutor. In recalling the rehearsals for the show, Delbert Mann

From the collection of Rosemary Acerra.

Nelson and the costars of *Our Town*, Eva Marie Saint and Paul Newman, in rehearsal for the NBC-TV special in 1955.

remembered, "Frank would show up once in awhile—once in a great while."

"We came to the middle of the rehearsals, when Frank became aware for the first time of our plan to have the orchestra in another studio entirely—not on stage where he could have visual contact with the conductor," the director continued. "He became very upset with that plan. Both Cahn and Van Heusen, who had been present at all the rehearsals, tried to persuade him that this was the only way to go for two or three reasons: first, we did not have room in the studio for the scenery and the orchestra as well. As a space consideration, we had to put the orchestra in the studio next door. But perhaps most importantly, the soundman was convinced that he simply couldn't get a proper balance of voice and orchestra if the orchestra was going to be in the same studio as the actors. He wanted them isolated so that he could mix the sound.

"When Frank finally agreed that that was the only way to go, that led him to feel even more insecure. He wanted us to change the musical director, Harry Sosnick, a sweet man who was the regular musical director of the Producers Showcase. We had to talk to Harry about retiring from the show and going back to New York."

Sinatra wanted a conductor he could count on, and that man was Nelson Riddle. Nelson recalled that one afternoon, "Frank made a phone call in the next room of his apartment on Wilshire Boulevard and returned to tell me that he had put things in order."

Before the show had even gone into rehearsals, Frank took a retinue of people up to Las Vegas, where he was performing at the Sands, and asked Mann and writer David Shaw, who had edited the play, to join them. "The benefit of that was clearly the fact that we met Nelson Riddle, who was conducting for him for the first time at the Sands," Mann pointed out. "I liked Nelson and got acquainted with him. We felt very comfortable with him."

This made it easier once Nelson began work on the production. The assignment was also an important test for Nelson, as this was the first time he had been given the musical responsibility for an entire television production—and a live television special at that. "Nelson moved in and took over the entire fifty-piece orchestra in the gentlest manner possible," Mann remarked. "He didn't want to make waves because he knew that everybody was uptight about the change. He gave Frank a sense of security with the orchestra in the other room and with his having to sing and also give a dramatic performance. A video monitor was set up for Nelson so he could watch the action of the show. From hearing the dialogue and seeing the show, he took his own cues."

Unfortunately, Frank Sinatra didn't like rehearsing. He felt it dampened his spontaneity and always believed the first take was his best. Regarding the preparation for the show, he told J.P. Shanley of the *New York Times,* "The rehearsals will have lasted about four weeks. It takes only four weeks to do some good movies. One day they're going to have to devise a method of cutting down rehearsals."

It therefore wasn't a total surprise, although it was a terrible shock to Mann, when Sinatra chose to skip the dress rehearsal the day before *Our Town* was to be aired. It left Coe and Mann in a panic. They immediately got in touch with singer Johnny Desmond, then appearing at a nightclub in Phoenix, who agreed to stand by. "If Johnny had to substitute, I'd have changed the show for him. It would have been a kind of hellacious operation, but we saw no other way out. We finally found out from Cahn and Van Heusen, who got in touch with Frank personally, that he would be there for the show. They were absolutely essential to that show going on the air," recalled Mann.

The assistant director of the play was none other than Dominick Dunne, today the bestselling author of tales of the rich and social. "During the rehearsal period, Nelson and I got friendly," he related. "He invited me to his home in Malibu. I was very touched by that. He was a very decent man. I remember that during the disastrous dress rehearsal, there was Bill Mims [Sinatra's understudy] singing this song with Nelson's magnificent music playing in the background. He was so hopelessly out of tune and out of sync."

"The night of the show I gathered the cast together, but I didn't even speak to Sinatra, nor did we even acknowledge each other," Mann recalled. When the show was over, he congratulated all of the actors except Sinatra, whom he never saw again. "Occasionally, I'd see Nelson at the Directors' Guild dinner or something of that nature, and we'd reminisce about *Our Town,*" he added.

Despite all of the *sturm und drang* surrounding the production, it was highly acclaimed by the television critics. *Variety* said, "There's no denying that as a TV show-case *Our Town* was an artistic achievement." Thornton Wilder, however, detested it. Mann immediately segued from this unfortunate experience to directing the film version of *Marty,* which he had originally directed for television; it won him an Oscar in 1957.

Nelson had only six days to prepare all the music for *Our Town.* In addition to the cues and incidental music, it also entailed arranging Sinatra's five songs as well as Newman's and Saint's songs. For his work, he received his first Emmy nomination for the musical direction of the show. The EP (Extended Play) 45-rpm album sold well, and the single by Sinatra containing Nelson's highly unusual arrangement of "Love and Marriage" (which won an Emmy for Best Musical Contribution for Television that year) reached #5 on the pop chart and spent fifteen weeks there. Despite the song's success, Sinatra didn't much care for it and rarely ever sang it in personal appearances. Today, it is still heard as the theme song of the television series *Married . . . with Children,* now in syndication.

★ ★ ★

Three events took place during an eight-month period extending from May 1955 to January 1956 that would change the face and sound of popular music forever. On May 14, 1955, Bill Haley, a chubby guitarist with a spit curl that hung over his forehead, who led a group called the Comets, saw his Decca record of "Rock Around the Clock" become the fastest-selling record in the country. Then, on August 20, 1955, guitarist Chuck Berry's "Maybellene" entered the *Billboard* pop chart and peaked at #5.

The third major development occurred on Saturday, January 28, 1956, on the "Fabulous Dorseys'" CBS-TV variety show, *Stage Show,* when Tommy Dorsey introduced Elvis Aaron Presley, a seemingly rebellious, greasy-haired former truck driver from Tupelo, Mississippi, whose swivel-hips gave an erotic twist to his provocative rhythm and blues singing. This event and what followed immediately put rock 'n' roll on the musical map.

It was apparent that Elvis had listened closely to the black Mississippi Delta blues singers who significantly influenced him. His eponymous RCA Victor debut soon became the biggest-selling album of the time.

Nelson Riddle and Frank Sinatra confer on an arrangement during a recording session for Capitol Records during the late 1950s.

The impact of Elvis Presley's music led to the emergence of a new youth culture, which began to question the middle-class mores of 1950s America. He was soon to become one of the most seminal musical figures in pop music history. A new kind of music for youngwhite audiences had suddenly taken hold as had happened exactly two decades earlier with the popularization of swing music. Once again, the new music had been "borrowed" from black musicians.

Frank Sinatra and Nelson Riddle were not immune to the changes taking place in pop music. However, not surprisingly, "Two Hearts, Two Kisses, Make One Love" backed with "From the Bottom to the Top," their first offering in the rock 'n' roll vein, did not cause a commotion when it was released. This was despite the fact that these two tracks also displayed elements of doo wop, with the Nuggets supplying the vocal background support. But their follow-up single record, "Hey, Jealous Lover," recorded thirteen months later, hit with decided impact and reached a high of #3 on the *Billboard* pop chart in November 1956.

★ ★ ★

The first step in the creative process when planning a Sinatra/Riddle album was a meeting between the two principals. Here Nelson's patience and thoroughness came to the fore. Despite Sinatra's inability to read music, these meetings illustrated the keen intelligence and surprisingly thorough knowledge of music that the singer possessed.

As Nelson described these meetings, "Whereas Nat Cole was relaxed and easygoing, Frank was often tense and businesslike. Though our meetings were invariably pleasant since they had to do with the subject of music, there was an air of excitement and expectancy where Frank was involved. I had learned in high school the knack of taking speedy, concise notes when someone was talking—notes which, even if referred to many weeks later, made sense, and retained clarity. [Sinatra later referred to Nelson as "a great secretary."] This ability was sometimes taxed to the utmost when conferring with Frank about an album to be recorded several months afterwards. At certain times he might be out of town and unavailable for rechecking any of the details.

"Frank accentuated my awareness of dynamics by exhibiting his own sensitivity in that direction. I would try, by word and gesture, to get the musicians to play correctly, but if after a couple of times through the orchestra still had not effectively observed the dynamics, Frank would suddenly turn and draw from [the musicians] the most exquisite shadings, using the most effective means yet discovered—sheer intimidation. He contributed a lot to the orchestral part of his own records just by leveling at the musicians a hostile stare from those magnetic blue eyes![19]

"In those days, twelve songs or more comprised an album. Frank would start with the most agonizingly specific comments on the first few tunes, often referring to classical compositions for examples of what he expected to hear in the orchestration. This hot, precise, demanding pace would continue for an hour or two, perhaps through the first four or five songs and then, as if he, too, was beginning to feel the strain, he would start to slack off, the comments gradually would grow less specific and perhaps a tune or so later, he would say simply, 'Do what you think best.' My headache would start to subside, my pulse return to normal and another Sinatra album would be launched."

"Most of our best numbers were in what I call the tempo of the heartbeat," Nelson explained at a later date. "That's the tempo that strikes people easiest because, without their knowing it, they are moving to that pace all their waking hours. Music to me is sex—it's all tied up somehow, and the rhythm of sex is the heartbeat. I always have some woman in mind for each song I arrange; it could be a reminiscence of some past romantic experience, or just a dream-scene I build in my own imagination. But to me a score for a vocalist to sing a song is like the soundtrack to some film sequence in which this imagined woman figures."[20]

While preparing the next project for the two male sensualists in 1955, which turned out to be *Songs for Swingin' Lovers*—my own choice as the apex of their twenty-four-year musical association—Sinatra made it clear he wanted "sustained strings" as part of the backgrounds. A thirty-five-piece orchestra consisting of a big band with a full string section was put together.

The album was recorded in what had once been a radio studio complete with seats for the audience at KHJ (now the home of Channel 9 in Los Angeles), which Capitol continued to use for recording purposes. Sinatra sang while standing on the floor of the studio with the orchestra on the stage. Incredibly, there were only two microphones for the strings, two more for the brass, and one for the bass, unlike today's digital recording wherein every instrument is miked. John Palladino had but three dials at his disposal to mix the sound of this varied combination of instruments and singer. Palladino explained, "Nelson understood recording, so if you told him, 'I can't control this . . .,' he would know exactly how to correct it within the orchestration. . . . By the time of the [recording] session, it was completely worked out."[21]

As if to confirm Bill Finegan's contention that Sy Oliver's arrangements were Nelson Riddle's major influence in writing in an up-tempo vein for Frank Sinatra, Nelson stated, "Perhaps unconsciously, my ear recalled some of the fine arrangements Sy Oliver had done for Tommy [Dorsey] using sustained strings but also employing rhythmic fills by brass and saxes to generate excitement. The strings, by observing crescendos in the right places, add to the pace and tension of such writing without getting in the way. It was a further embroidery on this basic idea to add the bass trombone [George Roberts] plus the unmistakably insinuating fills of Harry Edison on Harmon-muted trumpet. I wish that all effective formulas could be arrived at so simply. . . ."[22]

All the preparation in the world, however, couldn't replace the reality of having a core group of first-rate musicians challenged by having first-rate arrangements and interacting with a singer they respected who had emerged from the same big band background. This was one of the underlying reasons why *Songs for Swingin' Lovers* was such a standout album.

"The voice was just an extension of the orchestra," Bill Miller contended. "It was another instrument. Frank just fit in there, and he was on top. It was like we were playing for our band singer, but were really an important part of it."

Frank Sinatra's newfound confidence provided the impetus and the undeniable edge to his performances on this album. By now it was obvious that Nelson's arrangements had supplied the engine that had powered Sinatra's musical comeback. But it was Tommy Dorsey who was the unsung hero. His musical influence was certainly an important underlying ingredient in the success of this recording. It was he who had instilled in the collaborators a strong sense of discipline and excellence.[23]

I can still remember the first time I heard "How About You?," a selection from the album, on WNEW, when I was about to drive onto New York City's West Side Highway at 57th Street. I laughed so hard when I heard Sinatra's amusing reworking of the lyric ". . . and James Durante's looks—they give me a thrill" that I almost drove into a column supporting the upper level of the highway!

There wasn't a weak track on *Songs for Swingin' Lovers*. ("Memories of You" was the only song recorded but cut from the album.) Among its gems were "Sweets" Edison's muted trumpet bleats giving a whimsical twist to "Old Devil Moon" (French horn player extraordinaire Vince De Rosa rightfully referred to "Sweets" as "the salt and pepper," adding, "He had the knack of putting in just a few very right notes that were important.") George Roberts played a memorable bass trombone solo on Eddie Cantor's hit "Makin' Whoopee," which was also dressed up in brand-new colors, as was "Anything Goes."

Frank, Jr., recalled his father telling him that after completing the last recording session for the album on January 11, 1956, he got a call from Voyle Gilmore at one o'clock in the morning informing him that more songs had to be recorded the next night. An executive decision had been made that, in view of the anticipated success of this album, it would be better to include more than the usual twelve tunes on the 12-inch LP. (Sinatra's previous Capitol albums had been 10-inch LPs.) This unexpected news upset Sinatra. He had planned to drive to his Rancho Mirage home for the weekend the next morning.

For a few minutes, he contemplated the situation. Then he called Nelson at home, informing him that he had to arrange three more songs. "Sinatra [as Frank, Jr., often refers to his father] gave him three songs real fast. Either he had them already written down or he pulled them out of a hat," said Frank, Jr.

"Nelson got out of bed and started writing. By seven o'clock the next morning he got two songs to the copyist. He then had a few hours sleep and started writing again at about one o'clock in the afternoon. Nelson knew that 'you-know-who' wasn't going to be a very happy person that night because he did not want to be working. . . . With Doreen at the wheel of their station wagon, Nelson was in the back seat finishing the arrangement while holding a flashlight. When the Riddles arrived at the studio, Vern

Yocum, the copyist, had ten of his associates there. Sinatra recorded the first two tunes with Nelson and the orchestra while they were copying the last arrangement."

This last arrangement was the *pièce de resistance*—what Sinatra often called "Nelson Riddle's shining hour"—his arrangement of Cole Porter's "I've Got You Under My Skin." It became synonymous with Sinatra more than any other arrangement of his entire career. Milt Bernhart's epic trombone solo on the tune, recorded on January 12, 1956, was one for the ages. It followed on the heels of George Roberts's repeating, burping nineteen-bar bass trombone chorus, which served as its introduction. After the first complete take, the entire orchestra applauded Nelson.

The solo was completely improvised. "It took fifteen takes or more. I played every one of them differently before I got it right," Bernhart recalled. He went on to describe his solo: "It was a *montuna,* a musical figure that Afro-Cuban bands like Machito, Perez Prado, and Dizzy Gillespie had popularized. Dizzy's famous record of 'Manteca' is a perfect example."

Cole Porter's world was one of elegance and sophistication. He described it as "the best, the crest, the works, the top." If he had been asked his opinion of the Sinatra/ Riddle rendition of "I've Got You Under My Skin" (which he probably was), he no doubt would have used these same words in praise of it. It was the only musical arrangement cited by *Time* in its study of the most important entertainers of the twentieth century. Nelson was paid $150 for the chart.

At that time, Nelson was also beginning work with songwriter Richard Adler on arranging the score for the upcoming Warner Bros. film version of Adler's hit Broadway musical, *The Pajama Game.* Nelson invited Adler to this recording session. At its conclusion, Nelson introduced him to Frank Sinatra.

According to Adler, "Sinatra said, 'You're Adler. I'm Sinatra, the schmuck who turned down 'Hey There.'" Adler asked him, "Why did you turn it down?" Sinatra said, "I never saw the music. I thought it was a riff tune." The song went on to become a big hit for Rosemary Clooney.

Bob Bain, who played guitar on the recording session, remembered that the following weekend Sinatra invited Doreen and Nelson to Rancho Mirage (to make up for the previous lost weekend). Frank enjoyed Doreen's company. He believed she was the right kind of wife for Nelson. Doreen told Bain proudly, "Frank played the acetate of 'I've Got You Under My Skin' over and over during the weekend."

Initially, Sinatra had told Nelson he wanted a long crescendo in the arrangement, which caused Nelson to think of Ravel's *Boléro.* When Nelson discussed this with George Roberts, Roberts suggested adapting the section from Stan Kenton's record of "23° North, 82° West" that had featured him. Nelson proceeded to expand upon that idea.

Johnny Mandel stressed that an important ingredient in this historic arrangement was that it began in 2/4 time, went into 4/4, and reverted to 2/4 toward the end. "That was real Sy Oliver, right out of Jimmie Lunceford," he said. "I got excited when I heard that arrangement snowballing," the late jazz pianist Lou Levy added. "You can tell Frank is into it. They tore the world apart. It's one of *the* outstanding vocal arrangements—'My Way' and 'New York, New York,' if that's your bag, fine. But forget it, this one wipes 'em all out."

Jonathan Schwartz once asked Nelson if he didn't say to himself at the time he wrote the "I've Got You Under My Skin" arrangement, "This is awfully good." Characteristically, Nelson answered, "No, I probably said, 'Wow, isn't it nice that I finished it in time.'"

Paul Keyes, who wrote and produced several TV specials for Sinatra and also hired Nelson many times for various variety shows, owns the original manuscript of Nelson's arrangement, which Sinatra sent to him. It contains Frank's autograph along with Nelson's, and Nelson added, "Paul, sing it again!" Framed in red, it occupies a place of honor on the wall of Keyes's home in Westlake Village, California.

Playing alongside Nelson and Milt Bernhart in the trombone section that night was the talented valve trombonist Juan Tizol, whom Nelson often featured. Tizol had written "Caravan" with Duke Ellington and was featured with Duke's famous orchestra for many years. To complete the section was Jimmy Priddy, formerly a member of Charlie Spivak's band during Nelson's tenure there, continuing the tradition Nelson had established of hiring his former bandmates. Bernhart recently observed that Nelson's writing for his former instrument was heavily influenced by the bar-by-bar syncopations then being played by Bill Harris, who, along with J.J. Johnson, was the father of the modern jazz trombone.

It is also impossible not to recognize the fact that eroticism was at the very core of Nelson's arrangement of "I've Got You Under My Skin." Chris Riddle relishes telling of the time when, as a child, he overheard a heated argument between his mother and father. Doreen abruptly ended it by saying, "All you think about is music and sex!" Nelson countered with, "Is there anything else?"

★ ★ ★

On February 22, 1956, Frank Sinatra and Nelson Riddle were at Capitol, only this time, at the newly dedicated Capitol Tower on Vine Street, above Hollywood Boulevard, for the first recording session held at the new location. Sinatra conducted a sixty-piece symphony orchestra playing two original compositions by Nelson, "Gold" and "Orange," that were included with other pieces written by Victor Young, Alec Wilder, Billy May, André Previn, Elmer Bernstein, and Jeff Alexander for the album *Frank Sinatra Conducts Tone Poems of Color*. "Gold" opened with a heavy Germanic feeling (perhaps influenced by Wagner's Ring cycle) before venturing far afield to establish its primary theme, which is reminiscent of Alfred Newman's *Captain from Castile* score. "Orange," however, showed the influence of Rodgers and Hammerstein's "It's Been a Real Nice Clambake" from *Carousel* before segueing into a love theme displaying Nelson's familiar romantic use of strings. Both compositions made it abundantly clear that Nelson was eager to make his debut as a film composer.

Two weeks later, the dynamic duo was in the studio again to begin recording the *Close to You* album, their most unheralded artistic achievement. This time there was no big band or full orchestra, but rather a string quartet—a *formidable* string quartet. The Hollywood String Quartet consisted of Sinatra's frequent recording concertmaster, violinist Felix Slatkin; Paul C. Shure, violin; Alvin Dinkin, violin; and Felix's wife, violist Eleanor Slatkin. The idea for the album was derived from Frank's close friendship with the Slatkins.

The material consisted of the title song and such relatively obscure ballads as "Love Locked Out," "P.S., I Love You," "Don't Like Goodbyes," "It's Easy to Remember," and "The End of a Love Affair," a song that reflects the album's theme—Sinatra's favorite musical subject of lost love. "This was Nelson in his most classical vein," Johnny Mandel pointed out. "Although I still don't believe a string quartet can properly accompany a singer, this works."

The digital version of *Close to You* underlines the beauty of the string playing. It also demonstrates how the gorgeous tones of the instruments helped to define the tenderness of Nelson's arrangements. Paul C. Shure wasn't biased when he avowed, "It was the most stunning thing that Nelson ever did."[24] Nonetheless, the album received only mediocre critical acceptance and negligible sales when it was released during the winter of 1957.

Close to You exhibited a much different kind of writing than Nelson had ever undertaken. This led to his frequent consultations with Felix Slatkin and his musical cohorts during the writing process. He had no pad of strings to support him. A French horn (Vince De Rosa), clarinet (Mahlon Clark), and a very few other instruments were added on some tracks. Once again, he showed his musical debt to the French musical Impressionists, Ravel and Debussy, but also, according to Shure, to Brazilian composer Heitor Villa-Lobos.

Sinatra was left equally musically naked. For him to tackle such a project was quite a stretch, but he fit in quite easily with the quartet. He was in excellent voice, projecting a certain sweetness together with an understated interpretation of the bittersweet lyrics of the songs.

One of the tunes from the *A Swingin' Affair* album (which followed *Songs for Swingin' Lovers*), "I Won't Dance," hadn't been recorded by a major singer in years and served to reintroduce the Irving Berlin song first made famous by Fred Astaire. And having recently completed shooting *Pal Joey* for Columbia, Sinatra was justifiably enamored of his and Nelson's version of "The Lady Is a Tramp," which earlier had been sung only by female vocalists. This track was deleted from the record, although it is now included on the CD. Cole Porter's "From This Moment On," which had been cut from his score for *Can-Can,* was another memorable offering.

A Swingin' Affair has a particularly important place in my life. During the winter and spring of 1957, while an enlisted man in the peacetime army in South Korea, my good friend Frank Ceglia and I played this album on an almost nightly basis in the headquarters company of the Seventh Cavalry Regiment of the First Cavalry Division. Listening to it reminded us of home as we fantasized about getting out of the Army and starting our careers in New York.

Subsequently, about halfway through my sixteen months of duty in Korea, I was given leave and took the then-eighteen-and-one-half-hour flight from Tokyo to Honolulu. I was meeting my parents, who were flying in from the East Coast and weren't due to arrive until the next day. After registering at the hotel, I showered and changed clothes, and then read in the Honolulu newspaper that *Pal Joey* was playing at a local theater. I promptly took a taxi to go see it.

The leading role of nightclub singer Joey Evans was absolutely tailor-made for Sinatra. Nelson's chart of "The Lady Is a Tramp" became one of Frank's signature songs. This was one of several Rodgers and Hart songs he expertly arranged for Sinatra in the film. Film composer George Duning was helpful to Nelson in adapting the Rodgers and Hart songs.

The magical scene in which Rita Hayworth returns to the second-rate nightclub to see "Pal Joey" perform, staged brilliantly by director George Sidney, began with Frank kicking a magenta-colored upright piano into place as trumpeter Bobby Sherwood mounted the bandstand with his musicians. Sinatra then nonchalantly "played" a bluesy piano introduction (ghosted by Bill Miller), accompanying himself before rising up from the piano and hunching the padded shoulders of his blue dinner jacket as he exhaled smoke from a cigarette while seductively singing the final chorus of the classic tune. This was pure Sinatra and the best presentation of his musical persona ever captured on film.

"He seemed to take a particular delight in that song," Nelson recalled. "He always sang it with a certain amount of salaciousness; he savored it. He had some cute tricks he did with the lyric which made it especially his."[25]

★ ★ ★

It was the August 1956 world premiere engagement of another Sinatra film, the dreadful western *Johnny Concho* (Nelson's first film-scoring job), at the Paramount Theater in New York, that resulted in Frank's decision to work with Tommy Dorsey again after many years. The singer and the band provided the stage show to go along with the movie.

Tino Barzie, Dorsey's manager, remembered that often when driving with Dorsey in his Cadillac on the road, Tommy would flip the radio dial, eager to listen to his alumni Sinatra and Riddle's recordings of "It Happened in Monterey," or "You Make Me Feel So Young," which were then all over the airwaves. "Tommy would say, 'Listen to that son of a bitch—the greatest singer ever! He knows exactly where to go and what to do.'"

Hank Sanicola called Barzie from Spain, where Sinatra was making the film *The Pride and the Passion* with Cary Grant and Sophia Loren, to discuss how his client wanted to open *Johnny Concho* in New York with the Dorsey band. Upon relating the news to Tommy, the bandleader made it clear to Barzie that he and only he would lead his band during the engagement, "I conduct the orchestra. It's my orchestra," he said. Upon hearing Dorsey's edict, Sanicola conferred further with Sinatra and called Barzie back to explain that Sinatra would dispatch Nelson Riddle to New York to rehearse his charts with the Dorsey band for two days in preparation for the week-long engagement.

Jane Dorsey, Tommy's widow, told of the night Tommy brought two guests home for the weekend just before the Sinatra/Dorsey engagement began at the Paramount. "Tommy blew his (car) horn as he drove up out front, and I went to a window and looked down. There was Tommy with two gentlemen, one of whom was Nelson Riddle. The other was Dave Rose. Tommy, of course, was friends with both of them. He said, 'Hi, E-Flat.' That was his nickname for me. I'm told that on a trombone it's a very light note and very hard to reach. I think that was my first meeting with Nelson. I know it was the first time I had met Dave Rose." (Nelson said the reason he agreed to spend the weekend with Tommy and Jane was, "I had never seen him other than as an employer. I wanted to see what he was like just as a fella."[26])

Jane Dorsey recalled, "The first night we went to a wonderful French restaurant just over the New York state line called Le Cremellière. During dinner I gave Nelson the names of some great tunes that I thought Frank Sinatra should record. Nelson took out a pen and a piece of paper and, as he was writing them down, he said, 'Janie, I agree with you. You've got very good taste.'"

The next morning Jane awakened, looked out the window, and saw a solitary figure walking down the road next to the lake on the Dorseys' five-acre property. She quickly got dressed and joined Nelson, who was sitting on a white birch log tossing pebbles into the lake.

"I joined him and asked him what he was doing up so early," she recalled. "'Well, the quiet got to me. I wasn't used to such a quiet place,' he replied. We looked up at Tommy's bedroom, and he said to me, 'Janie, do you have any idea how much that man taught me?' I told him that I had a pretty good idea. He said, remembering his days with the Dorsey band, 'He taught me everything I know. Every note I write I learned from that man upstairs.' Nelson added, 'People rave over my arranging today, and I just think to myself, God bless Tommy Dorsey. If it hadn't been for him, I never could have done this.'"

The next night they ate at home. Over dinner, Tommy said to Nelson, "I really like the things you've been doing with Frank." Nelson then essentially repeated what he had told Janie, "I'll tell you the truth—much of the skill and ability to do these things came from my time with you," whereupon Dorsey began to cry. Nelson rushed over to embrace him and went on to say, "That's true, you're the one. You're the one who steered me."

In his depressed state, Dorsey exclaimed, "Nelson, I don't want Frank to come down to rehearsal and give me any orders or cast any aspersions toward me or embarrass me in front of my boys. I couldn't stand that." Nelson said, "He won't do that. Don't worry, Tommy, he won't."

"I got up and went over to Tommy and put my arm around him," Janie remembered. "I said, 'Tommy, you know he's not going to do anything like that. He wouldn't dare.'"

The next morning Nelson and Janie found themselves alone again waiting for the others to come downstairs. Nelson said to her, "I wish I had a wife who was something like you, Janie." "I was very surprised and shocked," Janie recalled. "I guess it was because it was a home atmosphere. We had children and it was relaxed and quiet in the country, and he saw that I had gone to Tommy's side. I don't know what made him say that. I didn't know anything about his personal life."

On Monday, in New York, Nelson and Tommy listened to several of Sinatra's records, which Nelson had arranged, and went over the scores that Nelson had brought along. Nelson realized that some of his arrangements for Sinatra were out of tempo and somewhat more complicated than Dorsey was used to. He found it odd showing Tommy how his arrangements should be played. But, as he admitted, "I'm a diplomat, heaven knows."

"Tommy was quick," Tino Barzie pointed out. "He had been studying the charts anyway so he knew exactly what they were about." They began rehearsing Sinatra's music with the Dorsey band. Nelson didn't stay for the opening. The day after he finished the rehearsals he returned to Los Angeles.

Dorsey confidant Eddie Collins caught a few of the performances during the first few days of the engagement. As he remembered it, "They were packed every day. The band was really good and so was Frank. Lee Castle played great lead trumpet and Charlie Shavers played some marvelous trumpet solos. What a thrill they were! It wasn't like the old band. The guys were playing all this stuff for Frank, of course—all the charts that Nelson had written, so they had Nelson's mark all over it."

That particular week I had been in New York in search of a job after graduating from the University of Virginia. I was in a cab going down Broadway en route to the Port Authority Bus Terminal when I looked up and saw the marquee at the Paramount announcing Frank Sinatra's appearance with the Dorseys. I told the taxi driver to stop immediately, got out of the cab, and was informed by the doorman at the theater, "No seats at all today, tonight, or tomorrow." Unfortunately, there were no more Sinatra performances the next day or any day after that. Sinatra caught a severe cold and Red Skelton, Jackie Gleason, Walter Winchell, Ed Sullivan and others were brought in to substitute for him to finish out the week. I was not to see Frank Sinatra perform until four years later, when Red Norvo introduced him as "my boy singer" in an engagement at the 500 Club in Atlantic City.

That summer of '56, Nelson's arrangements of "You're Sensational" and "Mind If I Make Love to You" for Sinatra were two highlights of Cole Porter's score for the MGM musical *High Society*. Frank sang the latter, a beautiful ballad, with great passion at the conclusion of a highly sensual love scene with Grace Kelly toward the end of the film. For some reason, to my knowledge this beautiful love song has never been recorded by a major singer since that time.

★ ★ ★

After more than three years of intensive recording, Nelson Riddle had been through many varied situations with Frank Sinatra. Paul Tanner related the amusing story of a weeknight in the mid-'50s when he got a telephone call from Nelson at 10:45 P.M. Nelson asked him if he could come down to Capitol at 11:30. "What in the world for?" asked Tanner incredulously. "Frank wants me to get the orchestra together," Nelson explained. "That means paying triple scale, you know," reminded Tanner. "Don't worry, you know he's good for it," Nelson said.

The now-retired trombonist and former music professor at UCLA showed up at Capitol with twenty-four other musicians, including "Sweets" Edison. Tanner recalled, "There was no producer in the booth, but there was an engineer handling the microphones and the control panel. We ran down about eight to ten tunes, but nothing was ever recorded. Kim Novak, his lady of the moment, was sitting in the rear of the studio with Frank Military. Sinatra merely wanted to serenade her. At the end, he thanked everybody and told us we'd all get paid for our efforts. Then he took Kim's hand and with Military walked out the door and into the night."

Vince De Rosa remembered, "During their first several recording sessions Frank would make fun of Nelson without his realizing it, but the orchestra caught it. He took advantage of his seriousness. Nelson was so serious that Sinatra would just kind of give him a jab. The musicians felt, 'Jesus, this guy's really nailing him.' But Sinatra was that type, ya know. However, obviously he had complete respect for him."

It is important to realize that Nelson's demeanor was almost always completely businesslike in the recording studio. Sinatra, however, approached the art of recording as if he were performing in a nightclub, often bantering with the musicians and invited guests. The basic difference between the two of them was absolutely palpable.

George Roberts and several other Riddle regulars told me of a few occasions when Frank would walk in and ask Nelson to have the orchestra run down the arrangements they were about to record that night. "I was on dates when Frank didn't like the charts, but it was usually because of the material. He would say, 'The date's over. You'll get paid,' and he walked out the door and that was the end. He wouldn't really say why he didn't like the charts, but you'd know why he was leaving," Roberts remembered.

At other times Sinatra would get on a musician for playing an uninspired solo or for hitting a "clam" (a wrong note). Publicist Jim Mahoney recalled Sinatra's adverse reaction to a particular guitar player's solo: "That guy needs a manicure."

Margaret Whiting also had frequent access to the Sinatra/Riddle recording sessions. She recalled, "Sometimes Frank would come in the studio, and he was looking at his watch as if [to say], 'C'mon, c'mon, let's get going.' He had a girl to see, or he was going somewhere. . . . Other times he was fascinated about an arrangement, and he would do it over and over. He'd say, 'Play it slower, play it softer,' and they would really get a record out of it. He loved some of the arrangements. Other times he was bored to tears and wanted to get out of there."

Donfeld, then Capitol's art director and later a four-time Oscar-nominated costume designer, remembered being at Capitol for an 8:30 A.M. meeting on December 10, 1953. Photographer Lee Friedlander had sent him an enlargement of a photograph he had made of Sinatra for use as a poster. When he asked Riddle his opinion of it, Nelson, looking even more forlorn than usual (having obviously been up all night following a Sinatra recording session), replied, "Sorry, Don, I'm not much of a Frank Sinatra fan this morning." Donfeld soon learned that Sinatra had insisted on doing twenty-eight takes of the tune "Rain," which immediately preceded the recording of "Young at Heart."

Trumpeter Uan Rasey pointed out, however, that if Nelson really felt strongly about a specific musical issue, he would speak his mind to Sinatra. "He would say it in a nice way. ["Suggest" was always the operative word in dealing with Frank Sinatra.] Frank would respect a suggestion coming from him because he knew if Nelson felt that strongly he was probably right."

Emil Richards concurred completely with Rasey's observation. "He respected Nelson's musicianship," he said. "You could see that in the way he talked to Nelson, and the questions he would ask him. Sometimes before he started to record, Frank would have Bill Miller, the guitarist Al Viola, and me go up to a room on the third floor at Capitol to vocalize and run over the tunes. Bill would play the melody. He played the chords so that Frank would know what the arrangement was all about. If I'm not mistaken, I think Nelson did that a few times because, of course, he not only knew the arrangement, but he could also play piano.

"Sometimes on the gig Frank would say, 'This ain't laying right for me. How do I do this, Nelson?' and Nelson would think for a minute and say, 'At bar 72, I want the trombones. . . .' Right away, before even answering Frank, he'd rewrite the little part and get it straight. He could rewrite it in his head. And, if Nelson said, 'Frank, I think we should do another one,' Frank would immediately say, 'All right, c'mon. We'll do one more for Nelson.'"

Don Raffell described the November 15, 1956, recording session for the *A Swingin' Affair* album: "We had rehearsed the music and we're sitting there. The double doors at Capitol open up and there's Sinatra. He's got a black hat on with a white band, black suit, black shirt, black shoes, white necktie—gangster. He doesn't say anything to anybody, walks into the recording booth, and says, 'You've had plenty of time to get the balance on this thing. I don't want any fooling around or it'll be your ass!' . . . He says that like a hoodlum. . . . We did one take on each thing that we did. One! That's it.

That's all he wanted to do. No slips, no nothing. He was an evil mother!"

André Previn related the story of the night when he had completed a recording session at United Recording for which he had written some arrangements. He wandered into the main studio when Sinatra and Riddle were at work and quietly took a seat in the recording booth. "I sat there unseen just in time to hear Frank suddenly wheel on Nelson and call him names and belittle him. Nelson was too sweet for his own good. He just took it. He stood there. I couldn't stand it, and I left and went back to my own recording date. About an hour later I met Nelson by the coffee urn, and I said, 'Nelson, how can you take that? I mean, there isn't anyone as good as you, not anyone in the world, and Frank owes you, as far as I'm concerned, a good fifty percent of whatever success he's had.'

"Nelson said, 'Oh well, you've worked for him, you've written for him. You know Frank—he doesn't even mean it.'"

Previn summed up the deep respect he had for Nelson when he added, "I do not have Frank's records with Gordon Jenkins, although they're good, or with Billy [May], although they're wonderful. But I think all the ones he did with Nelson—I have a lot of them—I personally think they're Nelson's records with a vocalist on! . . . What he wrote for Frank enhanced that which Frank was good at and minimized what he was not good at, and that was also a good trick. When the [movie] studios assigned Frank arrangers other than Nelson you could hear it. It just wasn't as good."

"Nelson said he was only afraid of one man, and that was Frank Sinatra," George Roberts related. "Not physically. He was afraid of him because he couldn't figure out what he would do . . . which is why Nelson wanted a first reading every time we played. He wanted it perfect the first time [so as] not to give Frank a chance to not like the chart. If he didn't like them, he'd have to redo them."

Roberts also recalled the time in January 1963 when Chris Riddle suffered a broken pelvis after being hit by a car while delivering newspapers. Nelson learned of the accident right in the middle of a record date. "Frank went into the booth and called three specialists and said, 'Get to Santa Monica Hospital right now and do what you need to do to save his life.' He took care of everything. That was really something, to see Frank really take charge and get those people out there—boom, boom—and then we finished the date."

There were certainly amusing situations as well. One night "Sweets" Edison was late for a recording session and, as a consequence, was caught speeding by the police. He explained that he was on his way to Capitol to record with Frank Sinatra and Nelson Riddle. His explanation was met by a "Sure, sure . . ." response. As the recording session was beginning, there was the trumpeter with two confirmation-seeking policemen accompanying him through the door of Studio A on the ground floor at Capitol. The policemen saw what was happening, laughed, and released Edison so he could play his trumpet parts.

Within two years of the 1953 release of *From Here to Eternity,* Frank Sinatra had disproved the judgment of the pundits. He had transformed himself into the most powerful force in Hollywood as an actor, recording star, and nightclub attraction. His enigmatic, chameleon-like ways, however, were often infuriating to those he worked with; he once admitted to writer A.E. Hotchner, "I'm my own worst enemy."

But in the eyes of the American public, he had reached the status of an icon. He had that rare and mystical ability to fascinate. It was said of him, "What Sinatra has is beyond talent." He epitomized style and exuded the unlikely combination of elegance and impending violence. The often-misused word "charisma" was practically invented by him. When he came to New York, the only thing Earl Wilson, the popular Broadway gossip columnist, had to write in his column was, "He is here." His readership would knew exactly who he was writing about.

Actor Henry Silva, a longtime Sinatra cohort, however, remembered witnessing a rare occasion when Frank Sinatra allowed someone to have a glimpse of his innermost feelings. "One night I was leaving Frank's old house up on Bowmont Drive at about three o'clock in the morning," Silva said. "I think I was the last one to leave after a party. As I was getting into my car, Frank looked over the carport toward the lights of the Valley and said, 'Many nights I've looked down there and envied the people who live there.' That showed me his pain and his loneliness."

★ ★ ★

Sinatra's June 9, 1957, live recording with Nelson Riddle at the Civic Auditorium in Seattle (released by Artanis Entertainment Corporation) illustrates the fact that, other than his close friend the late comedian Joe E. Lewis, he was perhaps the first performer who made a statement by drinking alcohol on stage. (Today, popular jazz singer Diana Krall swigs Evian water while her guitarist plays a solo!) He was one of the first singers to change lyrics by ad-libbing drug references, as when he sang "The way you smoke your tea . . ." while singing "They Can't Take That Away from Me." He was also one of the first to use profanity on stage while singing the last chorus of "The Lady Is a Tramp": "It's so goddamned cold and so damp."

But that same year, Sinatra had also started hiring arrangers other than Nelson— Billy May for "Come Fly with Me," Gordon Jenkins for "Where Are You"—even Felix Slatkin arranged and conducted "Monique," a song from Sinatra's United Artists war film *Kings Go Forth.* Nonetheless, between Sinatra's stints working with other arrangers, Nelson helped him enjoy hit recordings of "All the Way" and "Witchcraft." The former was from the biographical film about Joe E. Lewis, *The Joker Is Wild,* in which Sinatra starred; the latter garnered Nelson's first of eleven Grammy nominations as an arranger.

Publicist Warren Cowan remembered, "When Frank decided to record an album with Billy May, Nelson was very hurt. I think it surprised him. I remember him talking to me about it—'How could he do that to me—after all we've done together?' he said." In time, however, Nelson learned to deal with it, especially since he liked Billy

May personally and respected the powerful sense of swing and the puckish sense of humor he exhibited in his music. Sinatra once said, "Recording with Billy [May] is like having a bucket of cold water thrown in your face."[27]

The shock of his decision was cushioned by his naming Nelson the musical director of the *The Frank Sinatra Show* on ABC-TV, in 1957. Bill Richmond was then playing drums for Nelson. (This was a few years before he began working for Jerry Lewis; he later became a busy television writer and director.) Richmond recalled that for part of one season, Sinatra decided that the rhythm section of Al Viola on guitar, Joe Comfort on bass, and Richmond on drums should be prerecorded for all the tunes that were featured on the various episodes. "Frank was there dictating the tempos, and he would kind of sing, but to himself, as it wasn't being recorded. There was Nelson conducting these four guys! I don't know how many shows we did in those maybe two or three recording sessions in order to do thirteen shows."

"Sinatra refused to lip sync," Richmond continued. "He wanted to sing live on the show, but the band, which was all enclosed in glass, played to this track that had already been laid down. There were problems isolating the band from his track. This was years before tracking had even begun. He wanted it completely live.

"You always felt that when Nelson was recording with Frank he wanted it to be very special. Nelson would say, 'Now when Frank comes in, this has to be recording quality. He won't stand for anything less than recording quality.'"

★ ★ ★

In the mid-fifties Nelson brought Nelson, Sr., and Marie Albertine from New Jersey to live in Santa Monica. He invited his aunt and uncle, Ed and Bess Parker, to move out with them for companionship. Nelson also financed his parents when they set up a health food store, called Riddle's Vitamins, in Santa Monica on Wilshire Boulevard between 4th and 5th Streets.

Chris laughingly gave an example of how Albertine and Nelson, Sr.'s relationship continued in its usual vein after they moved to the West Coast: "She'd be yelling at him from the other room, and he'd say, 'Yes, dear.' Then she'd say, 'I bet you haven't heard a word I've said.' And he'd say, 'Every word.'" Rosemary added, "I think he adored Maman [the Riddle children's name for their grandmother]."

As in the past, Albertine ran the business. Within two years, however, she was diagnosed with breast cancer. Despite her earlier disapproval of Doreen, she grew increasingly close to her daughter-in-law. She also returned to the Catholic church during her illness.

Albertine passed away on May 9, 1958, at the point when Nelson was in the middle of his month-long work on *Only the Lonely,* his reunion album with Sinatra. Just three months earlier, Nelson and Doreen's baby daughter, Lenora Celeste, had died of bronchial asthma at the age of six months. In her memory, Nelson wrote "Lament for Lenora."

Only the Lonely is the album many Sinatraphiles consider Sinatra and Nelson's foremost artistic triumph. In addition, it was #1 on the *Billboard* pop chart for five weeks. Once asked if he had a favorite among all his recordings, Frank unhesitatingly chose this album. Nelson fully concurred with this statement. Perhaps the underlying reason for the success of this album hinges on the fact that the two of them fully understood the versimilitude of a man's heartbreak at the end of a love affair.

Laurie Brooks, Nelson's lover in his last years, observed, "People think that *Only the Lonely* reflected Sinatra's lingering sadness over Ava Gardner. They weren't aware of the sadness in Nelson over his mother's rapidly deteriorating health, which had an important effect on his writing. He was very devoted to her."

Paul Horn contended, "I'll tell you something with regard to Nelson's sadness: I think that's why he wrote [the way he] wrote. That all has a place. An artist can use everything that happens to him as a point of departure. Pain comes out in beauty. It's transmuted in the art."

In still another example of the uncanny developments that can be so much a part of a show business career, neither Frank Sinatra nor Nelson Riddle won a Grammy for *Only the Lonely* in 1958. This was the first year the Grammys were awarded. One would think that the album would have at least won in the Best Male Vocal Performance, Album of the Year, or Best Arrangement categories. Instead, the only Grammy *Only the Lonely* received was for its album cover, which was designed by Frank Sinatra! Unfortunately, since NARAS hadn't been established until that year, Sinatra and Riddle lost the opportunity to be honored for some of their most inspired work together during the mid-1950s.

The choice of songs for *Only the Lonely*—including "Blues in the Night," "One for My Baby," "Angel Eyes," "Guess I'll Hang My Tears out to Dry" (Bill Miller's favorite Riddle arrangement), and "What's New" (hardly coincidentally Ava Gardner's favorite song)—explored the depths of loneliness and despair as they had never before been recorded by the combination of a major pop singer and arranger.

In analyzing their work together, the fact that Frank Sinatra and Nelson Riddle were both only children born into families with dominant mothers and retiring fathers should not be overlooked. From the beginning, and throughout their lives, loneliness surrounded them both. Bill Miller, while readily acknowledging Sinatra's loneliness, also pointed out, "He wanted that to be known. The women dug it so he dug it; he was very smart in a lot of ways."

Nelson chose several instrumental soloists to communicate the essence of the music on the album. Harry Edison showed the somber side of his playing on "Willow Weep for Me." The late, great trombonist, Ray Sims, the unsung soloist with Les Brown and Harry James and brother of jazz tenor saxophonist stalwart "Zoot" Sims, delivered the finest recording work of his long career with a brace of meaningful solos. Bill Miller contributed several beautifully conceived piano solos. Felix Slatkin conducted the last few selections, since Nelson had to be out of town on a pre-arranged tour with Nat Cole.

Bill Richmond played drums on the album. Forty-two years later he called *Only the Lonely* "just fucking magnificent. It wasn't swinging and all those things Nelson could do. This was just plain artistry."

The *Nice 'N' Easy* album, released in the summer of 1960, consisted of the title song—written by the three-time Academy Award–winning lyricists and two-time Grammy winners Marilyn and Alan Bergman and composer Lew Spence—which was surrounded by a bevy of standards Frank had previously recorded between 1940 and 1950,[28] such as "Dream," "Nevertheless," and "That Old Feeling," the latter providing an excellent showcase for George Roberts and trumpeter "Cappy" Lewis.

ASCAP President Marilyn Bergman first met Nelson during the mid-'50s at The Hub music publishing company, then located at Selma and Argyle in Hollywood. Marilyn explained, "There was a time when Nelson wanted to write songs. That was around 1955." (No doubt he was already wary of the financial limitations of merely being an arranger.) The Bergmans wrote a song with him called "That's What It's All About," which was never recorded.

Marilyn said she and Alan came up with the idea of writing a song with the title "Nice 'N' Easy." "In fact, we wrote the lyrics for the first eight bars of it before we gave the idea to Lew Spence. We usually liked to have the music done first. Hank Sanicola had wanted Lew to write a ballad as a title song for an album with a nice easygoing, moderate tempo. Before that, in '58, we had had our first big hit with 'Yellow Bird,' which was #1 a couple of times during the calypso craze.

"But 'Nice 'N' Easy' was very important. Frank Sinatra was singing it. It meant a great deal to us. Nelson wrote the arrangement a little faster than we thought it should be, but he made it sexy at that tempo. It was terrific."

Over the next few years, Nelson also arranged their songs "Sleep Warm" and "Sentimental Baby," and their reworking of "Old MacDonald," which proved to be a perfect vehicle for a free-swinging Sinatra/Riddle track (now included on the *Sinatra's Swingin' Session* CD). Alan recalled, "Marilyn and I thought of doing a hip version of 'Old MacDonald.' We made Frank the traveling salesman in the public domain song, but our lyrics were all new. Bobby Darin had just recorded "Mack the Knife," which modulates with each chorus. We wanted to do something so that it would build like that. Nelson ran with it. His tempo was just perfect."

"The mark of a great arranger is somebody who has both a distinctive approach and a distinctive sound with an orchestra," Alan added. "When I hear a thing, I can say 'I know that's Nelson Riddle' or 'I know that's Johnny Mandel' by the chords, by the voicings of the strings or the band. That's what separates the journeymen arrangers from those of the first rank. There's a certain sound and a certain rhythmic impulse that Nelson had that swung. If you can do something that swings, that's really the highest compliment as far as I'm concerned.

"A great arranger is one who understands the lyrics of a song before he starts to arrange it," Alan continued. "Nelson always did that and so does Mandel because you're supporting not only the melody but what it's saying. That cushion, that support, the nuances in the lyric are important. Whether it's the underpinning of strings or brass or French horns or whatever—a good arranger takes into consideration the lyrics and the music when he decides how to score it." (This valuable skill is another important lesson that Nelson learned from Tommy Dorsey.)

The followup to *Nice 'N' Easy* was *Sinatra's Swingin' Session,* a collection of standards arranged in crisp 4/4 time. Nelson wrote the driving arrangement of "September in the Rain," that was the highlight of this album. It was one of Nelson's best—although sometimes overlooked—swing arrangements for Frank Sinatra.

The two-time Oscar- as well as Emmy-winning composer and arranger Ralph Burns stated, "Frank made orchestrators sound so wonderful. Not only that, they were inspired when they wrote for him." I asked Burns what really made Nelson's arrangements swing. "Sinatra," he said. "If you had a different singer up there it wouldn't have swung. When Frank got in front of an orchestra, the orchestra swung. Frank had authority, and he had incredible time. And those rim shots that Nelson wrote for him were right out of Lunceford-Oliver. Frank Sinatra sang like a drummer. Nelson was the perfect complement to Frank. . . . The two went together."

★ ★ ★

Nelson's film work with Frank continued unabated during 1960 with his scoring of the film *Can-Can,* which resulted in his receiving his first of five Oscar nominations. Not only did he arrange several Cole Porter songs ("I Love Paris" and "It's All Right with Me"), but also Sinatra's duets with Shirley MacLaine and Maurice Chevalier. It was the intricacies of the varied dance sequences (such as the "Adam and Eve" number, which called for both symphonic and big band arrangements) with MacLaine, however, that made this assignment an intense musical experience for Nelson.

The versatility of Nelson's writing for motion pictures was also well documented in the caper film *Oceans 11,* a cult classic that is currently being remade. Peter Lawford had originally paid $10,000 for the rights to *Oceans 11* five years before it was produced in 1960. He first thought of using James Dean in the lead role of Danny Ocean, which ultimately went to Sinatra.

To open the picture, Nelson cleverly made use of various percussion instruments, including a xylophone, as musical background for Saul Bass's unusually designed opening credits, which took the form of a flashing marquee. He also devised a bluesy harmonica-and-strings accompaniment for Sammy Davis, Jr.'s rendition of "EO 11," plus he arranged variations on this theme for a moody big band sequence that had a neo-Basie feel as background for the robberies of several Las Vegas casinos. Nelson reprised the "Tender Trap" arrangement he had written for Sinatra in a stripteaser's dance scene as well as his "Learnin' the Blues" chart in a lounge sequence.

This prolonged period of Nelson's artistic and commercial success was again

A 1960 scoring session at 20th Century Fox for *Can-Can*. Standing, left to right: dancer Alec Wilder, Shirley MacLaine, Nelson Riddle. Seated, left to right: musical coordinator Saul Chaplin, the late dancer and consultant Gwen Verdon, and choreographer Hermes Pan.

interrupted by sadness. Following Albertine's death in 1958, Nelson, Sr.'s health deteriorated rapidly. He finally succumbed to emphysema in 1960.

★ ★ ★

By the beginning of the 1960s, Frank Sinatra had a new passion in his life. It was not another "swingin' chick"; it was political in nature. During the 1940s he had greatly admired—and named his son after—Franklin D. Roosevelt. Now his on-again, off-again friend from MGM days, Peter Lawford, introduced him to Senator John F. Kennedy from Massachusetts, who was running for president. Sinatra relished being in Kennedy's presence and convinced his friends—the so-called "Rat Pack" (or "The Clan")—to campaign for him. Once again, he was attracted by the supreme aphrodisiac of power.

(The original Rat Pack consisted of Humphrey Bogart, Lauren Bacall, Frank Sinatra, Judy Garland, David Niven, restaurateur Mike Romanoff, literary agent Irving "Swifty" Lazar, and a few others. When this group flew to Las Vegas in June 1955 for Noel Coward's opening at the Desert Inn, Bacall remarked, "You look like a goddamn rat pack." The name stuck. When Sinatra and his cohorts started their "Summit" engagement at the Sands in Las Vegas in January 1960, the press, always looking for a catchy title, picked up the name and immortalized it.)

Riddle wasn't terribly interested in politics, but, according to Bob Bain, "Nelson thought John Kennedy would be good for the country." During this period, Nelson couldn't fail to remember the time in Ridgewood High School during the fall of 1936 when Mr. Miller, his homeroom teacher, conducted a mock national election. In this bastion of Republicanism, he and his fellow student Donald Quimby were the only students who had cast their votes for Franklin D. Roosevelt.

Nelson's tongue-in-cheek arrangement of "High Hopes," written by Cahn and Van Heusen for Sinatra's film *A Hole in the Head,* was adopted as the theme of Kennedy's 1960 campaign. It was therefore no surprise when Kennedy asked Sinatra and Lawford to produce the Inaugural Gala held at the National Guard Armory in Washington the night before the "New Frontier" came into power in January 1961.

As usual, Sinatra did things first-class. He flew Nelson and his orchestra as well as a contingent of such celebrated personalities as Ella Fitzgerald, Gene Kelly, Janet Leigh, Tony Curtis, Jimmy Durante, Joey Bishop, Milton Berle, Juliet Prowse, Cahn and Van Heusen, and others on a chartered twenty-nine-seat TWA plane furnished by Howard Hughes. At the rehearsal on January 21, 1961, Nelson looked even more fatigued than usual, preparing a huge assortment of music for these performers as well as for Ethel Merman, opera singer Helen Traubel, Mahalia Jackson, Harry Belafonte, and Nat Cole, all of whom had flown down from New York. Leonard Bernstein shared the podium with Nelson for part of the program. George Roberts recalled that when Bernstein began rehearsing the augmented Nelson Riddle Orchestra, he asked for Nelson's musicians to raise their hands. Addressing them in his often haughty manner, he said, "I don't want those piercing sounds. I want a big round sound."

Mahalia Jackson, Leonard Bernstein, and Nelson Riddle conferring during a break from the rehearsals for President John F. Kennedy's Inaugural Gala in January 1961.

At the completion of the concert, which raised $1.5 million (at $100 a seat) toward the Democratic National Committee's $2 million debt on the campaign, Kennedy thanked Sinatra and the cast, who had worked for nothing, saying, "We saw excellence tonight—the happy relationship between the arts and our long history I think reached culmination tonight." *New York Post* columnist Pete Hamill described the Kennedy Gala as being a kind of payback by the sons and daughters of those who had survived the Great Depression as a result of Franklin D. Roosevelt's New Deal. Reprise Records (Sinatra's new recording label) recorded the entire evening, but it was never released, most likely because of problems in obtaining the various necessary clearances.

Nelson later recalled that after the Gala was over he got roaring drunk at one of the hotel parties. He spotted the longtime Democratic Party benefactor, agent supreme Lew Wasserman and his wife Edie across the room, and in his excitement walked right through a fountain to get to them. Wringing out the sleeves of his dinner jacket, he said, "Good evening, Mrs. Wasserman, how are you tonight? Can I get you a drink?"

Three days before this event, Frank Sinatra had taped an appearance on the CBS-TV special *The Gershwin Years.* Making use of my old business card from MCA (where I had been an agent in the variety department), which I had purposely kept in my wallet for just such an occasion, I gained entrance to the Ed Sullivan Theater and watched him rehearse and then tape his portion of the show. After pitching two editors to see whether they would be interested in publishing my account of the taping, I took it to Judith Crist at the *New York Herald-Tribune,* who indicated that she would consider running it. The article appeared that Sunday as a half-page feature with my byline. The next day, Dorothy Kilgallen, as part of her long-standing feud with Sinatra, devoted a substantial part of her *New York Journal-American* column to one of her periodic diatribes against him, using my piece as ammunition.

At the time I was jobless, had recently been turned down by over sixty would-be employers, and had $27 in my bank account. A significant recession had plagued the country during the late fall and winter of 1960–61. There I was, desperately looking for a job. When I got a break and was published in a New York newspaper, I found myself in the middle of the feud between Frank Sinatra and Dorothy Kilgallen!

I knew that Henri Giné, a former MCA agent who had stood by Sinatra in his dark days, was now on retainer with him. I called Giné and learned that he had seen Kilgallen's column but not my piece, which I then dropped off at his Central Park South office. He explained that he was off to Washington to assist Frank in the production of the Kennedy Gala and would be in touch with me when he returned in a few days.

Giné called me that Friday and asked what I was doing that day. I told him I was still looking for a job. "Why don't you come over to Carnegie Hall about three o'clock. Frank's putting together a benefit for Martin Luther King. He would like to meet you."

I watched Sinatra rehearse a few songs and then a break was called. He leaned down from the stage, shook hands, and told me he admired my reporting in the article. As has been said many times over the years, when he turned those blue eyes on you, you couldn't help being affected. I wasn't immune.

A few minutes later, I was introduced to Sinatra's co-publicist, Henry Rogers of Rogers and Cowan, the most resourceful entertainment-industry publicist who ever lived. He tipped his smart-looking fedora and said, "Frank Sinatra thinks you're a very talented young man," and proceeded to give me a backstage pass for the benefit.

That night I sat on a couch in Sinatra's dressing room trying to appear cool, listening to him tell show business stories to the rapt audience of Dean Martin and Sammy Davis, Jr. At intermission Henry Rogers arrived to announce that a select few newspapermen and photographers would be coming up to interview and shoot them. "Bring the bastards up," said Sinatra. I was cropped out of the most frequently seen photographic image of Sinatra, Martin, and Davis.

Toward the end of the concert, which lasted over four hours, Frank entered through the back of the concert hall and sauntered down the aisle and onto the stage while singing "The Coffee Song." I couldn't believe that he had drunk what I remember being something like a dozen bourbon-and-waters in the upstairs dressing room!

The afternoon after the benefit, my cousin, John Epstein, called to inform me he was flying to Las Vegas the following Tuesday to participate in a skeet-shooting tournament. He said he had a ticket for me to join him at the Sands. Was I interested in meeting him there? Was I interested?!

That Tuesday, I reached Las Vegas before John did. I checked into our room and then walked into the lounge right off the casino. There, straightening up the bottles of liquor and glasses on his table, was Frank Sinatra, who saw me and asked, "What the hell are you doing here?"

Over the next five days, I saw Sinatra perform in the Copa Room of the Sands three times. Late one afternoon, I decided to take a steambath and headed for the steam room. There were only two people there, one of whom was Frank. We talked about the fact that Henry Rogers wanted to meet with me in his Beverly Hills office in a few days. "I think that would be a good move for you," he said. I couldn't help but notice the prominent scars on the left side of his chin, on his right cheek, and below his left ear, how pockmarked his skin was, and how his whole face was bloated from drinking. For years after that, I never saw him without makeup, even when he wasn't performing.

In May, I received an assignment to do a story on the shooting of Sinatra's film *Sergeants 3* from *Family Weekly,* a Sunday magazine supplement. With his usual largesse, Sinatra provided me with a round-trip first-class ticket to Los Angeles and a week at the Hollywood Roosevelt Hotel. While hanging around the set of this witless cavalry-and-Indians spoof, loosely based on the classic film *Gunga Din,* I interviewed all the principal stars—Dean Martin, Sammy Davis, Jr., Peter Lawford, Joey Bishop, and finally Sinatra. I was astonished at how really bright Frank was—his quick grasp of facts and his surprising vocabulary, which I later learned resulted from his voracious reading habits. I asked him about the truth of his reportedly telling Speaker of the House Sam Rayburn to "take your hands off the suit, creep" at the 1956 Democratic convention in Chicago. He denied it with a ready answer, but then I realized he had long since grown accustomed to being interviewed.

After spending that incredible week in Hollywood, I decided to move to Los Angeles that September. I was in Sinatra's company several times over the next three years, but I was hardly an intimate friend. More importantly, though, knowing him enabled me to be able to attend his Reprise recording sessions—a fascinating atmosphere that few were privileged to experience.

The recording studio is where Sinatra was most at home. After all, what he accomplished in the recording studio was his entree to the public. Warren Cowan referred to those who came to see him record at United Recording Studio as "his rooting section. They would have seats, and maybe there would be twenty to thirty people there if I remember [correctly]. They were all his friends along with some invitees. I've never seen a recording star who had an invited audience. I always thought that Frank liked to impress his friends, more so than all the fans. . . ."

I vividly recall that when he walked into the studio everyone's attention was suddenly riveted on him. Lust was written all over the faces of various young women as they watched him move jauntily toward the microphone, which was surrounded by a wooden screen that was open on one side and served to separate him from the orchestra. Yet its openness enabled him to "feel the warmth" of the orchestra.

As he strode into the room, the string players acknowledged his presence by lightly tapping on the throats of their instruments with their bows—the ultimate sign of respect among classical musicians. After he had settled himself behind the hanging microphone, the record producer would ask him if he was ready to begin recording, and he would spray one-liners—"Ready—baby, am I ready,"—attempting to free himself from his initial nervousness. After a few aborted takes, he would try to alleviate the tension in the room that was always there before he got the first take down by bandying with jazz musicians in the orchestra like Harry Edison, Frank Rosalino, or Joe Maini. He enjoyed the argot of jazz musicians. In the early '60s, jazz was still hip, and remaining hip was very important to Frank Sinatra.

Sometimes he would utter such lines as "I think I swallowed a shot glass" after a botched take. In those days it was nothing for him to complete four tunes in a three-hour recording session. Within the next few years, rock 'n' roll would take over popular music, and the tape revolution in the studio was at hand. One song might now require weeks to finish, and many times it was accomplished by overdubbing different instruments one at a time.

★ ★ ★

Sinatra's decision to leave Capitol in 1960 followed his demand to have the label finance his new record company. He proposed that he and Capitol would each own half of it, and Capitol would be its distributor. Profits would be split equally between them. In addition, Sinatra would get his usual royalty. Glenn Wallichs turned down this proposal.

When Alan Livingston returned to Capitol from NBC to assume the presidency in 1960, he called Sinatra to see if they could work out an alternative plan. According to Livingston, "Sinatra got furious at me and said, 'I'm going to tear that round building down, and you'll never see it again.' I told him, 'Frank, I'm sorry, I didn't know you felt that way.' He really wasn't against me but against Capitol—but his anger was directed at me."

To complete his contractual obligation to Capitol, Sinatra recorded two albums. In March 1961, he recorded an album with Billy May called *Come Swing with Me*. Despite Billy May and Heinie Beau's usual high-quality arrangements, the album sounded as if Sinatra had recorded every track in one take. The tunes included familiar standards like "On the Sunny Side of the Street," "Lover," "That Old Black Magic," and "Almost Like Being In Love."

His final Capitol album, arranged by Axel Stordahl, was recorded on September 11 and 12, 1961, and was appropriately titled *Point of No Return*. Bill Miller felt that on this album, "Axel borrowed some of those polytones from Nelson on two or three of the tunes." Nevertheless, the Sinatra/Stordahl rendition of "A Million Years Ago" was reminiscent of the magic they had created together in the 1940s, and because of that had a truly wistful quality to it. This album marked their last collaboration. A few months later, Axel Stordahl passed away.

Sinatra decided to call his new record company Reprise, but he pronounced it "reprize," suggesting "reprisal." Cynics tagged it "Revenge Records." The first Reprise album, released in January 1961, found Johnny Mandel arranging and conducting. *Ring-a-Ding-Ding* was titled after Sinatra's latest hip expression symbolizing action of one type or another.

It was while attending a Sinatra recording session on November 12, 1961, that I first saw Nelson Riddle at work. He had arranged the title song and conducted the orchestra and children's chorus (which included Christopher and Rosemary Riddle) for Frank's recording heard on the soundtrack of Frank Capra's film *Pocketful of Miracles*. I marveled at the way he seemed to coordinate the three elements so easily.

The billing on this record read "Frank Sinatra with orchestra and chorus." Nelson was long past ghostwriting arrangements for anybody, but he was still under contract at Capitol; the Vine Street company was not about to make things easier for Sinatra and his fledgling record company by letting Nelson out of his contract. He could arrange for Sinatra, but his name couldn't appear on a Reprise record label. Frank, Jr., informed me that in January of that year Nelson had written the arrangements for the memorable Cahn and Van Heusen ballad, "The Second Time Around" backed with "Tina," their musical ode to Sinatra's youngest child, on the same basis.

Three months later, I approached Geoff Miller, then editor of *Los Angeles Magazine,* about writing a profile of Nelson Riddle. After he approved my suggestion, I contacted Nelson's manager, Nick Sevano, about meeting with Nelson. A few days later Nick told me to meet Nelson for the interview at Nickodell's, the Hollywood music business restaurant of the time. I found Nelson kind, intelligent, and very forthcoming about his musical background. He didn't touch on his marriage except to say that he had several children and lived in Malibu.

Within about a half hour, Nelson suddenly turned morose as he revealed how upset he was that he could no longer get credit for writing for Sinatra. He expressed the feeling that his career was over. I reminded him that he still had a thriving television and motion picture writing career. (*Route 66* was then on its way to becoming a successful weekly series; Nelson had written its hit theme and was scoring the show.) I also mentioned that he was still arranging for Ella Fitzgerald, and she was the foremost female singer of the time. All of that failed to placate him.

"It's not the same thing," he said. "My association with Frank is what really got my career going. And now I can't work with him." I was astonished by how distressed he was. Here I was, a freelance magazine writer, listening to the anguish of the most respected arranger in popular music. In conducting interviews for this biography, I discovered, however, that Nelson had a penchant for relating his troubles to various people he had met for the first time.

At that time, a few publicity offices seemed interested in hiring me provided I could bring in some business, which was hardly an equitable arrangement, but at least it would provide me with steady employment and possibly a future. With this thought in mind, I approached Nelson about letting me handle his publicity. We had a few lunches to discuss this matter. From one meeting to the next, he would fluctuate in his thinking about its value—one day he would see its importance, the next time he said he couldn't handle talking about himself. Finally, he said, "Pete, I just can't afford it." I approached him one other time several years later, but we never formed a business association.

Guitarist Al Viola made a perceptive observation about Nelson when he said, "There was a lot of competition, a lot of great writers. . . . When he's trying to get in, he gets in on a fluke as a ghostwriter. When he finally gets established, I don't think he got the kind of recognition that he should have gotten right off the bat. I could see that in his face. I didn't see that much written about him as I saw about other writers. The other guys took advantage publicity-wise—'I've got something to sell.' Nelson was always holding himself back. He never took advantage of what he had."

Publicity could have been of vital importance to the development of his career, but he never did retain a publicist. It wasn't until two decades later that he finally got long overdue attention from the press. That was when he began recording with Linda Ronstadt.

★ ★ ★

During that year and the one following, Billy May arranged *Sinatra Swings* and Sy Oliver arranged *I Remember Tommy*. Other arrangers who worked with Sinatra in 1962 were Don Costa (*Sinatra and Strings*), Gordon Jenkins (*All Alone*), Neal Hefti (*Sinatra and Swingin' Brass*), and Robert Farnon (*Great Songs from Great Britain*, which was not released in the United States. until 1993), all of which preceded Hefti's production of the *Sinatra and Basie* album in 1963. Of all of these albums, the only real standouts were Oliver's successful tribute to the Sinatra/Dorsey era—which retained much of that period's original flavor—and Costa's album, which included magnificent renditions of "Come Rain or Come Shine" and "Stardust," the latter consisting of only the verse.

Frank, Jr.'s explanation of his father's use of various arrangers—"My father always believed in changing orchestrators from one album to the next to get a different sound"—doesn't tell the whole story. Nelson felt he was being frozen out.

In his attempt to establish Reprise as a major recording entity in 1961–62, Sinatra got Dean Martin to leave Capitol and Sammy Davis, Jr., to leave Decca. He approached

Eleanor Roosevelt autographs one of Nelson Riddle's arrangements during a break from the taping of a Frank Sinatra special. Nelson was musical director and the former First Lady was the special guest on the 1962 show.

Frank Sinatra, Jr. and Sr., and Nelson during a Reprise recording session in the early 1960s.

Bobby Darin's manager, Steve Blauner, about coming to the label. Blauner recalled, "After hearing Frank go on and on about who was coming to Reprise, I decided the best thing for Bobby was to go to Capitol. Besides that, I realized Nelson and Billy May were there. I knew how well they could work with Bobby." One can only speculate what an incredible pairing Darin and Riddle would have made as a Capitol recording duo. Blauner was not aware, however, that Nelson had already committed himself to joining Sinatra at Reprise.

For his first Reprise album, Nelson wrote a rather nondescript score for Sinatra's comedy western *4 for Texas* in 1962, his first film scoring assignment for the singer in three years. The only credited arrangements he wrote for Sinatra during this period were for the single record of "I Left My Heart in San Francisco" backed with "The Look of Love." Neal Hefti, however, conducted the orchestra. This single record was withdrawn soon after its release. It paled in comparison to Tony Bennett's smash hit version of the song.

Nick Sevano observed, "I think Frank got so far ahead of himself nobody mattered but him. I don't need anybody—that was his attitude. Nelson saw that. He saw it coming. That's why I wanted him to get involved with other people. Nelson had that feeling for Frank. He was a very loyal guy, and he was afraid of being left out because he knew Frank's habits. He had all that to contend with, and yet he didn't know how to handle it."

Shortly after Nelson signed with Reprise in January 1963, he and Sinatra returned to work together in the studio. Their first new endeavor was to record Cahn and Van Heusen's title song from Bud Yorkin and Norman Lear's Paramount comedy *Come Blow Your Horn,* which Nelson also scored.

Yorkin, the film's director, noted, "Nelson was a very gentle man—generous and easy to take. He was a man who tried to understand what you wanted and then would set out to accomplish it. We discussed themes—a theme for the young man [Tony Bill], a theme for the older brother [Sinatra], and maybe some kind of theme for the father [Lee J. Cobb]."

Nelson played piano as Sammy Cahn (easily the most frustrated performer I ever knew) sang the title song, which Frank was to sing over the opening credits. "I never thought it was going to be a hit or anything like that," Yorkin admitted. "But it was the kind of music that fit the times."

Cahn's lyrics—"Make like a Mister Milquetoast / and you'll get shut out"—blended perfectly with Sinatra's carefree singing style. The song also perfectly jibed with Sinatra's role as a "swingin' bachelor" in a plot adapted from Neil Simon's first Broadway hit comedy. Nelson's chart once again showed that he knew exactly how to write the right kind of up-tempo chart for Sinatra. Despite Cahn's tongue-twisting lyrics, Frank recorded it in one take and walked out the door.

"When Norman Lear and I began spotting [discussing where the music would fit] for the picture, Nelson came up with some wonderful ideas," Yorkin acknowledged. "He would say 'How about if we did this, it would be nice to segue from here to there.' He was very, very creative, which they [the arrangers] have to be because I have no idea how they can take a picture and sit down and write the music. We had quite a bit of music in that picture, if I recall. I think it was one of the few pictures in my life that I think damn near every cue that he wrote we used. And in a comedy you have to be careful that your music doesn't kill a laugh or fight the dialogue."

February 18, 1963, was the date of the first of four recording sessions for *The Concert Sinatra,* with Nelson conducting seventy-three musicians on a Goldwyn soundstage. This album completed the trilogy that had begun with *In the Wee Small Hours* and continued with *Only the Lonely.* Being present for the first recording session proved to be among of the most exhilarating musical experiences of my life.

As was Sinatra's usual practice, the album was recorded at night, when he felt his voice was strongest and most flexible. As Tina Sinatra once said, "The night was the time he found most pleasurable and the time he was the most vulnerable."

The idea behind the album was for Nelson to be given the vast canvas of a symphony-size orchestra to write elaborate backgrounds for a select group of the greatest pop standards for Sinatra to sing. He met the challenge magnificently, delivering some of his most memorable arrangements.

The album's annotator, Lawrence D. Stewart, cited the unusual combination of strength and delicacy in Nelson's work, "always subordinate to, and in support of, Sinatra's voice." The first song recorded was Kurt Weill's "Lost in the Stars." In this chart, Nelson wrote a beautiful crescendo of strings and gave Buddy DeFranco the opportunity to play a contrasting classical-type clarinet solo.

"Ol' Man River" found Sinatra going from the top of his upper register down to his lowest low notes and back up—an example of truly masterful singing. It took more than several takes before the singer finally said, "I can't do any better than that." Chris Riddle recalled, "I remember that my father had to make changes because, obviously, when you're conducting something and it's *rubato,* you have to simplify things so that it will work. You have to make changes here and there. He was an expert at doing that."

Throughout the album, the various colors of an orchestra were on full display—this was one of Nelson's foremost talents as an arranger—in his highly imaginative charts of Rodgers and Hammerstein's "I Have Dreamed" and "This Nearly Was Mine." These two tunes in particular could easily have been overdone, but restraint was an underlying element both in Frank's singing and Nelson's arrangements. Nelson's lyrical and haunting treatment of "I Have Dreamed" contained a particularly soulful passage underlined by Vince De Rosa's French-horn section.

The third and fourth of the Rodgers and Hammerstein songs, "You'll Never Walk Alone" and "Soliloquy" from *Carousel,* were songs that Frank had prerecorded with Alfred Newman in Hollywood a few years earlier before he walked off the set of the 20th Century Fox film in Maine. He never sang them with as much conviction as he did on this album. "Soliloquy" was recorded in sections since, as Nelson told British radio personality Stan Britt, "It was such an incredibly taxing thing."

Sinatra made extensive use of Nelson's *Concert Sinatra* arrangements in various concert performances during the last two decades of his career. They always elicited an especially favorable response from the audience. His spoken introduction to these songs also revealed just how much he treasured them.

After listening to *The Concert Sinatra,* Ralph Burns said of Nelson, "I admired Nelson. I copied from him. Listen, Beethoven built on Mozart. You copy from all the good ones. Nelson was like a big tapestry of instruments . . . probably, if he had written for Pavarotti, it would have been something wonderful to hear."

Two months later, Sinatra decided to record *Sinatra's Sinatra,* a collection of his biggest hits ("Nancy," "Young at Heart," "Witchcraft," "All the Way," etc.), this time in stereo, with Nelson conducting. The album, of course, included several of the arrangements Riddle had originally written for him; for Nelson, however, the album offered no new surprises. He wondered, justifiably, just how Sinatra was going to improve upon the original version. The purpose, however, was to produce a bestseller which, at the same time, would become an important catalogue item.

Shortly after Alan Livingston's return to Capitol, he had the company release a compilation of Frank's foremost tracks from previous albums entitled *The Best Great Years*. Livingston then instigated the plan to sell Sinatra's entire Capitol catalogue of albums at $2.98, thus undercutting the price of his Reprise albums. It achieved its intention by severely limiting the singer's Reprise album sales for a few years.

It was also in 1963 that Sinatra decided to adopt a repertory recording company approach to the scores from such classic Broadway musicals as *Kiss Me Kate, Finian's Rainbow, South Pacific,* and *Guys and Dolls*. Along with Sinatra, such artists as Dean Martin, Bing Crosby, Sammy Davis, Jr., Rosemary Clooney, Dinah Shore, Keely Smith, Debbie Reynolds, the Hi-Los, and Jo Stafford participated in the project. Billy May, Marty Paich, Skip Martin, and Bill Loose shared the bulk of the arranging chores while Morris Stoloff conducted the orchestra. Nelson arranged only Sinatra's tracks—"This Nearly Was Mine" and the wonderful duet Frank did with Rosemary Clooney on "Some Enchanted Evening," both of which were from *South Pacific*.

The artistry of these albums was mixed and resulted in only meager sales. The best of the lot was the *Guys and Dolls* album, for which Billy May arranged "Luck Be a Lady" for Sinatra. After a year the series was terminated.

On a much smaller scale, and despite the fact that Sinatra was using the services of several arrangers, it appeared that in the first year of his Reprise contract Nelson was becoming the "house arranger" again, writing albums for Mavis Rivers, Keely Smith, and other singers. Among them was Jo Stafford, for whom he wrote three arrangements that were contained in her *Getting Sentimental over Tommy Dorsey* album.

Throughout his long career, Frank Sinatra was extremely adept at publicizing and marketing himself. In line with Sinatra's hosting the Oscar Awards telecast in 1963, Reprise released an album of Academy Award–winning songs arranged by Nelson. While this was rather standard fare for the veteran collaborators, Frank's versions of "Secret Love" and "It Might as Well Be Spring" turned out to be different and more compelling interpretations of these tunes. "The Way You Look Tonight" was an example of one of Nelson's more delightful up-tempo charts, allowing Sinatra to swing at a romping pace.

On February 9, 1964, Ed Sullivan presented the Beatles, who made their American debut on his popular CBS-TV variety show. This date was recently cited by MTV as being the most important date in the history of rock 'n' roll. With this appearance, the age of the singer-songwriter was launched.

With songs written by John Lennon and Paul McCartney, the Beatles experienced overwhelming success, literally changing the world. A new and intriguing kind of pop music had suddenly been established, and the sales of traditional pop music plummeted. A new generation wanted its own kind of music—one with which it could totally identify.

Sinatra and Riddle continued on with their kind of music. In what could conceivably have been another *Guys and Dolls,* in 1964 Sinatra produced and starred in *Robin and the Seven Hoods.* The film was the saga of a 1920s gangster and his henchmen, using the tale of Robin Hood as a premise. It starred Sinatra, Dean Martin, Sammy Davis, Jr., Bing Crosby, and Peter Falk. Inferior direction by Gordon Douglas and a fast shooting schedule resulted in little more than a mediocre musical. Still, Cahn and Van Heusen were at their zenith as songwriters in this film, contributing a splendid group of songs highlighted by "My Kind of Town" (a song Sinatra enjoyed singing in tribute to his good friend, Mafia don Sam Giancana), "I Like to Lead When I Dance," and the much overlooked "Style."

Nelson was particularly inspired in his work on this score, starting with his lively overture. In addition, while handling secondary songs such as "Mr. Booze," "All for One," and "Don't Be a Do-Badder" he displayed his keen sense of humor.

I remember sensing how disconcerting it was for Nelson to have to conduct his soundtrack arrangements of "My Kind of Town" and "I Like to Lead When I Dance" for Sinatra during the same recording session in which Frank recorded the song "I Can't Believe I'm Losing You" with Don Costa. As I recall, Costa was completing the final take on the song while Nelson waited patiently in the recording booth. When he had finished, he and Nelson exchanged pleasantries and Costa left the studio. Nelson then went in and mounted the podium to conduct the songs from the *Robin and the Seven Hoods* score.

Almost three years earlier, Nelson had been extremely upset by Frank's decision to use Costa as the arranger on *Sinatra and Strings.* As a result, he began to refer to Costa as "Don Co-Star," a term which indicated more than a touch of envy.

Emil Richards made a significant point when he said, "When it came to Don Costa and some of the other guys that were writing for him at the time, Frank kind of told them what he wanted, but with Nelson, he asked."

New and original ideas for the Sinatra-Riddle combination were now becoming scarce. *Moonlight Sinatra* consisted of a potpourri of "moon" songs, i.e., "I Wished on the Moon," "The Moon Was Yellow," and "The Moon Got in My Eyes," along with "Moonlight Serenade," etc. "Moon Love," adapted from the main theme of Tchaikovsky's Fifth Symphony, displayed Nelson's ability to highlight its beautiful melody while retaining its classical origin.

And then suddenly, out of nowhere, in this period of grave uncertainty for mainstream pop music practitioners, Frank Sinatra enjoyed his first #1 "Adult Contemporary" (a newly-minted term to describe the changing marketplace) and *Billboard* #1 single record. The song was "Strangers in the Night," arranged by rhythm and blues writer Ernie Freeman.

Nelson was brought in by his old friend and musical colleague Sonny Burke to

Nelson conferring with Sammy Davis, Jr., while Dean Martin and Bing Crosby listen. This photograph was taken during one of the 1964 recording sessions for the soundtrack of the Warner Bros. film *Robin and the Seven Hoods*.

build a hit album using "Strangers in the Night" as the title song. This 1966 album, subtitled for the youth market *Sinatra Sings for Moderns* (although less than half of the songs were even of '60s vintage!), contained Nelson's popular "Summer Wind" arrangement which, when it was released as a single, like "Strangers" became another #1 Adult Contemporary hit for Sinatra. (Their recording of the tune was later heard under the opening titles of the 1984 MGM movie *The Pope of Greenwich Village*.)

It's my feeling that their versions of "On a Clear Day" and "All or Nothing at All" from the *Strangers in the Night* album were almost in the same league as "I've Got You Under My Skin." They sounded as if they were directly inspired by the latter. "All or Nothing at All" began at a hearty medium tempo—much different from the original Sinatra/Harry James version—but after Artie Kane's organ solo the band began to roar with Sinatra on top wailing to the finish.

Ray Briem, the longtime Los Angeles radio personality, remembered the time he interviewed Nelson on his program. "I played the endings of some of the things he did with Sinatra—just the endings. Nelson said to me, 'Do you know that's the nicest thing anyone has ever said to me—that you love my endings? I take great pride in them.'" As Briem observed, "Most arrangers' endings are just a board fade."

Despite this great success, Frank Sinatra and Nelson Riddle didn't record together again for over two years, although in 1965 Nelson scored the absurd Sinatra, Dean Martin, and Deborah Kerr comedy, *Marriage on the Rocks*. Frank also brought both Nelson and Gordon Jenkins to Miami Beach to co-lead a large orchestra which featured arrangements by both of them in a February 1967 engagement at the Fontainebleau Hotel. Over the years, Nelson had helped Jenkins repair certain arrangements when he had reached an impasse in his writing. In Pete Hamill's opinion, "Unlike Gordon Jenkins, Nelson Riddle was always too hip to clog the music with a lot of sugar."[29]

In the interim, in addition to Don Costa, others including Quincy Jones, Ernie Freeman, Gordon Jenkins, Torrie Zito, Claus Ogerman, Billy May, Billy Strange, and H.B. Barnum arranged Sinatra's albums and singles. Nelson had plenty of work in motion pictures and television as well as with other singers, but he deeply regretted the gradual unraveling of their once close musical relationship.

★ ★ ★

There was, however, one recording session that could have been one of the most significant and historical pairings of all time. It's unfortunate that the proposed album involving Frank Sinatra, Ella Fitzgerald, and Nelson Riddle and his Orchestra was never recorded.

Frank Sinatra began two days of rehearsals for his third *A Man and His Music* special on NBC-TV on October 1, 1967. The show was taped on November 3 and aired on November 13. Sinatra's musical guests were Ella Fitzgerald and the Brazilian George Gershwin, Antonio Carlos Jobim. Nelson Riddle conducted the orchestra. Sinatra and Ella sang two long medleys arranged by Nelson on the show.

The next day the two superstar singers, along with Nelson and his orchestra, began rehearsals for the album with the intention of duplicating the feeling contained in their medleys from the television special. They also planned to record some additional songs by Cy Coleman. The rehearsals went well and continued for two more days in anticipation of the recording session scheduled to take place at Western Recorders on November 9, 10, and 11, 1967.

The best-laid plans of Frank Sinatra and Norman Granz, Ella's manager, however, were not to be realized. Their problems with each other had started almost a decade earlier when Sinatra had tried unsuccessfully to buy Verve Records, owned by Granz. Granz's true feelings toward Sinatra were evident during the first recording session of the 1962 *Ella Swings Gently with Nelson* album in March 1962, which I attended. That night Granz welcomed Mo Ostin, his former treasurer at Verve but now the president of Reprise Records, by saying, "Ella's singing so badly tonight she's about ready to record with Sinatra." When Sinatra and Granz had another row in the autumn of 1967, the recording sessions were abruptly canceled.

Nevertheless, in 1974, Ella and Sinatra worked together with Count Basie and his orchestra at Caesar's Palace in Las Vegas and in '79 at the Uris Theater in New York. Nelson conferred with them before their Vegas date, transposing the keys so that they could sing duets on his original arrangements.

I later saw Ella and Frank perform together at the Society of Singers dinner on December 3, 1990. Their beautifully executed medley of songs followed the presentation of the organization's "Ella" award by Ella to Sinatra. The genuine respect they held for one another was rekindled that night before a star-studded show business audience at the Beverly Hilton.

In August 1968, Nelson recorded a Christmas album, *Wish You a Merry Christmas,* with Frank, Frank, Jr., Nancy (who had recently become a pop star starting with her smash record of "These Boots Are Made for Walkin'"), and Tina Sinatra with the Jimmy Joyce singers. Three months later Nelson backed Frank on Cahn and Van Heusen's title song from the Julie Andrews 20th Century Fox film, *Star,* which was based on a portion of the life of the celebrated English stage star Gertrude Lawrence. There were great expectations for the song and the movie. Unfortunately, both turned out to be failures.

By this time, Don Costa had become established as Sinatra's regular arranger. Justifiably, Frank admired the consistency of his writing, particularly for strings. It is also important to realize that Costa arranged Sinatra's hits "Cycles," "My Way," and "New York, New York."

By 1971, Frank Sinatra knew the party was over. Music had changed too radically for him. While he had loathed what Elvis Presley represented back in the mid-1950s, he was bewildered and angry about what was taking place in popular music a decade and a half later. Saxophones and brass no longer carried the melody; the guitar, Fender bass, and drums, formerly primarily rhythm instruments, suddenly were at the forefront of the new music.

Sinatra's attempts to keep himself contemporary by covering current hit songs and involving himself in projects with Eumir Deodato, Rod McKuen, and Bob Gaudio were indicative of a fading performer, now well past fifty, struggling to keep himself musically apace with the new generation. Young people considered his kind of singing, backed by a large orchestra playing charts by Nelson Riddle, passé.

He announced that his farewell to show business would take place at the newly opened Los Angeles Music Center on June 13 for the benefit of the Motion Picture and Television Relief Fund. At the benefit concert, Nelson debuted his arrangement of George Harrison's "Something" for Frank to sing with the Los Angeles Philharmonic Orchestra under the direction of Zubin Mehta. Following the end of the orchestra's rehearsal of the arrangement, Mehta referred to Nelson as "The Gustav Mahler of Popular Music."

Mike Lang, one of the most sought-after pianists in Hollywood recording circles,

Frank Sinatra and Nelson Riddle are shown rehearsing at the White House for the concert that preceded the state dinner for Prime Minister Andreotti of Italy on April 17, 1973. This concert performance indicated that Sinatra was about to end his self-imposed retirement. And who did he choose to work with? None other than his former collaborator Nelson Riddle.

interpreted Mehta's compliment this way: "Nelson brought that kind of harmonic orchestral skill to pop music. I think Nelson's arrangements, depending on the material, were capable of being very serious, very romantic, very beautiful, very emotionally affecting, maybe in the way that Mahler's lyrical things were."

In true dramatic Sinatra fashion, for his closing number, Frank chose Nelson's arrangement of "Angel Eyes." As he sang the last line, "'Scuse me while I disappear," he strolled off into the darkness.[30]

But after a break of less than two years, Sinatra had to return to show business. He didn't need the money, but he desperately needed the approval of a live audience. Preceding the recording of his comeback album with Don Costa, Frank brought Nelson to Washington on April 17, 1973, to join him at the Nixon White House to conduct the Marine Band in a performance following the state dinner for Prime Minister Andreotti of Italy.

Throughout the remainder of the 1970s, Nelson and Frank Sinatra had a "hide-and-seek" relationship. Nelson steered clear of him, and Sinatra would call him only when he wanted to work with him. Away from the recording studio, concert stage, or nightclub floor, Nelson's laid-back manner simply was hardly a perfect match for Frank's freewheeling, mercurial personality. Nelson realized it wouldn't work for him to involve himself in Frank's action-filled lifestyle with his celebrated group of friends. Instead, he did much of his drinking alone. In years gone by, his and Frank's only real socializing together had taken place after a recording session or at occasional parties or industry functions. After awhile, they were rarely in touch with one another.

Joe Smith, the retired one-time CEO of Warner Bros., Reprise, Elektra/Asylum, and Capitol/EMI, dealt with Nelson in his years at Warner Bros. Smith recalled, "Nelson was never on the inside with Frank. He used to ask me, 'Why won't he ever socialize with me? Why won't he go to dinner with me? He goes with everybody else!' Nelson would bemoan the fact that Frank never was warm with him."

Beginning in the early 1970s, however, every year at Christmastime Nelson took great care in sending Sinatra an expensive piece of Baccarat crystal. Sinatra would send him an appropriate gift such as an expensive small crystal Christmas tree. This tradition ended in the mid-'70s when Nelson sent him another piece of crystal and Sinatra reciprocated with a tin of Poppycock popcorn. Frank knew that Nelson liked peanut brittle, which he often put in his side pocket, and the fact that he also enjoyed having caramel corn in his pockets with peanuts. But while this may have been meant as a humorous gift, Nelson didn't view it that way. Their exchange of Christmas gifts was finished for all time.

In the musical wilderness in which Frank Sinatra now lived, he found a good piece of material in November 1976 in Cy Coleman's "I Love My Wife," the title song of Cy's recently opened Broadway musical. Sinatra sought out Nelson to arrange the song for him. The record got good airplay but generated only mediocre sales. Four months later, Frank came up with an idea derived from this song—the notion of recording an album with the titles of the songs based on women's names. He approached Cahn and Van Heusen to write a song devoted to his fourth wife, the former Barbara Marx, ex-wife of Zeppo Marx of the Marx Brothers.

Nelson and Frank recorded six tracks together that included "Barbara" and "Nancy." In addition, Nelson recorded several more instrumental tracks such as "Josephine," "Stella by Starlight," "Ruby," "Tina," "Laura," and "Michelle" for Sinatra to overdub. Against his better judgment, Frank had recently given in to overdubbing, which was now a common practice in contemporary pop music recording. Several arguments arose, however, between Nelson and Sinatra about the direction of the music during the recording sessions. Sinatra finally lost interest in the album's concept, and it was never released.

A few years after it was scrapped, Nelson was quoted as saying, "I think Frank felt it was an old-fashioned premise. . . . In other words, to madly scramble for twelve girls' names on songs might end up with about eight really good songs and four efforts that were mostly there because of the girls'-names connection."[31] Some of these Sinatra/ Riddle tracks were later included in a Reprise collection. Throughout the 1970s, Sinatra continued his difficult search for a hit, recording material written by the new pop

From the collection of Betty Rose.

At a testimonial dinner at the Century Plaza Hotel in Beverly Hills on April 16, 1978, sponsored by ALYN Orthopedic Hospital and the Symphony Arts Foundation, left to right, Sid Caesar, John Gavin, Gregory Peck, Nelson Riddle, and David Rose. The dinner had been postponed to accommodate Frank Sinatra's schedule so that he could present Nelson with an award. However, he sent Gregory Peck in his place.

composers—such as Paul Simon's "Mrs. Robinson" and Jim Croce's "Bad, Bad Leroy Brown." Both were further ill-advised attempts on his part to appear contemporary.

In an October 1981 bylined British magazine article, Nelson, in an overview of his association with Sinatra, said, "From about 1953 until, say, 1963, we were able to keep people very much interested in what we were doing. Then Frank became concerned because his need—at least at one time—was to remain contemporary. He didn't want to be thought of as a star of yesteryear. . . . He recorded 'Watertown' and some more of those things—trying to make sense out of that [material]. I think he realized reluctantly that one cannot reach over the decades forever, so he just decided to sing good music."[32]

In spite of the disputes that had taken place during the recording of their last album, Sinatra realized that he could rely on Nelson for the huge musical undertaking involved in his ABC-TV special, *Sinatra and Friends,* which aired on April 21, 1977. This unusual television special had no dialogue except during the introduc-tion and the conclusion of the show. The amazing potpourri of guest stars included John Denver, Dean Martin, Natalie Cole, Tony Bennett, Robert Merrill, Loretta Lynn, and Leslie Uggams. In his letter to Nelson complimenting him on the success of his difficult assignment, producer Paul Keyes said, "You are the dearest and most talented man in town."

The capper to Nelson and Frank's now twenty-five-year relationship took place in the spring of 1978. The Sunaire Foundation for Asthmatic Children, the ALYN Orthopedic Hospital, and the Symphony Arts Foundation collectively honored Nelson at a testimonial dinner at the Century Plaza Hotel on March 18. The evening was titled "A Tribute to Nelson Riddle." Gordon C. Luce, the dinner chairman, approached Frank Sinatra about presenting the award to Nelson.

Although Sinatra was booked for a concert engagement scheduled to open at the Sunrise Theatre in Fort Lauderdale, Florida, on March 13, he agreed to be in Los Angeles to present the award to Nelson. Unfortunately, on the fifteenth, he came down with a bad cold or the flu and left that afternoon to fly to his Palm Springs home. He immediately advised Nelson that he would be unable to show up for the dinner. The date for the dinner was then changed to April 16.

On April 13, Sinatra returned to the Sunrise Theatre to make up five canceled concerts but promised he would be in Los Angeles on the sixteenth to present the award. A large contingent of the Hollywood music community was in attendance to honor Nelson—the Henry Mancinis, David Roses, Lalo Schifrins, Pete Rugolos, etc.

The last of the substitute concerts, however, was on April 16. He never notified Nelson or Gordon C. Luce that he would be unable to attend the dinner. Instead, his good friend, actor Gregory Peck, took his place as the presenter of the award. Nelson was justifiably livid at being snubbed.

Frank Sinatra, Jr., blames his father's failure to show up on someone else. He said, "It was another person who had brought that about, an intermediary who took it upon himself to speak for Frank Sinatra, who sent Gregory Peck in his place. . . . That person should remain anonymous. It kept the two of them [Riddle and Sinatra] apart for several years. I find that unfortunate." I believe that the person he was referring to was the late Mickey Rudin, Sinatra's attorney for many years, who attended the dinner.

The dazed and hurt expression on Nelson's face is apparent in the photograph taken at this dinner showing Nelson standing alongside Peck, arranger David Rose, actor John Gavin (then ambassador to Mexico), and comedian Sid Caesar. "How would you look?" said Frank, Jr. "How would you feel if that happened to you that night? That would be tough to take for anybody. That would hurt an awful lot."

Chris Riddle recalled, "Dad said, 'I'll never work for that man again, ever!'" Milt Bernhart said, "Nelson went around mumbling about it saying, 'He let me down.' It was a big blow!"[33] The relationship between Nelson Riddle and Frank Sinatra appeared as though it had finally come to an end.

In the summer of 1979, Sinatra prepared to record a three-part album that would be entitled *Trilogy.* The album was to musically examine his past, present, and future, and was to include the arrangements of the three men he had worked with most frequently—Nelson, Billy May, and Gordon Jenkins.

Film producer Rob Fentress was a close friend of Sonny Burke, who continued to be Sinatra's record producer. "I had come to know Nelson through his recording sessions over the years," Fentress recalled. "One evening I was at a supermarket in Westwood and came upon Nelson. I told him that Sonny planned to use him for the upcoming Sinatra album. Nelson said to me, 'I used to work with Mr. Frank Sinatra, but that was some time ago. I don't plan to work with him again!'" The vehemence with which Nelson made the statement prompted Fentress to call Burke and inform him that Nelson would not be interested in participating in the *Trilogy* project. His only contribution turned out to be the aforementioned "Something" arrangement.

In analyzing their musical relationship, Nelson once cited Sinatra's "stupendous phrasing, the extremely masculine and meaningful quality of his voice, and his complete knowledge of the inner meanings of the lyrics that he was performing. Frank stood for quality." He added, "I think that he brought out the best in me, and I like to think that at times I brought out the best in him."

The best musical years of Nelson and Frank's lives had ended abruptly. For a long time, Nelson told close friends that Frank never complimented him for the important contribution he had made to his career. Yet, Frank, Jr., informed me that his father had told him, "Of all the orchestrators I've ever worked with, Nelson is the finest musician of them all." In 1962, Sinatra had remarked to his biographer, the late British author Robin Douglas-Home, "Nelson is the greatest arranger in the world—a very clever musician—and I have the greatest respect for him. He's like a tranquilizer [what Sy Oliver had called Bill Finegan]—calm, slightly aloof. . . . There's a great depth somehow to the music he creates. . . . Nelson's quality of aloofness and way of detachment give him a particular kind of disciplined air at sessions and the band respects him for it."[34]

The Congressional Record of 1971 contains a tribute delivered to Sinatra in the United States Senate. In it, Senators Tunney, Javits, Percy, and Hubert Humphrey heaped praise upon the singer. Sinatra sent a copy of it to Nelson with a note signed on his stationery that read, "Dear Nelson: You are as much a part of what was said about me by these great men in the Senate, and at the risk of my doing something hokey, I wanted you to have a copy of the enclosed. All the best always. Love, Frank."

Nelson Riddle never recorded with Frank Sinatra again. However, their superb body of work, which consisted of some 318 records—including sixteen albums for Capitol and Reprise—seven movies, and about twenty-five television shows, comprises some of the most outstanding and sophisticated popular music ever recorded. That is sufficient in itself.

Photo courtesy of the Nelson Riddle Memorial Library at the University of Arizona School of Music and Dance, Tucson, Arizona, and the Naomi Riddle Estate.

CHAPTER 7

A Flourishing Career

Nelson Riddle referred to Nat Cole's effect on his career as supplying "the wedge." If Nat Cole was the wedge, Frank Sinatra's importance was in supplying the force—in effect, breaking down the door for Nelson in the music industry. Due directly to his musical association with Sinatra, Riddle was now in demand as the most talked-about arranger in Hollywood.

In a three-hour KCRW Los Angeles National Public Radio tribute to Nelson, which first aired in July 1985, Nelson acknowledged Sinatra's vital role in his career: "He was very good to me. For this was a tight, scared, greedy crew—the music world in this town. . . . Even in those days when work was a lot more plentiful, there were eighty musicians for every job."

Aside from the singers mentioned earlier, in the early 1950s Nelson arranged and conducted single records for such diverse performers as Jimmy Wakely, Georgia Carr, Tommy Leonetti, the Four Knights, Bob Graham, Tex Ritter, and Betty Hutton. His association with Hutton—the exuberant blonde actress and singer, then an established Paramount star married to Alan Livingston—began with the single of "Goin' Steady" backed with "No Matter How I Say Goodbye" in November 1953, which was followed by three more singles in the next year.

Songwriter Jay Livingston recalled Hutton's admiration for Nelson's work: "I was then doing all of her musical material. She was a perfectionist, and she could be a problem because she was very insecure. Because she liked Nelson's work so much, he wrote a lot for her nightclub act.

"In the summer of 1954, Nelson even conducted for Hutton during a two-week engagement at the 500 Club in Atlantic City," Livingston pointed out. "When she was asked to star in the NBC-TV ninety-minute special *Satins and Spurs,* she insisted that she would only do the show if we [Livingston and his partner, Jerry Evans] and Nelson did the show with her." Nelson became the musical director for the show. His work earned him his first Emmy nomination.

In addition to working with Hutton, Nelson arranged "Three Little Stars" backed

Preceding page: Nelson with his two favorite artists, Ella Fitzgerald and Nat Cole.

with "Take It or Leave It" for another prominent film actress of the time, Yvonne DeCarlo. Years later, he said that DeCarlo could have made a greater impact as a singer because she had a real talent. It was she who, in 1971, introduced Stephen Sondheim's incisive anthem to show-business survival, "I'm Still Here," while starring on Broadway in the original cast of *Follies*.

With his suddenly burgeoning career, Nelson needed help in making the right career decisions. He therefore signed a personal management contract with the late Fred Benson, who had helped to mold Ray Anthony into a successful bandleader and Capitol recording artist. Anthony enjoyed such important hits as "The Bunny Hop," "Harbor Lights," the theme from *Dragnet,* and later in the 1950s the theme from *Peter Gunn,* in addition to several bestselling albums. Still active leading his own band, Anthony remembered Nelson as a very shy and diffident man, saying, "He let his music speak for itself."

Anthony's records were produced by Lee Gillette who also produced not only Nat Cole, but also Stan Kenton and the Four Freshmen. Nelson arranged two single records for the Four Freshmen, another one of Benson's clients, whom Nelson rightly referred to as "the precursors to the Hi-Los." Bob Flanigan, a member of the original group, remembered that the first tune Nelson arranged for the Four Freshmen was an *a cappella* version of "Indian Summer," which was included on the album *The Four Freshmen in Person.* "It was the most phenomenal thing I've ever had to sing! We had to cut half of it because we couldn't sing it all. His harmonies were just too much," Flanigan related.

"I originally became close to Nelson because of my association with Gillette," said Benson. "He was very bitter about Les Baxter, and I tried to help him out of that bitterness. He wanted personal attention, and I am good at that."

Benson and his associate, Sid Garris, negotiated Nelson's record deal with Alan Livingston at Capitol. Riddle's first single, "Brother John," received considerable airplay. As a result, Nelson began to become nationally known by disc jockeys.

Former Capitol executive Fred Grimes recalled, "Nelson called 'Brother John' 'a KMPC hit,'" referring to the heavy airplay it received on the Los Angeles pop music station that programmed the better grade of popular music; this didn't necessarily mean the record was a major hit, although "Brother John" did reach #23 on the Billboard pop chart. What also made Nelson a longtime favorite on KMPC was the fact that he willingly appeared on the live annual radio program, *The Show of the World,* for which Capitol promotion man George Russell's wife, Tess, booked the talent for nine years.

"Nelson had a little apartment in Hollywood, which he had taken 'cause he was often writing all night," Russell remembered. "He was beginning to arrive. One morning I woke him up. He was sleepy-eyed and I got him going. I filled him up with coffee, and we went first to Music City for him to sign some autographs and to do some promotions there. I took him to all the radio stations around L.A. They welcomed him with open arms because they loved his work. He had great product, and it was easy to promote. It just took a little elbow grease."

After the completion of a disc jockey tour they worked on together, in appreciation, Nelson hired Russell, who was also a guitarist, for an upcoming record date. "He introduced me to the orchestra by saying, 'He's not only playing on the date, but he's going to go out and promote the record and make it a hit!' That was the best introduction of my life," Russell proudly recalled.

It wasn't, however, until his sixth single, "Lisbon Antigua," that Nelson had his first unqualified hit. His record was #1 in the country for four weeks and it remained on the *Billboard* chart for twenty-four weeks. It became a gold single record, the only million-selling single record of Riddle's entire career.

"Lisbon Antigua (In Old Lisbon)" was originally a Portuguese song written by Raul Portela, José Galhardo, and Amadeu do Vale in 1937. The lyric was written by Harry Dupree in 1954. Carlos Gastel by this time had succeeded Fred Benson as Nelson's manager. The song was originally suggested to Lee Gillette by Gastel's sister, Chiqui, who was living in Mexico, where it had been a big hit with a band called Los Churambeles. When Gillette met with Nelson to discuss recording the song, he suggested that he should emphasize the melody by writing choruses of tremolo strings for the violins. He said, "The disc jockeys will like hearing that, and the record will get good airplay."

But another important element in the record's success was the late Arnold Ross's softly romantic piano solos. (Nelson referred to them as "Arnold's little filigree.") Ross came into Nelson's life in an unusual way. "I had just finished a Mel Tormé date at Capitol for Van Alexander. At the end of it, this guy came in with a batch of music under his arm. I didn't know who he was. They let the band go but kept a nucleus, and I was one of them. Dave Klein [the recording contractor] said, 'Stick around because we have somebody else coming in,'" Ross recalled.

Ross, one of the outstanding but unsung bebop piano players, had worked for Harry James, Lena Horne, and Frank Sinatra, among others, and was revered by all of them. He sightread the piano parts perfectly on the first take of "Lisbon Antigua," which was recorded on October 19, 1955. "Sweets" Edison played a brief trumpet solo, repeating the same figure Arnold was playing on the piano, thus incorporating a *soupçon* of jazz into the arrangement.

After the first few takes, Gillette insisted he needed to hear more strings. "That will make it a hit," he insisted to Nelson. Nelson, who hated the tune, showed his disgust for the quiver-and-hesitation device that Gillette wanted. He muttered to George Roberts, "If this thing's a hit, then I'll have to play it a lot." After the record became a hit, its popularity led to its being incorporated into the Ray Milland-Maureen O'Hara film *Lisbon,* made for Republic Pictures in 1956, which Nelson scored.

During this period, Arnold Ross was a heroin addict, and as a result, he was off the musical scene and didn't work for Nelson for another six years, while he went through recovery at Synanon. After that he was one of Nelson's regulars for over twelve years. In analyzing Nelson's work, he offered the observation that, "Nelson used a lot of flatted fifths, which were big in the early days of bebop, and he incorporated a few bebop figures, but not much—he was a swing arranger. That worked for him. I wasn't that crazy about all of his arrangements. Harmonically, they weren't advanced enough, but they were good arrangements. They swung. His were mostly basic chord structures. He had a knack for little figures."

For all of the chart successes Nelson helped create for Nat Cole, Frank Sinatra, and other singers, as well as his own succession of hits, in 1955 *Billboard* recognized Nelson as "The Arranger with the Most Record Hits." Following up the success of "Lisbon Antigua," his next two singles—"Port au Prince" in April 1956 and the theme from *The Proud Ones* (a western starring Robert Ryan) in August of that year—were also back-to-back Top 40 hits.

For the next few years, however, Riddle failed to come up with any other hit singles. This was partially due to the fact that he was unable to write any unusual or highly original pop material. In addition, Capitol was unable to provide any potential hit material for him. Nelson later reflected, "I think I was too close to the record business to back off and think what might be good for me."

He made several attempts to recreate the string gimmick that had been so successful on "Lisbon Antigua" on several other single records during this period, such as "Alone Too Long." He even adapted it when he arranged a new version of "I'm Getting Sentimental over You." Regarding this time in both of their careers when they were forced to arrange considerably mundane material, Billy May said, "There's good crap and bad crap."

Years later, in explaining why his instrumental records were not successful, Nelson said, "They had a slight stiffness about them. They were strictly studio-type jazz—too many orchestral tricks to really make it good jazz writing, and I know that [now]."[1]

Despite the fact that Capitol was not providing quality material, Van Alexander, then also under contract to Capitol as an arranger and bandleader, believes that being at the label had its advantages: "At Capitol, things were recorded better. It was the beginning of hi-fi and then stereo. Everything sounded so much better than it did in the early dance band days with the echo chambers and all those things, plus Nelson's knowledge of combining sections helped him. And he had a sound—there's no doubt about that."

In its constant search for a hit single record, Capitol had the misguided belief that if a record incorporated the singing voices of Stan Kenton, Nelson Riddle, and Billy May, it could be a smash. As a result of this twisted thinking, the three were recorded singing "Belly Up to the Bar," a song from the hit Broadway musical *The Unsinkable Molly Brown*. Since I was unable to find a copy of this "historic" recorded event, I asked Billy for his opinion of how well the "singers" came off in their renditions. The jovial arranger and composer burst out laughing and simply said, "You'll have to listen to the record."

After Nelson's series of singles, it was finally time for him to record his first album.

Capitol had already recorded and released the soundtrack of the Todd-AO musical film of *Oklahoma!* starring Gordon MacRae and Shirley Jones. Nelson was asked to arrange his own instrumental album of the popular Rodgers and Hammerstein score.

F.M. Scott was in charge of albums at Capitol at the time. "We were looking for ancillary promotion for the film album," he remembered. "I said to Nelson, 'Do what you think is good.' He came up with a marvelous artistic kind of thing, but commercially it was just terrible."

In a 1982 radio interview with Jonathan Schwartz on WNEW that discussed *Oklahoma!*, among other things, Nelson remarked, "Some of my interpretations bore little or no resemblance to what was going on in the [film] cast version," and added in his usual self-deprecating manner, "which may have partly accounted for its stunning lack of sales."

Schwartz informed Nelson that as a fourteen-year-old he had played the album for Richard Rodgers, who was renowned for trying to control the way his music was played. "Rodgers thought it was sensational," he said, "and he had a favorite track, 'I'm Just a Girl Who Can't Say No.'" Nelson went on to sheepishly admit that "Sweets" Edison's humorous take on the tune and Champ Webb's English horn solo had made his rendition special.

Ralph Burns heard a tape of Nelson's *Oklahoma!* album for the first time forty-five years after it was recorded. While listening to the title track, he remarked, "Listen to those French horns and his chords. Immediately when you hear this you know this is Nelson's touch. He had those wonderful rich chords above the melody. It's Nelson at his best in writing for an orchestra. That's his sound—the trombones holding the lower chords and the strings and woodwinds up high. It's full and rich. He sure knew how to voice for horns—for everything."

Nelson's next successful venture with a singer came about when Capitol signed Judy Garland and assigned Nelson to work with her. After being written off by the film industry because of her myriad personal problems during her last years at MGM, Garland had made her first of several amazing comebacks with a much acclaimed engagement at the Palace Theatre in New York. Then Warner Bros. backed her version of *A Star Is Born*, which had returned her career to major proportions.

While Garland could be difficult to work with, she immediately sensed that Nelson was a highly accomplished arranger, and she also realized how helpful he was to her in the studio. He knew exactly how to write music that would complement the passion and pathos she brought to singing. About Garland, he said, "She had a rhapsodic frailty of her own. She came to the record dates knowing the songs. That's all anybody could expect."

Sid Luft, Garland's husband and manager during the 1950s, sensed what Nelson meant to her. He said, "Judy had the greatest respect for him. There was a rhythm that they understood about each other, not only the music but the rhythm of people—timing is another way to say it."

In the 1985 KCRW interview, Nelson said of Garland, "I remember her as a very warm and appealing female. I think one wanted to protect her. . . . I was attracted by her voice, that warm, almost overdone vibrato, which she used but nevertheless made your hair stand on end. It was a very special thing she brought, which no one else brought." Nelson also said of Garland (it also could have been said of Sinatra), "She put the words before the music, instead of the other way around, treating the lyrics with all the reverence due them."[2]

Nelson's laudatory comments about working with Garland ignored the fact that, according to Donfeld, a considerable part of their second (and last) album together *Judy In Love* was overdubbed in Capitol's small Studio C because the singer didn't show up for some of the recording sessions. This was at a time when overdubbing hardly existed.

Their collaboration produced twenty-four arrangements. Among them were two of Nelson's most memorable and dynamic charts, both of which perfectly suited Garland: "Zing Went the Strings of My Heart" and "Come Rain or Come Shine." These songs were also two highlights of her subsequent *Judy at Carnegie Hall* album triumph. I remember witnessing a zealous fan of Garland's being so moved by her performance of "Zing . . ." at her July 1961 outdoor concert at the West Side Tennis Club in Forest Hills that he ran down the steps of the stands before an audience of 16,000 people screaming in ecstasy and sprinted about seventy-five yards toward the stage, only to trip over a giant speaker.

Nelson recalled that he wrote the "Come Rain or Come Shine" chart following the vocal line that Roger Edens had originally put together for Garland at MGM. However, he actually first wrote it for Rosemary Clooney a few months earlier. When Clooney went backstage to see Garland after one of her performances at the Palace Theatre in New York in the late 1950s, she was confronted by Judy, who said, "You stole my arrangement!" Clooney was so taken aback by Garland's outburst that she was speechless. Finally, she explained that she had recorded the song when she had her own television show, but because Nelson was under contract to Capitol he couldn't be credited as the arranger. Clooney suddenly figured out that Nelson must have been pressed for time and had copied the arrangement for Garland's recording session. This realization caused her to be angry at Nelson for a time.[3]

In April 1956, Nelson arranged and conducted for Garland in a General Electric–sponsored television special in which Ronald Reagan, then the spokesman for General Electric, delivered the commercial messages. Sid Luft then brought Nelson to Chicago in 1957 to conduct for Judy when she was booked for a week of concerts at Orchestra Hall. "Nelson was Judy's kind of musician—pleasant and unassuming, but he knew his business," Luft said. "He could also zing you and it would be effective, like a dart! He had become the guru of modern conductors of that kind of music. . . . I must tell you, I liked him immensely. I've met some modern conductors recently who were

Nelson looking surprised and a bit uncomfortable with Judy Garland on his lap following one of their mid-1950s Capitol recording sessions.

involved with Judy's material. Not that they're bad guys, but they just didn't have the heart and soul of Nelson Riddle."

Luft played me Garland's collaboration with Nelson on her signature song, "Over the Rainbow" (written by E.Y. "Yip" Harberg and Harold Arlen), which was recorded in 1956. It was played by a music box he hoped to have mass-produced in China. Luft pointed out that this was one of only a few times Garland had done a studio recording of her immortal hit from *The Wizard of Oz*. "That was as good as she got," he observed. Nelson's sympathetic use of strings behind Garland indicated that he knew precisely how to write for her.

His ability to bring out the best in girl singers wasn't limited to the recording studio; often it extended to the bedroom as well. In the early '50s, he met Joanne Greer at the office of the Hub Publishing Company. Greer was an excellent band singer who was later featured for many years with Les Brown's band. She also dubbed Rita Hayworth's singing voice in *Pal Joey*. At the time she and Nelson met, Greer was sharing the singing for Ray Anthony's band with Tommy Mercer, Nelson's former compatriot in the Merchant Marine band.

In 1953, Mercer and Nelson got together again at the Croyden Hotel in Chicago, where the Anthony band was staying while working an engagement at the Aragon Ballroom. Mercer recalled Nelson pouring his heart out about how much he was in love with Joanne, even crying as he explained how much he wanted to marry her.

Lois Duning, the widow of Nelson's longtime friend George Duning, said, "Joanne came and spent a weekend with us [in the 1980s] in Borrego Springs when she was okay [Greer currently suffers from Alzheimer's disease] . She told us that she and Nelson were able to pick up their affair after long separations. They kept it quite silent. She felt that some day they would be together, and it would all work out. That may have been wishful thinking on her part. I felt that at the time she was telling us. It was so sort of homespun. . . . She'd cook for him. She adored him."

★ ★ ★

At home, Nelson and Doreen's life together had become increasingly tense. Nelson continued to spend long days in Hollywood, often not returning home until 10:00 P.M. He also had many out-of-town dates with Cole, Garland, and Sinatra. Further, there were what musicians referred to as "casuals"—dance dates or concerts in which he led a big band in order to generate additional income.

Nelson also spent considerable time on the *Dornel*, a twenty-eight-foot auxiliary sloop he kept in Long Beach and later in Marina Del Rey, continuing to satisfy his need to for solitude. This practice had begun almost two decades earlier in Rumson, New Jersey. Nelson's second-oldest daughter, Bettina (Tina) Bellini, believes, "If he didn't like music so much he probably would have spent his whole life on a boat. He just loved his sailboats. I mean, sometimes I think my mother was ready to give up between the music and the boat!"

Alto saxophonist Bud Shank said, "His heavy wooden boat would be more at home in the Northwest or in the Northeast where there are heavier winds and rougher waters. Southern California has very light winds and gentle tides—it's a gentleman's place to sail. I do know, however, that he loved that boat. I would have imagined that if he was really fond of sailing he would have had a different kind of a boat, but people fall in love with a boat for a whole lot of different reasons."

Referring to her father's absences from home, Tina recalled, "Sometimes he would be gone maybe for a month in New York, and I wouldn't even notice," Tina recalled, looking back on the years she spent as a child in Malibu. "You know, parents in those days didn't say anything to the kids. Maybe, if he had time on the weekends, Dad would like to help paint the house. He and my mom would always pick out the colors when they were repainting the house."

Nelson was pleased to have his own music room in the Carbon Canyon home. There, seated at his black Steinway grand piano, he worked on his arrangements. He had a sweeping view of Santa Monica Bay, his "Sea of Dreams," which became the title of one of his Capitol instrumental albums.

Doreen always deferred to Nelson in all decisions, even about what movie to see. She protected him from anything that interfered with his writing. Doreen's mother, Annah Moran, counseled her about trying to develop some interests unrelated to Nelson and the children, but apparently to no avail.

Doreen had few friends of her own other than Jean Bain, Bob's wife. The Riddles' entertaining was devoted to having Nelson's clients—Sinatra, Nat and Maria Cole, Judy Garland and Sid Luft, Rosemary Clooney and Jose Ferrer, and Johnny and Ginger Mercer—to their home for parties designed to further Nelson's career.

Nelson and Doreen's family roles were clear: She ran the household and was in charge of the children's welfare, while he was the provider. "That was the fairy tale," observed Barbara Ernest, Doreen's sister. This was the 1950s, after all.

Nelson once said to Barbara's husband, Virgil, "You don't have the opportunities that I have." The question arises: Was Nelson referring to the fact that he had an ideal home life for a creative person or was he alluding to his opportunities to play around?

Tina believes that her father's philandering was based on an attitude he had developed: "Can I get away with it?" "I think it was something left over from his childhood that he never quite fulfilled," she continued, "and it got the better of him. I don't think there was any way to fix it, and I don't think there was anything my mother could do."

Nelson had started out as an introvert, but his years touring with big bands had changed him. He developed a constant yen for women, and he saw that the bandleaders he toured with always attracted them—both on the road and in the recording studio. Now that he was the leader of an orchestra himself, he seemed to feel justified in behaving as the others did.

Drummer Norm Jeffries, whose musical association with Nelson dated back to

Fort Knox, had another angle on Nelson and Doreen's relationship. According to Jeffries, "She was jealous of his success, more or less." He felt that Nelson grew past his wife as his career began to take off. "She sort of hung onto his coattail wherever he went," Jeffries said. "He was embarrassed about her because she drank so much."

It was during Nelson's frequent trips away from home on various assignments that Doreen had begun to drink. In addition to her problems with Nelson, life had not been easy for her as one of eight children in a struggling Irish Catholic family with a dominant mother. After her father's death when she was eight years old, her mother had brought a man into the household who was a heavy drinker. Jeffries stressed, "Doreen was a real nice lady, though, when you caught her when she was straight."

The drummer was referring to the few times Nelson and Doreen left Malibu for parties or other social gatherings. She encouraged Nelson to attend more industry events, but he didn't really enjoy them unless they were parties given by fellow musicians. On those occasions he could relax and feel at home. Years later, he said of himself, "I wouldn't call myself a party animal, maybe a party dinosaur."

I asked Barbara Ernest if she had ever talked to Doreen about her drinking. "It was hard to say things to her," she said. "She was my big sister. She was always my mentor. She had so much on the ball. But I'm sure my mother talked to her about it."

★ ★ ★

Capitol continued to pick up Nelson's option, and he was now allowed to arrange occasional outside projects. One of these was *Phil Silvers and His Swinging Brass* for Mitch Miller at Columbia Records. In 1955, Silvers was all the rage because of his portrayal of the freewheeling Sergeant Bilko on the CBS-TV show of the same name. Nelson was brought to New York to arrange an album of tunes associated with the army. He arranged the entire album except for a few songs arranged by Frank Comstock.

Trombonist Chauncey Welsch remembered, "The whole album was done in one day—a morning session and then an afternoon session. I was hired to play bass trombone by the contractor, Hymie Shertzer [also one of the best lead alto players of all time], although I really played regular [tenor] trombone. But when I first heard George Roberts playing with Nelson on records, I got myself a small bass trombone and learned to play it. I started to get a little bit of a reputation for playing it, but I was nervous as hell because I knew what Nelson was writing for George, and there was no way in the world I could handle most of what George was doing.

"Nelson's arrangements were beautiful, and we had some great players on the date—Artie Baker on clarinet, Boomie Richman on tenor saxophone, Urbie Green on trombone, and the trumpets were Bernie Glow, Jimmy Maxwell, and Charlie Shavers. The bass trombone was included in every arrangement. It was at a minimum four pages. That night I went to play for Elliot Lawrence. I could hardly play above a middle D. The next day I sold the instrument.

"Fifteen years later, I came out here to do a television show with Peter Matz for

Sammy Davis, Jr. At Shapiro's drugstore, I was having breakfast and looked across the room and there was Nelson with some kid. He introduced me to his son Chris and said, 'Chauncey is a bass trombone player [as is Chris].' I hadn't seen him in all that time and hadn't touched the instrument. Isn't that amazing? What a memory!"

In 1957 Nelson returned to writing for a girl singer—a most imposing girl singer—when he wrote the charts for Peggy Lee's *The Man I Love* album. The conductor was Frank Sinatra. The idea for the album was Frank's; he brought Lee a list of songs, from which she selected what she wanted to record. On the KCRW show, she described how elated she was to be working with Sinatra and Riddle, saying, "I thought I'd died and gone to heaven. Frank was an excellent conductor, and I'd say, more sensitive to a singer than most. He designed the cover and did the whole production. As a matter of fact, he wanted me to have a misty look on that cover so he had someone spray menthol in my eyes."

Lee's longtime accompanist, pianist Lou Levy, recalled, "Nelson composed beautiful beds for those people to perform on. They were pads of harmony that made those people feel good. *The Man I Love* was a lovely project. Frank was very easy to follow. Nelson did a great job, and Peggy sounded wonderful."

As usual, Nelson perfectly tailored his arrangements to the singer's strengths. His eloquent use of flutes, French horns, and strings supplied the perfect backdrop for Lee's soft and wistful singing style. Her renditions of "That's All," "Then I'll Be Tired of You," and especially "The Folks Who Live on the Hill" are among the very best of the Lee recorded canon. Her rendition of "Folks," along with that by David Allyn, are *the* definitive recordings of this Jerome Kern classic.

A year later, Nelson showcased another side of Lee's singing abilities when he arranged an album called *Jump for Joy*. These charts were written to show her ease in handling more rhythmic, up-tempo material, something she had mastered while singing with Benny Goodman.

Nelson was now close to the peak of both his creative powers and his ability to build a comfortable career with his talent. The mention of his name immediately elicited respect. David Abell, a music aficionado and one of the kindest and most respected business people in Los Angeles as owner of Abell Pianos, observed, "I think in a way when we first started doing business with Nelson [in the early 1960s] I was somewhat in awe of him because his reputation was so strong, and obviously I was pleased he was doing business with me." Their relationship continued to the end of Nelson's life.

With his newfound success, in 1956, Nelson's business manager, Charles Brown, encouraged him to seek out a business venture that could serve as a tax write-off. Shortly after Virgil Ernest graduated from California Polytechnic State University with a degree in dairy husbandry, Nelson purchased a farm near Tulare, California, that the Ernests found for him. It was a registered Holstein dairy farm with seventy-six acres of land. Nelson asked Virgil to run it for him.

"Virgil was taking care of the soil, rotating crops, and doing the thing with the

Holsteins," Barbara remembered, "which may or may not be what you want to do if you're trying to make everything run at a loss." The Riddle family spent Thanksgiving and Easter at the farm with the Ernests on an annual basis.

★ ★ ★

In 1955, Berle Adams, one of the leading MCA agents, selected Nelson to become the musical director of the new syndicated Rosemary Clooney television show. "We decided to sell Rosie in a thirty-minute filmed show," Adams recalled, "rather than in a taped show because I wanted to preserve the sound of the recording studio. We recorded the show at Radio Recorders on Highland in Hollywood. We had the sound I wanted with Nelson, who led something like a twenty-three-piece orchestra. His arrangements were perfect. We had the Hi-Los as permanent cast, and we brought guest stars in.

"When we first started, Rosie said to me, 'I forgot to tell you, Berle, I'm four months pregnant.' I said, 'Well, we've got the commitment.' We had to finish the thirty-nine shows for Foremost Dairies. She was beautiful in those days. To conceal her pregnancy, we hid her behind plants, half-opened doors, walls, fences, and big chairs."

Toward the end of the show's first episode, Rosemary introduced Nelson to the home audience by asking him to come up to the microphone and appear on camera with her. When he joined her—and this may or may not have been spontaneous—she gushed, "Isn't he just the cutest thing you ever saw?" Nelson seemed to turn green and shyly sauntered out of camera range.

"Nelson was a wonderful guy to work with. You could make suggestions. You could really talk to him. He was terrific," Adams said. In view of that, one day Clooney said to Nelson, "I think you are the best *singer* who ever lived because you know just what to do on any given word or any particular note. What you write conveys exactly what I'm feeling. Exactly!"[4]

After the completion of the contracted shows in 1957, *The Rosemary Clooney Show* got a new sponsor—Lever Brothers, the soap manufacturers. It had now graduated to the NBC-TV network with Nelson continuing as its musical director. According to Adams, Clooney told him that she was three months pregnant with her second child during the first week of shooting.

Riddle and Clooney began recording together, but once again Nelson's latest Capitol contract prevented him from being credited. He wrote the arrangements for three of the tracks for her next Columbia album, *Ring Around Rosie*: "Love Letters," "I'm in the Mood for Love," and "I'm Glad There Is You." He also he arranged six single records on Columbia for her under the name "Joe Seymour."

★ ★ ★

After having five children with José Ferrer, Clooney began to have serious problems with Joe (as he was known), among them his flagrant infidelities and his often violent behavior. And who was close by to discuss her problems with but her musical director—who was easy to relate to and always willing to listen? They soon became close friends and

Photo by Charlie Briggs.

Nelson and Doreen visiting Nelson's old friend Charlie Briggs in Allentown, Pennsylvania, in 1956, during an eastern disc jockey tour. The warmth of their relationship at the time is evident in this photo.

they discovered that their birthdays were close together—hers on May 23 and his on June 1. They celebrated them together, at first with a group of people and later alone together.

Finally, in 1957, after they had been working together for about a year, a serious love affair between Nelson and Clooney began. Their six-year liaison was to become the most intense relationship of their lives, next to their marriages. In 1991, Clooney said, "It was the best blending of my job and my personal life that I've ever had."[5] Clooney has also often been quoted as referring to Nelson as "the love of my life."

Despite my having had a friendly two-decade-long relationship with Clooney that began when I was her publicist in the early years of her incredible comeback, she chose not to be interviewed for this book. She has been happily married for several years to Dante DiPaolo, who stood by her during the terrible years she endured in the late 1960s and early '70s, when she was addicted to prescription drugs. There were aspects of her relationship with Nelson that she didn't wish to share and which weren't revealed in her 1999 autobiography, *Girl Singer*.

A story related to me by Bob Bain illustrates exactly how absorbed Nelson and Clooney were with each other. One afternoon, Bain was at the Riddle home in Carbon Canyon when Nelson said to him, "Bob, come and buy some liquor with me." "He didn't need any liquor," Bain recalled. "We went down the long circular driveway and there was Rosemary with [her manager] Joe Shribman in a car. She was on her way to New York or someplace, and they said goodbye at the bottom of the driveway. I said to Nels, 'This is really getting out of hand.' I told him, 'You're crazy.' He said, 'I know.'

"I finally got over coming home and mentioning anything about Nelson 'cause it got to be where Judi [Bob's wife] would say to me, 'Jesus, you're so depressed. You've been with Nelson again.' He'd lay all this garbage on me. He always had to talk about it.

"I also remember the time Judi and I went up to San Francisco. Nels said to me, 'Don't tell anybody about Rosemary Clooney.' So when we got there I bumped into Buddy Cole, who was playing piano for Rosemary at the time. He said, 'Hey, you know Nelson and . . .' I said, 'Oh, shut up!' Everybody knew about this thing, but Nelson said, 'Don't say anything.' He'd tell anybody over lunch. And he had a habit of blaming Doreen entirely. It was her fault, her fault." Rosemary Acerra said, "He hurt our mother and us so much."

Skip Riddle, in discussing his father's relationship with Rosemary Clooney, said, "It was a romantic, sexual relationship. He needed somebody to take care of him to have a good relationship, not somebody that he had to take care of. He couldn't handle somebody with emotional highs and lows. . . . He was looking for somebody to make peace . . . but he was attracted to women who [were disruptive] so *he* could slip into the role of making peace and then take out his anger on them. And I'm sure he did that to every woman that he's ever been with." Skip added, "Here were a lot of very driven, really talented, deeply emotional people who behaved badly because they didn't know how to behave another way."

Tina Bellini recalled the moment in 1962 when she believes her mother suddenly discovered what was going on between her father and Clooney. "I well remember that night. There was some sort of an odd atmosphere at a party [attended by José Ferrer and Rosemary Clooney], and I was just a little thing. When I grew up, I realized just why I remembered that night. I think my mother knew that night. She realized there was something going on."

When the party ended, Doreen began interrogating Nelson about Clooney. As he had with several previous minor escapades, he finally admitted the affair, but swore it wouldn't continue.

At that time Nelson was working very closely with Eddie Forsyth, the music supervisor at Screen Gems. Nelson told Forsyth how he had told Doreen the truth about his affair with Clooney. "I couldn't stand it anymore," Nelson reportedly told him, "and I told her, 'Yes, I've been having an affair.'" Forsyth remembered replying, "'You're doomed!',", continuing, "and he *was* doomed. I don't care what the situation is, you never, never, ever admit the infidelity thing to a woman because 'a woman scorned. . . .' Doreen was a tyrant in this case. The Catholic thing with her was so oppressive—the discipline, the recrimination."

According to Skip Riddle, Nelson continued to see Clooney after he admitted his infidelities with her, and Doreen knew it. "That blonde—your father is with that blonde again," Doreen would say when addressing her children about their father's whereabouts. Forsyth informed me that Nelson told him he would sometimes meet Clooney at the Hollywood Roosevelt Hotel. Nelson said that she would check in and he would climb up the fire escape to meet her in the room; he was afraid of being recognized in the lobby.

Doreen's discovery proved to be the second terrible link that led to her severe alcoholism. The death of the Riddles' little girl, Lenora Celeste, of bronchial asthma on February 11, 1958, at the age of six months was the first. It caused her to undergo a nervous breakdown. According to Rosemary Acerra, the attending physician, Dr. Roger Makeman, said, "Keep the children away from her. She's exhausted, she's depressed, and she needs time to recuperate."

"She lived in the bedroom and controlled everything from there," Barbara Ernest said. "She went through a post-partum depression, but it went beyond that. She was living with a lot of things we didn't know about."

"Mom started to detach more," Rosemary recalled. "Dad had already shown that he wasn't that much help to her on her emotional side. When she was totally on track for him . . . everything was okay. But when she needed something, he couldn't handle it."

Decades later, Nelson rationalized about the aftermath of Lenora's death by explaining that Doreen felt especially bad about it because she had previously had an abortion; he claimed she thought it was God's punishment. He was obviously trying to relieve himself of any responsibility for his failure to support Doreen emotionally.

Rosemary said that her father later deeply regretted his inattention to her mother's needs at this terrible time in Doreen's life.

"It was horrible," Tina remembered. "That just sent my mom right around the corner. And every year for years afterwards, Lenora's birthday and the date of her death meant my mother was going to put herself and us through hell on those two days."

To make matters worse, Albertine was diagnosed with breast cancer at almost the same time. In the final months of her life, Doreen, who by then had recovered from her own illness, took complete care of her, and Albertine came to depend on her.

Maria Cole said that once Doreen found out about Nelson and Rosemary, she underwent a drastic change, sinking into a state of madness that was exacerbated by her excessive drinking. This led her to call Louella Parsons, the leading Hollywood gossip columnist, and pour out the problems she was having with Nelson.

Barbara Ernest emphasized Nelson's role in his wife's decline. "Nelson destroyed her self-confidence. She had nothing left. It was like he gutted her. He was self-centered because that's how he was raised. The only thing I want to impress upon you is the goodness of what he had at one time. My sister wasn't perfect, but she was the epitome of wife, motherhood, family, and all of that. Once she started to drink, however, she became the epitome of awful."

★ ★ ★

On the musical side of Nelson's life, things couldn't have been much better in 1957 and 1958. His back-to-back albums *Hey . . . Let Yourself Go* and *C'mon . . . Get Happy* both hit the *Billboard* chart at #20 for one week. On *Hey . . . Let Yourself Go,* Nelson's enjoyment of using jazz musicians as soloists was once again illustrated by Stuff Smith's delightful violin solo on "Have You Got Any Castles, Baby?" and Juan Tizol's solo on "You and the Night and the Music," and "Sweets" Edison was featured on several tracks.

Reflecting on his successful albums during this period, Nelson said, "I could never count on the big acceptance that some singers commanded, but I always knew that they would get well played if they were [any] good. I knew that the disc jockeys would take the time to listen to them and play them, and that's quite an achievement."[6]

Nelson returned to film scoring, his favorite musical endeavor, in 1956 with the Jane Powell-Cliff Robertson RKO musical, *The Girl Most Likely,* with words and music by Blane and Martin. In those years, Hollywood was still producing a considerable number of film musicals. Capitol released the soundtrack album two years later when the film finally reached theaters.

The songs were nowhere near as good as those the songwriters had written for Judy Garland for the MGM musical *Meet Me in St. Louis,* and Cliff Robertson, while always a very creditable actor, was not a formidable singer. The best tune in the film was actually the title song, which was written by Bob Russell and Nelson.

Jane Powell fondly remembered working with Nelson on both *The Girl Most*

Likely and the Frank Sinatra television show: "He had such a sly sense of humor. He always had a twinkle in his eye."

One of the most versatile screen composers and a particular favorite at Paramount for decades was Walter Scharf. He scored a total of 280 films in a career that lasted fifty-five years. Among them were *Road to Rio, Hans Christian Andersen, Winchester '73, The Joker Is Wild, The Nutty Professor,* and *Funny Girl,* "and about 1,000 television shows," as Scharf described it.

Scharf first met Nelson at Paramount in 1957 when Nelson arranged "All the Way" for Frank Sinatra to sing in the Joe E. Lewis biographical film *The Joker Is Wild.* As Scharf recalled, "Actually, Nelson wrote the music that played over the main title for the picture and also scored a few nightclub scenes. Victor Young was set to score the picture, but he had a heart attack. Frank got me off the picture I was supposed to be working on and got me the job. I was on *Joker* for seven months. It was a dramatic picture.

"I don't think Nelson ever fulfilled what he could do in pictures. He never had the opportunity to work on dramatic films. I think he was afraid to take a chance. And I'll tell you something, he had the greatest chance. He was flying high, and people liked him. He never embarrassed anybody or himself. I told him, 'If you let yourself go and do dramatic films, you will leave a legacy. I own the [musical] copyrights to eighty of my pictures.'"

As mentioned earlier, in 1956 Nelson wrote arrangements for the Warner Bros. film version of the musical *The Pajama Game,* starring Doris Day and John Raitt. It was probably due to contractual obligations that Day and Nelson never were able to collaborate on an album.

★ ★ ★

Nelson also found a musical rapport with another female singer, Keely Smith, then a sensation with her husband, trumpeter Louis Prima, in their lounge act at the Sahara in Las Vegas. Part of Prima's 1956 deal with Capitol called for Smith to have her own Capitol contract. Voyle Gilmore assigned her to record with Nelson.

Their first album was *I Wish You Love.* The tune became Smith's theme song and her rendition with Nelson was nominated for Best Performance by a Female Vocalist in the first year of the Grammy competition.[7] "When Day Is Done," from the same album, was one of the most memorable arrangements Nelson ever wrote for a singer. After Smith's second vocal chorus, he wrote a string background on top of a throbbing rhythm section with a full percussion section that reaches a thrilling climax. This was yet another example of Nelson's use of eroticism in music.

Out of their second album, *Swinging Pretty,* for which Nelson rewrote some of Smith's small band charts, came his notable arrangements of "It's Magic" and "When Your Lover Has Gone." His interpretation of the latter tune was an example of how Nelson could transform a mournful ballad, usually written with strings (as he had done for Sinatra for the *In the Wee Small Hours* album) into a big band swing chart, without

Smith losing sight of the melancholia in the lyrics. She admired his work so much that he also contributed two arrangements for the film she and Louis starred in, *Hey, Boy! Hey, Girl!* in 1957.

Smith admitted, "Louis always had a say-so over everything. But I think because Nelson was Sinatra's arranger, Louis decided not to tell him what to do, just go let him go ahead and write. So that's why when people ask me about 'When Day Is Done' and 'When Your Lover Has Gone' and things like that that have those up-tempos, I always give Nelson the credit because they were his ideas. Working with Billy May was a lot different from working with Nelson, because Nelson was laid-back and kind of quiet, until you crossed him, and then he would let you know who's boss. But he was very kind and very charming, and very tender with me because I was so young. . . . He kind of knew how to talk to me."[8]

★ ★ ★

Nelson's old friend Lou Brown from the Coast Guard band was now conductor for Jerry Lewis, an association that lasted forty-eight years. Brown amusingly described Jerry's 1957 NBC-TV special for which Nelson was musical director: "Jerry wanted a name conductor for the show, and of course, he had also recorded with Nelson for Capitol. The show had wall-to-wall music so Nelson had to get a few other guys to help him with the writing.

"I worked with him all week with Jerry's music plus all the cues. The show was 'live,' but from the very beginning he was lost. He gave a downbeat to the musicians with absolutely no preparation, like *BOOM!* It was mayhem! None of the guys knew where they were. He didn't know what he was doing. He was up there throwing his arms around. His downbeats were so indistinct. After the show was over, he said, 'I'll never do a 'live' show again as long as I live. It's the worst experience of my life in the music business.' And it *was* awful!"

Following that unfortunate experience, Nelson began work on one of his favorite projects, the *Cross Country Suite* album, which showcased the brilliance of Buddy DeFranco. This recording took place at the time when DeFranco was the winner of both the *Down Beat* and *Metronome* polls as the leading clarinetist eleven years in a row. It also won Nelson his first Grammy in the category curiously designated as Best Musical Composition First Recorded and Released in 1958 (Over 5 Minutes Duration). The Suite was also nominated for Best Performance by an Orchestra.

It's ironic that after Nelson was shut out in the first year of the Grammy competition for his work on *Only the Lonely,* and Keely Smith received a nomination for Best Vocal Performance, Female for singing his arrangement of "I Wish You Love," and he was nominated for his arrangement of "Witchcraft" for Frank Sinatra, it was the *Cross Country Suite* that won him his Grammy.

Cross Country Suite had its premiere performance at a Hollywood Bowl concert that Nelson conducted for Nat Cole. Despite a strong response from the audience, its

Nelson Riddle playing one of his "casuals." Clarinetist and saxophonist Willie Schwartz is shown in the foreground. Other Riddle "regulars" included drummer Stan Levey, seen at Nelson's right, and, in the trumpet section, Cappy Lewis on the left and George Werth on the extreme right.

notices were negative. One reviewer called it, "Nelson Riddle's pathetic attempt at a Ferde Grofé composition with a clarinetist."

DeFranco revealed that *Cross Country Suite* originated as a piece for him to play at a Le Blanc Clarinet clinic. "I felt it should be a combination of a big band, jazz, and an orchestra [which turned out to be forty pieces] so I got hold of Nelson at a time he was extremely busy writing for Nat Cole. I'm glad he accepted the offer because it turned out to be one of the best things he ever wrote. It was his idea to write two long compositions containing eleven musical sketches of various parts of the country in it. My friend the music contractor Jack Lee got Randy Wood at Dot to record it."

I wondered how the two musicians found a musical common ground, since DeFranco was a bebopper and Nelson was grounded in swing. "Well, we didn't," answered DeFranco. "It kind of spilled itself out, in a way. Nelson kept the swing idea and the element of the swing band, but he had never stopped growing harmonically and rhythmically. He would always be at the forefront of modern arranging even if it wasn't considered bebop . . . and although I was considered a bebop clarinetist, my fundamental background was in swing. There [actually] was a common ground."

DeFranco recalled that when the recording session began the orchestra ran down the suite twice, with Nelson making a few changes along the way. Milt Bernhart, who played trombone on the date, emphasized that the makeup of the musicians really made it work—trumpeter Don Fagerquist, French horn player Vince De Rosa, clarinetist Willie Schwartz, pianist Pete Jolly, guitarist Billy Bean, bassist Red Mitchell, and drummer Stan Levey—a perfect combination of the best studio musicians mixed with the right jazz musicians. "Nelson was even more serious than usual. He really took pride in his composition," DeFranco said.

DeFranco related that for the album's cover photograph, the Dot Records art director dressed him in a sweater, slacks, and white bucks. "It was exactly what Pat Boone would have worn. You see, Pat was Dot's biggest artist in those days," he pointed out.

Cross Country Suite was an artistic success, but not a big seller. Interestingly, today, twenty-five percent of the requests on Buddy DeFranco's Web site are for a CD copy of it; unfortunately, it has never been released on compact disc.

★ ★ ★

In the music business, as in other businesses, there are people who deserve to become a major success but for various reasons never do. One of them is Sue Raney. She was signed by Capitol at the age of seventeen, and now, decades later, is still a fine but underappreciated singer.

Nelson arranged and conducted Raney's first album, *When Your Lover Has Gone,* in 1958. It's amazing how mature Raney sounded at this young age. The title song was given an up-tempo treatment that differed greatly from the version Nelson had written for Keely Smith a year earlier. This album served as the beginning of a long-lasting musical relationship between him and Raney.

Looking back on her recording debut, Raney reflected, "I'm telling you, the excitement. . . . I can hear this scared little girl singing these songs, but there was something comforting obviously about Nelson Riddle because he didn't scare me. . . . It was an orchestra of thirty to thirty-two musicians, and it was pretty overwhelming. In those days, of course, you just sang and that was it. You didn't go back and fix anything. . . . Now if I could only have those tracks and sing them again, would I love that! Because you're older and wiser, you're more content with who you are." Speaking further of Nelson, she added, "He was like a dad to me. He didn't make you feel intimidated. I don't know— there was a softness about him."

Raney later worked with Nelson as his "girl singer" when his band did concerts or dance dates in places like Palm Springs and Bakersfield, as well as in major cities like San Francisco and Salt Lake City. "I would drive to the gigs with Nelson and [trumpeter] Shorty Sherock. There were times you saw fun in him, that he might be having a good time, and it was great. He was always good to me."

Not everyone saw this side of Nelson when he was performing. F.M. Scott remembered seeing Riddle leading a big band at a party after the Grammy Awards one year. "Scotty" remarked, "I remember thinking he had that peculiar look on his face that clearly said, 'What am I doing here?'" This was just one example of how uncomfortable Nelson was when leading his band on dance gigs.

In addition to working with him in the studio, Bill Richmond played drums on

Nelson's "casuals" in the mid-1950s. "He had a dance book which was very small," Richmond related. "The arrangements sounded like they were somebody's vocal arrangements minus the vocal." (They probably were arrangements Nelson had written for various singers.)

The late bandleader Les Brown said, "I know that he hated to front a band. I understand he'd never look at the audience. And when he'd play an arrangement that had been written with strings in it, and there weren't strings there, it just didn't sound as good. He was just taking the money and running."

Richmond more or less agreed: "Nelson was just an arranger, he wasn't a band-leader. He never was. He wasn't Tommy Dorsey, in other words. Because, you know, all of those guys—Harry James, Tommy Dorsey—they had a strong presence on a stage. They knew who they were. I remember seeing Tommy Dorsey—he wore clothes that he'd obviously never sat down in. Nelson couldn't look like that. He looked like he slept in his clothes. 'And now, here he is, Nelson Riddle, right from the bed!' And, of course, as far as talking, he had no personality to project. Even Benny Goodman in his heyday had more personality than Nelson. But by the same token, Nelson had to be acutely aware of the fact that there was money involved when it was 'Nelson Riddle and his Orchestra.' Prime agents, I'm sure, said, 'You want Nelson there in person, you want Nelson Riddle?' and everybody's thinking, 'Yeah, Frank Sinatra . . . .' so agents could get good money for that."

Sandi Shoemake sang on some of these dance dates. She said, "He loved the musicians and he'd just walk around, up and down—pace the stage! But I thought he was very special. I was completely in awe of him 'cause I knew what he had accomplished. . . . He would also get his horn out once in awhile and play. But he wouldn't play out in front into the mike, however."

★ ★ ★

For over three decades years, Ed Townsend has been established in the rhythm and blues world as a record producer and songwriter. He wrote and produced the classic "Let's Get It On" for Marvin Gaye, as well as various songs for the Impressions, the Shirelles, Dee Dee Warwick, Chuck Jackson, and others, but he started out as a singer.

In 1957, Nat Cole brought Townsend to Capitol. "I got to meet a lot of people at a time when you got to know almost everybody on the label," he recalled. "Nelson Riddle was one of those people. We got to like each other an awful lot, and I admired his work."

Right away, Townsend had a hit single called "For Your Love," which he wrote. It reached a high of #13 on the *Billboard* pop chart at the end of April 1958 and remained on the chart for twelve more weeks. He followed that up with a modern version of "When I Grow Too Old to Dream." As his producer at the time, the redoubtable Tom Morgan, observed, "Ed wanted to be classy. He wanted to work with Nelson Riddle."

Morgan soon began to confer with Nelson and his associate, Gil Grau, at Nelson's office in Hollywood on Gower, below Sunset Boulevard. "I would say, 'Look, here's a tune, let's do it this way. We'll have Ed do the verse and then you go into a chorus and a half, and if you could do a key change. . . .' and Nelson would turn to Gil and say, 'Well, you know what to do. Do this and that. . . .' Nelson didn't really have to sit down and score anything. I think he laid it out in eight-bar segments.

"The album was all standards. . . . The dumb thing was we never put 'For Your Love' in the album that was called *New in Town*," Morgan continued. "That was right before record companies started putting hit singles into albums and naming the albums after them."

Their first album was successful. Townsend claims that the second album he recorded with Nelson, *Glad to Be Here,* was also beginning to sell when the Capitol pressing plant went on strike, which inevitably impeded its sales.

"The kind of songs I was doing were not considered R&B," he explained. "Nelson didn't treat me like an R&B artist. I was a ballad singer, pure and simple. He treated me like any other artist. If you listen to the arrangements, they were really great pop arrangements, right down the middle.

"I think Nelson might have been color-blind because I never once felt that he had any animosity or any dislike for anybody based on race. He often remarked how much he enjoyed working with me, so it was a very good relationship."

Townsend particularly remembered recording the "The More I See You" track with Nelson. "It was the first time I had recorded with a full orchestra. . . . It was a very tearful moment for me. I don't think you know what it means to be born in Tennessee and longing for the day when you could walk into the studio with Nelson Riddle and record with a full orchestra at Capitol. When I got to the part where he went into a sort of a bolero beat and changed the tempo with a very beautiful modulation—it just sent chills down my spine."

Two other singers, who were anything but young and emerging pop stars, record-ed with Nelson in the late '50s—Mavis Rivers and Dinah Shore. Capitol "naturally" had Nelson arrange their first albums for the label. The Samoan-born Rivers, more of a jazz singer, unfortunately never followed up the favorable impression Nelson helped her make with her Capitol debut album, *Take a Number.*

The effervescent Shore acknowledged the fact that Nelson's being a Capitol artist was an inducement for her to sign with the company. She was already an established star on radio, records ("I'll Walk Alone," "The Anniversary Song," "Shoo Fly Pie" and "Buttons and Bows" were big hits of hers), and with her own highly popular NBC-TV variety show. She was given the patented Riddle swinging treatment and reveled in it on *Dinah, Yes Indeed.*

A singer one might have thought would be musically incompatible with Nelson was Tommy Sands, who had several hit pop singles and albums in the late 1950s before being paired with Riddle. The truth of the matter was otherwise, as shown by the two albums they recorded together. Signed by Capitol as the clean-cut answer to Elvis Presley, Sands, like so many young pop stars of the time, was recorded singing both rock 'n' roll and traditional pop songs. This practice was followed in order to ensure the retention of one audience if the singer didn't register with the other.

The first of two albums Sands recorded with Nelson was produced in 1959. *When I'm Thinking of You* featured standards like "Fools Rush In," "Always," "It Had to Be You," and "The Nearness of You." Then, in 1960, there was *Dream of You,* which was highlighted by their versions of "It's So Peaceful in the Country," "Lazy Afternoon," and "Faraway Places." What becomes apparent when listening to these two albums is that Nelson's arrangements on it were as original and stimulating as any he wrote for any singer, and obviously Sands was musically comfortable with him.

Sands recalled that the first time they met was at Nelson's home. "He sat at his piano and played while I sang. I remember he said my voice was like a viola. I think he was speaking mainly to what my vibrato was like in terms of a string instrument. Nelson did a lot of things that Johnny Mathis's arrangers did. He ended an instrumental interlude on the same note as the vocal begins. [You can hear it] in the arrangement he wrote for me on 'I'll Be Seeing You'; [it's] similar to what you can hear in Johnny's famous rendition of 'Misty.' You would end a note never knowing that Nelson was going to write something special for it. Then you would listen to the playback and you'd hear that your voice at the beginning of what you were going to sing was coming out of a group of instruments that sounded just like your voice. . . .

"We only had one difference of opinion; that was on the second album, *Dream of You,* when I felt the tempo on the tunes should be slower. We recorded the album at the tempo he wanted. After they were done I took them into another studio and slowed them down. I sang live but I had my voice on one track and the orchestrations on another track.

"Looking back, I can say that Nelson was the best arranger I ever worked with. He had his own distinct sound. [He confirmed for me] what I probably gained even before I worked for him, and that was the sense of what could be accomplished in popular music through the right sounds, the right instruments, and the right kind of arrangements."

"Nelson was the guy who brought romance to swing," Sands concluded. "That style of arranging is as current today as it was then. He was also a fabulous ballad arranger—one of the best that ever came down the road."

★ ★ ★

By the 1960s, Nelson Riddle was well established as the foremost arranger in popular music. To follow a succession of albums entitled *Music Minus One* on the Command label, which were recorded so that the musician at home could play his instrument in front of a tight rhythm section, Capitol designed a similar experience for at-home singers when it released *Sing a Song with Riddle.* The cover of the album showed a microphone in front of a weakly smiling Nelson wearing a polo shirt and slacks and giving a simulated downbeat. With the playing of this album, a would-be singer had access to the best background he or she could ever experience in his or her musical life. (Could it be that this was the forerunner of the karaoke movement?)

In order to acquire some insight into what makes a recording studio musician—at least the high-caliber musicians who worked for Nelson Riddle—I discussed the matter with vibraharpist and percussionist Frank Flynn. Flynn had been one of the standout performers on the Sinatra/Riddle album *Swing Easy*. He noted, "Among the ingredients of a really good studio musician are that you have to be able to go in and do almost anything—any style they want. You can't do it all well, but you can do enough things well. It helps to be flexible and be able to play jazz. [Also,] you can't let things bug you."

The monotony of recording-studio work is sometimes thankfully broken by unusual occurrences that take place. As a perfect example, Lou Levy remembered the recording session in 1958 when Gene Barry, then starring as Bat Masterson in a weekly television series, entered the studio. Barry came directly from the set in his costume for the role, complete with a deep blue shirt, a black tie, a houndstooth suit and vest, cowboy boots, a walking stick, and a derby! "Maybe I just imagined that he wore the hat," Levy said. "I can vouch, however, that Gene wasn't much of a singer. The tunes were like "When the Red, Red Robin Goes Bob, Bob, Bobbin' Along." Levy wasn't sure the album was ever released; I have yet to find it listed in any discography of Nelson's work. "The quality of Nelson's work, no matter if it was for Gene Barry or Sinatra or Ella, remained on a certain level," Levy added.

Two instrumental albums, *The Joy of Living* in 1959 and *Love Is a Game of Poker* in 1962, found the Nelson Riddle Orchestra at its recorded peak. The first provided a stunning example of George Roberts's often whimsical bass trombone playing, and the second was highlighted by several displays of "Cappy" Lewis's muted trumpet. Cappy had begun to take Harry Edison's place at recording sessions, since "Sweets" was often working out of town.

On both of these albums, his orchestra demonstrated Nelson's ability to both demand and succeed in getting his musicians to play with a recognizable precision and zest. At the same time, these tracks showed that he indeed was at the height of his powers as a highly imaginative arranger.

Nelson compared his repeated use of the same musicians as being, "Like my piano at home, which was the first piece of furniture that my wife and I purchased after we were married. . . . An orchestra can become as familiar and reliable as a well-known, well-worn piano. You know what to expect from it—which is very reassuring. You're able to write strictly for that."[9]

★ ★ ★

Norman Granz was for many years at the forefront in jazz, first as a concert promoter beginning in 1944 with his "Jazz at the Philharmonic" concerts in Los Angeles and then as a record producer with his Clef and Norgran labels. He recorded several of the JATP concerts and, soon afterwards, individual albums with many of the artists who had appeared in these concerts. Granz was the first true jazz impresario and the first to insist on non-segregated audiences for his concerts.

Taking over the management of Ella Fitzgerald in December 1953, after featuring her on several JATP concert tours, formed the cornerstone of his career. Without question, throughout the next four decades Ella proved that she was indeed "The First Lady of Song." Granz's career direction brought her out of the jazz ghetto and into the major nightclubs and concert halls of the world without sacrificing a scintilla of her presentation as a jazz singer. What he accomplished on her behalf makes him the most resourceful manager in the history of jazz.

One of Granz's first important strategic moves in managing Ella was to obtain her release from Decca Records in exchange for allowing Universal-International to use his exclusive recording artists Teddy Wilson, Gene Krupa, and Lionel Hampton on the Decca soundtrack of *The Benny Goodman Story*. After that, knowing full well how Ella could interpret the best popular music standards, he set upon a plan to produce Fitzgerald on his newly inaugurated Verve Records in a series of "songbook" albums. These recordings provided a concentrated look at the best of the vast catalogues of the American popular music pantheon—Cole Porter, Duke Ellington, Rodgers and Hart, George Gershwin, Irving Berlin, Jerome Kern, Harold Arlen, and Johnny Mercer.

Granz realized he needed the work of a brilliant and flexible arranger to work closely with Ella in order to properly structure the songbooks. He had attempted to sign Nelson Riddle for his first of these, the Cole Porter songbook, in 1956. Due to Nelson's newly signed exclusive six-year contract with Capitol, Granz had to settle for Buddy Bregman, who had earlier arranged a few singles for Ella. Milt Bernhart played on these recording dates for the album. "It was very obvious how much Norman wanted Nelson for the job," Bernhart noted. "Bregman tried to write the charts in a Riddle vein, by copying Nelson's approach note for note."

In researching a musical biography, one comes upon often unforeseen bits of information. This is precisely what took place when personal manager Alan Eichler suggested that I talk to his client, the totally unique jazz singer Anita O'Day.

"I was recording for Norman Granz in the early '50s," Anita recalled. "He wanted to use a big orchestra on this recording date. I told him I had found a guy named Nelson Riddle, and Norman said, 'Who's he?'

"I first got to listen to Nelson on a record of some sort, and then I met him and talked with him and thought, 'Hey, this guy's really got something,' so I took him up to meet Norman. Norman says, 'I'm sorry. I'm in a hurry. I've got to leave. I'll talk to you when I get back.' By the time Norman got back, and I was trying to hold Nelson for us, Sinatra gets in! I said to Norman, 'You're too late, we lost the best guy in town.'"

Nelson did, however, arrange one of Ella's singles, "Beale Street Blues," in the mid-1950s. Never let it be said that Norman Granz didn't recognize talent! Hiring Nelson to collaborate with Ella on the five-volume George Gershwin songbook (for which recording began at Capitol Records's Studio A in March 1959), cost him considerably more money than it might have had he followed O'Day's suggestion.

The situation with the Gershwin project begs the question: Why would Capitol suddenly allow Nelson to participate in such a full-scale project with Ella Fitzgerald when earlier the company had prevented him from getting billing on Rosemary Clooney's Columbia album and had quashed his participation in Ella's Cole Porter album? Unfortunately, no one seemed to be able to answer that question. Alan Livingston, who had left his post as Vice President of A&R in 1955, speculated, "If I had been in the job, I would have certainly allowed Nelson to participate in this project. He had a big family responsibility then so he always needed money. Besides, having Nelson work with Ella would have done a lot for him, and the company would have certainly benefited from it."

Ella Fitzgerald Sings the George and Ira Gershwin Songbook, accompanied by Nelson Riddle and his Orchestra, was unquestionably the foremost combination of vocalist, composer, lyricist, and arranger in the recorded history of popular music. This was Nelson Riddle and Ella Fitzgerald at their absolute best. By coincidence, this masterpiece was recorded only nine months after the magnificent Sinatra/Riddle collaboration on *Only the Lonely* was completed.

Ella Fitzgerald's long career had begun with her winning the famous amateur night contest at the Apollo Theatre in Harlem in 1934. She was soon discovered by her mentor, the little hunchback drummer, Chick Webb, with whose orchestra she toured for five years until his death, at which time she assumed its leadership. Over the years, the only real musical criticism she received was for her limitations in interpreting lyrics. Arranger Johnny Mandel believes, however, "She sang Ira Gershwin as well as anybody."

In the *Gershwin Songbook,* in addition to her superlative treatment of important Gershwin standards like "Soon," "Love Walked In," "They Can't Take That Away from Me," "The Man I Love," and "Love Is Sweeping the Country," her humorous treatment of less important songs such as "The Real American Folksong" and "By Strauss" stood out.

It was apparent that Riddle had devoted considerable time to arranging various other "book" songs from Gershwin's Broadway musicals such as "Aren't You Kinda Glad We Did?" or "Slap That Bass," as he had with the composer's more familiar songs. John A. Tynan of *Down Beat* opined, "A high point of the collection is the treatment of 'Just Another Rhumba.' This becomes a riot of abandonment and a workout for singer and orchestra as Riddle keeps building instrumentally to reach a climax."

A total of fifty-three songs were contained in the five-volume Gershwin album, which was recorded over an eight-month period. They were about equally divided between up-tempo and ballad arrangements. Ella and Nelson's musical compatibility is

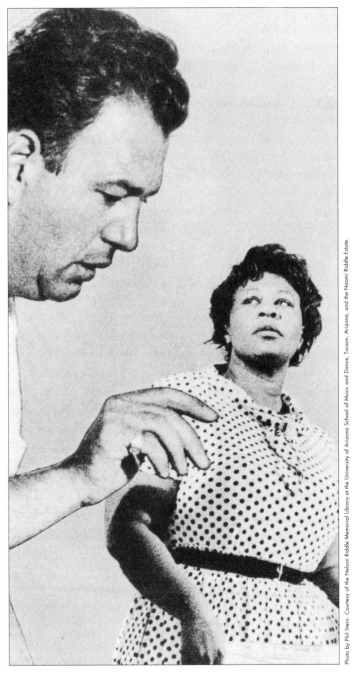

Photo by Phil Stern. Courtesy of the Nelson Riddle Memorial Library at the University of Arizona School of Music and Dance, Tucson, Arizona, and the Naomi Riddle Estate.

Nelson and Ella Fitzgerald rehearse one of the fifty-three songs recorded for the *Ella Fitzgerald Sings the George and Ira Gershwin Songbook* album in 1959. This collaboration was one of the crowning achievements in the careers of both Fitzgerald and Riddle.

readily apparent throughout the entire recording, as exemplified by Nelson's comment: "Not a note was changed in any arrangement, no key was altered, no routine was restructured. . . . That's quite a tribute to a great artist and wonderful human being."[9]

André Previn was astounded by the incredible versatility of Nelson's approach to Gershwin's music. While recording the songbook, Nelson also arranged six Gershwin instrumentals: "Promenade," "March of the Swiss Soldiers," and "Fidgety Feet," as well as the three piano preludes. These were later added to the CD version of the album. Nelson often featured the first three songs (under the title "Ambulatory Suite") in his later concert performances with a large orchestra.

Herb Ellis, the jazz guitarist acclaimed for his work with the Oscar Peterson Trio, who played on the album, recalled, "Nelson knew precisely how she sang and what she needed in her accompaniment. He was also aware of what she didn't need. Ella knew the melody to all the songs she sang. Nelson realized that and he arranged so that she could sing the melody, and it would not conflict with the harmonies that he had written for her. He also wrote in a way that would give her a lot of freedom to scat sing. In other words, she was the star, and he made it possible for her to be the star that she was."

Lou Levy remembered, "Ella would come in and sing with her hand over her ear in that little isolation booth . . . and we would crank them out one after another. The funny thing was that they never sounded as if they were cranked out. Riddle did a fantastic job. We did them pretty rapidly considering the quality of the music.

"In that album there's a song called 'Sam and Delilah.' Nelson utilized the sound of the lyric to indicate just what the lyric was about: Delilah was a vamp or siren. She tempted people, so he used the oboe to play music you would charm a cobra to. It was very, very smart orchestrating, and you could tell it affected Ella when she sang it. That's when he was really hip."[11]

Although the retail cost was a then-exorbitant $25.98 for the entire set of recordings, which came complete with individual Bernard Buffet paintings on the cover of each volume, it reached #12 on the *Billboard* pop chart. *Ella Fitzgerald Sings the George and Ira Gershwin Songbook* continues to be a consistent seller more than forty-two years after its release.

Ella and Nelson were to record four more albums together during the 1960s: *Ella Swings Brightly With Nelson* and *Ella Swings Gently With Nelson* (both released in 1962), *The Jerome Kern Songbook* (1963), and *The Johnny Mercer Songbook* (1964). While all of them have several highlights, individually they weren't able to match the excellence of the *Gershwin Songbook*. Interestingly, Nelson's by now familiar sound was more prevalent in these later albums.[12] In retrospect, it also seems as though their approach to recording became somewhat formulaic after awhile.

Ralph Burns, who worked for Norman Granz many times, contends that Granz wasn't terribly concerned with the recorded sound of Nelson's orchestra or even the quality of his writing. "The writers that I knew listened to Nelson because with Frank [Sinatra] the orchestra was beautifully recorded. The engineer was very important to Frank, but the sound on Norman's records was shitty, no matter who was writing. Granz didn't care about the writing. He wanted it done in one take, and that was it. He would go on to the next tune."

Regardless of Burns's feelings, Lou Levy said, "When we did the Hollywood Bowl concert with Ella [July 24, 1959], Nelson conducted the orchestra. Norman and Nelson treated each other with respect. The orchestra always treated Nelson with a lot of respect. The guys loved Nelson because there was a lot of work involved with what they did with him, but the quality of the music was always great.

"I can remember another time when we were coming back from a European tour. At the airport, Norman said to me, 'Put this on your wrist.' I looked down and there was a beautiful Patek Philippe watch. He said, 'I want you to wear it through customs. It's for Nelson Riddle.' I was honored to bring something to Nelson like that. It would be a thank you for all the wonderful knowledge that I absorbed from working for him."

According to drummer Stan Levey, who worked on several of the Fitzgerald/ Riddle sessions, "Ella loved Nelson, and thought he was the greatest, and for her he was terrific 'cause she's a down-the-middle swing singer, and he's a down-the-middle swing arranger. Straight ahead. His specialty was swing. They had a very real camaraderie."

Emil Richards remembers Ella as "the only person I saw Nelson be human with. They spoke to each other like they were friends. . . . Like I said, I never saw Nelson smile in the studio. Well, I remember seeing him smile, be jovial, and maybe even laughing with Ella. Every word you could say about camaraderie or friendship emanated from him with Ella. They didn't only talk music, they could talk incidental stuff and have a rapport. I never saw him have a rapport with anybody else. . . ." (Richards did admit that he only worked on a couple of recording sessions for Nelson with Nat Cole.)

Nelson said that working with Ella Fitzgerald was utterly devoid of problems. "She's almost always willing, cheerful, and cooperative. It's only when the demands of her incredible schedule sap her strength that she's a bit short-tempered or irritable. She went on occasional tirades against Norman about the ambitious series of personal appearances he has set up for her or about the choice of songs to record, but there is a real respect and affection they have for each other."[13]

Ella's friendship with Nelson extended to his family. When she first met Rosemary, she started calling her "Dimples." Rosemary still proudly wears a bracelet with a charm inscribed "To Dimples, Love, Ella."

Regarding Ella's amazing talent, Ralph Burns said, "Ella had this natural gift. She just sang. Singing to her was like cooking. But sometimes, if you're listening to her with Nelson, the music competes with her. She didn't have authority. She was the greatest, but she didn't have the authority that Frank had. His voice was that big. It was always Frank and the orchestra."

Burns's colleague, Johnny Mandel, commented on Nelson and Ella's rendition of Burns's composition "Early Autumn" from the *Johnny Mercer Songbook*: "She's listening to the background, and she's blown away. She just loves it, and she's really gotten into it. She's got this beautiful curtain of sound that Nelson set up. It's the kind of sound he got on *In the Wee Small Hours*—it's very atmospheric. It's one of those times when everything's going right."

Regarding their work on "Midnight Sun," from the same album, Johnny commented, "It's a song with so much content and notes and everything that less is more. And what Nelson's doing here is perfect in my opinion."

Bassist Wilfred Middlebrooks, who worked with Ella Fitzgerald from 1958 to 1963, described an unusual way Nelson had of correcting him on an arrangement written for Ella. "He never said anything. The way he would do it was with humor. If there was a unison part that I had to play with the horns he would draw a picture of a pair of glasses, which meant he'd want me to read that part of it."

To illustrate how prepared Nelson was for a recording session with Ella—and vice versa—Middlebrooks remarked, "On one of the albums, we came back from Lake Tahoe and went right into the studio. We played the arrangements down one time and recorded them. We had no problems whatsoever. Most of the time with Nelson there was never anything wrong. And Ella had such an incredible ear. She always knew all of her arrangements. She was very comfortable with Nelson and complimentary to him."

All told, Ella and Nelson recorded eleven albums encompassing 132 tracks over a period of twenty-three years. They also worked together on television and in concerts in New York, Hollywood, London, San Francisco, Washington, Minneapolis, Detroit, Ravinia (outside Chicago), and other cities. From the beginning, next to Nat Cole, Nelson liked and respected Ella Fitzgerald more than any other artist he ever worked with.

During this period of intensive writing, which was also giving him both artistic and commercial acceptance, Nelson was saddened by the death of his father from emphysema in February 1960 at the age of sixty-nine. Chris Riddle remembers that he personally put several quarters in Nelson, Sr.'s coffin during the viewing. As he related, "This was to replace all the quarters I got from him over the years."

★ ★ ★

After having scored *Our Town, Johnny Concho, St. Louis Blues, Li'l Abner,* and *Can-Can* (the last two movies having resulted in Oscar nominations), in 1960 Nelson ventured into weekly network television scoring. His first project was to write the music for the pilot of *Route 66* for Screen Gems, then the television division of Columbia Pictures. For another Screen Gems show, *Naked City,* Billy May wrote the original theme and scored the show for most of its four seasons on the air, but he grew tired of the grind of turning out cues and variations on the show's theme week after week. He later said, "Good God, there's only an eight-bar melody in there. How many times could I turn it around? If I'd known the show was going to be a hit, I'd have written a more complicated theme."

These two programs averaged nineteen to twenty minutes of music for each hour-long episode. Herbert B. Leonard, the executive producer of both shows, insisted that each episode had to be scored with original music. Therefore, the musicians were doing well financially for their work, but it was a laborious chore for the weekly composer.

Jack Lee introduced Nelson to Eddie Forsyth, the post-production executive who supervised the music for all of the Screen Gems shows. Forsyth recalled, "In the fall of 1961, about a year after Nelson started working for me, I was mentioning my problems one day to him with Billy, and he said, 'I want the job!' I had Nelson working on scoring the weekly episodes of *Route 66* at the same time.

"I told him, 'You're mad, man. You can't do that. My God, that's double the load, forty minutes of original music!' But I knew he could do it. The man was an incredible talent. At the same time I thought I was leveling a death penalty," he said laughingly. "But he begged me, 'No, I want to do it.' He was a workhorse."

Forsyth was pleased with how perfectly Nelson captured the feeling of New York in his music. Nelson went on to score those episodes of *Naked City* that Billy didn't want to work on. "Nelson thought it was creatively important to use Billy's original *Naked City* theme and his cues," Forsyth said. "That meant Billy would continue to get performance royalties. In those days, writing the title theme of a network television series was good for $10,000 a year. Of course, now the figure is astronomical."

Toward the end of the 1961–62 *Naked City* season, Nelson wanted to write his own theme for the series. After conferring with Leonard, Forsyth got the go-ahead to use Nelson's new theme, which was also recorded for Capitol but was never used on the soundtrack.

"In the course of writing four years of *Route 66* plus his work on *Naked City,* Nelson's thematic content was never repetitive," Forsyth declared. "He wrote individual themes for individual situations."

Some observers felt that Nelson created a new trend in television scoring with his work on *Route 66.* Nelson, however, said, "It was Henry Mancini who really set a trend in TV writing for me by his use of jazz in all the most impossible situations where it would never have been used previously. His utter disregard for what was going on, constantly [writing music] *against* the scene created quite a good thing for him."[14]

In his writing, Nelson was faced with constant deadlines. Forsyth remembered how obligated Nelson was to Frank Sinatra during the presidential campaign in the fall of 1960, which often caused problems. Sinatra would call Nelson, and Nelson would tell Forsyth, "I've got to go." This meant having to cancel recording sessions for shows about to go on the air and then rescheduling them when Nelson flew off to New York to back Sinatra at a Kennedy rally. To save time, Forsyth would spot the music (decide where it belonged on the soundrack) for Nelson, and Nelson came to rely on his judgment.

While supervising the music at Screen Gems, Forsyth introduced Nelson to Naomi Tenen (originally Tenenholtz), who had come into his office one day in search of a job. She was hired as Nelson's secretary and became very important to him in the next few years, assuming firm control of his business life.

Actually, Tenen had originally met Nelson in 1954, while she was working for Jack Denovic, the producer of *The Telephone Hour,* a local television variety show where Nelson was the bandleader. She had dinner with him twice during that period.

Forsyth described Tenen as "a very difficult personality. It was hard for me to figure out the depth of understanding between Nelson and Naomi. Their relationship was incomprehensible to me and to his contemporaries. The musicians called her 'The Gray Ghost.' She had such a negative personality that it affected everybody in the [recording] band. She was the biggest wet blanket I ever encountered. You just got depressed being in her presence." One recording executive who was working with Nelson on a project mentioned that his assistant hated calling Nelson's office because she would have to deal with Tenen.

Forsyth went on to describe how dark Nelson's office suite was kept, with no sunlight coming in—something I recalled from when I first met Nelson. The oppressive atmosphere in the office was perhaps not only indicative of the dark aspect of Nelson's personality, but also reflected his secretary's biting and sarcastic nature.

★ ★ ★

Nick Sevano took over from Carlos Gastel as Nelson's manager in 1960. Previously, Sevano had been Nelson's agent at Goldstone-Tobias. Mickey Rudin, Sinatra's lawyer for many years, said, "Nelson wanted Nick because he had worked with Frank." This was only part of the reason. Sevano had relationships with the music supervisors at the movie studios, which meant important potential work for Nelson.

Among the jobs Nick secured for Nelson was writing the score for Frank Capra's last film, *Pocketful of Miracles,* which he never completed. He recalled, "Nelson never finished it because Frank Capra told me about the problems Nelson was having at home and how his wife was ill, so I put Walter Scharf on the picture."

Shortly after that, Nelson began to assume an even greater load of weekly television scoring work; he had not only *Naked City* and *Route 66,* but later the Desilu production of *The Untouchables* and others. According to Sevano, "He begged me to get those jobs."

Nelson's theme for *The Untouchables,* which concerned Elliot Ness's crusade to destroy the Al Capone gang in Chicago, was one of the most fitting and identifiable weekly television themes ever written. It received a Grammy nomination in 1960 in the category of Best Sound Track Album or Recording of Music Score from Motion Picture or Television. *The Untouchables* had a long life in syndication after its four-year run, which was halted by congressional pressure concerning violence on television. Nelson never really scored the series, however, as the music was derived from music library sources.

It appears evident that Nelson saw the dissolution of his marriage with Doreen and the financial calamity that lay ahead of him. I remember being concerned at the time that this incredible amount of weekly television work plus film scoring and recordings would have an adverse effect on Nelson's health, but Sevano explained that he had others ghostwriting for him. Recalling this period of intense work, Sevano said, "You know Nelson had that fear he was going to lose it. He didn't realize how good he was. He never realized that he had a tremendous range. He had to have the money. In some respects, he hurt himself. He was doing too much.

"I also remember that in those years Naomi made out the [commission] checks. She wasn't prompt with her payments. I wasn't concerned about being stiffed by any means, but she knew how to stall things."

What Sevano was referring to in this instance was that Naomi saw herself as the gatekeeper at Nelson's office. Although Sevano was his manager and had the job of getting film and television music writing assignments for him, she wanted to exert a measure of control over all his business affairs. Both Buddy DeFranco and Eddie Forsyth mentioned that Jack Lee, who got Nelson and DeFranco the record deal for *Cross Country Suite* and who actually introduced Nelson to Forsyth, was suddenly removed from Nelson's business life because of Naomi's influence on Nelson.

After I had interviewed Nelson for *Los Angeles Magazine* in March 1962, at which time we struck up a rapport, he asked me to call him again in a few weeks to have lunch with him. I waited and called him twice about scheduling a lunch date. Each time I called, Naomi informed me that he was out on the scoring stage, which was close to his office on Columbia's Hollywood lot. I fully believed her, but I never received a return call.

A few weeks later, I saw Nelson at the conclusion of a recording session. When I said hello to him, he asked, "What ever happened to you? I haven't heard from you." I explained what had happened. After that I saw him for a few lunches to discuss publicity. I discovered in the process of conducting interviews for this biography that what transpired with me was similar to what close to a dozen other people encountered.

★ ★ ★

When it debuted in the fall of 1960 on CBS-TV, *Route 66* was an immediate hit, and its leading man, George Maharis, became an instant sex symbol. The show's premise owed something to the coast-to-coast wanderings of Jack Kerouac and Neal Cassady in Kerouac's popular Beat Generation novel, *On the Road*. Maharis and his costar, Marty Milner, traversed the country in their dashing Chevrolet Corvette.

The popularity of Nelson Riddle's theme was another important reason for the success of the show. Capitol Records wanted to capitalize on its popularity. Nelson recorded the "Route 66" theme, which was highlighted by Bob Bain's guitar solo. It peaked at #30 and remained on the *Billboard* pop chart for three weeks.

Nelson characterized his theme by saying, "I think it [captures] the intriguing mysticism which often generates at the beginning of a trip. There's a big question mark, that notion that this is going to be a little different. There is the persistence of sound, of motion, the romance of seeing them drive down this highway."[15]

When the single was recorded, it seemed natural to build an album of other TV themes around it. Tom Morgan produced the single record, the album, and later a sequel. "When we began work on the album, Nelson said to me, 'You choose the tunes. Tell me how you want it done,'" Morgan recalled.

"Lee Gillette was trying to lessen his artist roster. He decided I should work with Nelson. I'd, of course, already produced two albums for Ed Townsend with Nelson. I was concerned about the sound. I remember I suggested bringing in a Fender bass. I wanted to have the Fender bass and the string bass play the same identical notes together, and they would be just a bit off to make an unusual sound. We used that idea on Nelson's version of Billy May's 'Naked City' theme. I had Plas Johnson [normally Nelson's tenor saxophone soloist] play maracas on it, too.

"We needed the *Naked City* theme as a follow-up single to 'Route 66.' I said to Nelson, 'I noticed you wrote the same piano figure in 'Naked City' that you did on 'Route 66.'' He said, 'Well, I thought you wanted kind of the same record.' That's why I featured the maracas to make this version sound different. When I played it for Lee Gillette at the A&R meeting, he said, 'That's the best instrumental I've ever heard.' God, was I proud! Lee wasn't the kind of guy to give compliments, either." It turned out, however, that this sequel to the "Route 66" single and the album *More TV Hit Themes* weren't nearly as successful as the originals.

In the next few years, Nelson's association with Screen Gems led to his scoring several episodes of *The Farmer's Daughter* starring Inger Stevens, as well as the late actress's TV special, *Inger Stevens in Sweden*. He also wrote the music for the pilot and the television series *Wackiest Ship in the Army*; for the series *Redigio*, which aired only briefly; and for the pilot of *The Eve Arden Show*.

While Nelson didn't mind scoring for TV, Doreen did not consider the work important enough. She shared her thoughts on the subject with her children, saying, "Ideally, by 1970 I want your father not to have to do any more of this shit-ass television. Then I want us to move to Europe, where your father can write."

There was still a market in those days for instrumental versions of movie soundtracks and Broadway shows. In spite of the meager sales of his *Oklahoma!* album back in the mid-1950s, Nelson recorded albums of the songs from the films *Can-Can* and *Merry Andrew* (a Danny Kaye comedy which he had also scored), as well as the Broadway musicals *Tenderloin* and *The Gay Life* in 1960 and 1961. These albums were designed to appeal to those who were still dancing the fox trot.

In 1960, Billy May needed one more tune to complete his *Billy May's Big Fat Brass* album for Capitol. He wrote an amusing parody of Nelson's arranging style and his repeated use of counter-melodies, and called it "Solving the Riddle." The song was recorded in a concert version (five French horns and six trumpets plus percussion) and was a dead-on imitation. "Nelson thought it was kind of a left-handed compliment," May laughingly remembered.

Nelson continued to arrange albums and singles for singers. Among them were Anna Maria Alberghetti, who referred to Nelson as "a lovely human being and a stupendous arranger." Despite Nelson's work on her *Warm and Willing* album, she never made the transition from success in opera at a young age to stardom as a pop vocalist.

Another project for Nelson in the early 1960s was *This Time I'm Swingin'!* with Dean Martin, which, in my opinion, was the most musically successful album Martin ever recorded. The album was recorded in 1960, four years after the much talked-about split between Martin and his comedy partner, Jerry Lewis. Martin was still in the process of becoming an important personality on his own following his costarring role with Sinatra in *Some Came Running*. The track "I Can't Believe That You're in Love with Me" from this album was heard over the opening credits of the 1996 independent film *Swingers,* and their version of "Ain't That a Kick in the Head" is currently heard in a Pacific Bell television commercial.

Frank Sinatra showed up in the studio to supervise Martin's interpretations of Nelson's splendid arrangements. Dean Martin fascinated Sinatra because Martin was naturally funny and Sinatra simply wasn't. Despite having the best comedy writers to work with, Sinatra didn't have the timing, much less the comic delivery, that Dean Martin had. Martin parlayed nonchalance into an art form.

Alan Wright, editor and publisher of the Nelson Riddle newsletter *Nelson's Notes,* described Nelson's musical approach on *This Time I'm Swingin'!* as his applying "a very gentle swinging style totally compatible with Dean's relaxed approach" and "in some ways a parody of Sinatra's *Songs for Swingin' Lovers* and *A Swingin' Affair.* Performances of "I Can't Believe That You're in Love with Me," "On the Street Where You Live," "Please Don't Talk About Me When I'm Gone," and particularly "Just in Time" stood out. In 1961, Nelson teamed up with Martin again for *Cha-Cha de Amor,* which was mediocre at best.

Jeannie Martin, Dean's second wife, said, "I think Dean's best recordings were made with Nelson. I really never knew Nelson very well. I would love to tell you about their rehearsing together at our home, but that never happened. Dean didn't believe in rehearsing for his recording sessions."

★ ★ ★

Although Rosemary Clooney had left weekly television by the early 1960s, she and Nelson continued to work together while maintaining their affair. *Rosie Solves the Swingin' Riddle* was the provocative title of their 1961 RCA Victor album, which was also a twist on the title of Billy May's composition. The opening track, Lerner and Loewe's "Get Me to the Church on Time" showed how perfectly Clooney fit in with Nelson's orchestra and how she understood his intentions in his writing and the nuances in the band's phrasing. Her work with Nelson here was reminiscent of the best combinations of female singers with bands—Helen Forrest with Harry James, Jo Stafford with Tommy Dorsey, and Doris Day with Les Brown.

There were several other standout tracks on this album. One was Clooney's version of Arthur Schwartz and Howard Dietz's "By Myself," which had been revived by Fred Astaire in the MGM musical *The Bandwagon*; her version contributed even more toward the rediscovery of this poignant ballad. Nelson wrote one of his trademark arrangements, which began at a slow tempo and then built to a dramatic peak before trailing off. Another important track was the familiar jazz tune "Limehouse Blues," in which Nelson displayed his sardonic humor in musical terms by his use of a gong in the arrangement, which Clooney sang with obvious delight.

The most outstanding of the three albums they recorded together, however, was *Love,* which celebrated their love affair and was coincidentally recorded shortly after she and José Ferrer separated. Clooney selected all of the songs. *Love* was recorded in 1961, at the height of their relationship, and, inspired by Nelson's superb writing, Clooney turned in the most passionate performance of her entire recording career.

The sincerity with which Clooney conveyed the personal meanings inherent in such ballads as her longtime neighbor Ira Gershwin's lyric for "Someone to Watch over Me" and Walter Gross and Carl Sigman's "How Will I Remember You?" indicated exactly how autobiographical the songs were. The latter is very likely her most stirring and *personal* performance.

Nelson used a full orchestra, which included twenty-three strings plus harp, brass, and reeds to tell the story. The album's annotator, Jim Gavin, quoted Clooney as saying, "The sessions were just intensely emotional. When we got a good take, everybody knew it."

Multi-Grammy Award–winning engineer Al Schmitt, who worked on the album, recalled, "You could see [that] the relationship between Nelson and Rosie was special—it wasn't just arranger and singer. There was a lot of touching, and whenever there were breaks they were together talking."

Due to Clooney's slumping record sales, RCA shelved the *Love* album. It was finally released by Reprise in September 1963, but it wasn't until 1995 that Warner Bros. Records's Gregg Geller decided that it should be released on CD. It was only then that it received long overdue attention.

Clooney told Terry Gross, host of NPR's *Fresh Air,* "He [Nelson] was the first arranger who really looked at the words to a song and asked what they meant to me. . . . He understood my feelings about what I was trying to say or sing. He would advance that. If there was something difficult to sing, if it was to be full out at the top of my range, he would have seven brass under it so that I would have such support. . . . He knew when to slow down, when I had to make a point dramatically. He knew that moment. I never worked with anyone—ever—who could do that."

Continuing her interview with Gross, with regard to the fact that their love affair had to be conducted in a clandestine manner, Clooney said, "[The feelings] could be let out in the songs. They had to be pent up in our everyday living, but not in the music—never in the music."

★ ★ ★

On August 26, 1961, Bob Bain married Judi Clark. This second marriage followed the death of Bain's first wife, Jean. The wedding ceremony took place at the Church of the Good Shepherd in Beverly Hills, and Doreen and Nelson acted as matron of honor and best man. After enjoying a wedding dinner at the home of their friends, screenwriter Jim and Sue Webb, the newlyweds spent their wedding night at the Beverly Hills Hotel.

They were abruptly awakened by a telephone call from Doreen at 5:00 A.M. Bain recalled, "She sounded like she was out of her nut. She said, 'You've got to come down here and get Chris [who was not yet eleven and whose middle name was Robert, named after Bob] because Nelson just left me, and I don't know what I'm going to do.'" The Bains quickly got up and drove to Malibu.

They learned that as Nelson and Doreen were beginning the drive home after the wedding dinner, Nelson had announced, "I'm leaving you tonight." Doreen was in such a state that she tried to jump out of the car in the middle of traffic. Nelson managed to get her back in the car, but when they reached home they had another serious row, and he abruptly left.

"We picked up Chris," Bob said. "We dropped him off at Judi's aunt's house in Fullerton on our way to San Diego for our honeymoon. After that, [Doreen's] drinking got bad. She would call at various hours of the night and want to talk. I tried to talk to her, but she was going around in circles. Finally, I would hang up and leave the phone off the hook."

When it was obvious that there was a true separation, Doreen said to the children, "Daddy has to go away now." Speaking of his mother and father's relationship, Skip Riddle remarked, "They were terribly wrong for each other, except in the beginning. She had found a purpose in life, and he found somebody who would take care of him. In those days she absolutely adored him."

Looking at his father's way of conducting his marriage, Skip Riddle said, "He was able to say 'Fuck you' to my mother by having affairs. He was able to hurt her by going to the extent of rubbing her nose in it. That was his way of saying, 'Stop behaving badly toward me.' He couldn't say that out loud to her. It always had to be indirect. It fed a thing that he had that began when he was a kid. His mother wanted him, his father wanted him, his wife wanted him, and his girlfriend wanted him. . . . 'I've got it all. I'm back into familiar ground again.'

"As a teenager," Skip said, "I found out my way of having a relationship with my dad was to be his priest. The same with my mom. They talked to me about their angst and their frustrations."

After a few weeks, Nelson wanted to talk to Barbara Ernest in person. "When we met," Barbara recalled, "I asked him, 'What do you want? You can't have your cake and eat it, too.' He said that he and Doreen were going to have a meeting over lunch at a hotel in Malibu. I said to him, 'That's not real life, that's storybook life. Come home, figure it out. . . .' He was very weak. He had so much to offer. I ended up being very angry at him, although I must say he was scared to death to divorce Doreen. He said, 'I'll be ruined.' It was all about him—ruination, gloom, gloom. Well, it takes two to tango!

"'He's stupid,' we used to say, because he was so damn dumb. He wasn't an evil person. He did things that you shouldn't be able to get away with," Ernest concluded. Within a few weeks, Nelson left the apartment he had rented in Santa Monica and went back home.

Another person who knew Nelson and Doreen well during this period was Laura Mako, who for many years has been a well-established interior decorator in Beverly Hills. During this period she lived on Carbon Beach in Malibu as well as in Beverly Hills.

"Doreen didn't want to practice birth control. That was their big problem when I came into the picture," Mako remarked. "Nelson was trying to paint the house when they lived in Carbon Canyon. The house was kept in terrible shape. I felt sorry for Nelson. He was having a struggle. I went down to his office one day to pick up a check. I asked him if Doreen drank, and he said, 'Yes, it's a problem.' He also told me about his love for Rosemary Clooney.

"Nelson was a very sincere, down-to-earth man, and I loved his music," she continued. "He wanted to pull his marriage together and fix up the house and try to make something of it. But I must say that the house and the yard were a shambles. He tried hard to be a good father."

On the night of February 17, 1962, while Mako was remodeling the interior of their Carbon Canyon home, the Riddle family temporarily moved to a house on Pacific Coast Highway. Chris remembered that on that night, "My mother heaved a flower pot at my father and missed. I later asked her about that. She said, 'If I had wanted to hit him, I would have hit him.'" Nelson got into his car very hurriedly and pulled away.

Later that same night, Doreen got into her station wagon, and while trying to locate Nelson in Malibu, hit a parked car and injured two people. She was arrested for drunk driving and lost her license for a year. Nelson made an out-of-court settlement to take care of the damages involved.

Shortly thereafter, Doreen attempted to get in touch with Frank Sinatra, but he wouldn't return her call. He was aware of the drunk driving arrest. Women who drank too much always irritated Sinatra, perhaps because it reminded him of Ava Gardner's behavior when she was drunk.

Laura Mako noted while Henry Mancini—like Nelson—wasn't that comfortable socializing, his wife Ginny learned how to do it. Then as now, attending parties was an important ingredient in being a member of the show business community. Simply speaking, showing up at these parties often led to work. "Ginny was a key part of Hank's success," she said.

Ginny Mancini remarked, "My first recollection of Nelson was that so many men from the Tex Beneke band settled here in California. Jimmy Priddy was a friend of both Henry's and Nelson's. That's how we met Nelson and Doreen. I recall that Nelson was such a gentleman.

"I just think the most important thing is raising your children. And even though there are problems, they are your problems, but Nelson would turn away from them, and I think in desperation Doreen went the direction she did. She couldn't get his attention, I guess. Nelson worked far into the wee hours of the morning on his arrangements. I don't think he paced himself very well. I must say that Henry always did."

Mancini had first hit with his themes from director Blake Edwards's *Peter Gunn* and *Mr. Lucky* TV series, which were of considerable importance in bringing jazz into television and motion picture scores. Through scoring films for Edwards, he composed such important songs as "Moon River," "Days of Wine and Roses," and "Dear Heart" along with the hit themes from *Hatari* and *The Pink Panther.* He also composed such other successful movie title songs as "Charade" and "Two for the Road."

Mancini's many hit songs and movie scores led to his successful concert tours with Andy Williams, Johnny Mathis, and other singers that began during the late 1960s. With only two significant hit records, Nelson, on the other hand, was not in a position to be paired with an important singer for concert tours (i.e., he didn't have enough hits on his own to fill up the first half of a concert program). Of course, if relations in the mid-1970s between Frank Sinatra and Nelson had been cordial when Sinatra started doing concerts in a big way, the situation might have been different.

★ ★ ★

In the spring of 1962, Rosemary Clooney's divorce from José Ferrer was granted in Santa Monica Superior Court. She kept the house on Roxbury Drive in Beverly Hills and was to receive $1,500 per month in child support. Nelson was not named as corespondent in the proceedings.

Nelson was off to London in late May to score *Lolita* for producer James B. Harris, the famed director Stanley Kubrick, and MGM. Naomi reserved rooms for Nelson and Clooney at the Plaza Hotel in New York, where they celebrated their birthdays before Nelson flew on to London.

Recalling this romantic weekend, Clooney said, "After dinner, we walked along Central Park South on this sweet spring night, holding hands. Near the entrance to the Plaza, on one side of the fountain where F. Scott Fitzgerald [and Zelda] had splashed, we kissed. 'Champagne's waiting upstairs,' I reminded him.

"And, along with the champagne, a message: from the way he sat on the edge of the bed, his shoulders hunched, I knew who'd called. 'My wife,' he confirmed in a subdued, pained voice, 'to wish me a happy birthday.'"[16]

Clooney had begun to weigh the factors of being "the other woman." She remembered saying to Nelson during the course of that weekend, "'I don't think we can keep this up.' 'I think you're right, Rosemary,' he said finally. I waited for him to say the rest, but he never did." The next day at the airport, while they were saying their goodbyes, the singer repeated what she had said the previous night, but nothing definite was resolved.[17]

Clooney wrote to Nelson in London under cover, putting her letter in an envelope addressed to Stella Magee, the secretary who was assigned to work for him in London. In an incredible coincidental twist, José Ferrer later met Stella and married her after his second divorce from Clooney. She is now his widow.

Years later, Clooney said of her romance with Nelson, "I knew that I was in love with this caring man. He was one of the two men in my life who loved me just for myself, as a person. Like Dante DiPaolo, he didn't just appreciate my strengths and overlook my weaknesses; if anything it was the other way around. . . ."[18] Over the years, she said several times, "Except for the birth of my children, my time with Nelson was the happiest of my life."

★ ★ ★

Vic Lewis, the English bandleader and personal manager, began visiting California in 1960 and met Nelson through his friendship with Bill Wagner, then the manager of the Four Freshmen. Lewis and Nelson had lunch at Musso and Frank, where Nelson ate almost every day when he was working in Hollywood. A few weeks after they met, Nelson invited him to Malibu for the weekend. This marked the beginning of a close personal and business relationship. They called one another "Victor" and "Nelly." "I don't think we ever had one cross word in all the time I knew him," Lewis recalled.

"When we met, Doreen was marvelous," he remembered. "I had this cold, and she kind of looked after me. But I could see there was a tension between her and Nelson. That first night I stayed overnight I could hear them shouting at each other."

Early on in their friendship, it struck Lewis that "Nelson was working his fingers to the bone to support his family." He also saw that Nelson never was given anything substantial to compose other than the movie soundtracks he was doing. "I think he was heartbroken that he never got to really write something of importance. I think basically he wasn't confident," said Lewis. Over a period of years, Lewis was helpful in rectifying this situation.

In 1960, Nelson visited Great Britain for the first of several visits. Lewis saw to it that Nelson and Sue Raney appeared on the BBC TV show *The Best of Both Worlds* that summer; he appeared on the same show in 1964 with the fine Australian singer Matt Monro. Raney recalled, "Doreen was going through a very bad time. I noticed how very caring Nelson was with her during the time we spent together in London. He was trying to work on the marriage."

In 1962, when Nelson came to London to score *Lolita,* Vic Lewis also negotiated deals for him to arrange albums for Shirley Bassey (*Let's Face the Music*) and Danny Williams (*Swingin' for You*). As a token of friendship, Nelson arranged Lewis's tune "I Can't Get You out of My Mind" for the Bassey album. He and Bassey did several concerts together in Scotland as well.

One night during this particular visit to London, Nelson dropped in on a recording session for Frank Sinatra's album *Great Songs from Great Britain,* arranged by the Canadian-born arranger, Robert Farnon. Farnon, who has long been respectfully referred to by musicians as "The Governor," related that unfortunately this was the only time he ever met Nelson.

After one of Nelson's recording sessions, Lewis told Nelson that he would be glad to drop him off at the Westbury Hotel, where he was staying. Nelson asked him to instead take him to Claridge's. He explained that Rosemary Clooney was staying there, referring to her as "the girl of my dreams" and "the girl I'm in love with."

A few days later, Lewis and his wife Jill joined Nelson and Clooney for dinner together several times. Doreen found out about Nelson's liaison with Clooney during this visit to London when, one morning at 5:00 A.M. London time, she drunkenly called Nelson at his hotel, only to discover that he was not in his room.

★ ★ ★

Stanley Kubrick had admired Nelson's artistry in *In the Wee Small Hours* and *Only the Lonely.* This was the basis of his interest in hiring Nelson to score *Lolita,* his film version of Nabokov's licentious novel. The veteran film composer Bernard Herrmann, who Nelson revered, had turned down the job. Nelson had Gil Grau join him in London to work closely with him on the film. Nelson's enjoyment of the film scoring process is shown by the statement he made in a radio interview with Jonathan Schwartz: "Scoring for pictures was better than just making other composers rich," decrying his status as merely an arranger for hire.

During the film scoring process, Kubrick and James B. Harris were both overly cognizant of not allowing any hint of depravity in the music. Harris was bothered by the fact that Nelson had written the main theme of his score in a minor key. The musicians were suddenly ordered to cease playing as he and Kubrick conferred with Nelson. They wanted a simple love theme; they believed any form of dissonance in the music would make Humbert Humbert appear too lascivious to the audience. It was decided that Bob Harris, James's brother, should write the main theme for the film.

As it turned out, Nelson's score was one of the few original film scores ever written for a Kubrick film.[19] His popular "Ya Ya" theme written in collaboration with Harris perfectly captured the humor of Humbert's lust for the teenybopper, and the twanging guitars he used as a backdrop predated the sound of pop music that was to sweep America within two years. In retrospect, I'm struck by the satirical edge to the piece; it appears as though Nelson wrote it as a less than subtle putdown of the rock generation.

Nelson followed *Lolita* with the films *Come Blow Your Horn, Paris When It Sizzles,* and *What a Way to Go!* during 1962 and 1963. *Paris When It Sizzles* was intended to be a sophisticated love story featuring Bill Holden and Audrey Hepburn, who were rekindling their real-life romance from when they made *Sabrina* years earlier. Unfortunately, the film was bogged down by Harry Kurnitz's tedious and uninvolving screenplay. Nonetheless, Nelson was obviously greatly moved by Hepburn's gamine charm and wrote a delightful Gallic-sounding theme for her character of Gabrielle.

Perhaps if the film had received creditable notices it might have helped elevate "Gabrielle" to hit status. One of the lingering curses of Nelson's career was his realization that he never was associated with a certifiable box office smash, unlike his colleague Henry Mancini, who had the gift of being not only prolific but also the composer of hit songs from many of the movies that he scored.

What with Nelson's series of successful musical undertakings with various singers, it was only natural that the newly emerging singing sensations were anxious to work with him. It was therefore no surprise that Johnny Mathis and Nelson collaborated in the fall of 1961 on the *I'll Buy You a Star* album, which was released in early '62.

The enduring pop singer began his description of his association with Nelson by saying, "When I worked with Nelson, I was a kid. I was much too young [he was actually twenty-seven]. I never dreamed that he would work with me. If I could do it over again I would certainly do it. . . . The album was less than wonderful. I was going to Max Jacobson, the infamous drug doctor, at the time I was making this album. I was half conscious and half unconscious. I wanted it so much to be wonderful, but it was less than wonderful, and Nelson was so kind. Nat Cole was the reason that I thought I would love to sing with Nelson. In my estimation Nat was Jesus with tonsils, and he never did anything wrong in his entire career.

"Anyway, we did the first album, and a few things turned out all right," Mathis continued. "Nelson wrote a classic version of 'Love Look Away' from *Flower Drum Song*. I still sing it with all the symphony orchestras that I work with. There were several others, like the title song of the album, 'I'll Buy You a Star,' and 'Stairway to the Stars.'

"When I saw Nelson at a function in Hollywood about a year later, he said to me, 'Ya know, John, we should do something else again.' And before I could break out in a grin, he said, 'Because you were awfully unsure of the notes on the first album.' He didn't want to waste his time with someone who didn't get the notes right. I was so happy he gave me a chance to do another recording with him.

"I'll always remember that Nelson treated me as if I knew exactly what he wanted to do. And, of course, I didn't. I was guessing all the way. But fortunately my voice was flexible enough to take advantage of all the wonderful sounds he created orchestrally for me when we made those albums.

"Nelson was as important as the performance of the singer who was singing," Mathis added. "He was a true artist in his own right, and because he had that kind of

The triumvirate of Johnny Mathis, Nat Cole, and Nelson Riddle, photographed in Mathis's hotel suite following his September 21, 1961, opening at the Coconut Grove in Los Angeles. Cole was Mathis's favorite singer; he dubbed him "Jesus with tonsils." Nelson arranged two albums for Mathis.

malleable personality to get along with these inflated egos, that give him even more stature in my estimation."

The second Mathis/Riddle album was *Live It Up,* which unfortunately has never been released on CD. "'Just Friends' is very representative of the best in the album. It's Nelson at his best and me being restrained, and," as Mathis laughed, "for once, not trying to sing every note that I can possibly muster up. "I Won't Dance" is the wonderful song that was immortalized by people like Frank Sinatra. I tried to choose those songs that loped along rather than raced along because Nelson was wonderful with loping songs. . . . I never did what I felt was a definitive record with him, something I could put in front of people and say, 'This is my Nelson Riddle song.' There are, of course, arrangements that Nelson did for me that I take great pride in singing to this day.

"I never saw him after that. The last time I inquired about him I was told he had some health problems, and he wasn't very well. I felt so bad. You have to count your blessings in this business. Even though I didn't get the definitive Nelson Riddle record, I was privileged to be involved with him at one point in his great career, so when I fantasize and think about people of that stature I can get a feeling of fulfillment."

Toward the end of 1962, Nelson began to seriously question his future with Rosemary Clooney. He consulted with Alan Livingston. "You've been through all this [a divorce]," Riddle said. "I need some advice. I don't know what to do." He told Livingston how much he loved Clooney. "It cannot work," Livingston responded. "You don't make enough money to support ten kids. [He and Doreen then had five children and Clooney and Joe Ferrer had another five.] Hard as it may be, you've got to walk away from it some way. . . . It's an impossible situation."

Nelson felt guilty about what he had done to Doreen and also panicked about what divorcing her would mean to him financially. In this period of Nelson's indecision, Clooney had dinner with Frank Sinatra. She asked him if he would intercede with Nelson by persuading him to finally get a divorce from Doreen. Frank gave Clooney the same advice that Alan Livingston had given to Nelson. He, too, felt there were too many children involved to make it work.[19]

Shortly thereafter, Nelson went to see Rosemary and reluctantly told her their relationship had to end. Clooney was doing her own soul-searching; she soon after reconciled with Joe Ferrer and they eventually remarried.

A few years later, Sue Raney was having problems with her mother, who was being terribly controlling. She came to Nelson for advice. It was then that Nelson shared with her his own difficult situation. Raney remembered him saying, "I was madly in love with someone, but it ended. It took me four days of staying alone in this office before I could get over my decision. It was the hardest thing I ever did in my whole life." She knew that he was referring to the end of his love affair with Rosemary Clooney.

The end of the affair did not resolve the lingering problems at home. During the summer of 1964, Nelson brought Doreen, Skip, Rosemary, Chris, and Tina with him to England on the *Queen Mary* after stopping off in New York at the Plaza. While in New York, Nelson took the family to the World's Fair that was taking place that year and also to see Eartha Kitt, who was headlining at the Persian Room of the Plaza.

In one of her rages, Doreen wrecked their stateroom on the ship. Nelson later noted, "What the German Navy was unable to succeed in doing in WWII—sink the *Queen Mary*—your mother nearly accomplished."

He also said, "What the Luftwaffe was unable to do in WWII, your mother almost succeeded in doing when she nearly leveled the Mayfair Hotel in London." There, Doreen tore their entire suite to pieces and threw a large bust of some prominent figure at Nelson, who fortunately ducked. He was afraid it was going to go through the window and hit someone on the head down below. Fortunately, there was bullet-proof glass in the suite's windows.

While in London the family attended the world premiere of *What a Way to Go,* starring Shirley MacLaine, which Nelson had scored. Vic Lewis arranged for them to have a chauffeured Phantom V Rolls Royce limousine at their disposal in London. Afterwards, they toured Ireland, France, and Italy.

★ ★ ★

All through this period and extending to the end of his career, Nelson gained a reputation for snapping relentlessly at musicians. Rosemary Acerra believes, "His viciousness came from his lack of self-esteem." It's also important to realize that Nelson was a perfectionist in the studio.

Buddy DeFranco worked for him frequently, including on all the *Route 66* shows. He recalled that during the television adaptation of John F. Kennedy's Pulitzer Prize–winning *Profiles in Courage,*"I was having problems with my clarinet. Nelson said to me, 'Can't you get the goddamn thing in tune? That's not like you!' It was Tommy Dorsey revisited."

Saxophonist Don Raffell had a major hassle with Nelson at Universal one day over his interpretation of a nine-bar passage. It ended up with Nelson berating Raffell in front of a large orchestra. According to Raffell, this rift resulted in his losing work at the studio for several years. Riddle "regular," trumpeter Shorty Sherock, called Raffell at home after the recording date was over and told him, "Nelson said, 'I don't want to hear the name Don Raffell again the rest of my life.'" The two old friends later made up when they encountered one another at the Musicians' Union on Vine Street. "So I was back in his good graces," Raffell remembered, "but then the same thing happened again.

"I think his intolerance derived from his mother. He had to have something [to complain about] in order to assert himself. He once said to me, 'My notes are solid gold. Don't change one damn thing!' He also had to find a whipping boy. Shorty Sherock was it," Raffell remarked. Sherock commented, "The Nelson Riddle recording sessions began at 8:00 P.M. You were supposed to be able to play high Cs, play with perfect pitch and perfect dynamics right from the beginning." After working six to eight hours before these sessions, the lips of most trumpet players were blown out.

Nelson seemed to be unaware of his thoughtlessness, which sometimes came through even when he was attempting a compliment. One of several off-base remarks in the studio was directed at an Italian violinist whom he used many times: "Before I met you, I thought only Jews could play the violin."

Chris Riddle recalled that while playing the final cues during the scoring of the pilot for Jack Webb's 1972 NBC-TV series *Emergency!*, "Cappy" Lewis, speaking for the trumpet section, raised his hand and asked Nelson, "Would you like to hear that played on flugelhorns?" Nelson replied, "Have you got them with you?" Whereupon Lewis said, "We have them right here." Nelson's response was, "Good! Shove 'em up your ass."

On one record date, a saxophonist, one of Nelson's former colleagues from NBC who occasionally worked for him in the recording studios, listened to Nelson pour out his marital problems. "He told me how he would come home after a record date, and she [Doreen] wouldn't be there. Then she'd storm in and shout obscenities at him and wake him up. It made a nervous wreck of the guy. Even before that, when I did *Johnny Concho* with him, he was kind of putting everybody down. He would embarrass musicians by making smart remarks about intonation."

The saxophonist further recalled having lunch with Nelson at the Brown Derby on Vine Street in the early 1960s. "I told him how a lot of the musicians we both knew were talking about how rough he was in the studios. I told him I thought he'd changed considerably, and not for the better. He didn't take kindly to that. I never saw him again."

Saxophonist and composer Johnny Rotella said, "He always had a salty attitude. . . . You'd never know when it was going to come at you. That's the way he was. But I respected the man anyway. I also remember he never smiled."

"He wasn't like Billy [May]. . . . He wouldn't let himself get out that far," said trumpeter Uan Rasey. "He had tunnel vision. He couldn't laugh at himself—he couldn't see that one's overall life could be happy and that one could have a good time, which would include the music. We even called him 'The Iron Curtain.'

"One time I worked for him near Christmas, and we all thought he was going to break down and say, 'Thank you, guys.' Instead, he said something like, 'If those goddamn saxes had been in tune, we would have gotten out of here a half-hour earlier.'"

With it all, Riddle continued to get prime writing assignments. In 1963 he wrote an album for the Oscar Peterson Trio, arguably the foremost jazz group of that time. The idea for *Oscar Peterson and Nelson Riddle,* released the following year, was conceived when Nelson came in one night to see the Trio perform at the London House, the now-defunct Chicago jazz club, while he was on a Reprise Records promotion tour. He and Peterson discussed how their admiration for one another's work could result in the kind of album which would coordinate both of their musical concepts. Nelson believed that Peterson's pianistics could be presented in a setting not too far afield from the sound of the old Claude Thornhill band.

The album was recorded in three sessions in Hollywood early that November. While attending their initial recording session, I remember how pleased Oscar Peterson was to be able to record on a Bosendorfer grand piano. The first half of the album found Peterson's Trio backed by Nelson's symphonic setting of ten cellos, five French horns, five flutes, a percussionist, and a harpist. The remainder of the album had the Trio backed by a swinging band with strings format.[20]

Peterson praised the experience: "When we went into the studio I was a little bit nervous because the Trio hadn't recorded with a big orchestra in several years. I really liked the way he arranged 'Someday My Prince Will Come.' I thought that was an especially good arrangement. I really enjoyed working with him, and I think the album turned out well."

Nelson said, "I had always admired Oscar's dexterity, his 'star shower' way of cascading note upon note in a dazzling display of technique that impressed many concert pianists. Oscar has a way with harmonies that is particularly his own, and his frequent

The intensity involved in the recording process of the Oscar Peterson and Nelson Riddle album is captured as the two artists work at the Bosendorfer piano.

use of polyphony arouses my own sympathetic vibrations. . . . My favorite [selection] is 'My Ship,' a wonderful standard from the show *Lady in the Dark* [which was] played more slowly than most people would consider tasteful, but, to my way of thinking, permitted Oscar to weave a spell the likes of which I've seldom heard even from him! His own composition "Nightingale" is a standout addition to an album which will remain one of my favorites."[21]

The superb bassist Ray Brown first met Nelson when he came to see the Trio at another jazz club, Shelly's Manne Hole in Hollywood. "Every time we played there Nelson would be in the audience." Regarding the Peterson/Riddle album, Brown noted, "When I heard that sound Nelson created with the French horns, all I know is it was a sound like I hadn't heard before, something really different.

"I also remember that when I first came to town [after Brown left the Peterson Trio] I did a concert with him. He stopped the band right in the middle and said, 'I have a report that this guy I'm about to call down here knows how to play the bass exceptionally well. I haven't heard him do it but I'm going to listen to him right now.'"

A few years later, Brown did all the Sinatra TV specials with Nelson and also worked for him on the Smothers Brothers' CBS-TV show. "Nelson was not a songwriter," he declared, "but he was a prolific arranger of the first order. There ain't nobody any better than him at arranging. He was a bitch!"

Peterson's drummer, Ed Thigpen, my oldest friend in the music business, recalled, "We did a song called 'Judy' on which I had a break of about two-and-a-half beats. The fill was something else. When I heard it played back . . . I wanted to tell Buddy Rich right away. Look out! Of course, when I'd do that I was always putting Buddy on, and he would laugh and say, 'Well, you're getting it.'"

Speaking of Nelson, Ed added, "The man was fantastic. The sound was so lush and his orchestrations were just beautiful, so it was a really wonderful setting for me to be playing his music with that orchestra. . . . But more important to me than all that was his kindness and encouragement . . . whenever he would see me, whether it was playing or whenever we'd run across one another in an airport."

On March 1, 1965, Nelson continued writing in a jazz vein, although in a different context, when he debuted a four-part suite as a vehicle for Buddy DeFranco under the title of *Il Saltimbocca,* subtitled *A Recipe in Music* for presentation by Stan Kenton's Neophonic Orchestra at the Music Center in Los Angeles. Each part of the suite was named for some type of food: 1) "Il Vitello"; 2) "Il Prosciutto"; 3) "Il Spinace"; and 4) "Sono Combinati." It was a one-time experience, and was never recorded. The "high falutin'" plans for the Neophonic Orchestra, which was designed as a repertory orchestra to premiere new works, never jelled, and Kenton returned to the road with his regular band. The popularity of rock music was by then so strong that such an idea had very little chance of succeeding anyway.

★ ★ ★

In an April 1965 *Life* magazine article, Frank Sinatra wrote, "Of the male newcomers, Jack Jones is the best potential singer in the business. He has a distinction, an all-around quality that puts him potentially about three lengths in front of the other guys." Unfortunately, the combination of a lack of drive, the wrong attitude, and the difficulties involved in trying to overcome the onslaught of rock 'n' roll eventually stymied the growth of Jones's career. Still, Jones remains one of the leading singers of traditional pop material today.

Nick Sevano then managed both Jack Jones and Nelson Riddle, which enabled him to convince Kapp Records to record them together in June 1965. Riddle and Jones melded easily on the album, *There's Love and There's Love.* Nelson's romantic strings, French horns, trombones, and flutes were a perfect complement to Jones's treatment of such well-chosen ballads as "The Night Is Young," "Young at Heart," Lennon and McCartney's "And I Love Her," and "True Love." The standout performance on the album was "A Lovely Way to Spend an Evening," where Jones sang with understated passion following Dick Nash's beautiful introductory trombone solo, which was reminiscent of Tommy Dorsey's beautiful sound.

"Nelson knew what the trombone could do, and he wrote there," Dick Nash declared. "When you came into a Nelson date you were on pins and needles, because he was going to tax you. I remember that Jack was having a little trouble hearing this note since it was out of the ordinary. Nelson said, 'It's *this* note!' He started to get mad at him. Jack had to tighten up and get his act together. After three or four takes, he got it right."

But the most *beautiful* album that Nelson ever arranged in his entire career was *The Wonderful World of Antonio Carlos Jobim,* recorded in 1965. It is really the inner workings of the Jobim/Riddle combination—the tenderness and sensuality that predominated throughout this recording—that revealed how much Nelson and "Tom" Jobim were soulmates. And what Jobim melodies! "She's a Carioca," "Agua de Beber," "Surfboard," "A Felicidade," "Bonita," and "Dindi." The latter song, pronounced "gingee," compares favorably with Sinatra's version. Moreover, there is an intrinsic beauty that Jobim brought to his performance as its composer that even Sinatra couldn't quite match.

Nelson used a mixture of flutes, trombones, and strings to perfectly convey the romanticism of the samba. Jobim's Portuguese and heavily accented English vocals and guitar blended seamlessly with Nelson's arrangements.

Albums with two other singers followed Nelson's projects with Jones and Jobim. Eddie Fisher had made a significant comeback after being cuckolded by his wife, Elizabeth Taylor, while she was working on *Cleopatra.* A combination of a bad gambling habit and speed dispensed by Dr. Max Jacobson, however, led to problems with other drugs and caused his ultimate downfall.

Despite all of his obvious problems, RCA Victor still believed in Fisher. Going very much against the grain of pop music in 1966, RCA hired Nelson to work with him on the single record of "Games That Lovers Play." Somewhat miraculously, he and Fisher came up with a semi-hit (#45 on the *Billboard* pop chart).

Al Schmitt produced "Games That Lovers Play" and the album titled after it that followed. "When I called Nelson about being available to arrange the tune, he said, 'Yeah, sure.' When I told him the artist was Eddie Fisher, there was a pause. The feeling I got was that he didn't want to do it, but he said 'Okay,' since it was just the one song I originally wanted him to do. It was Nelson's arrangement that made it successful—the kind of arrangement you would think came from Nelson Riddle.

"We overdubbed Eddie later, otherwise we wouldn't have gotten anything done. I think it was one of the first albums that Nelson did in which the singer overdubbed his vocals. Eddie was blessed with a sound, but he had no sense of time and no sense of pitch," Schmitt concluded.

Many really well-equipped pop singers never made it. Johnny Hartman and David Allyn should have become important singing stars, but unfortunately neither of them did. Vic Damone came considerably closer to becoming a major star, but despite his having the best voice of any pop singer of the postwar generation, it never happened for him either. In 1967, Nelson recorded five songs to make up one side of a Damone album on the obscure Loota label. They were "A Day in the Life of a Fool," "Desafinado," "A Dreamer's Holiday," "Games That Lovers Play" (again), and "Mean to Me," which were finally released on CD on a 1988 British album entitled *Games That*

Lovers Play and again in 1989 on another album called *The Look of Love*. Nelson's writing proved to be rather uninspiring, as was Damone's singing of these tunes.

Nelson's film-scoring career continued despite the fact that he worked on such minor fare as United Artists's poor adaptation of John O'Hara's *A Rage to Live* starring Suzanne Pleshette, for which he was paid $15,000; the "other" production of *Harlow* toplining Carol Lynley; and Paramount's *Red Line 7000*, directed by Howard Hawks, an auto-racing saga starring James Caan.

Nelson was still heavily involved in scoring for weekly television, working on the prestigious NBC-TV series *The Rogues*, with David Niven, Charles Boyer, and Gig Young as the leads. Herschel Gilbert, composer and conductor, was then music director for Four Star Productions that produced *The Rogues* in 1960.

Gilbert recalled, "I was enamored of the way he wrote. He wrote right in the parts—I could never do that—most composers can't do that. In other words, he wrote a trumpet part, wrote a second trumpet part, and wrote a third trumpet part and kept it all in his head. That's a highly advanced way of scoring. He saved all that time and he saved all that money because, in effect, that took care of the orchestration fee as well. You can count the number of people in our business in any given year at five, if that many, who can do that. It seemed to pour out of him."

Gilbert got to know Nelson personally. "He was actually very sweet. That was one of his problems. He was too kind. I remember his once discussing his problems he was having with his ex-wife. He said, 'She's going to get all that money. What am I going to live on?'"

Other weekly series that he worked on in the mid-'60s included *Tarzan* (which did well for him financially because the series played worldwide), *Sam Benedict,* and *Voyage to the Bottom of the Sea*. His well-received soundtrack from *Profiles in Courage* also kept him in demand.

★ ★ ★

America was changing at a rapid pace. Camp entertainment was suddenly "in." A perfect example of this was the television series *Batman,* starring Adam West, which became a national rage in the spring of 1966. The hit theme for the show was written by Neal Hefti, who eventually made enough money on it and his familiar *The Odd Couple* television theme to retire. Nelson scored the show for three years. The emotions expressed by "pow!," "oops!," "bam!," "wham!," and the like were underlined by his musical cues. Though not artistically gratifying, *Batman* did wonders for his BMI (Broadcast Music Incorporated) earnings.

Nelson's work on television was so prevalent that on Rowan and Martin's popular *Laugh-In* show, Dick Martin often concluded his announcements of the week's guest stars with ". . . and Nelson Riddle and his Orchestra." By the mid-1960s, through his various musical endeavors, Nelson was grossing $300,000 a year.

Surprisingly, for the John Wayne/Robert Mitchum Howard Hawks–directed western *El Dorado,* in addition to supplying standard music for a western, Nelson added several contemporary musical touches complete with a flagrant use of guitar and Carol Kaye's perfect Fender bass punctuations. The score also had a Latin flavor because all the action took place in a Mexican border town. The film performed well for Paramount and made Nelson a favorite of Bill Stinson, who then headed the film-scoring department for the studio.

Time magazine's March 17, 1967, review of United Artists's *How to Succeed in Business Without Really Trying* read, "The movie implements Frank Loesser's score with inventive arrangements by Nelson Riddle." Nelson allowed that, "I think I did a good job on it, but I was hampered by the contractual obligations to Frank Loesser, whereby you couldn't change a note."[22] (Shades of Richard Rodgers!)

How to Succeed wasn't a triumph for Nelson, however, because he wasn't given a qualified singer to work with among the cast. And then again, the film version was a rather static duplication of the Broadway musical, which brilliantly satirized the corporate world.

Despite the financial windfall he was enjoying, Nelson's life remained anything but tranquil at home. The Riddles moved to a beachfront house in the Malibu Colony in 1966. Their neighbors included actress Deborah Kerr and her husband, the writer Peter Viertel, as well as actors Jim Hutton, Ben Gazzara and his then-wife Janice Rule, and Dorothy Malone. As he had during his years in the Carbon Canyon house, Nelson swam almost every day. Doreen's drinking continued unabated.

They each consulted with various psychoanalysts plus a marriage counselor, but nothing made life any better. Doreen made it clear to one of her doctors that she wanted Nelson to acknowledge to a much greater degree the sacrifice she had made for him and her children. Nelson, however, once mentioned a sacrifice of another sort when he said to Chris one day, "I spent over $70,000 for psychiatrists for your mother and myself." Looking back on those years, Rosemary Acerra observed, "They went in and played games with their psychiatrists."

From 1960 to 1965, Monsignor James O'Callaghan was the pastor of Our Lady of Malibu, the Catholic church the Riddles attended. According to Father Jim, as he was called, "Nelson was very respectful to our Catholic faith and to me." (Nelson at one time had taken instruction in the Catholic church but never converted; the children attended Catholic school.)

The Monsignor had had a nonreligious background of working at RKO and 20th Century Fox for four years. He had started as a janitor and graduated to working with Fred Astaire and Hermes Pan in RKO's choreography department. "It gave me enough bread to keep going for the priesthood," he said.

Father Jim remembered the time when Fred Astaire, Nelson, and the choreographer Hermes Pan attended a bossa nova concert in Santa Monica (most likely an appearance by Stan Getz in his "Girl from Ipanema" period). "After the concert, they came over to my house for some food. They started discussing the tempo of the bossa nova. Fred and Hermes thought it went one way, but Nelson saw it differently. It was quite a discussion. The next day Nelson called me. He realized that Fred and Hermes were right, and he wanted to tell Fred." It wasn't too long afterwards that Nelson recorded with Antonio Carlos Jobim, and more than a decade later he was to record a tribute album to Fred Astaire.

"Yeah, they [Nelson and Doreen] had problems," said Father Jim. "I hope I advised them properly. They were good people, but they had all those kids!" (Cecily, their fifth living child, was born on January 26, 1960. She now resides in Rancho Mirage, California, with her husband Mike and two children, and is a senior teller at the Bank of America. Maureen, the sixth child, was born on November 16, 1962, when Doreen was forty years old. Maureen is now an associate professor at Rutgers and recently earned her doctorate in Twentieth-Century American Literature and Cultural Studies.

Father Jim remembered that when he left the parish for his current assignment in Hacienda Heights, Nelson tearfully presented him with a painting he had purchased in Italy. He was extremely appreciative of everything the priest had done for him and his family.

As a result of his problems with Doreen, his uncertain future with Sinatra, and the constant pressure of deadlines, Nelson's drinking increased. Don Raffell observed, "He didn't drink when he was young—didn't drink at all. He didn't drink 'til he came out here. No drugs. Oh, he drank. Christ, he drank! I don't know how he could walk around."

Maureen's childhood memories of her mother are of "a screaming harridan." She recalled her mother saying abruptly to Nelson, "I can't be your mother anymore. I've got six children to take care of."

Another major setback for Nelson was the situation that ensued when Charles Brown made several bad investments for him, which resulted in severe income tax problems. This necessitated his taking on an even more substantial load of weekly television shows and arrangements for various singers.

Tax problems notwithstanding, it has often been said that Nelson took too many arranging jobs for too many years at very low fees. Bobby Helfer, who was an important recording contractor, had admonished him about this several years earlier, saying, "Nelson, you're going to be offered a lot of jobs. You're going to have to learn sometimes to say no." Apparently, he never did.

Chris Riddle believes that his father took almost every job offered him because of his terrible lingering memories of the Great Depression. "His idea was you had to take any work offered to you to keep the wolves at bay. Besides writing cheaply, he wrote fast—that was one of his other significant talents, but not necessarily one from which he reaped many benefits."

On top of his other problems, the farm in Tulare run by Virgil and Barbara Ernest suddenly became immersed in financial problems. Barbara Ernest revealed, "The cotton crop failed. We wound up selling the Holsteins. We had to declare bankruptcy in order to get out from under."

Through the years, Naomi Tenen had maintained a good relationship with Doreen and the children. Given her loyalty to Nelson, it was no surprise that, according to several sources, she rented an apartment in her name for Nelson and Rosemary Clooney to use for their assignations. When Nelson encountered his financial setbacks, Naomi and her cousin, who was an accountant, took charge of the situation. It took them a few years, but they finally stabilized his finances. This development only served to tighten the control Naomi exerted over Nelson.

Where once he would take his children to an expensive restaurant like Scandia, Nelson now took them to places like Jack in the Box. In order to provide the fast-food establishment with some degree of cachet, he jokingly referred to it as "Jacques in the Box."

★ ★ ★

Immediately preceding the "Summer of Love" in Haight-Ashbury, the epicenter of hippie culture in San Francisco, the Monterey Pop Festival took place from June 16 to 18, 1967. Such new and innovative musical artists as Jimi Hendrix, Janis Joplin with Big Brother and the Holding Company, Otis Redding, the Mamas and the Papas, and the Grateful Dead emerged from the Festival as stars. The important recording-company moguls were in attendance and immediately grasped the fact that America suddenly had its own homegrown corps of contemporary pop music stars. No longer did they have to count on the steady succession of pop groups—the so-called "British Invasion" of the Beatles, the Rolling Stones, the Dave Clark Five, the Kinks, and the Animals.

Instead, an entirely new kind of music business was at hand. All of a sudden the term *marketing* became of primary importance. The question became, "How do we tap into the biggest youth culture in the history of the country (the baby boomer generation)?"

Middle-aged executives removed their ties and jackets for good, started wearing tight-fitting shirts and bell-bottom trousers, and wore their hair well over their shirt collars, often in Prince Valiant style. Their necks were often adorned with beads or gold chains—anything to look young. Suddenly, records (or "product"), if they were outstanding, were labeled "far out," aping the parlance of the jazz world. If a record wasn't successful in the marketplace, it had "stiffed."

"They didn't want the ballads, the prettiness—they wanted '60s caca because '60s caca was what was happening and selling," observed Emil Richards. "Swing was on the back burner, way on the back burner. . . . There were other guys that were doing what Nelson could do in a more contemporary way, like Quincy Jones and others. There were no more upright bass players, and the one guitar player on a recording session became eight or ten guitar players on every session!"

The great popular music tradition of the past forty years was coming to an abrupt end. With this development came a decrease in the demand for even the most talented exponents of this tradition, including Nelson Riddle. It was obvious that indeed "the times, they [were] a-changin.'"

CHAPTER 8

The Difficult Years

Despite the fast-changing state of the music business, Nelson was hired by the producing team of Saul Ilson and Ernie Chambers to be the musical director of *The Smothers Brothers Comedy Hour* during the 1967 and '68 seasons on CBS-TV. In those days, the job of musical director of a network variety show could still be given to a musician from the pre-rock era.

Saul Ilson recalled, "I first met Nelson Riddle when I was a junior writer on a Bing Crosby special in 1960. Our relationship started out in a unique manner because I think Nelson was appalled by me. I'd come from Canada and this was my first venture in Hollywood. I told him the tempos were wrong in a spot I'd written for Bing and Johnny Mercer on this ABC-TV special. He said, 'I know in most cases you want it to swing, but I think it has to have an edge to it, and not only that, all the tempos should remain the same, no matter what the song is.' When I think about it now, I shudder. Here I am telling him about it, and he's saying, 'Okay, okay.' Later on I learned that he couldn't believe it, he was so stunned. Anyway, he went ahead and changed it to what I suggested, and it worked."

After that awkward beginning, Riddle and Ilson worked together on another ABC-TV special, this time with Crosby and Maurice Chevalier. During the preparation for the show, Nelson invited Saul to his Malibu home for a meeting and dinner. When he met Doreen, "I remember thinking, frankly, 'She's drunk.' She was slurring her words. I left their home that night on my way to the [San Fernando] Valley feeling sad and very depressed."

Shortly thereafter, Ilson produced the CBC-TV special, *The Swinging Sound of Nelson Riddle,* on which Rosemary Clooney was a guest star. During rehearsals, Nelson approached him, saying, "Listen, I've been rehearsing the script, and I want to know, do you want me to say exactly what's written?" "It's funny you should ask," Ilson replied. "The musicians were asking, 'Do you want me to play exactly what you wrote?'" Nelson said, "I get the message."

Preceding page: Nelson's concentration and anguish are captured as he listens to a playback at a recording session from the 1960s.

Nelson Riddle and Rosemary Clooney during a CBC-TV special in the early 1960s.
The happiness they shared is captured in the photograph.

Upon being signed to produce for the Smothers Brothers, Ilson immediately informed Tommy Smothers that he wanted Nelson as the show's musical director. "Tommy was excited. He loved the work Nelson had done for Sinatra. In fact, Nelson had appeared with Frank on one of his specials about a month before.

"When I first spoke to Nelson about the job, I said, 'I don't think you'll want to do this show. It's a comedy show. I don't know how much music there's going to be. . . .' He said, 'No, no, I'd like to do it.' We paid him $5,000 a show with twenty-six shows—plus arrangements. I think he got half of that for reruns. He'd write six to ten arrangements a show."

Tommy Smothers and his brother, Dick, had first emerged during the folk era of the early 1960s. Their musical sensibilities weren't necessarily in line with Nelson's kind of music, yet Tommy spoke of Nelson with great affection. "I was a stickler for perfect sound, so I put the orchestra in a separate room. [Bassist Max Bennett called it "Smothering Heights" because it was located in the basement.] I used to spend a lot of time watching Nelson rehearse with the musicians. He was all business, but he always had a twinkle in his eye. I would just revel in the sound of the orchestra and marvel at what Nelson accomplished."

Proving once again that appearances can be deceiving, Tommy Smothers added, "Anyone with the creative spark that Nelson had had to have some great joy in his life."

His obvious affection for Nelson was shown in a comedy skit on *The Smothers Brothers Comedy Hour* in which Tommy and Nelson played a duet, the cohost on harmonica and Nelson, of course, on trombone. Nelson's inability to handle himself as the foil for an experienced comedian was highly apparent. This was compounded by his outwardly gruff manner. Tommy played his usual low-key, deadpan self, and Nelson, unfortunately, had to carry the scene. Still, he saved it musically by illustrating his basic ability as a trombone player.

Trombonist Kenny Shroyer, a member of the Smothers Brothers Orchestra, recalled that Nelson looked out for musicians who needed help. Shroyer called Nelson, "a really ethical guy and humane. He used some guys in the saxophone section who were kind of down on their luck. There were a couple of black guys and a Spanish guy named Anthony Ortega. Nelson didn't know him that well." Riddle also used trumpeter Maynard Ferguson, who was going through bad times but would later re-form his band and go on to pop jazz stardom, and pianist Arnold Ross, who was coming back from years at Synanon, one of the first major rehabilitation centers for drug addicts.

★ ★ ★

Cecily Riddle Finnegan recalled, "Moving to the [Malibu] Colony from Carbon Canyon, from what I hear [she was only seven years old at the time], only made things worse. They didn't leave anything [any of their problems] at Carbon Canyon—they took it all with them, and they were magnified. Some of my earliest memories . . . are standing at the top of the staircase . . . hearing what was happening. And it was what many divorces unfortunately bring: fighting and breaking things and yelling and crying.

"Mom would forgive him over and over and bring him back into their bed, and then he would betray her again. . . . If he were late from work, even if he were working, I'm sure she would just assume the worst and then the drinking would start. Even if he was half an hour late, she'd already just wallowed in the fact that he was probably with somebody else and had drunk too much. . . . By the time he walked in the door, she was ready for a battle. Why would he want to come home? It was all like a cycle.

"I definitely remember my dad coming home and one of the first things he'd do was put me on his shoulders and we'd walk around the house and clap my feet together 'til I would scream. . . . He must have read Mother Goose to me every night for I don't know how long, cover to cover, and then back again and back again. . . . I always remember the time he spent with me as being special, so all I can relate today is that those times must have been few and far between; they must not have happened very often."

Chris Riddle remembered the night of April 20, 1968, when Nelson left home for the second and last time. "He shouted to Mom downstairs, 'You had to have all those kids!' My brother and my sisters looked at each other and thought, 'He must mean you. He couldn't be referring to me!' . . . I helped him get his suits together to put in the car."

Cecily also remembered the pain associated with that night. "It was raining and we were all outside. My mother hung on to the car [door handle] and tried to stop him from leaving as he pulled away. Daddy was driving a brand-new burgundy Cadillac convertible." Chris recalled that his father was so angry that he backed up over a series of speed bumps in order to get out of the Malibu Colony as fast as he could.

"It must have taken awhile for visitation [rights] because I think there was quite a period of time when I didn't see my dad," Cecily added. "Maybe it was only six months. And then they set something up so we could see him every Wednesday and every other weekend. . . . Almost inevitably it was Knott's Berry Farm or Disneyland —something wonderful—and then you would come home to a very angry mom a lot of the time. . . . I hated coming home. She very often had been drinking all day, and she was in so much pain."

Nelson was equally hurt by the final breakup with Doreen. After concluding a rehearsal late one afternoon, toward the end of the first season of *The Smothers Brothers Comedy Hour,* he came into Saul Ilson's office at CBS Television City and blurted out, "I don't think there's anything left for me." "You're a lost soul," Ilson replied. "I've been a lost soul for a long time," Nelson responded.

There were also humorous moments when Nelson tried to hide his pain. Ilson recalled the time in 1968 when his partner, Ernie Chambers, was lonely and going through his own divorce. One evening at Nelson's apartment on Fountain and La Cienega in West Hollywood, the three colleagues did quite a bit of drinking that went on until two o'clock in the morning. "Ernie said he'd move in with Nelson if he would be his friend. Ernie was trying to persuade him that he needed a friend. Nelson said, 'No, I'm not committing to that. I won't be your friend. I don't find you good company. I don't personally like you very much.'"

Ilson, in an attempt to negotiate, said, "Can't you at least be his friend part of the

Photo courtesy of the Nelson Riddle Memorial Library at the University of Arizona School of Music and Dance, Tucson, Arizona, and the Naomi Riddle Estate.

Nelson conducting. His limited ability as a conductor never approached his extraordinary talent as an arranger.

time?" but Nelson protested, "No, I don't want to be his friend," and then, with a hint of a smile, said, "He can be my neighbor."

"Nelson was the kind of guy who would give just a *soupçon* of a smile," Chambers remembered. "Very rarely would he burst out laughing, but the one thing I loved was when he did smile. He had that wonderful, wonderful smile."

"For a guy with such a [musical] gift, I think his self esteem was in the toilet," Ilson opined. "I never knew anyone who knew so little about himself. I think he knew what to do musically—I'm not talking about his career, he was a genius—but what to do with himself, that was another thing. I told him one night what I felt, and I think it really hurt his feelings. Another time I said to him, 'You're Nelson Riddle! Don't you know who you are?' He said, 'Yeah, yeah, yeah. That's *that* world,' pushing it aside. How can a man have any self-esteem about his personal life when he has no self?

"It was so interesting to me," Ilson noted. "We would be sitting having a conversation, drinking coffee, and we'd sit and we'd talk. . . . He was a festival of sadness. I could see the sadness coming out of his pores.

"And then the music contractor would come over to me and say, 'Okay, five's up!

224 SEPTEMBER IN THE RAIN

Let's go!' I'd watch Nelson walk over to the podium and a transformation took place. . . . I loved the way he conducted. Moving within a radius of maybe three inches! And a cigarette sometimes hanging out of his mouth. . . . But to me, the man was conducting and a sound was coming out. I enjoyed his creativity. He never let me down. Even when he wrote some little comedy piece it would be right on the button, and it wasn't a cliché. It had that feeling."

"He had such a phlegmatic, stoic kind of personality," Ernie Chambers said of Nelson. "The only thing I know is that he was incapable of dealing with interpersonal relationships—he just didn't have it in him. He couldn't stand up to a strong woman. For the richness, romanticism, and emotion of the arrangements he wrote, as a person he was just a real flat guy—laconic, about as animated as an animatronic figure in a department store window. You could never dream that they could come out of this man. Obviously, he was a romantic inside."

★ ★ ★

Vibraharpist Terry Gibbs led sextets for Steve Allen and Regis Philbin on their television shows during the early and mid-1960s. In 1968, he was signed to lead a sixteen-piece band on the ABC-TV show *Operation Entertainment,* which emanated from Army and Navy bases on Friday nights. "I wanted to prepare myself for my new job, so I studied with a symphony conductor," Gibbs recalled.

"Now, the difference between conducting symphonic music and conducting television music—everything is on the nose in television. There's no preparation—you don't have time—cue, boom, right into it, whereas with symphonic music you can give them a preparatory beat. You have to lift your arms in a certain way so the whole band knows where you're at. After studying awhile, I figured I'd go and watch some of the heavyweight conductors and see what they were doing. I went over to watch Nelson Riddle conduct for the Smothers Brothers.

"Every time he lifted his arm, I couldn't figure how the musicians came in. I never knew where he was. I went to Irv Cottler, who was playing drums for Nelson on the show and who was Frank Sinatra's drummer, and I said, 'Irv, how do you know when to come in?' He said, 'When he lifts his arms up in the air, the moment they go up in the air, before they come down, we come in. Conrad Gozzo [the lead trumpeter] and I come in, the whole band comes in, and we're perfect.'"

"Actually, Irv was taking it away from Nelson," Gibbs said. "The musicians didn't follow him at all. He lifted up his arms, and they became the bandleaders. I don't think anybody knew where he was, and I was trying to learn from him!"

Emil Richards related how Nelson, while conducting, would indicate the beginning of an up-tempo musical passage by extending his hands diagonally downward—exactly the opposite of what the musicians would expect. One could conclude that Nelson, despite his obvious musical genius, had somewhat of a problem communicating with his musicians—just as he did with people generally. He made use of his high IQ to write arrangements and compose, yet, as Maureen Riddle put it, "He could figure out a 47-piece orchestra but he couldn't figure out six kids and a wife."

Maureen related another incident which sadly gives even more depth to this observation. At the age of six, she asked her dad, "Was I a mistake?" His response was, "As far as I'm concerned, you were all mistakes."

★ ★ ★

Nelson's obvious discomfort with the "new music" became increasingly apparent. In the spring of 1968, arranger Artie Butler got a call from the late, well-known jazz critic Leonard Feather, who asked if Nelson Riddle could call him. Butler replied, "Of course. Why?" Feather said, "He wants to attend a recording session where they layer the instruments; he's never been to one where they make rock 'n' roll records. . . ."

Butler related, "A couple of days later, Nelson called me. 'Artie. . .' I thought it was a bass trombone. 'It's Nelson. I'd like to come to a recording session to see how you make these modern American records.' I said, 'Nelson, I'd be delighted to have you. Let me get to my next project. I think you'd enjoy watching the process.'

"I don't remember what it was, but it was at a studio right off Sunset Boulevard on McCadden Place. I called the record producer and asked permission for Nelson to attend because he didn't want anybody in to hear their latest, greatest thing, so I wouldn't think of bringing a guest without asking. I brought Nelson in, and he sat there for the full three hours and watched a drummer, a bass player, and a guitar player working on one tune. First we did the drums, then the bass, then the guitar.

"When we had coffee afterwards, Nelson said, 'You're not making records, you're making soup.' We were putting in a little of this, a little of that—that's what he meant by his comment. He was used to the grand old days of the big orchestras, which, thank God, I still get a chance to work with. To him it was just unbelievable because he was used to working with Sinatra and Ella and all the guys in the orchestra. Frankly, we all miss that."

Through their mutual agent, the late Charles Stern, who represented them for commercials, Riddle and Butler got further acquainted. Butler recalled, "I saw him at dinner parties and bar mitzvahs, and at parties at the Magic Castle [the Hollywood club for practicing magicians], where I was a member. I was infatuated with magic. We were sitting in one of the smaller rooms where they do close-up magic. They have maybe fifty to sixty seats where you sit down in a stadium-seating setup. The magician would come out and say, 'What magic tricks would you like me to perform?' Nelson said, under his breath to me, 'I wonder if he can make rock 'n' roll disappear.' I, of course, broke up," Butler recalled. "This was when the Beatles were at their peak."

Another time, at one of Charles Stern's barbecues, Paul Frees, who was then the actor of choice for voiceovers on commercials, told Nelson and Butler the big news about the major rock star (probably Neil Diamond) who was getting $3,000,000 to headline concerts in a new venue about to open in Las Vegas. Nelson quipped, "Yeah, he's getting a million for each chord he knows." The sardonic humor Bill Finegan noted in Nelson back in 1938 was still very much alive in him more than thirty years later.

In a diplomatic yet still condescending *Los Angeles Times* interview, Nelson said, "I'm not identified with rock 'n' roll, but [I] don't sell it short. Think of all those millions of records sold. I've adopted a live-and-let-live philosophy about that type of music. One can't supplant it, but one can concentrate on bucking it with good, well-constituted music."

Butler, who scored the 1992 CBS-TV miniseries, *Sinatra,* stated, "When you talk about arrangers that can swing, you talk about Nelson Riddle and then you list the other arrangers. His arrangements can never be called corny because they don't age. They are like fine wines. They get better, they don't get old. No matter what we write, we took from him. He's as important as oxygen. I don't know a bigger compliment to pay him."

★ ★ ★

Chris, of all of Nelson's children, was closest to him. At the age of eight, Chris started working as the bandboy for his father's casuals—looking after the music, setting up and tearing down the music stands, and serving as an aide-de-camp to his father. "I was his footstool many times," said Chris. Nelson's regulars started referring to him as "Half-Nelson."

He decided to take up the bass trombone and began taking lessons on the instrument from George Roberts at the age of twelve. As Chris explained, "It was a way of being with my father. I think he thought that I was more like him than any of the other children. Not that he cared for me more than any of them, but we had a lot in common. . . ."

Like Chris, Cecily said, "I wanted to be involved in music because I thought it would bring me closer to my dad. I took piano and voice lessons. I see it even more clearly now." She later attended Juilliard briefly, but was homesick for Southern California and returned home. "Part of me wishes I'd stayed because I could have grown as a musician." Cecily spent the next few years working at United Western Recorders, where her father got her a job as a recording engineer.

Regarding learning the etiquette of the recording studio, Chris remarked, "I had the discipline drilled into me at an early age that when the red light goes on you don't say anything to anybody. You don't move, you don't even breathe. . . . My father would come in, the band would be sitting around having a cup of coffee. Of course, there was the usual fumbling around about who was going to sit lead trumpet, and then Conrad Gozzo would walk in two minutes before the session began and Shorty Sherock or "Cappy" Lewis or I guess whomever had selected the lead chair for themselves would graciously slide aside because obviously Conrad was going to play lead. And then my father would start running the charts down to make sure there weren't any copying errors and to make sure the band got the right feel."

Chris recalled when his father was commissioned by the government of British

Columbia in 1968 to write a suite which would serve as a musical portrait of the beautiful and majestic province. He and his father were flown to Victoria and stayed at the Empress Hotel. For a week they were flown all over British Columbia in a twin-engine Piper Cub. Chris took photographs and Nelson took background notes before starting to write the piece. Prime Minister W.A.C. Bennett gave Nelson a beautiful pair of cuff links as a gift that Chris now wears on all of his Nelson Riddle Orchestra dates.

During much of the 1968–70 period, Nelson and Chris lived together, except for a period in 1969 when Chris was studying in London. On his return, he moved in with his father in West Hollywood. Chris remembered, "He had a gorgeous apartment. I thought Dad and I were doing great together. I was taking care of him. He'd come out of the shower, and I'd say, 'Get back in there and wash something.' He would wash his hair and that was it. I had our laundry done and all the rest of it. At the time, I wasn't even twenty yet."

Chris Riddle's first recording session took place on March 29, 1971, when he worked on the Frank Sinatra, Jr., album *Spice* (released by Daybreak Records) and soloed on the title song. After that, even though Nelson was constantly afraid of being accused of nepotism, he began hiring Chris to fill in for George Roberts, who occasionally had conflicting recording dates. On a few occasions, Chris even took jobs that were meant for Roberts.

Even while he provided Chris with opportunities to learn and grow as a musician, Nelson was conflicted about his son coming into the business full-time. In addition, having played the instrument, Nelson admitted, "I'm hard on trombone players." He also hated the business of music, which was perhaps still another reason he was often quick to criticize Chris. Among other things, he didn't want Chris to face the uncertainties of employment and the music business politics that he had faced.

Two musicians told me of separate occasions when Nelson tore into his son, once for playing a musical passage that wasn't to his liking, and another time for failing to bring his tuba when it was required for a particular recording date. Both times he reprimanded Chris in front of the entire orchestra, rather than taking him aside. Despite his father's harshness, however, Chris was insistent on becoming a musician. One of the musicians believes strongly, "Chris was always looking for something that Nelson was never going to give him, and that was approval."

Approval was something Chris absolutely did not get from Buddy Rich. In 1972 Nelson called Rich, with whom he had worked in the Tommy Dorsey band, to ask if Chris might join his band, which would enable Chris to gain valuable experience. Rich agreed, and before Chris left Los Angeles to fly to St. Louis to join the band, Nelson asked George Roberts to give him a quick lesson. Chris drove over to George Roberts's home in Pacific Palisades. At the completion of the lesson, Roberts knew he wasn't ready to face the volatile bandleader. True to his prediction, Chris lasted one set and flew home the next day.

Nelson Riddle stands proudly between his good friend, bass trombonist George Roberts, and his son, Chris Riddle, who was then studying with George.

★ ★ ★

Saul Ilson and Ernie Chambers produced the CBS-TV special *Francis Albert Sinatra Does His Thing* in the fall of 1968. After serving as musical director for Sinatra's three consecutive annual NBC-TV *Man and His Music* specials, Nelson was passed over in favor of Don Costa. "He was really hurt," Ilson remarked. "After that, Frank called him to do a benefit. Nelson told me that he had said to him disgustedly, 'Why don't you hire me for the real job? Then I'll do your benefit.'"

Ilson and Chambers left *The Smothers Brothers Comedy Hour* in 1969 and Nelson began working for producer Alan Bearde. The season did not go well. Tommy Smothers's constant barbs about the futility of the Vietnam War and the CBS censors' inability to allow him to continue his highly political stance ultimately caused the show to be canceled.

Out of the Smothers Brothers show, however, Nelson got the job as musical director for the *Pat Paulsen for President* CBS-TV special. The comedian had been a popular member of the show's cast. *The Leslie Uggams Show* in the fall of 1969 was another musical variety show on which Nelson was musical director.

That same year, at a time when big-budget musicals were finally going out of style, Paramount gambled on the questionable commercial potential of the Alan Jay Lerner/Fritz Loewe musical *Paint Your Wagon,* which was set during the 1848 California gold rush. The studio assigned the highly respected Broadway director Josh Logan to direct. Lee Marvin, Clint Eastwood, Jean Seberg, and Harve Presnell were the leads. Nelson scored the film, which resulted in his fourth Oscar nomination. He was paid $30,000 for his work, exactly double what the studio had paid him for *El Dorado* two years before.

Though hardly a singer, Marvin, one of the truly outstanding character actors, had a turntable hit with "(I Was Born Under a) Wanderin' Star." Eastwood, a qualified jazz aficionado, proved to be a less-than-convincing ballad singer in his attempt to convey Lerner's poetic lyric in the film's other principal song, "I Talk to the Trees." The choral work by the Roger Wagner Chorale, however, was outstanding. The picture's budget spiraled out of control, as did its length, but in spite of that the soundtrack album went gold (indicating sales of 500,000).

But after completing these two major movies, Nelson scored three second-rate pictures in a row. They were *The Great Bank Robbery,* a comedy western starring the unlikely duo of Kim Novak and Zero Mostel; *The Maltese Bippy,* with Rowan and Martin, (which Dick Martin still thinks is one of the most ridiculous things that he and his partner ever did); and *Hell's Bloody Devils,* a biker picture starring Broderick Crawford, which was once called *The Fakers.*

Paramount gambled on Alan Jay Lerner as screenwriter and lyricist again in 1970, when he collaborated with composer Burton Lane in *On a Clear Day You Can See Forever,* which Lerner had originally written for Broadway. Barbra Streisand was cast in the leading role of Daisy Gamble and Yves Montand played the Columbia University professor entranced by her tales of ESP and reincarnation. The problems with the book, so apparent in the Broadway production, were never solved in the film version, either.

Neal Hefti was initially hired to score the film version, but for some unspecified reason his work did not meet the approval of La Streisand. Barbra told the film's producer, the late Howard W. Koch, "I don't want to work with this guy. I want Nelson Riddle."

"She was trouble. Nothing was good enough for her," remembered the producer. "But she and Nelson were like a team from the time we switched."

Nonetheless, Nelson had his own difficulties with the perfectionist star. He complained about her domineering ways while admiring her incredible instrument, which he compared to an oboe. Riddle and Streisand blended beautifully on the formidable score, which included "What Do I Have?," "She Isn't You," "Melinda, " "Come Back to Me," and the title song.

"There was nobody like him in the world who had that kind of magic," Koch added. "He was the kind of a guy for a man to be with and work with."

I can scarcely forget the first time I heard the film's soundtrack. In the winter of 1970, I started representing Alan Jay Lerner while working for John Springer Associates. When I was ushered into the library of his 67th Street townhouse to meet "The Master" for the first time, he was listening intently to the recording of "On a Clear Day" that concluded the film. Before even saying hello, Lerner exclaimed excitedly, "Listen! Listen to that!" Streisand held the last word of the closing chorus "forever and ever-more" for an astounding length of time—which I later clocked at an uncanny twenty-four seconds!

Nelson made use of his familiar trombone sound on his "Come Back to Me" chart. Jack Nicholson appeared in an ill-defined character role playing a sitar. For some unknown reason, to date this Columbia soundtrack album has never been released on CD by the company's Legacy division.

★ ★ ★

In 1968, America came apart as a result of the Vietnam War, the assassinations of Martin Luther King, Jr., and Bobby Kennedy, and the riots that took place during the Democratic Convention in Chicago. In that same year, the Nelson Riddles officially broke apart as well. Doreen began divorce proceedings on August 9, although the couple would not officially go to court until September 1969. Separating appeared to be the only possible solution to her problems with Nelson. Following his usual practice of having other people clean up his messes, Nelson agreed to pay his attorney, Abe Marcus, an astounding five percent of his future BMI royalties for taking care of his divorce.

After their parents' separation, the children lived with Nelson for a time in a house in the Cheviot Hills section of Los Angeles, adjacent to the 20th Century Fox studio. Later, the children returned to Malibu to stay with Doreen. Cecily remarked, "As children, we didn't believe my mother could live without us because we didn't know who would take care of her. [After the divorce] my mother had abusive relationships, unfortunately, especially with one man."

The children were now in a state of limbo. One afternoon Nelson came out to the Our Lady of Malibu School, scooped up the three younger girls, and left them with friends of his. Doreen reciprocated by taking them to stay with her hairdresser, where they lived during the entire summer of 1969. Doreen came to see them only four times during that period.

Nelson attempted to get full custody, accusing Doreen of being an unfit mother. He hired private detectives to report on her behavior with the children. This included occasions when she would spend hours in bars with little Cecily and Maureen.

During the divorce proceedings, Skip, Rosemary, and Christopher were compelled by their father to testify against their mother. The younger children, Tina, Cecily, and Maureen (all under sixteen), met privately with the judge in chambers. They reiterated their fear of what would happen to their mother if they didn't live with her. Cecily later said, "I'm glad we did, because, I have to be honest with you, I don't think she would have lived as long as she did [if she had not won custody]."

After nine days of court proceedings that ended on December 29, 1969, on January 22, 1970, Nelson Smock Riddle, Jr., and Doreen Moran Riddle were granted a divorce in Superior Court of Los Angeles County by Justice Goscoe P. Farley. Doreen was awarded full custody of the children, and Nelson was given the usual visitation rights. He was ordered to pay child support of $400 a month per child for the three minor children, all medical expenses exceeding $50, and all existing life insurance policy premiums for them. Doreen was to receive $1,200 a month in alimony, plus, Nelson was responsible for paying legal and accounting fees which alone amounted to slightly over $40,000. Finally, Doreen was to receive half of all the earnings from his corporation (Nelson Riddle Productions), as well as from BMI and the Dornel Publishing Company, among other joint properties. The marriage had lasted fourteen years, three months, and twelve days.

★ ★ ★

Back in 1963, during one of Vic Lewis's yearly visits to California, which always included considerable time spent with Nelson, Naomi Tenen drove Lewis out to the Riddle home in Malibu for a weekend visit. "She admitted to me how much she was in love with Nelson," Vic recalled. "She told me what a terrible life he had.

"I remember saying to Nelson, 'There is somebody under your very nose who's in love with you.' He asked, 'What do you mean?' I said, 'Naomi, she's in love with you.' I don't know if he had even thought about that.

"And I don't think that Doreen would have had any thought that Nelson would have any attraction towards Naomi other than as his secretary. She thought she knew all the others. Because I opened Nelson's mind to the fact that somebody was in love with him, Naomi was always friendly towards me."

Her devotion to Nelson continued despite his complaints to Doreen that she wasn't a good bookkeeper. Doreen suggested he keep her as she realized how much he depended on her. By the end of the 1960s, a romantic aspect had been added to Nelson and Naomi's relationship. They began having dinner together on a regular basis.

Chris remembered driving home one night with his father during the early days of the courtship. Nelson had just dropped Naomi off at her Beverly Hills apartment on Palm Drive when he burst into tears and exclaimed, "Naomi told me she had sex with a black man." (Presumably, this liaison was with Harry "Sweets" Edison.)

Chris was absolutely stunned by his father's outburst. He recognized the nature of Nelson's racist remark: "It was Dad's 1920s New Jersey background speaking." This was in spite of Riddle's close friendship with Nat Cole and other African American musicians over the years. He had also been one of the first conductors to frequently use black musicians, such as saxophonists Buddy Collette and Plas Johnson, clarinetist Bill Green, and bassist Joe Comfort in the recording studios. The remark was also troublesome to Chris because his mother had spent considerable time indoctrinating all of her children with the importance of racial and religious tolerance.

"That somehow sullied Naomi in his eyes. . . . He still wanted to be with her, but he didn't know if he could now," Chris recalled. Somehow or other, "the problem" sorted itself out. Shortly thereafter, when the divorce proceedings started, Nelson moved in with Naomi.

Reportedly, Rosemary Clooney also was in touch with him during this period. When she asked him why they couldn't get together, Nelson replied, "It's too late." More than a decade later, Nelson admitted to his daughter, Maureen, "I was never able to be alone."

One night Nelson told Chris of his plans to marry Naomi, explaining, "She's been loyal to me. I feel I owe it to her." On April 11, less than three months after his divorce from Doreen was finalized, Nelson married Naomi in a civil ceremony at Abe Marcus's home. They were both forty-nine years old. Chris was Nelson's best man. A European honeymoon followed, which included a visit to Alsace-Lorraine to see Albertine's hometown of Milieu. Sometime later, Doreen remarked to the children, "Your father has finally succeeded: he married his mother."

Bob Bain, who, with his first wife, Jean, had been extremely close to Doreen (Jean was Cecily's godmother) wasn't invited to the wedding. In fact, the only reason he found out about it was that George Roberts, who *had* been invited, called Bain in distress when he couldn't locate Marcus's home. Bob asked why he needed to know where it was, only to be told that Nelson was getting married that afternoon.

Shortly after they were married, Nelson, realizing what a heavy smoker Naomi was, vowed to stop smoking and succeeded. He had seen the deterioration of his father's health from a longtime smoking habit ten years earlier, and had also seen Nat Cole die a similar death. The couple consulted with a specialist to help them drop their habit, but Naomi started smoking again only months after stopping. She continued to smoke incessantly to the end of her life.

Over the next few years, the Riddle children witnessed their father tearing down their mother while putting Naomi on a pedestal. Rosemary attributes this to Naomi's Svengali-like psychological hold on their father. Despite this, the children worked hard at trying to impress Naomi with how lovable and intelligent they were. At that time, the younger girls especially were in desperate need of affection after feeling rejected by their mother and watching her slowly destroy herself.

Rosemary, being the oldest daughter, became "Deputy Mom" (as Cecily and Maureen, the two youngest girls, called her) before she went east to Monmouth College (now University) in New Jersey, at which time Tina took over the role. When life with their mother became unbearable, the younger girls would seek Tina out at her apartment in Brentwood. They finally came to live with Nelson and Naomi for a time in 1970. According to Rosemary, however, "Naomi made their lives hell. They ended up going back to Mom." After that, since it was obvious that Naomi didn't like having them around, Nelson would pick them up and spend the weekend with them at the Beverly Hilton.

Betty Rose, the lovely widow of arranger David Rose, recalled, "If the children couldn't stay overnight he'd have dinner with them and then he'd go back to the house. He really loved his daughters and his sons, and he talked about them all the time when Naomi wasn't around. I couldn't understand why she had such animosity. She would never tell us why."

Naomi believed strongly in the value of an education. Joey Acerra, Rosemary Riddle's husband, like his wife, is a retired schoolteacher; Naomi, therefore, had immediate respect for him. Joey recalled that during their Christmas 1978 visit to California, "Naomi was playing with our little son, Michael. Michael was trying to break away from her as she was holding him. She had him in a lock. He started to scream and cry, but Naomi was going to more or less break him and wasn't going to let him go. . . . He had to stop crying first. Finally I said, 'Let him go!' She wouldn't let him go until he succumbed to her. That gave me a big insight into her, a very big insight."

Naomi's background helps to shed some light on her domineering personality. Her father, Eli Tenenholtz, who was born in Russia, began a career as an actor in the Yiddish theater in 1906 on New York's Lower East Side. After a few years as an actor he founded the Yiddish Art Theater and also operated the Amphion Theater in Brooklyn. Additionally, he acted in repertory theater for eight years. During this period, he got to know the future film stars Paul Muni and John Garfield, who had been prominent actors in the Yiddish theater as well.

Sandy Krinski, the Emmy-winning writer for such television series as *Donny and Marie, Alice, Three's Company,* and *The Nanny* first met Nelson when they worked together on the Golden Globes, back when it was a local television show. Krinski also became a close friend of Naomi in her later years and learned about her early life. Of those days, he said, "The family was always moving—to Los Angeles, and then back to New York, and then back again. Her father was difficult, and she always felt that he wasn't a particularly good provider. He would spend money on other actors and nothing on his children. Her mother basically supported the family. [However,] Naomi did like him."

Eli Tenenholtz's various coast-to-coast jaunts with his family—which consisted of his wife, Ethel, and his daughters Naomi and Miriam—were made to fulfill acting jobs in silent films. When talkies came in, he was signed to MGM for three years where he played a number of comedic character roles.

Like many actors, Tenenholtz had a sizable ego and a sense that he was always right. In that way, he played the role of the autocratic lord of the household. He also was apparently a frequent philanderer. In a photo of Naomi with her mother, most likely taken in the 1970s, Mrs. Tenenholtz had the appearance of a woman who has gone through years of anguish.

The Tenenholtz family finally settled in Los Angeles. Naomi graduated from Hollywood High School and was on her own by the time she was eighteen. She went to work during the war years at Douglas Aircraft, and she was a fashion model in Los Angeles for a time after the war. Eventually she moved into television production.

A little over a year after their marriage, and after the Malibu Colony house was sold, Nelson and Naomi bought a bungalow on two lots for $75,000 at 1616 Bel Air Road on the edge of Bel Air. Built in 1963, the 3,000-square-foot Japanese-style house had a blue tile roof and three bedrooms, plus a music room, a living room with fireplace, and a den. There was a pool and spa in the backyard.

After Naomi contracted hepatitis in 1972, they set up separate bedrooms, an arrangement that continued throughout the marriage. "Sex was one of the only ways he found pleasure, and it was taken away from him," reflected Maureen.

Their marriage provided Naomi with the security which she had longed for throughout her life. After years of dedication to Nelson, she assumed even greater power upon becoming his wife. It seems apparent that the years she, Miriam, and her mother spent living in a deprived and itinerant state had made an indelible impression on Naomi. She was not going to allow anyone to control her fate, certainly not her husband. She was also reluctant to see his children receive more love and attention than she had received as a child.

"I wouldn't say I liked her," Saul Ilson candidly remarked, "but I got along with her. She could have been a keynote speaker at a victim's conference. The bitterness in her had an effect on her looks. She had that dour look about her. She could have taken Johnny Mercer's song and made it into 'You've Got to Accentuate the Negative and Eliminate the Positive!'"

During their first years together as husband and wife, Nelson was strapped with heavy alimony and child support payments. To compound that situation, his career went into a steady and prolonged slump.

Krinski commented on the nature of Naomi and Nelson's marriage: "She was always gruff and opinionated, but she was also fiercely loyal to Nelson. . . . Their names for each other were 'Pookie' and 'Snookie'—'Pook' and 'Snook'—and sometimes they reversed it. They really had a kind of teenage romance even though they were both over fifty. She really cared a lot about him.

"She was also generous. She helped people with no credit. [Both Chris and Maureen vouched for her generosity during the early years when she was their step-mother, in spite of their later feelings about her.] She was very liberal in her thinking, maybe from that early leftist Jewish upbringing. Her favorite programs were on NPR. She had been a big jazz fan for years, and I think at one time she had an affair with "Sweets" Edison before Nelson knew him. She was difficult, and I understand that, and I made allowances for that," Krinski concluded.

Naomi no longer worked for him, but Nelson continued working out of his office in Hollywood, which he moved to Larchmont Boulevard. Naomi forbade him from writing any arrangements at home. His small office was furnished with a twenty-year-old gold sofa that needed reupholstering and his thirty-year-old baby grand piano.

Naomi didn't cook, so they ate most dinners in a restaurant. They were frequent theatergoers, attending plays at the Schubert Theater in Century City and the Ahmanson in downtown Los Angeles as well as on Broadway during their visits to New York. In addition, they attended classical concerts and dance recitals in Los Angeles.

There was little socializing with friends at their new home. Instead, Nelson spent evenings reading poetry (Robert Frost was a favorite poet) or the history books he enjoyed. Nelson was a serious Civil War buff and had a profound respect for Carl Sandburg's poetry.

Back in 1959, when Nelson had been musical director of Gene Kelly's NBC-TV special on which Sandburg was a guest star, Nelson had the pleasure of writing an underscore for Sandburg's recitation of some of his poems. After the show was over, Nelson told Sandburg how much he had enjoyed his Abraham Lincoln biography and wanted to learn more details about Sandburg's Spanish-American War service. As Nelson recalled, ". . .With a wave of his hand, he cut me off in mid-phrase and said, 'Let's forget about all of that junk and just talk about jazz!'"[1]

★ ★ ★

In the fall of 1970, Nelson began working as the musical director of *The Tim Conway Comedy Hour.* The show lasted thirteen weeks. This deal was made by Nelson's then-agent, the late Phil Weltman of the William Morris Agency, who was also Conway's longtime agent. During the summer of 1971, Nelson worked on a CBS-TV variety show called *CBS Newcomers* in the same capacity.

By 1970, he had been without a recording contract for two years. Reprise had dropped him after the disappointing sales of *Nat–An Orchestral Portrait,* his 1965 Cole tribute album. Solid State Records (a division of United Artists Records) then signed him to a one-album contract. Liberty Records, the Hollywood-based independent label, tried unsuccessfully to sell albums on which he arranged contemporary material—*The Bright and the Beautiful* and *Riddle of Today,* in '67 and '68, respectively. But Nelson's kind of music was completely out of step with the pop music of the time, and his recording output was soon restricted to soundtrack albums such as those for the afore-mentioned *El Dorado* (Columbia), *Paint Your Wagon* (Paramount, now Universal Records) and *On a Clear Day* (Columbia).

But an even more serious change was at hand. With the abrupt change in the music, longtime pop singing stars such as Bing Crosby, Vic Damone, Andy Williams, Robert Goulet, Dinah Shore, Keely Smith, Rosemary Clooney, and many others were dropped by major record companies, depriving Nelson of countless arranging opportu-nities. A significant part of Nelson's income was suddenly taken away from him.

Among the pop stars of the late '60s to early '70s, Nelson admired the purity of Judy Collins's magnificent singing voice. However, no one approached him about working with her; Nelson wasn't in a position to attract the interest of any major recording label in such a collaboration. He greatly admired the composing ability of Stevie Wonder and arranged certain favorite tunes of Wonder's for his own concerts. He also admired the singer-songwriter Joni Mitchell and called Stephen Sondheim "The Great White Hope of the American Theater."

Another pop star, Barry Manilow, who never knew Nelson personally but who appreciated his contributions, said, "Not only was he respectful of the singer and of the composer, but he was saying something, too. He had a very muscular way of writing—you knew he was there. That's the difference between him and everybody else."

Nelson yearned to record with Tony Bennett. Unfortunately, their only involve-ment was sharing the bill at a Royal Festival Hall concert in London, which was broad-cast on the BBC in 1976.

★ ★ ★

In 1970, Nelson flew to London, where he had been building an audience through his albums with English recording artists (Shirley Bassey and Danny Williams), BBC appearances, and concerts. While there, he recorded an album with the 101 Strings for Marble Arch Records. Although he had shown an aptitude for effectively making use of the Fender bass in his score for *El Dorado,* Nelson was completely out of his element on this album, trying to sound contemporary with the combination of keyboards, Fender bass, and guitars backed by the large string orchestra. He also wrote four instrumentals for the album, but none had any appreciable melodic content.

Several years later, in speaking of his attempt to become more "with it" in his writing, Nelson said that the Marble Arch album was recorded "during a transition period. I was

Nelson Riddle, his English manager Vic Lewis, and Shirley Bassey take a tea break during a 1963 concert tour of northern England.

starting to pick up on the other things but I hadn't gotten there yet. I'm a lot closer now."

One of the dangers veteran pop and jazz artists constantly face is the ever-changing nature of the music. For example, in the post-WWII period, the advent of bebop compelled Benny Goodman and Harry James to alter their musical presentations. James was somewhat more successful than Goodman in making the transition, but after about a year both returned to what made them successful in the first place and continued with their popularity unabated. For Nelson, whose musical roots were also steeped in swing, to incorporate rock 'n' roll into his presentation with a large orchestra was a losing proposition.

"The main thing that happened at that particular time was that the rhythm section became king," bassist Max Bennett recalled. "Nelson didn't understand that. He never got the message about the intricacies and the importance of the rhythm section." Drummer Stan Levey remembered one of Nelson's record dates that included a tune called "Hula Hoop." "It was supposed to be a jazz arrangement and yet it had a rock 'n' roll beat to it. He went that route, and it didn't work."

Guitarist Mitch Holder began working for Nelson in 1976 in the recording studios. He noted, "He didn't know the contemporary electronic effects that keyboard players and guitarists were using. But I noticed that his *Route 66* theme was remarkably advanced polyphonically. It sounded so simple, yet harmonically it was ahead of its time."

Veteran composer and arranger Buddy Baker, who respected Nelson's arranging, worked with him during this period, trying to show him how to work with a click track. The click track, invented by Walt Disney, for whom Baker scored all kinds of films for decades, is a metronome that enables musicians to hear the beat by wearing earphones while recording.

As Baker explained it, "You lay out the music to a certain tempo—a click track. Hearing that click in his ear bothered Nelson because he liked to be free. Nelson told me, 'I can't stand it.' He liked to hear a rhythm section. There are times in scoring a picture where it's stupid not to use a click track when, for instance, you have a long chase sequence in a western and you're trying to keep up with the horses galloping. It's [also] easier for the orchestra."

Although he was four years older than Nelson, Baker was able to adapt to modern film scoring techniques, but Nelson simply couldn't. While critiquing Nelson's writing for television, Baker also made the point that "Nelson's writing on *Route 66* was closer to phonograph writing than out-and-out motion picture writing because it consisted of all kinds of tempo stuff and movement."

★ ★ ★

Toward the mid-1970s, Naomi once again took a serious look at the financial ledger, which reflected the obvious fact that Nelson's services were much less in demand than they had been in the past. She decided to put Nelson on a spending allowance. He received $250 a week in cash—$50 a day for daily expenditures, Monday through Friday. During this period, musicians would often ask him to have lunch with them during the break in an all-day recording session, and sometimes he would beg off, saying, "I don't have any money." This bewildered several of his regulars, and after a time, they blamed Naomi.

Naomi's sarcastic, poker-faced presence inspired trumpeter George Werth to refer to her as "Ma Barker," alluding to the leader of the notorious 1930s Barker family gang; Stan Levey called her "The Serpent." Levey recalled, "We were doing a big band recording date. We were playing 'Spanish Eyes.' All of a sudden I see a foot over there . . . and it's her sneaking around the studio to see if everybody is really doing their best. . . ."

Nelson wanted to help his youngest daughters, who, along with his other children, were, by Naomi's decree, barred from their Bel Air home. He had trouble getting Naomi to write checks to them for their various needs, but finally managed to figure out a way of circumventing her edict. When he worked for Ella, he sometimes had Mary Jane Outwater (who ran Ella Fitzgerald's production company, Salle Productions), make out checks to one daughter; when he wrote arrangements for Frank Sinatra, Jr., the checks would be mailed to his post office box in Hollywood. By the early 1980s, his need for money got so bad that he asked Billy May if he knew of any work he might get where he could be paid in cash.

Nevertheless, Nelson's sterling musical reputation afforded him the opportunity to work on radio programs sponsored by major corporations, such as the *Sears Radio Hour* and *Sears Mystery Theater* on CBS Radio in 1970 and 1971 and for an Avon Christmas promotional album in 1978. Similarly, he was retained by Sea World, San Diego's famous oceanarium, to arrange and conduct the orchestra for the music/light/water spectacular *Water Fantasy* in April 1971. These projects may have paid Nelson well, but they were of negligible importance in helping him to maintain a thriving career.

★ ★ ★

When Nelson and Frank Sinatra, Jr., coproduced Frank, Jr.'s album *Spice* in 1971, Nelson arranged and conducted several orchestra tracks using forty-eight musicians as well as others using an intermediate-size orchestra of thirty-two musicians that included French horns and strings. Nelson had previously arranged two single records for Frank, Jr., when the singer was recording for RCA two years earlier.

"I borrowed $20,000 from the bank to pay for the recording, the musicians, and the arrangements," Frank, Jr., recalled. "Since I was then on the road with an octet, I also wanted to record some songs with those guys. I remembered that when I was a kid, people used to say, 'Variety is the spice of life,' so I said, 'That's what we're going to call this album, *Spice*.' In twenty minutes I wrote the title song.

"Nelson wrote for this album like he hadn't written since the old days with Nat [Cole]. Sonny Burke was in the booth while I was rehearsing with Nelson. My old man walked in with Lennie Hayton, and they played back "Spice." He asked, 'Whose tune is that?' I walked in and said, 'Mine.' He said, 'You wrote that?' I said, 'Sure.' Then he said, 'You wrote the music and lyrics for that?' I said, 'Yeah.' He said, 'You're full of shit!' I said, 'Yeah, it's true, but I still wrote it.'"

The first track on the flip side of the *Spice* album is "Black Night," which is derivative of Leadbelly's "In the Pines." "This was a folk song that I remembered from summer camp in 1959," said Frank, Jr. "Black Night" vividly demonstrates Nelson's knack for creating incredibly imaginative arrangements.

The record begins with a faintly strumming acoustic guitar and the sound of a few violins as background for Frank, Jr's vocal. In the middle of the tune, to emphasize the downbeat nature of the lyric, out of nowhere comes the sinister sound of a contrabass clarinet played by Bill Green. This is followed by a crescendo of strings—similar to the introduction to Milt Bernhart's solo on "I've Got You Under My Skin"—and which leads immediately into a torrent of roaring brass at the climax of the arrangement, which is punctuated by a baritone saxophone solo by Walt Borys. Nelson had deftly transformed a brooding folk song into a dynamic big band flag-waver!

Larry O'Brien, the affable longtime leader of the Glenn Miller Orchestra, recalled that when he came into the studio to record the bossa nova tune "So Many Stars," he found that Nelson had arranged it in a different key from the one used by Frank, Jr.'s octet. Nevertheless, O'Brien's superior phrasing on trombone, along with Frank, Jr.'s singing, made this one of the best interpretations of the tune ever recorded—and it was done in one take.

Frank, Jr.'s compelling singing on this album is easily the best he ever exhibited on records. Unfortunately, as often happens with rare recorded treasures, *Spice* did not fare well in the marketplace and was never released on CD.

According to Frank, Jr., "Nelson trained me in harmonizing and the use of instruments. For all intents and purposes, by this time he had outlived his usefulness. I used to invite him and Naomi to the Frontier Hotel in Las Vegas where I was performing with the octet. Sometimes they would spend ten days to two weeks there as my guests.

"After the eleven o'clock show, all the writers in the group and half the musicians in town would come backstage and Nelson would sit at the piano. He would look at the scores that the guys had played, and he would hold court. He'd say, 'Try this,' and all my writers would study with him. . . . I was so proud of that—that Nelson was able to help these young writers. They studied with Nelson, and he was delighted to do it.

"I began to get somewhat close to Nelson, and I admired him so much. He has been such an influence in my life," Frank, Jr. maintained. "He was a musical schoolmaster to me."

I asked Frank, Jr., if Nelson might have been a surrogate father to him. "No, no, it was not that kind of a relationship," he answered. Despite his response, it's my feeling that the two of them spent more than a little time discussing the completely unpredictable behavior of one Frank Sinatra, which seriously affected both of their lives.

When I asked Frank, Jr., his feelings about Naomi, he replied, "Well, Naomi was not only famous, Naomi was infamous. Nelson's second marriage was to a woman who at the time was forty-nine years old and had never been married," he continued. "Suddenly, she is married to a man with six children and an alcoholic ex-wife, so there are going to be problems there, obviously. That's purely my speculation; I think it's pretty accurate."

Frank, Jr., and Nelson did another album, *His Way,* the following year for Daybreak. In 1973, RCA ended its agreement with Daybreak Records.

By now Nelson's past was catching up with him. In October 1971, he flew to London again, this time to participate in a Festival of Music concert at Royal Albert Hall. He conducted his *Route 66* theme, "Mona Lisa," "Wanderin' Star," and his *Untouchables* theme, in addition to a Frank Sinatra film suite. The other conductors on the program were Frank Chacksfield, David Rose, and Maurice Jarre.

Next, Nelson recorded two albums for MPS, the German label: *Communication* (1971) and *Changing Colors* (1972). The former was devoted to the work of young German composers and the latter contained several standards. Neither was noteworthy. In addition, Sonny Burke had him arrange the album *Vive Legrand* for Daybreak as a tribute to Michel Legrand, the French arranger-turned-composer who was then challenging Henry Mancini with his ability to deliver hit songs from motion pictures.

Contained in this album was an eight-bar solo by Chris Riddle on "What Are You Doing the Rest of Your Life?" At the time, Chris was studying with trombonist

Tommy Shepard, one of Nelson's veteran regulars. After the recording, Shepard said to Nelson, "What a spot to put your kid in, but how great he was to rise to it."[2]

In 1972 Nelson reunited with one of his old friends, Ella Fitzgerald. Norman Granz had sold Verve Records to MGM and Ella, too, was without an exclusive recording contract. Granz brought Ella and Nelson back together to collaborate on a new Cole Porter album, *Ella Loves Cole,* which was supposed to have been recorded sixteen years earlier. After its completion, the album was sold to Atlantic Records. With the recording of an additional track, "Dream Dancing," in 1978, *Dream Dancing* replaced *Ella Loves Cole* as the title of the album and marked the first album released by Granz on his new Pablo Records label.

Nelson delivered a superb group of arrangements for songs Ella had recorded initially in the *Ella Fitgerald Sings the Cole Porter Songbook* album, as well as some of his more overlooked songs like "Down in the Depths" and "After You." They were perfectly tailored to Ella's voice, allowing her to soar on her astounding vocal flights. However, there was one serious problem that interfered with the success of the album: her once beautiful and pliant vocal instrument was beginning to unravel. She was now constantly plagued by a shaky vibrato.

Following Lou Levy's departure, Paul Smith served as Ella's accompanist. Smith remembers being on the road with her "about forty-six weeks" during 1962. He returned ten years later when *Ella Loves Cole* was about to be recorded. While listening to a playback during one of the recording sessions for the album, Ella remarked to Smith, reflecting on her vocal problems, "Now I'm Mary McQuiver."

In 1972 Nelson returned to television in a big way. First, he scored the pilot for *Emergency!,* the medical drama produced by Jack Webb's Mark VII Productions, which starred the late husband and wife team of Bobby Troup and Julie London. That same year, Julie Andrews ventured into television with her own ABC-TV variety show, and on André Previn's recommendation Nelson became her musical director.[3] Lorimar, another television production company, inaugurated the miniseries format with its adaptation of Joseph Wambaugh's *The Blue Knight* starring Nelson's old friend, Bill Holden; Nelson won an Emmy for his impressive score.

Unfortunately, Jack Webb felt that Nelson was too involved with *The Julie Andrews Hour* and after a few episodes of *Emergency!,* Nelson was replaced by Billy May. May recalled that he was brought in after Nelson had to go to London to work. "Joe Friday" (Webb's *Dragnet* character) was entirely correct in his judgment, because in addition to working at *Emergency!* and *The Julie Andrews Hour,* Nelson was also the musical director for Ralph Edwards's *This Is Your Life.*[4] Three years later, however, Webb brought Nelson back to score his *Mobile Two* series, which toplined Jackie Cooper.

Julie Andrews is surely one of the most stunning talents of the last five decades. After enjoying successive triumphs in *The Boyfriend, My Fair Lady,* and *Camelot,* on Broadway, she conquered Hollywood with *Mary Poppins* (for which Nelson was

Nelson Riddle on trombone and Henry Mancini on piccolo serenade Julie Andrews during a rehearsal for her 1972–73 television show.

originally asked to score the music, but which he turned down), *The Americanization of Emily, Thoroughly Modern Millie,* and *Victor/Victoria.* During a fallow period in films in the early 1970s, Andrews made the natural transition to hosting her own television show.

The Julie Andrews Hour only lasted one season—twenty-four episodes. It was produced by Nick Vanoff, well-respected for his variety shows, such as *Hollywood Palace.* It was also one of the most artistic and creative musical shows ever produced on television and deservedly won seven Emmys out of ten nominations. In his usual fashion, Nelson refused to nominate himself for his work scoring the show. If he had, it might very well have enabled him to win back-to-back Emmys.

Very likely there was more music on the show than perhaps any variety show in television history. "Nelson wrote for the show like it was a concert—medleys, combined medleys, key changes, and all good," said guitarist Al Viola. George Werth, who also played on the show, called it "wall-to-wall music. And when Nelson would get irritable from time to time, Julie would say, 'Now Nels, we can cool it!'"

Nelson had so much to write (he called the shows "songbooks") that he was compelled to seek out seven other arrangers, including Billy Byers and Joe Lipman, to assist him. He concentrated on arranging Andrews's solo numbers. Needless to say, the musicians made a great deal of money as a result of all the rehearsals and the long taping sessions.

The popular star perfectly captured Nelson's essence by nicknaming him "Eeyore," after the sad, forlorn donkey that was such an important character in the classic children's book, *Winnie-the-Pooh*. (Similarly, Billy May had once said of Nelson, "He has the personality of a stale cigarette.") "He was always troubled, always pretending to be slightly grumpy but with that brilliant wit," Andrews recalled. "His droll observations were hugely funny."

Regarding Nelson's failure to nominate himself for an Emmy, Andrews said, "If that isn't an 'Eeyore' thing, I don't know what is. We were so angry with him about it, and he was so self-effacing. He said, 'If I'd been nominated, they wouldn't give it to me anyway,' or something like that. He would have won, hands down!"

Speaking of the hard work her show entailed, Andrews explained, "It killed all of us. Wednesday night was our night to prerecord, and a great deal of the show was prerecorded. It was the best night of the week. Tapings were Thursday and Friday nights. Sometimes we'd tape until 4:30 A.M. The first two weeks of the show he and I were on our own in the sense that he didn't have anybody helping him. I was very much in awe and not too sure of how much to tell him. A very good friend [who became her conductor], Ian Fraser, was brought in and things went smoothly after that. The two of them helped me to stretch and grow so much on that show. I've never done such a body of work. I worked with the greats like "Sweets" [Edison], the trumpeter. I may be wrong but it felt like we had thirty-eight to forty musicians. We had some great times. Mostly it was quality. And the arrangements he did for me! . . . They were so beautiful.

"I once said to him, 'Nelson, you used to do a lick for Sinatra—a particular musical phrase such as in that arrangement of 'I Have Dreamed.' It's almost a little trademark of yours, and it's beautiful. And he said, 'Oh, that's really Frank's—I don't know if I can do that,' and I said, 'Oh please, will you do it for one of my arrangements? It would be so lovely.' And he did."

Unlike his classic arrangement of "I Have Dreamed," the version Nelson arranged for the *Andrews Hour* began with a string quartet introduction. This was followed by the full string section carrying the melody, which built steadily before returning to the string quartet. Andrews recalled, "After we recorded it, he said, 'Well, I guess it's yours now.' That was so lovely of him—so adorable. I did love him very much." She admitted, "I envied the hell out of Linda [Ronstadt] when he did her albums."

"Nelson arranged about fifty percent of all the music on the show," said Ian Fraser. "He worked so hard. Sometimes Julie would lip-synch the songs and other times they were done live. Each show was the equivalent of doing a TV special. Nelson sometimes wrote as many as six arrangements a show, which occasionally included medleys. He would have to write between Monday evenings, when he had our meetings, and three o'clock on Wednesday afternoon, when we started to prerecord the music."

Nelson reflected on the experience years later, saying, "Julie managed to maintain a generally sunny disposition, which indicated a self-discipline characteristically British. [However] the ratings were bad. Nobody could identify with Julie. America is folksy, I'm afraid. . . . I think Julie Andrews was too good for them. She sang to them from a position of intellectualism. I never want to work that hard again in my life for anybody."[5]

In the late 1960s, after many years of being disgruntled at having their music rights usurped by CBS, a group of prominent composers banded together to sue the network. Finally, at the beginning of the 1972–73 television season, the $300,000,000 class action suit that Nelson, Henry Mancini, Elmer Bernstein, Marvin Hamlisch, David Rose, and 61 other composers and lyricists had filed was resolved. Their legal victory returned to the composers the rights to all music written for CBS-TV shows and established that all future contracts would give the music rights to the composers. as opposed to having the networks own the music that had been performed on television. In 1978 the same suit was filed against all the other television networks and motion picture companies and was settled out of court. As president of the Composers and Lyricists Guild of America, Bernstein had been instrumental in starting these legal actions. The gracious veteran composer said, "Nelson really backed us up on our grievances and was extremely helpful in allowing us to retain our rights."

★ ★ ★

With his wife, Eydie Gorme, Steve Lawrence continues to keep the tradition of quality music alive in their concert and Las Vegas performances. In 1973, he recorded *Portrait* with Nelson for MGM Records. Nelson's laid-back behavior in the recording studio gave Lawrence the mistaken impression he was from the Midwest. "He was very bright and instinctive," the singer said.

The close friendship Steve and Eydie enjoyed with Frank Sinatra during Sinatra's last years gave Lawrence a reason to reflect on Nelson's work with Sinatra: "Riddle expanded Frank's musical horizons. As great and as innovative as Frank was musically and as an interpreter lyrically, Nelson gave him a sound that up until that point he didn't have orchestrally. From then on, it gave him an identification that they both really wallowed in—the straight quarter notes tied to each other became the driving force. He really overpowered Frank, lifted him up to that climax, threw him over the top, and then brought him back to where they wanted to settle. There are only a handful of people that you can think of who understood each other so well. Both of them became bigger because of each other.

"When we were recording his wonderful arrangement of 'In the Still of the Night,' during the instrumental portion of it, I got so enthralled listening to it I almost forgot to come in," Lawrence remembered. Listening to the recording, you can actually hear Lawrence snapping his fingers to the beat. This chart displayed Nelson's patented gusto and made use of his "Under My Skin" vamping device. In arranging "Ain't No Sunshine," also included on the album, he cleverly utilized the combination of bongos and percussion to create a rock backbeat.

"Riddle was a terrific guy to talk to," Lawrence went on to say. "He contributed not only verbally, but musically. . . . We took everything that we were doing, and said, 'How can we make [the music] not only special and make it fit into the album, but make it different than anybody has done before?' Nelson really had a lot to offer on a lot of levels."

In Lawrence's opinion, "If Costa and Riddle and Billy May were living in the seventeenth or eighteenth century, they would have been Mozart and Brahms and Beethoven. These guys were so underappreciated. Frank was one of the few people—and Eydie and I always do it, too—to pay tribute to and mention the guys who wrote those arrangements.

"I liked him a lot," Lawrence concluded. "He was a gentleman, and I admired that about him in a business where there's a lot of shorthand that goes on. He was not a typical musician or writer. It was very deceptive. You would never think that that [magic] would come out of this guy, and that added to it. . . . I think his contribution to the overall music business was a very heavy one. He left a great musical legacy behind for many generations to enjoy."

★ ★ ★

Helen Reddy, growing up in a show business family in Australia, was very aware of who Nelson Riddle was through his records with Frank Sinatra. Starting with "I Don't Know How to Love Him," from Andrew Lloyd Webber's *Jesus Christ Superstar,* Reddy had several hit records, including the huge "I Am Woman," which was the anthem of the women's movement in the early 1970s. In 1973, she hosted an eight-week NBC-TV summer replacement show.

"When he was assigned as the musical director of the show, I had a few moments of doubt," the singer recalled. "This was a time when there was such a decisive thing going on in music. . . . Not that I didn't respect his work. I had enormous regard for his work, but because we were going to have so many rock acts as guest stars I thought perhaps it was a mismatch. At the very first meeting, when Nelson and I met with my lead guitarist Michael Warren and they were going over music together, he turned to no one in particular and said, 'Boy, I love these young guys. I can learn so much from them.' I was blown away. I mean here was a man who was a maestro, and he was excited at the prospect of learning something!"

Mike Berkowitz was Reddy's drummer. "Helen was very loyal to her band," Berkowitz said. "We all had really long hair, and we were all about twenty-three years old. Nelson brought a metronome to that first session. He would start the tunes off with it—count us off just to get the tempos—and we'd [begin to] play. At the end, he'd turn the metronome back on to see if I had rushed or dragged the tempo. I don't know if he did that to test a new drummer. I think he was unfamiliar with Helen so he wanted to make sure he had the tempos right."

According to Reddy, the broad spectrum of songs she sang (besides her hits), made him the right choice for her show. "I came out of a jazz background, and I dissed rock 'n' roll for years," she related. "It was only when I got to the States and saw Simon and Garfunkel and the Blues Project, who were into complex harmonies and were obviously true musicians, that I changed my opinion. That was a big breakthrough for me, but there were a lot of people from Nelson's era who put down the younger set, and for him to have that enthusiasm made me understand his greatness."

"He was a large man physically, almost intimidating in size," she continued, "but he was so gentle and soft-spoken—a lovely, lovely man." Indeed, by the 1970s Nelson was a large man. He had put on weight after dousing his smoking habit. In addition, his hair had turned gray and his hairline had receded. He now had a distinguished aura about him.

Berkowitz recalled the day he needed a monitor in order to see a visual cue while working on the Reddy Show. Nelson said, "Just play, and we'll get you a monitor," but Mike protested, insisting he needed it right away in order to do right by the show. In usual Riddle fashion, Nelson asked the young drummer, "How, at twenty-three, do you have the same bad attitude it took Irv Cottler fifty-five years to get?" Sometime after the Reddy show was history and once Frank Sinatra started doing concerts on the road, Berkowitz began working for Nelson for several years, replacing Cottler.

In 1974, Nelson and Sammy Davis, Jr., collaborated on *That's Entertainment* produced by Mike Curb, the President of MGM Records, for the label. It was one of only a few albums Nelson arranged for a singer during the 1970s. Nelson and Davis had previously worked together on several Sinatra projects, including *Robin and the Seven Hoods*, but never before on one of Davis's solo albums. The concept for the album was to feature a series of important songs from movies.

"Unfortunately," as Gregg Geller, the producer of *Yes, I Can! The Sammy Davis, Jr. Story*, the Rhino boxed set, observed, "the music emerged as being overwrought. Both Sammy and Nelson were trying too hard. Sammy had had two hit singles in 'Mr. Bojangles' and 'Candy Man.' The follow-up records were failures. With this album they returned to a middle-of-the-road format." Even so, the project was a delight for Nelson, whose arrangements underlined Davis's ability to swing and his jazz-inflected phrasing. One particularly outstanding track was "Lover Come Back to Me."

After having worked on the back-to-back Andrews and Reddy weekly variety shows, Nelson became the musical director for Lucille Ball's March 1975 CBS-TV special, *Lucy Gets Lucky*. He also wrote two arrangements for Dean Martin, who was a guest star on the special. That same year, he composed the music for the pilot and scored two episodes of *Caribe* starring Stacy Keach, the *Mobile Two* pilot, *The Runaway Barge, Barnaby Jones, Manhunter, Medical Center,* and *Movin' On*. He was paid anywhere from $1,600 to $2,000 an episode for these series—which showed exactly how much the demand for his work had slipped since his 1960s heyday as a film composer.

The following year Nelson scored several episodes of another TV series, *City of Angels*; another Lucille Ball special, which had Jackie Gleason as guest star; and *What Now, Catherine Curtis?* (starring Lucille Ball and Art Carney), also produced by Lucille Ball Productions. The latter was the follow-up to Ball and Carney's teledrama *Happy*

Anniversary and Goodbye for which Nelson was paid a paltry $4,000.

Continuing in the no-man's-land of weekly television composing in '77, he scored six episodes of *The Blue Knight,* a series based on the miniseries for which he had written an Emmy-winning score. He also worked on six episodes of another series called *Executive Suite.*

★ ★ ★

David Merrick, the leading Broadway producer from the 1950s to the 1980s, was as celebrated for his confounding ways of conducting business as he was for his artistic and financial successes. He brought a glamorous approach to Paramount's 1974 film version of F. Scott Fitzgerald's *The Great Gatsby.* (The studio had also filmed a version in 1949.) Included in Merrick's package were Robert Redford and Mia Farrow in starring roles. Francis Ford Coppola, fresh from his two *Godfather* successes, was the screenwriter, and Ralph Lauren, the latest rage in fashion, was the costume designer. Despite having this winning team, the movie was an overproduced, unwieldy mess.

André Previn had originally been approached to score the movie. "I had absolutely no desire to do it," he remembered. "I didn't find it interesting. I didn't want to score one of Mia's movies [she was then his wife] for many reasons. *The Great Gatsby* ran longer than *Gone with the Wind* when I first saw it. I also knew that with all that '20s source music it was going to be a pain in the neck to do."

When he turned down the job, Previn suggested Nelson. Although David Merrick's initial reaction was, "Who?," Riddle got the assignment. Nelson was in the middle of a rehearsal for a Helen Reddy concert when he was notified that he would have to proceed immediately to London to screen *The Great Gatsby* in order to "spot" the music. Five weeks later he was back on the Paramount scoring stage beginning work on the film.[6]

Director Jack Clayton, like Merrick, wanted an authentic 1920s soundtrack. In his nearly one hour of music, Nelson captured the restless spirit of "The Roaring Twenties" with muted trumpets, bracing cornet solos, wah-wah muted trombones, oompah tubas, and the "potted palm" sound of violins and tinkling pianos. In reality, he was re-creating much of what he had heard at home while growing up in during that era, and, in effect, displaying his talent as a music historian. He managed to get Paramount to hire Tom Mack, an old friend from the Charlie Spivak band, to produce the album, which went gold.

Tommy Dorsey's legacy was not lost in Nelson's writing for the *Great Gatsby* score. He virtually duplicated Dorsey's original chart for "Who," and got pianist Jess Stacy, who had been on the Dorsey band with him thirty years earlier, to play a two-chorus solo on "Beale Street Blues." The piano was modified to sound tinny in order to provide a player-piano aura.

The highlight of the score, however, was seventy-six-year-old Nick Lucas's rendition of Irving Berlin's classic, melancholy ballad, "What'll I Do?" Nelson also managed a skillful blending of the Berlin ballad and an original countermelody, freely admitting that he had utilized a technique practiced by his good friend George Duning in his adaptation of "Moonglow" and in his own *Picnic* theme.[7]

On his fifth nomination, Nelson finally won the Oscar in 1975 for his *Great Gatsby* score. Regarding his experience in writing it, he said later, "*The Great Gatsby* rejuvenated me." Nelson sent Previn a pair of cuff links in appreciation; Previn remarked, "I still wear [them] on occasion. I wear them with pleasure because Nelson gave them to me."

Nelson's best original composition in the film, "A Long Time Ago," featured a haunting bluesy clarinet solo by his veteran clarinetist, Mahlon Clark, one of several excellent solos Clark contributed to the soundtrack. That year, the Tex Beneke band, which included Clark, was playing at the Governor's Ball that follows the Academy Awards ceremony. Nelson approached Clark when he was standing around with a group of fellow musicians on a break, and said, "I owe a good part of this [shaking the Oscar] to you."

"I suddenly remembered back to when I first met him at a Decca Records recording session back in the late '40s," Clark recalled. "At the end of that session, he had said to me, 'You're quite a clarinetist!' I said to him, 'And you're quite an arranger!'"

"Gonna Charleston Back to Charleston" as well as various standards were removed from the soundtrack of the video version of the film due to the fact that Paramount, like other studios, would not allow the use of these songs unless the studio could obtain a buyout from the publisher. (Paramount simply would not pay a royalty per song for the video version.) As a result, the soundtrack contains only Nelson's original music—including a tango—and library music, instead of the original film score.

A decade earlier, Nelson had been quoted as saying, "An Oscar ups a music man's price $10,000 a picture."[8] One would think that after winning the Oscar, Nelson would have been deluged with offers. He said to Mike Berkowitz, "Now that I've won the Oscar, maybe somebody'll hire me." As it happened, the opposite was the case. Winning the Oscar and being on the cover of *Time* have often been the kiss of death to a career.

Nelson didn't get a bona fide offer to compose his next film score for over a year. Was it because he won his Oscar for a predominantly adapted score rather than for an original score? Or was it because Henry Mancini, Quincy Jones, Johnny Mandel, and Michel Legrand were sharing the assignments for most of the A-movies?

"I think that Nelson wanted to emulate the days of David Raksin and the other quality film composers," Mike Berkowitz contended. "Mancini and Lalo Schifrin, to some degree, were two writers who changed movie music because songs had suddenly become more important. No longer was there a great title piece like 'Laura' with all the music related to that [sprinkled] throughout the movie." To echo Berkowitz's statement, David Raksin commented, "Bernard Herrmann never composed a great melody, despite which he wrote some of the best film scores ever composed."

Nelson's next film scoring job was again an adaptation—supplying the overture for *That's Entertainment, Part II* (1976), MGM's second salute to its glorious decades of

Photo courtesy of the Nelson Riddle Memorial Library at the University of Arizona School of Music and Dance, Tucson, Arizona, and the Naomi Riddle Estate.

Nelson beams after receiving his 1975 Academy Award for his score for *The Great Gatsby.*

movie musicals. This medley consisted of his arrangements of the title song, "Temptation," "Hi-Lili Hi-Lo," "Be a Clown," "Good Mornin'," "Broadway Rhythm," and "Have Yourself a Merry Little Christmas." This assignment was followed by two decidedly B pictures in 1978—*Harper Valley PTA* (with Barbara Eden) and *Goin' Coconuts,* which starred Donny and Marie Osmond—along with various television projects, including the documentary *America at the Movies.*

It was Eddie Forsyth who, when asked by Warner Bros. to secure a composer for *Goin' Coconuts,* called Nelson. Nelson asked his old friend how much the job paid. "$25,000," said Forsyth. "Try and get it for me, Eddie," he replied.

In the middle of this barren period, Nelson's longtime friend Victor Bay, the violinist and conductor for the Santa Monica Symphony, made him a different kind of offer. The city of Santa Monica was celebrating its centennial year in 1975. Bay commissioned Nelson to write the *Santa Monica Suite* for presentation, with Henry Fonda as the narrator, at the Santa Monica Civic Auditorium on May 18 of that year.

Through his friendship with Bay, Nelson had been a patron of the Symphony and had attended several of its concerts over the years. Bay, in turn, had premiered Nelson's one symphony, the approximately nine-minute-long "Sinfonia Breve," in 1969. I heard this piece performed by the University of Arizona's Symphony Orchestra at the gala concert commemorating the opening of the Nelson Riddle Archives on February 3, 2001; it sounded to me as though it was actually more of a film score than a symphony.

Bay also commissioned Nelson's last serious work, a waltz entitled "M.A.," which Nelson dedicated to Marie Albertine.[9] As Sheila Wells, who handled publicity for the Santa Monica Symphony, observed, "In Victor, Nelson found a man who loved and respected him." Bay joined Bill Finegan, Alan Shulman, and Mario Castelnuovo-Tedesco as Nelson's true mentors.

When asked why he had agreed to write the *Santa Monica Suite,* Nelson replied, "Because it's a good thing to do—a good thing for the town, and a good mental exercise, which composers of commercial music seem to need."[10] Two years earlier, Nelson had commented about such commissioned work, "You get a performance out of it, plus some kind of fee which doesn't even cover the copying expenses, but you absorb the rest and charge it off, and you've been given the incentive to write."[11]

Walter Arlen of the *Los Angeles Times* said of Riddle's work, "Like the suites of that longtime Santa Monica resident, Ferde Grofé, the *Santa Monica Suite* is a descriptive piece of slickly arranged music for a large orchestra."[12]

During the remainder of the 1970s, Nelson took whatever jobs came his way, which were mostly from television movies and miniseries. The TV movies were the previously mentioned Jack Webb opus *Mobile Two; Promise Him Anything* with Eddie Albert; *The Runaway Barge* with Nick Nolte; *A Circle of Children* with Jane Alexander; and *How to Break Up a Happy Divorce* with Barbara Eden. The miniseries were Harold

Nelson and Naomi Riddle at New York's Loews State world premiere of *The Great Gatsby* in March 1975. This overproduced version of the F. Scott Fitzgerald novel was a critical and box-office failure; nevertheless, Nelson's score for the film earned him his first and only Oscar after five nominations.

Robbins's *79 Park Avenue* starring Lesley Ann Warren, which paid Nelson $15,000, and *Seventh Avenue* starring Jane Seymour. In addition, there were more pedestrian writing chores: another documentary, *Oscar Presents the War Movies,* which dealt with various war films that had won Academy Awards; and thirteen episodes of *Project U.F.O.* (again for Jack Webb), as well as episodes of *CHiPs* and *The Love Boat.*

An obstacle to getting additional television work was Nelson's tendency to have disagreements with producers concerning the musical content for their shows. As saxophonist Ted Nash said, "Nelson wasn't a phony. He treated bigwigs in the same manner as he did musicians. He didn't kowtow; therefore, they didn't feel too warmly toward him. Nelson would get down in the mouth if they threw out a cue—you don't do that with producers. We always felt uneasy about it when he'd have those little tiffs. We'd look at each other and say, 'Well, here goes this show.'"

Perhaps Nelson's awareness of the difficulties he was encountering with television producers was one reason why throughout most of the 1970s he shopped at Alan Adler, the silversmith in Beverly Hills, for elaborate Christmas presents that were sent to many of the producers he had worked for over the years. This practice helped him to ensure more scoring assignments.

Mike Melvoin is a highly experienced studio musician who I knew would be able to evaluate Nelson's career in this period. The veteran pianist, who first worked with Nelson on the *Route 66 and Other Hit TV Themes* album, is convinced that Nelson was indeed a jazz writer. He said, "He didn't have confidence in himself as a jazz writer, but on that occasion he emerged to me in his real identity."

Melvoin understood Nelson's lack of confidence and his feeling of desperate uncertainty in the 1970s. He began by saying, "I think part of the reason Nelson was sad was that he came out so infrequently as who he really was. Somehow or other, he felt that he was forced into this box with those famous singers, and that was his career.

"He had this persona of the subservient arranger-conductor father figure for these people. That's where he got those big merit badges because he was absolutely the guy that a singer could trust to be unobtrusive and supportive—to cocoon them in total safety. He would never write or play anything that would spook them in any way. He knew that it was his role, and somehow or other we're dealt this hand, and we play it.

"Nelson got bagged as being the ideal music director for these singers, but at the cost of his own musical identity. I think that got to him sooner or later. He was a reticent person, and he didn't think he could play in that Hollywood arena as the socialite. Unfortunately for him, a lot of business was done at those dinners and parties."

In an interview for the *Halifax* (Nova Scotia) *Chronicle Herald* on October 23, 1976, which was published in conjunction with a local concert appearance, Nelson said, "I've been told that I don't have a large enough ego, and if I did, I'd have gone a lot further. Well, one can adjust a personality slightly, but you can't change basic traits. . . ."

★ ★ ★

Sue Iwasaki and her attorney husband, Bob, were longtime neighbors of Nelson and Naomi on Bel Air Road. They first met the Riddles at a party at the home of Akiko Agishi, the Japanese concert promoter who had arranged for Nelson to be a guest at the Tokyo Music Festival—an appearance that led to subsequent visits to Japan for concert dates in the 1970s.

The two couples socialized frequently and even traveled to Hawaii together. Sue referred to Nelson as "such a kind person and a very approachable man. He was very compassionate, kind, and honest. I always said if there were tons of Nelson Riddles in this world we wouldn't have wars!"

She characterized Naomi as "a very direct person who was a little harder to understand. Once you got to know her she was a loyal friend. She also disliked a lot of people. She didn't want any part of anybody who liked Nelson [too much]."

When asked about Naomi's decision that Nelson's children weren't permitted in the house, and that Nelson wasn't allowed to call them from the house, Sue responded, "I don't know who mistreated whom unfairly at the beginning. Somehow it just fell apart. I think Nelson wanted to keep it as peaceful as possible. He just didn't want to create any waves. That's the kind of man he was."

Bob Iwasaki recalled, "At the Bel Air gate there is a telephone booth. Many times I'd drive through the gate, and I would see Nelson. He was talking to his children on the telephone. Naomi wouldn't let anybody get close to Nelson except us. I think that's because we were Japanese Americans. She loved going to Japan and she loved the Japanese traditions over there. Otherwise I think she would have treated us like anybody else."

★ ★ ★

By the end of the 1970s, it was obvious that Nelson was having severe difficulty in getting offers to score major movies. His adaptation Oscar was now several years old. He was typecast as a screen composer who was only adept at adaptation. Yet, the Motion Picture Academy still considered him a composer of importance and had him conduct the orchestra for the 50th Academy Awards telecast on April 3, 1978.

At this point Nelson made a move that would seem to contradict his best interests as a screen composer. According to Walter Scharf, one night at a meeting of the music branch of the Academy, Nelson stood up and said to the members, "Why should we have a separate Oscar for adaptation? I don't know why we're giving out two Oscars. We should give only one for the best score."

Scharf further remembered, "This quiet guy [Nelson] complained about how musical themes from old pictures were being put into current films and were being allowed to qualify for Oscar nominations. He was shaking a little bit and trying to find his words. Everybody was a little surprised, but he made a big deal about it, and, as a result, we changed the rules."

Composer Elmer Bernstein commented, "It was strange for Nelson to do this because he was really the best person at adaptation, but then he had a way of running down his own work. His was a very conservative point of view." Nelson's suggestion was approved by the Academy, however, and in 1980 the "Adaptation" Oscar was removed, only to return two years later.

Nelson's first film scoring assignment of the 1980s, Paramount's *Rough Cut,* again for producer David Merrick, resulted in one of the best examples of his arranging skills and also showed his musical allegiance to Duke Ellington. *Rough Cut* was a caper film with obvious chemistry between Burt Reynolds and Lesley-Anne Down. It also starred David Niven, but it suffered from a confused and unresolved ending.

Trombonist Bill Watrous played a memorable solo on "Mood Indigo" and was a standout on the other Ellington selections on the soundtrack. Unfortunately, Nelson's score was never released as an album.

The two Hollywood trade papers, *Daily Variety* and *The Hollywood Reporter,* both praised Nelson's score, with the *Reporter*'s Ron Pennington remarking, "It's too bad there wasn't more interesting action for this lovely score to support." Ironically, Nelson probably would probably have earned an Oscar nomination for the high quality of his adaptation were it not for his own suggestion before the Academy.

The high caliber of his work on *Rough Cut* had no effect on his difficulties in getting offers to score major movies. His next picture was a horrid Mexican/Spanish/Panamanian production, *Guyana: Cult of the Damned,* starring a bevy of yesterday's movie leading lights. Stuart Whitman played the notorious Jim Jones (called Rev. James Johnson in the film) with Yvonne DeCarlo, Joseph Cotten, Gene Barry, John Ireland, and Bradford Dillman in support.

Agent Carol Faith, who represented Nelson as a film composer from 1979 to 1981, said, "I saw him as kind of a beaten, defeated man, and it was sad. I wish I had known more about his early years—I don't know if that would have been better or worse, though, as far as our working together . . . those had to be the best, the glory years with Sinatra and all that."

The veteran agent also recalled that Nelson always brought his dog Christopher, a cockapoo (whom he later called "Chrissy Boy"), with him to the scoring stages. "The pictures I'm getting now are of seeing Nelson holding the dog or the dog on the leash— flat face, no animation, nothing." (One wonders if man's best friend wasn't *truly* his best friend during this down period of his life.)

"He was doing [television] episodes of this and that. I think this town wouldn't accept him as a composer, he was an arranger. His Oscar didn't mean anything."

Faith went on to deliver an extensive list of pilots for television, in addition to TV specials, television films, and movies for which Nelson had been submitted. "The one big film that I was able to get for him was *Rough Cut*. He got $25,000 plus orchestrations. In those days that wasn't bad. He apparently got $20,000 for *Gatsby* five years before that." Her last film scoring deal was *Harper Valley P.T.A.,* for which Nelson got $10,000. He also scored an episode of *Strike Force* for Aaron Spelling.

Elmer Bernstein commented, "I don't think Nelson wanted to deal with the particular kind of nonsense he encountered. He didn't want to be on the firing line. Nelson just didn't have the stomach for it. He wasn't an in-your-face person. He wasn't by nature a performer. I started life as a concert pianist and was accustomed to the idea of being a performer. For him it was a little different.

"With the films he did for Sinatra, he was doing them from a fairly protected, familiar atmosphere. . . . I don't know how he fared on a day-to-day basis in the Sinatra world, which was not an easy world. He would have liked to have been doing primarily films, but he was stuck. Film scoring was not his deal."

★ ★ ★

On December 30, 1979, while dining with Naomi at L'Hermitage, a chic Los Angeles restaurant, Nelson began to feel weak while sipping a glass of wine. He was scheduled to play a New Year's Eve date the next night, but he awoke that morning feeling extremely ill. At Cedars-Sinai Hospital, he was diagnosed with cirrhosis of the liver. He welcomed in the new decade from a hospital bed. He later said, "I liked a glass of vodka, but I never drank so that I was inebriated. As soon as the doctor told me the problem, I stopped cold right there, which alcoholics cannot do. I had a weak liver. I suppose I was one of those guys who should never have had anything to drink."[13] It appears as though Nelson was underestimating his drinking problem.

★ ★ ★

The decade after Doreen's divorce was lonely and dismal for her. By then Skip, Rosemary, and Chris were grown up and Tina, Cecily, and Maureen were away much of the time attending private schools. She restlessly moved around a great deal, living for short periods in Lake Arrowhead, La Jolla, and El Segundo.

On April 9, 1980, twenty-two years to the day after the death of her infant daughter Lenora, Doreen died of lung cancer, which was perhaps exacerbated by her alcoholism. It was also two days before Nelson and Naomi's ten-year anniversary. At her own request, Doreen was cremated, and her ashes were sprinkled into the Santa Monica Bay. At that time Nelson said he wanted the same for himself on his death.

Frank Sinatra, Jr., called Nelson on May 27, shortly after hearing of Doreen's passing. Nelson was in the hospital for the second of three visits during that year, this time with bleeding from the rectum. He needed blood transfusions to replace the blood he had lost. During one of the transfusions he was infected with hepatitis B. His doctors decided to install a portacaval shunt in his liver in order to shut off the weakened vein at the base of his esophagus, which had burst.

Frank told his friend and mentor, "Nelson, I just wanted to tell you how sorry I am about the death of the mother of your children." "He burst into tears on the telephone—big, big tears," Frank recalled. "'I tried to save her! I tried so hard to save her!' he said."

"Nelson must have been a very emotional man, a sweet man," added Frank, Jr. "I had previously only seen that kind of emotion coming from Nelson in his music."

Less than two months later, Frank, Jr., approached Nelson to arrange Rupert Holmes's song "The People We Never Get to Love" for an upcoming engagement at the Sahara in Las Vegas. He brought a tape of it to Nelson and waited for him in his Larchmont Boulevard office. Frank later remembered that as he watched Nelson walk in, he was hoping his face didn't reveal his shock at his friend's appearance. "I hadn't seen Nelson in a long time. His hair had gone completely white. He came into the office, and I sat down at the piano and played the song for him while he sat on the couch.

"While I was talking to him, he began nodding off. His head was going back and his eyes were closing. Then he was sitting up, and I was looking at him; and I thought, 'Something's wrong here.' He looked around his office. It was the kind of office where you can't open any windows. He said, 'I think there's something not straight with the air in this room. You know what I'd like to do, Frank? I'd like to walk outside to my car and sit there and get a little fresh air!'

"It was after 5:30 at night and everybody was gone from the building. We went down the elevator one flight and walked toward the parking lot. I was walking behind him when Nelson fell right down, right on his face, BANG! I don't know if you've ever been so scared that you wet yourself. I wet myself and I said, 'Nelson!' I grabbed him, and his face was the color of your shirt [blue]. I turned him over. His flesh was clammy.

"I began giving him CPR when all of a sudden he opened his eyes, and he looked around and said, 'What the hell happened?' I said, 'Don't talk, just breathe.' I sat him up against the wall. I reached into my pocket. I had a bunch of keys and I threw them across the floor, and I said, 'What's that?' He said, 'What?' I said, 'What's that?' He looked, and he said, 'Look like keys.' I said, 'How many?' I was trying to get his autonomic functions to take over. I took his pulse and his pulse was going fast. It was almost imperceptible. I said, 'Nelson, keep breathing. Just sit there, for God's sake.' He said, 'No, I'm better now.' He tried to stand up, and he weighed nothing at that point. He was about six feet tall, but he was skinny.

"I picked him up and put him in his four-door Cadillac. He sat behind the steering wheel, and by now he was doing better. He gave me his keys and asked me to go back up to his office and get something with sugar in it. In his office I picked up a container of orange juice and then dialed his home number. There was no answer. I locked the office and went down to the car.

"The color was back in his face, he was breathing the air, and he was feeling better. I gave him the orange juice, and he started drinking it. He said, 'What took you so long?'" Frank, Jr., explained to him that he had called Naomi, whereupon Nelson became furious and said, "Why the hell did you call her for? Now she won't talk to me for another six months!" Frank tried to explain to him that he had come very close to dying only a few minutes before. "You were dead a minute ago," he protested.

Nelson suddenly started his car and wouldn't listen to Frank, Jr.'s pleas that he shouldn't leave—what if he had another seizure? Nelson drove off and left him standing there extremely alarmed and dumbfounded. He figured the reason Nelson wouldn't take his advice was that he was too young for Nelson to take seriously. (He was then thirty-six.)

Frank, Jr., then called Sonny Burke, but he wasn't home. He told Burke's wife, Dotty, what had happened and asked her to have Sonny call Nelson at home and scream at him about the seriousness of his condition. There was silence. "Frank," said Dotty, "Sonny is in intensive care at St. John's Hospital in Santa Monica. He has cancer in both lungs. They don't expect him to last until the end of the week. I don't know if he can talk, let alone bawl out Nelson, but I'll see if I can get him to. . . ." Frank, Jr. said, "I'm sitting here and I'm listening to this. Now her husband's a few days away from death." Dotty said, "Are you all right?" Frank, Jr. said, "This has been some swingin' day!"

Later that night, Sonny Burke called his old and dear friend, Nelson Riddle, and told him what an idiot he was and how foolish he was to drive home after what happened. According to Frank, Jr., "He didn't tell Nelson anything else. And I don't think Nelson ever found out that on that day that he died right in front of me, or that when Sonny called him that night to bawl him out, Sonny was dying. Sonny Burke died four days later on May 31, 1980. I was present at his funeral."

For Nelson, the shadows were lengthening. His career was in terrible shape, his marriage was in a hopeless state, and his health was now a serious problem. What was ahead for him?

CHAPTER 9

Linda Ronstadt and the Last Hurrah

Indicative of the declining state of Nelson Riddle's career by 1980 are the four days he spent that year rerecording thirty to forty of his foremost arrangements for Muzak, Inc. Although his music was no longer palatable to an increasingly youth-oriented culture, it was perfect to serve as a background in elevators and in dentists' and doctors' offices. This led to Riddle's commenting, "Yesterday's hits are today's Muzak, and today's hits are tomorrow's Muzak."

John Palladino, the Capitol engineer-turned-record producer, hadn't seen or spoken with Nelson in years when he received a call from him one night in the early '80s. Nelson wondered whether Palladino was working on anything in which he might be able to participate. "By then I had retired," Palladino recalled. "Poor guy. I felt sorry for him."

Whenever he was going through a down period, an offer to work in London provided Riddle with an inspirational lift. In "Nelson Riddle Talking," one of several bylined pieces in the English jazz magazine *Crescendo,* he said, "When I come over here, I find they treasure the past; by treasuring the past they fasten me firmly in the present—which is nice, I must say." And so it was when he and Naomi flew there so that Nelson could record with two of the world's most accomplished musicians, Sir Yehudi Menuhin, the renowned classical violinist, and the premier jazz violinist Stéphane Grappelli, formerly a member of Django Reinhardt's classic Quintet of the Hot Club of France.

The album, *Puttin' on the Ritz,* was recorded on July 15 and 16, 1981, for Angel, Capitol/EMI's classical label. It consisted of songs first introduced and made famous by Fred Astaire, with Nelson conducting an instrumental ensemble in support of the complementary talents of Menuhin and Grappelli. Riddle used much of the same setup he had employed eighteen years earlier with Oscar Peterson, namely the combination of English horns, flutes, and celli.[1]

While the arrangements were not among his most sterling efforts, he relished the opportunity to work alongside the two masters. Menuhin and Grappelli had actually recorded several of the songs for the album in 1973, '75, and '78 with an accompanying

Linda Ronstadt and Nelson during one of the last recording sessions of their *For Sentimental Reasons* album. The severity of Nelson's illness is evident.

small group. Nelson's remaining twelve orchestral tracks with them completed the album.

Considering the astonishing richness of the Astaire canon, it's unfortunate that Nelson and Astaire never were given the opportunity to record together. As noted earlier, they had enjoyed a warm personal relationship dating from the early '60s. But by the time Nelson began working on a freelance basis, Astaire had stopped recording. Given the focus of the post-mid-'60s music industry, it's unlikely that any major label would have devoted the kind of budget necessary to bring together these two stalwarts from another era.

Bud Yorkin, who produced Astaire's two truly special television "Specials" said, "Fred loved Nelson . . . he wanted to have Nelson arrange André Previn's hit, 'Like Young,' for one of the shows." According to Yorkin it didn't work out because David Rose, the musical director for the two Astaire shows, remarked—justifiably—"If I can't arrange that one, I can't arrange anything; it's basically all strings."

★ ★ ★

Although the central reason for his visit to England in the summer of '81 was to participate in the Menuhin/Grappelli recording sessions, in addition, the Grosvenor House in London had booked Andy Williams and Sarah Vaughan for a June 22–27 engagement and asked Nelson to be a part of it. During the 1970s, Williams had sought Nelson out to write five arrangements for him, among which was "New York, New York."

"You could pick out Nelson's arrangements anywhere," Williams recalled. "He had developed that definite style. I think he appreciated me. I told him the combination of things I wanted to do, and he said, 'Terrific.'"

Since Andy Williams and Henry Mancini had worked so successfully together, I asked Williams to compare Mancini and Riddle's writing. "They're both wonderful to sing to because they're both great accompanying arrangers. They don't take away from you, they add to you. Nelson wasn't writing to show off. His charts were always nice and swinging. He didn't scream with high brass, didn't get nutty; he stayed within the range of most people's abilities. I found that out in England. You could go through his things in half an hour. I found Nelson very easy to work with and extremely nice. I would have loved to have him write on our television show, but he wasn't available. He would have been my first choice. I liked him so much."

At the Grosvenor House, Williams and Vaughan each did forty-five minutes preceded by Nelson conducting a large orchestra for thirty minutes. "It was great for all three of us," Williams said.

Following the London engagement, it was planned that in August Vaughan and Nelson would attempt the umpteenth recorded approach to the George and Ira Gershwin score from *Porgy and Bess* for Pablo Records. Nelson looked forward to the project, but it was just another album that never happened. In anticipation of arranging it, he said, "Such events are very valuable because, once again, some of our fine voices are stilled on record, due to the record business having changed so drastically."[2]

★ ★ ★

Two of Nelson and Naomi's closest friends were David and Betty Rose. Arranger and composer David Rose first became celebrated in the 1940s for his hit single "Holiday for Strings," and again two decades later for "The Stripper." He also spent more than thirty years in television as musical director of *The Red Skelton Show* and another fourteen years as composer for the popular Western series *Bonanza,* in addition to scoring several films. Most importantly, David Rose was one of the premier string arrangers in the history of popular music.

Aside from respecting Rose's considerable talent, Nelson was drawn to him by his likable and urbane personality as well as his ability to take a break from his musical career when he so chose. This was a trait Nelson admired but was completely unable to emulate. For one thing, Nelson was never able to take a real vacation from music.

The Roses spent more time socially with Nelson and Naomi than with any other couple, getting together two or three times a month. Betty remembered, "Naomi was finicky about food, so she liked certain things and to David and me it didn't really matter. We mostly ate at Italian and Japanese restaurants. Nelson ate plain food at the Italian places. When Nelson went to Japan or Australia or England he'd take Naomi with him. And he was a big gun there. Everybody wined and dined them. That she loved."

Although Betty tried to instill in Naomi some sense of what she could gain from having a relationship with her family, Naomi was estranged from her sister Miriam at the time, and had no contact with her mother at the end of her mother's life either. Betty recalled, "I told her that she was missing so much out of life not being a stepmother. But she said, 'I don't have time for that.'"

In September, Nelson returned to Cedars Hospital to have portacaval shunt surgery. According to Betty, Naomi never visited Nelson once during the more than two weeks he was in the hospital. She remarked to Betty, "I don't want to see him suffering like that."

After his liver surgery, Nelson was told he had to eat plenty of fruit and vegetables and to avoid fried foods. Betty remembered, "Naomi was informed that she would have to prepare certain things at home for him. She said, 'No, I'm not going to do that.' Just like that. So, all of his friends helped out. I sent fruit baskets, and sometimes I'd go over with some soup and hand it to the maid. The maid would cook a little bit, I think.

"I used to get half-gallon orange juice containers for him so that he could drink it when they would come over for dinner. In September, Nelson had been informed by Dr. Gerald Blankfort, his attending physician, that he had never had a liver case such as his that held up more than five years, six years at the most."

It took Nelson the better part of three years to regain his strength. During that time he tried to increase his endurance by once again doing a lot of swimming. He was finally able to do thirty laps a day before he went to work.

In discussing his illness, he said, "It taught me something. It taught me that just to swing your feet over the side of the bed every morning is its own reward. Nobody knows how long you're going to be around, so you might as well enjoy it."[3]

Nonetheless, Nelson's outlook on life was unchanged. "One day I had lunch with him at Musso & Frank," Saul Ilson recalled. "I said to him, 'Can't we go somewhere else?' 'No! Not negotiable.' He was talking about having recently gone to some party, and he was observing. He said to me, 'I felt so bad watching those happy couples, all those people together enjoying life. . . . I'm not one of them. I don't belong to that group.'

"He also mentioned that he hadn't had sex with Naomi for years. He said he talked to her about it and said, 'Do you realize that we haven't had sex for two years?' She said, 'Really, is it that long?' He'd get real melancholy."

The Roses were not the only of the Riddles' friends to note Naomi's adverse effect on Nelson's life. Nelson's first cousin, Bob Runyon, was about to accept an upper-level executive job with the Denny's Restaurants chain in 1980 and relocated to Southern California. On their arrival, he and his wife Jean were picked up at the airport by Nelson and the three of them spent the day together. They hadn't seen one another in sixteen years, at which time Nelson and Doreen had still been married.

Nelson spoke candidly to the Runyons about his marriage to Naomi. He explained that when he decided to marry Naomi, "It seemed like the easiest thing to do." He also explained in terms of a justification, "She would take care of me." Later that day he added, "You know, Bob, I think when I married Naomi I married my mother."

During the next two and one-half years Runyon repeatedly experienced Naomi's standard operating procedure of failing to deliver Nelson's messages. He and Jean saw Nelson only twice more during these years. "I knew how Naomi felt about Nelson's children and, after all, we were family, too," Runyon resignedly pointed out.

After a decade of having been married to Naomi—whom he often referred to as either "The Ice Queen" or "The Dragon Lady," complete with a rolling of his eyes—Nelson was ripe for another affair. Several musical colleagues, such as Lalo Schifrin and Bill Watrous, had witnessed public spats between them. Saul Ilson said, "In his first marriage, Nelson gave away his power, and in his second, he gave away his life."

Nelson had originally met attractive redhead Laurie Brooks, who was working at the Robertson Boulevard Animal Hospital, in 1971, when he brought his dog Chrissy Boy in for treatment. Their affair, however, didn't begin until 1979. "We began as friends, talking friends," Brooks recalled. "One day we had lunch and decided maybe there was something there. It was a walking, talking relationship in many ways. . . . He needed a person maybe out of the industry to talk to. We laughed a lot—he had a marvelous sense of humor. It would usually be because of something he'd said—about anything."

For the next six years, while Nelson was working in Los Angeles, he and Brooks saw each other almost every day, often meeting at Holmby Park or at his office and then strolling down Larchmont to have lunch or dinner.

Nelson was open to talking to Brooks about both of his marriages. "I think that

An early 1980s photograph of Nelson and his friend, arranger Billy May, taken at a music industry function.

his marriage to Doreen was happy at the beginning," she said. "I think the kids would concur that she was an alcoholic. He was very unhappy. He felt that he had failed somehow. Here they had all these kids, and then his getting involved with Rosemary Clooney.

"He was working so much. He really was a workaholic. There were times when he would write four arrangements in a night. As my daughter said once, 'Mom, he's very grumpy.' He had that kind of demeanor . . . but there was a sparkle in his eyes.

"He was a very loving, very kind man. He sent me a card a day for practically the entire six years. That's why I could never understand his marriage to Naomi. He felt he owed it to her somehow. He believed she couldn't take care of herself, that she would have to have someone take care of her. I was very happy being with him, and I knew he loved me very much."

Brooks went on to relate that Naomi was dead set against the Riddles having a Christmas tree in the house, something which Rosemary Acerra and Chris Riddle readily confirmed. Nelson would meet Chris at Skip's house on Christmas day and exchange presents with Brooks and the other Riddle children. "Here was a guy in a man's body but a kid at heart who wanted in the worst way to have all his kids around him at Christmastime," Brooks said.

★ ★ ★

To compensate for his lack of film, television, and album-writing assignments, Nelson began playing dates conducting symphony orchestras for pops concerts—a practice that had begun in 1977. These dates were with the likes of the Boston Pops, the Chicago Symphony, the San Francisco Pops, the Denver Pops, the Phoenix Pops, the Vancouver Symphony, and the Houston Symphony. André Previn secured one of these dates for him when he was the conductor of the Pittsburgh Symphony.

"Nelson came and conducted an absolutely wonderful pops concert," Previn recalled, "except his diffidence was so great that he tended to disappear from the stage. I took him out to dinner [afterwards]. . . . He asked if I had anything to say. Then I said, 'Well, not musically, because musically we can all take lessons from you.' But I said, 'For Christ's sake, assert yourself a little bit.' At that point, his wife [Naomi] came to life and said, 'You hear that, Nelson, you hear that? Now, get some advice on how to conduct without looking like such a jerk.' I said, 'Hey, wait a minute! Wait a minute!' I got so upset that I then, as graciously as I could, excused myself and left the table."

On February 4 and 5, 1982, Ella Fitzgerald and Nelson Riddle recorded their last album together. Despite an array of such formidable soloists as tenor saxophonist Bob Cooper, alto saxophonists Marshal Royal and Willie Schwartz, trombonist Bill Watrous, flutist Hubert Laws, guitarist Joe Pass, pianist Jimmy Rowles, and drummer Shelly Manne, the album, *The Best Is Yet to Come,* simply wasn't the best. In fact, it was a near disaster.

The raggedy tone of Ella's voice couldn't be disguised. It marred the impact of her more meaningful lyric interpretations at this stage of her career. In addition, the several organ solo spots that Nelson wrote for Art Hillery were intrusive. He wrote several charts for a combination of four flutes, eight cellos, and four French horns. As he explained it, "By superimposing the flutes or cellos on the horns, I was able to create a sound similar to the blend Debussy achieved in 'La Mer.'"[4] However, these settings, while marking a slight change in his musical direction, simply didn't provide the kind of support Nelson had furnished Ella in the past.

During the recording sessions, Riddle deferred to Norman Granz rather than asserting himself. Bill Watrous recalled that he specifically designed his solo on "Lady Be Good" behind Ella by choosing to play only a few particular notes. "I had started to abandon the multi-note attitude that I had earlier in my career," Watrous said. "When an instrumentalist is accompanying a singer, his responsibility is really to stay the hell out of the way." Granz, however, wanted Watrous to deliver a more extravagant kind of a solo by playing more notes.

"Nelson and Norman didn't exactly go 'round and 'round during the entire session, but there was tension," Watrous remarked. "Norman was set in his ways as to how he wanted things to be, but Nelson was every bit the dignified professional. When we listened to the playback, Norman overruled us. Nelson said, 'There's no accounting for taste.'" As usual, Nelson didn't want to rock the boat.

His aversion to conflict was also displayed one night when he was sitting alone in a restaurant at a table right across from Max Bennett and his wife. Bennett recalled that he and his wife were having a serious argument. Max looked over at Nelson in the middle of it, which led Nelson to remark to them, "No matter what's wrong, you guys should work it out and stay together." Bennett said, "He showed real compassion for people. That was really heartwarming to me."

In reality this was not merely compassion, but was another example of Nelson's thinking: avoid confrontation with your wife at all cost. It was Nelson Smock Riddle, Sr.'s behavior toward Albertine all over again.

And despite the fact that Charles Brown had made some serious investment mistakes with his money a few years before that, when Meyer Levin, another of his business managers, wanted to defend Nelson against the IRS's contention that some of his deductions weren't allowable, Nelson caved in to the IRS rather than stand up and fight for his rights. He told Levin to pay the money rather than deal with the confrontation.

★ ★ ★

Another disappointment for Nelson occurred a month after the *The Best Is Yet to Come* recording sessions. While he had been signed to score the limited run of the CBS-TV series *Cagney and Lacey,* which initially starred Tyne Daly and Meg Foster, he was not retained to write the music when the show was picked up by the network. The series wound up spanning six seasons and would have been the most financially lucrative television series he had ever scored. Bill Conti, who had made an auspicious screen composing debut with his *Rocky* score, was signed to score for the rest of its run and wrote an entirely different kind of theme that ultimately became synonymous with the show.

But all was not lost for Nelson in television. In 1981 and '82 he scored the two-hour *Mike Hammer: Margin for Murder* movie starring Kevin Dobson in addition to *Help Wanted: Male* starring Suzanne Pleshette. He also scored the *Harper Valley P.T.A.* series, a spinoff from the inane film he had scored three years earlier.

An important break came Riddle's way under strange circumstances. Bob Newhart, who has spent the major part of his incredible comedic career starring in television situation comedies, recalled, "In 1983 [my wife] Ginny and I used to walk over to Armand Hammer Park, formerly Holmby Park [in West Los Angeles on Beverly Glen]. Nelson often talked to his children from the pay phone there.

"After we had seen him there many times, he approached us. He looked familiar and introduced himself. He started walking with us, and we found him a curmudgeon. . . . We really were in awe of him because we wondered, how did he do that [write arrangements]? What kind of a mind does it take that hears all the instruments playing in harmony?

"And when we got to talking, I found out that Nelson knew everybody in the park. He had a story about everybody. At one point, I think I mentioned his doing the music for the show, and he said, 'I'd love to do that.'"

Once again, though, Nelson found himself in Henry Mancini's shadow. Mancini had already written the theme for Newhart's third situation comedy, *Newhart,* which began airing on CBS-TV in 1982. It featured Bob as the proprietor of an inn in Vermont. After the meeting in the park, Nelson was signed to score the show on a weekly basis, a chore he performed until early in the 1985–86 season. As Newhart described Riddle's work: "It meant transitions from one scene to another, kind of setting the mood for the next theme. He used a combination of two woodwinds, a harmonica, and a string quartet.

"Nelson featured trombones more than most composers," Newhart also noted, "and he made use of them during the most romantic part of the arrangement. He used the trombone section as the emphasis—interesting because that was his instrument. He would use a piece of Hank's theme. Very often when a scene would end, and there'd be laughter, it would be cut off because it couldn't carry over into the next scene. He'd use the music [as a transition]. Nelson's music was often as funny as some of the scenes."

★ ★ ★

At this juncture in Nelson Riddle's declining career, a rock 'n' roll superstar, of all things, entered his life and created a major turnaround. Maria Linda Ronstadt had left Tucson in the late '60s, intent on establishing herself in the folk-rock scene in Los Angeles. Her first boyfriend in L.A. was the singer/songwriter J.D. Souther, also a folk rocker who later wrote several of the Eagles' hits (including "New Kid in Town"), as well as Ronstadt's "Faithless Love." Music was at the very core of their relationship; Bob Dylan was their muse.

It was Souther who reintroduced Ronstadt to the music of Frank Sinatra backed by the arrangements of Nelson Riddle, which she had first heard as a seventeen-year-old high school student. He brought to her attention the classic nature of the *Only the Lonely* album, and she immediately fell in love with the arrangements.

Ronstadt diligently pursued her career in pop music for the next fifteen years. Reaching the pinnacle of her profession, she became *the* female voice of rock of the 1970s with such hits—both with her first band, the Stone Poneys, and later as a solo artist—as "Different Drum," "Silver Threads and Golden Needles," "Heat Wave," "You're No Good," "When Will I Be Loved," "Blue Bayou," "It's So Easy," "Ooh, Baby, Baby," and "Hurt So Bad." In all that time, she never lost sight of the high musical standard that the Sinatra/Riddle combination offered.

As a child, Ronstadt had been exposed to many genres of music; she had learned Mexican song standards from her family and listened to Wolfman Jack, the noted rock 'n' roll radio personality on XERB radio, which beamed up from Mexico. She loved Bavarian music, Jamaican music, and even the Jewish liturgical music sung by cantors. She had long been open to expanding her musical horizons and felt a need to explore other, even more diverse kinds of music.

One of Ronstadt's latest passions was the operettas of Gilbert and Sullivan. Her mother had played their music on the piano to her when she was a little girl. When Joe Papp, who headed New York City's Public Theater, announced in 1980 that Linda Ronstadt would star in a Delacorte Theater production of *The Pirates of Penzance* as part of the Public Theater's Shakespeare in the Park program, it seemed completely incompatible with her image. Many people were skeptical that a thirty-four-year-old pop star could make her mark in such an alien musical environment and, perhaps more importantly, questioned how it would affect her superstar status in the rock field.

Not surprisingly, Ronstadt knew exactly what she was doing. The New York critics and theatergoers enthusiastically endorsed her starring appearance in *The Pirates of Penzance* both in Central Park and when it moved to Broadway. In the fall of 1984, when she played in the even further afield English adaptation of Puccini's opera, *La Bohème,* the reviews were equally favorable. Her powerful voice, coupled with her keen intelligence, enabled her to successfuly interpret these two very different types of repertoire, which were thousands of miles away from the anthems that had initially made her a star.

Reflecting on these varied musical pursuits a few years later, Ronstadt said, "They were amazing experiences, but I'm a seat-of-the-pants singer without a trained operatic or legitimate voice. I've been told I would have sung in that style if I had started training when I was much younger. Technically, the bottom of my voice is overdeveloped, while my high voice is patterned after my brother's boy soprano. . . ."[5]

But there was still another kind of music that intrigued her: American pop standards—music from the era that predated Ronstadt's entrance into the music business. And it was none other than one of her lovers, Mick Jagger, who further piqued her interest in this kind of music. Jagger gave her a Norman Granz–produced jam session album of standards featuring saxophonists Charlie Parker and Ben Webster, which she played constantly.

"In the '60s, people drew artificial lines between what was hip and what was not," Ronstadt remarked. "That confusion of ideology and music, I think, was wrong. I refuse to be an ideologue who memorizes rules about good taste and good art. I have to go by feeling, by exploring my own roots, by following my bliss."[6]

In 1982, during the run of *Penzance,* the renowned record producer Jerry Wexler, despite Ronstadt's protests to the contrary, was convinced that she could successfully interpret the songs originally made famous by Mildred Bailey, such as "A Ghost of a Chance," "Lover Man," and "Someone to Watch over Me." "Jerry kept saying, 'You've got the chops. You can do it!'" Ronstadt recalled. "We did a demo record with the jazz pianist Tommy Flanagan and a bassist and drummer. I felt seduced by the music. In fact, I was completely gone."[7]

After she left the show, Wexler convinced Ronstadt to work with tenor saxophonist and arranger Al Cohn on an album he (Wexler) would produce for her. Joe Smith, then the president of Elektra/Asylum, gave tentative approval to the Cohn project. As Ira Koslow, then Ronstadt's tour manager and later her personal manager, pointed out, "Linda had sort of earned her right to pick her own music."

Ronstadt wanted to rehearse with the band before attempting to record the album, a practice she had long since adopted. She felt this would enable her to rework the arrangements, if need be. Wexler was dead set against it, citing the prohibitive cost of such rehearsals. The album was completed in three days and didn't work out. Cohn's arrangements reportedly put Ronstadt in a strictly jazz context that wasn't at all suited to her. She played it for J.D. Souther, who said, "No, that just doesn't cut it."

Joe Smith told her, "You are not Sarah Vaughan, you are not Carmen McRae, you are not Ella. You are different. They can't do 'Heat Wave.' On this recording, you sound like you're always trying to catch up on it." According to Smith, at that point Ronstadt walked over and hugged him.

After Smith informed Wexler that Elektra/Asylum wouldn't release the results of the sessions, he had lunch with Ronstadt and said, "If you want to do those standards, there are three guys you can do them with: Don Costa, Gordon Jenkins, and Nelson Riddle."

Ronstadt then flew to London to film *Pirates of Penzance*. She returned to record the *Get Closer* album, a mixture of rock 'n' roll oldies, country material, and pop ballads. The thought of working with Nelson Riddle, however, wouldn't go away. As she said later, "I would have sold out my best friend to figure out a way to get into the studio with Nelson. I honestly didn't know if he was still alive, if he was still working, if he had ever heard of me, or if he thought I was horrible."[8]

Her manager and record producer, Peter Asher, also wanted her to work with Nelson. "At that time, we were discussing various options for a forthcoming album," Asher remembered. He called Nelson in May 1982 to discuss the possibility of his writing charts for a few songs. One of them was "Guess I'll Hang My Tears out to Dry," which had been one of the memorable tracks from the *Only the Lonely* album.

Laurie Brooks, on a break from the animal hospital, was visiting Nelson in his office at the precise moment when Asher called. "When he hung up, he looked at me and said, 'Who's Linda Ronstadt?'"

When Nelson met initially with Asher and Ronstadt at a recording studio, his terse reply to Asher's query was, "I don't write arrangements, I write albums." He realized that if he wrote an individual chart it would be included in an album with several other arrangers' work.

When they next met, at Ronstadt's home in Brentwood, Nelson had her sing some of the songs she was considering recording. "He didn't like much of the stuff she had selected," Brooks recalled. Chris Riddle remembered, "What Dad [first] told me about Linda was that she had a wonderful instrument, but that she had never been taught what to do with it. He told me that he had urged her to listen to Frank Sinatra's records and listen to the attention to detail he gave to a lyric and how he perfectly molded the syllables in with the chord changes."

Shortly thereafter, a three-album deal was signed. For the first album with Ronstadt, Nelson was to be paid a royalty of one percent of all retail sales of discs and tapes and one-half percent if sold by an Elektra/Asylum licensee. There were also different royalty breakdowns for various major countries. For the other two albums, he was paid the same one percent of retail, but the figure escalated to one and one-half percent for sales in excess of 500,000 albums sold and to two percent of sales in excess of 1,000,000 albums, with the same deal as before for Elektra/Asylum licensees.

Riddle was also paid a fee of $2,000 per song arrangement for each album and an advance of $500 for each master. For each song released on a different record, an additional advance of $500 would be paid within thirty days, following the release of that album.

Joe Smith recently called the deal "only fair." "Nelson could have asked for even more money, and I think Linda and Peter might have given it to him."

Once they had agreed to work together, Ronstadt asked Nelson how he worked in the recording studio. Nelson said, "We usually do three or four tunes in four hours." She responded, "In rock 'n' roll we try it over and over, and if we can't get it then, we go and play video games." Nelson concluded the discussion by saying, "We don't work that way." It would be incorrect, however, to assume that Ronstadt expected to work in her usual manner with Nelson and an orchestra.

Ronstadt relished the fact that Nelson brought his original conductor's notes for the Sinatra session of "Guess I'll Hang My Tears out to Dry" to one of their first meetings. "It was so freaky to see him cross out Frank's key. He took his pencil and crossed it out very casually and put my key at the top and started making new notes. It seemed to me that that piece of music should have been framed."

Ronstadt and Riddle began recording together at the Complex Studio in West Los Angeles, owned by the respected recording engineer George Massenburg, on June 30, 1982. Peter Asher was the producer. Ronstadt, with Nelson and his orchestra, cut "Guess I'll Hang My Tears out to Dry," "What'll I Do?," "Someone to Watch over Me," and "What's New?" (Ronstadt had recorded some of this material with Al Cohn, and it had also previously been included on the *Only the Lonely* album).

Afterwards, she played the results of the first session for her jury of J.D. Souther, singer/songwriter Andrew Gold, and comedian Steve Martin, all of whom encouraged her to complete the album. "I was never happier singing," she enthusiastically recalled. "I just never had as good a time as I did doing that record."

One musician who attended the first recording session reported, "I remember Nelson being furious at Linda the whole time because she was singing very sharp.

Afterwards, he was grumbling. He said, 'She can't sing two notes in tune!' There would be this beautiful take with the orchestra, and she would be out in left field, and they'd have to do it over again. If you listen to the title cut, Tony Terran was playing lead on that tune. He played it beautifully. The take that was used had Tony playing sharp—when trumpet players get tired they play very sharp. But that was because they had to do so many takes."

In the midst of the first Riddle recording sessions, Ronstadt candidly told Robert Palmer of the *New York Times,* "I'm just determined to make an album of those standards. It's not easy for me to sing that stuff. I've always sung in a less disciplined style than these songs require. Your phrasing has got to be perfect, and I think phrasing has always been my biggest problem." When asked how long it would take until she had a finished album, she answered, "Long enough for me to get it right."

The six recording sessions for the album eventually titled *What's New* weren't completed until March 4, 1983. On the album's release in September, the national airplay was meager, but New York stations went on it and stayed with it. Rock stations and Adult Contemporary stations left it alone. Jonathan Schwartz of WNEW made promoting the album his personal crusade by constantly playing it. He not only admired how well Ronstadt and Riddle had succeeded, but he was also personally fond of both of them.

★ ★ ★

Trombonist Chauncey Welsch had relocated to California in 1972. On the recommendation of Tommy Shepard, who had also become Nelson's contractor, Welsch began doing several of Nelson's casuals—gigs at the Beverly Hills Hotel, the Century Plaza, the Beverly Wilshire, the Beverly Hilton, the Bullock's store on Wilshire Boulevard— and then graduated to playing on his *Sears Mystery Theatre* radio shows on CBS. After Shepherd had a heart attack, he was still making calls to secure musicians for Nelson's record dates. He hired Welsch for the final *What's New* recording date with the admonition, "It's only one trombone, and you'd better bring your lip."

The narrow musical framework for the Ronstadt album was completely different from the structure of a typical Sinatra or Ella Fitzgerald album, which most often used a big band, strings, and added instruments. The instrumentation for the *What's New* album consisted of a full string section, woodwinds, no saxophones except for tenor saxophonist Bob Cooper, no other brass except for trumpeter Tony Terran, and a rhythm section. "Nelson never gave me an idea of what he wanted me to play. I was left completely on my own," Welsch recalled.

During the recording of "Lover Man," Ronstadt complained to Nelson that she was distracted by the sound of what she thought was a violin, but in reality was Welsch's trombone. In later years Ronstadt admitted to Welsch, "Until I heard you play, I always thought a trombone should have a boxing glove at the end of it." "That was what trombones were to her. They were like marching band instruments. What she heard from me was something lyrical and loving," he said.

As a result of his solo on "Lover Man," Welsch began to work at all of Nelson's casuals. At a dance date at the Beverly Wilshire, he asked Nelson, "Is there anything happening with Linda's album?" "Oh, yeah," Nelson replied. "We're editing it, and it's going to be great, and you've got a lot to do with it."

This was an inspiring moment for Welsch. He realized he had succeeded in approaching "Lover Man" the way his trombone idol, Urbie Green, might have. He later did the other two Ronstadt/Riddle albums, *Lush Life* and *For Sentimental Reasons,* and had several solo opportunities on "My Old Flame," "'Round Midnight," "You Go to My Head," and "Bewitched."

During one of the recording sessions for *What's New,* drummer John Guerin was attaching his cymbals to his drums and saw the title tune on his music stand. "I thought, 'Why are we doing this? It's been done.' Nelson had written an intro for "What's New" for Sinatra that had knocked me out. I went up to Nelson and said, 'How are you going to top that intro?' He said, 'I've been up half the night.' But what he wrote was wonderful. He wrote it quite a bit differently. That's a very difficult thing to do."

On its September 13, 1983, release, *What's New,* which consisted of nine songs ("Never, Never Will I Marry" was recorded but not included), went gold in a month and then went platinum. It zoomed to #3 on the *Billboard* Pop Album chart and stayed on the chart for an incredible twenty-five weeks. "Everybody was buying it for their mother or grandmother," remarked Guerin. It has gone on to sell an amazing total of over 3.4 million copies.

Ronstadt had once again proven her versatility. The musical combination of Ronstadt and Riddle had surprised everyone except the two of them. Many members of the media thought Nelson had retired; suddenly he was in vogue again. *People* published a highly complimentary story, complete with a photo of Nelson and Naomi kissing in their Japanese garden.

Nelson told *People* writer Todd Gold that recording with Ronstadt was "damn fun. Just think of the miracle to tie into somebody who's as reliable as Linda Ronstadt to record this type of music and be on the charts." He said, "The same principles guided me on the arrangements for this album that have always guided me. That is to give the singer room to breathe."

Nelson continued by admiring Ronstadt's "strong, beautiful voice which has really unbelievable power," and praised her intonation. "When she belts out the song, 'What's New,' you really believe it." He acknowledged the fact that "she took a real risk doing this album." He added in his usual off-center slant, "I don't think I would have the nerve to leave all those millions of rock 'n' roll dollars lying in someone else's pockets."

Nelson called Ronstadt "a lady who I think is a combination of people. I think part of her is very grown up. She's a bright, dependable human being, and on the other hand there's a little girl who enjoys her toys and a fresh area to think about."

When asked about what made *What's New* such a resounding hit, Nelson replied, "I think it's a freak. This type of music is not eminently salable these days. I don't know what to say except that people have learned a few new songs in spite of themselves that have strong melodies and non-suggestive words, just good songs."

Relishing the fact that he was once again involved with a successful album, and asked whether he would become more active in the record business as a result, Nelson said, "We'll see. I don't have any plans. I was the king. I don't need to be coronated again. Just to have been on top once was enough. That's more than most people get."[9]

A September weekend concert engagement at Radio City Music Hall in New York was booked specifically to tie in with the release of the album, and also to generate interest from the press. Along with a few other essential musicians, bassist Ray Brown, who was featured on the recording, was brought to New York as part of the orchestra to ensure that the performances would be of a high caliber.

John Guerin remembered seeing people dressed in World War II uniforms in the front row of the theater. "I think there was only one cry from the balcony in the whole concert saying 'Blue Bayou' or rock 'n' roll.' Mind you, the album hadn't been out that long."

During her performance Ronstadt was enchanting in her obvious delight in singing these classic standards in the great hall, even though she wasn't yet totally comfortable with all of the material. She opened the concert wearing a black sheath with sequins, her hair up, standing by the piano, with the curtains closed, encircled by a spotlight. She began singing the verse to "I've Got a Crush on You" ("How glad the many millions. . . ."). When she got to the bridge, her hand went down and the orchestra—with Nelson at the front on a riser—emerged, playing as it rose from the pit at the front of the stage.

When Ronstadt took a break, Riddle led the orchestra in a medley of songs from the album. The staging and the production for the concert were exemplary. Ronstadt's entrance to open the second half of the performance was equally striking. Wearing a black dress with crinolines, she reclined on a crescent moon that was left over from singer/songwriter Peter Allen's engagement. She and the moon slowly descended to the stage at the moment Nelson's orchestra again ascended from the pit and began to play.

Immediately after their return from New York, Linda and Nelson performed on the ABC-TV show *Live and In Person*. The show was taped on September 29, 1983, at the Shrine Auditorium in Los Angeles. During the break between the rehearsal and the taping of the show, Nelson approached saxophonist and flutist Gary Foster and the rest of the reed section from Peter Matz's orchestra. He said to them, "I hope you guys know why I don't hire you." Foster recalled, "We perked up and thought, 'What's going to come next?' Then Nelson said, 'I'm very loyal to the people I came up with.' I think it made everyone feel good because it was very sensitive on his part to even address an issue like that with us."

Pianist and arranger/composer Alan Broadbent worked frequently for Nelson during his last decade. "Nelson was one of the few, if not the only one, of the arranger-composer echelon in Tinseltown who had loyalty to his musicians," he said. "He had a real love for those individuals who said nothing but nasty things behind his back about him. [Even so] I think they all loved him."

★ ★ ★

Stephen Holden in the *New York Times* called *What's New* "a pop masterpiece. While the record pays its full respects to the idealistic romantic traditions and the naïve formal glamour of a bygone pop era, Miss Ronstadt's serene folkish vocal personality is a voice very much of the rock era. . . . The voice is ideal for Miss Ronstadt's goal of delivering simple, fluid line readings of great melodies while refraining from imposing heavy psychological or dramatic concepts."

Jay Cocks in *Time* offered, "*What's New* is one of the gutsiest, most unorthodox and unexpected albums of the year. . . . Emotionally it can bring a sweet rush of feeling that is immediate, direct, and for all of its sumptuousness, almost recklessly intense."

The incredible success of the album had much to do with the producing ability of Peter Asher, who, in addition to managing Linda Ronstadt, James Taylor, and several others, produced many of their records as well. Asher had been one half of the Peter and Gordon duo who had amassed nine Top 20 records (three of them gold) during the mid-'60s.

Being a fervent Gilbert and Sullivan admirer since his childhood in England, Asher had also produced the *Pirates of Penzance* stage and screen cast albums, although the latter was never released due to the failure of the film version. Being a former musician, he not only had admirable musical instincts but also extreme patience and exhibited strong but subtle leadership in the studio.

Years later, Asher left personal management and record producing to become a senior vice president of Sony Music (Columbia Records), where his main focus is the international aspect of the record business. Based in New York, he travels extensively for his work and is still involved in signing and the preproduction of new artists.

Whether he intended to or not, Nelson served as a mentor to Ronstadt and was her musical guardian throughout their association. Asher said, "He wasn't sure what to expect, but it would take a lot to make Nelson apprehensive about working with Linda. He'd sort of seen it all, and he'd heard her sing. He was impressed, certainly initially with the amount of homework that she had done. The way she had talked to me [about what she wanted to record], I had imagined it, rightly or wrongly, slightly more cabaret-ish and slightly less big production. Once he started working with her he realized what an incredibly good singer she is—Linda's one of the best female singers ever, and just happened to be first known in the rock 'n' roll tradition.

"The thing that was new to Linda was that the orchestra would follow her. In rock 'n' roll you're entirely used to singing to a track which is in strict time. That's why a lot of the vocalists end up being overdubbed. Linda would be holding a long note and waiting for the orchestra to show her where to go next. Nelson would be waiting, hands in the air, for her to be heading to the next note so he could bring the orchestra in. That was a major misunderstanding for a long time.

"We started out in the studio by walking out and standing next to Nelson. Linda would sing in his and my ear as the orchestra would run down the arrangement, and we'd make whatever adjustments were necessary. But, of course, that had been preceded by several meetings around a piano [with Don Grolnick] before he'd written [anything]."

As the sessions for the three albums progressed, Nelson began to take direction from Asher. It started with Asher's suggestion about editing part of an arrangement—removing a woodwind passage—which Nelson agreed was entirely justified. Asher recalled, "Sometimes, when my instinct was that things were just a little bit overdone, leaving not quite enough space for Linda, he would agree all too readily, which actually sort of scared me. I'd be nervous about suggesting something because he'd sort of just rip the page out."

The Ronstadt/Riddle pairing was not the first recording by an important rock star of the '60s generation singing standards with a large orchestra. It had been done by the late Harry Nilsson (or Nilsson, as he was called) with arrangements by Gordon Jenkins in the early 1970s. But at that time, Nilsson's album was considered a novelty and insignificant in comparison to what Ronstadt and Riddle had created with *What's New*, much less their other two albums. On top of that, Nelson won his second and third Grammys (out of eleven nominations) for his arrangements for *What's New* and *Lush Life* (the second album he recorded with Ronstadt).

Asher made the point that, "Even though at that particular time he [Nelson] may have been less than he was before, there's no question his reputation today would be just as intact as with or without Linda. But I think Linda added something to it and was proud to do so. . . . She kept saying about these American standards, 'They have this reputation as elevator music.' The initial album with Nelson could be called the 'Save the American Standards from the Elevator' project . . . so to do something different is, I think, a better risk than getting stuck in a rut."

Asher said the budgets for these albums were relatively the same as for Ronstadt's rock 'n' roll albums. He described the albums as, "More people for less time and less experimentation. We did most of the experimentation [earlier] around the piano."

"In recording the albums, the trick was following the score, marking the bits that didn't work, maybe doing another take and watching to see if those bits were correct or perhaps doing some edited pieces. We got better at doing that as the thing went on. . . . You will find there are mistakes on the first album, certainly. We got much better at learning how to fix things, partly because we started using more digital technology, which was coming in around that time."

★ ★ ★

The sudden attention Linda Ronstadt brought to Nelson had absolutely no bearing on his film scoring career. Based on the Hollywood homily, "You're only as good as your last movie"—and the fact that despite his brilliant use of Duke Ellington's music in

Rough Cut, the film was not a box-office hit—he was still not in demand for major films. After adapting various standards for the overture of *That's Entertainment, Part II,* which did nothing for his career, he scored the dreadful *Chattanooga Choo Choo,* starring Barbara Eden and pro-football-quarterback-turned-actor Joe Namath, in 1984.

During the shooting of the film he even flew to Sacramento to conduct the city's 100-member drum and bugle corps for a wedding scene with the two leads at the California State Railroad Museum. He continued to work in television, scoring episodes of *Matt Houston* and *Hotel.*

At about the same time, Saul Ilson was doing a television pilot at Columbia Pictures for a new series to star comedian Buddy Hackett. He wanted to sign Nelson to do the music, but the executive in charge of the show wouldn't go for it. As Saul remembered, "He wanted somebody hipper. Nelson was very bitter about that."

A month after finishing the *What's New* recording sessions, Nelson was completing an album for Discomate, a Japanese record company. He had arranged a series of swing-era vintage tunes to feature vocalist Kei Marimura. The basic tracks had been recorded in Japan during one of Nelson's visits.

Trumpeter Harry James was scheduled to overdub three tunes on the album playing behind Marimura, plus one track alone. It had been exactly forty years since Nelson had arranged "Comin' in on a Wing and a Prayer" for James's band, although Nelson had seen the James band several times in the Los Angeles area within the last few years.

The famous bandleader had been operated on for a cancerous growth on his neck at Sunrise Hospital in Las Vegas on April 4, 1983. The photograph on the back of the album revealed how physically devastated James looked. He wore a scarf to cover the scar from his surgery, and his face had the appearance of a death mask. Nelson, now much thinner, had also aged considerably as a result of his liver problems and looked much older than his almost sixty-two years.

Being aware of the gravity of James's condition, Nelson contacted trumpeter Rick Baptist, whom he had been using as his lead trumpet player on recording dates (such as the Ronstadt sessions) and pops concerts. He paid Baptist the supreme compliment by referring to him as "the new Conrad Gozzo," acknowledging his prowess as a lead trumpeter.

Trumpeter Louise Baranger, then a member of the James band and Baptist's wife, remembered, "When Nelson called, he sounded kind of frantic. He said, 'I've got this session tonight with Harry James,' and then he mentioned the tunes. He told Rick, 'If Harry can't do it I need to be able to call on you to play his part.' This is the only time I ever saw Rick practice. He took out his trumpet and tried to play with Harry's vibrato because Nelson had said, 'You have to sound like Harry.'"

James was very aware of Baptist's ability, having seen him play in Las Vegas. In fact, he had told Baranger, "Rick has more technique than any trumpet player I've ever known."

On April 12, James flew to Los Angeles to record despite his weakened condition. When the recording session began, he almost immediately became disoriented and encountered serious difficulties trying to figure out exactly where his solos fit in. He asked his manager, Sal Monte, to have Nelson come down from the recording booth to conduct for him. For James, his performance on these tracks was the nadir of his long recording career. He sounded tentative at best, and his playing was completely devoid of any musical expression. Sadly, he sounded like a novice trumpet player. Nelson's charts were also anything but awe-inspiring. They sounded as though they had been farmed out to another arranger. After the session, Nelson called Baptist and told him it was the most pathetic thing he had ever heard.

Baptist related a story that was indicative of Nelson's often testy nature. "It was the most interesting New Year's Eve I've ever played in my life, and it involved Nelson. It was at the Sparks Nugget Hotel in Reno. After about two hours into the gig, several people asked Nelson to play 'In the Mood.' They knew Willie Schwartz, Glenn Miller's original clarinetist, was in the band. They wanted to hear that and other Miller tunes. At twenty minutes before midnight, Nelson walked up to the microphone and said, 'I know you've all been asking for Glenn Miller.' The people said, 'Yeah!' Then Nelson said, 'I'm going to play 'Moonlight Serenade' and I wish you would not ask for any more Glenn Miller.'

"He did the same thing one other time. When we were playing on Catalina Island at the Avalon Ballroom, he said to the audience, 'You keep asking for 'In the Mood.' Well I'm not going to play it because I'm not in the mood.' That was his exact line and typical Nelson. He had that gruff exterior but underneath he was a loving guy."

★ ★ ★

Engagements at the Greek Theater in Los Angeles and the Concord Pavilion in Northern California immediately followed the *Live and In Person* television show for Ronstadt and Riddle, after which they toured Australia and Japan. These latter concerts helped stimulate the important international market for *What's New.*

By early 1984, their first album, which was helped by Ronstadt's appearance with Riddle on the February 28 Grammy Awards telecast, had become a nationwide sensation. Appearances at the Orpheum Theater in San Francisco from February 29 to March 4 served as a warm-up for the HBO television special that was excerpted from two concerts at the ornate Arlington Theater in Santa Barbara on March 9 and 10.

Entering the Arlington Theater is like walking into a Mexican plaza at night. The walls are decorated with balconies that are painted like houses, and the roof is covered with stars. The audiences for the two taped concerts were requested to dress in 1930s costumes to create additional ambience.

In a calculated attempt to bring even further attention to the album, Linda and Nelson, leading a big orchestra, performed at the NARM (National Association of Recording Merchandisers) annual convention that took place March 21–23 at the Diplomat Hotel in Hollywood, Florida.

★ ★ ★

That spring Skip Riddle returned from Tokyo where he had been successful in the advertising field to manage the Los Angeles office of the Dancer-Fitzgerald-Sample (now Saatchi & Saatchi) advertising agency. "I moved back to L.A. for business and other personal reasons. However, I also realized that I needed to get closer to my dad, as he was ill, and I didn't know how many more opportunities I would have. Our usual way of meeting, the occasional lunch, would not be enough.

"Dad and I started meeting on weekdays at the Holmby Park about 8:30 in the morning. I would delay my work day so that we could meet there. The solitude gave way to a sense of camaraderie. Dad needed to talk to rid himself of the considerable angst he felt about the disappointments and frustrations of his personal life . . . and to feel that he was with someone who cared about him without wanting anything other than his company. He was not an assertive man; his sensitivity and deference in molding arrangements to a singer's professional style and personality went hand-in-hand with a fear of confrontation. He told me that 'peace' was what he longed for most. This was mostly in the context of relationships with difficult and demanding personalities.

"His work with Linda Ronstadt was rejuvenating his life. . . . He respected Linda more than most as a courageous singer and artist; he appreciated her willingness to stretch her ability and to experiment musically. He also genuinely cared for her on a personal level, almost as a daughter, and felt that she cared about him, too.

"I needed him to listen to me, as well, and to somehow develop a dialogue with him that would bridge the gulf that had grown between us. On reflection, I'm not sure how much honesty we exchanged, but we both made a stab at it . . . and for this I will always be grateful."

★ ★ ★

The first concentrated American tour did not begin until June 27, 1984, when Ronstadt and Riddle headlined at the New Orleans World's Fair. This was the beginning of an eight-week-long tour that included dates at Poplar Creek in Chicago, Pine Knob in Detroit, the Blossom Music Center in Cleveland, Merriweather Post Pavilion outside Washington, D.C., and Chastain Park in Atlanta, among other venues. After an engagement at the Sands Hotel in Atlantic City from July 18–24, the musical nomads returned to California to appear at the Costa Mesa Amphitheater on August 14 and then from August 16–22 at the Universal Amphitheater in Los Angeles. The songs from the album were coupled with new arrangements by Nelson, which included the title song from the follow-up album, *Lush Life,* as well as "Skylark," "Can't We Be Friends?," "My Old Flame," and others.

On these concerts Nelson conducted a forty-seven-piece orchestra and a singing group called the Red Hots supplied a break from Ronstadt's ballad renditions. In addition, a group of six traveling musicians (tenor saxophonist Plas Johnson; trumpeter Tony Terran; trombonist Chauncey Welsch; pianist Don Grolnick; bassist Bob

Magnusson; guitarist Bob Mann; and drummer John Guerin) and a full road crew of lighting, sound, and equipment men traveled with them by plane and bus.

"We had our set designer reproduce all of the sets that we had at Radio City," recalled Ira Koslow. We built our own Peter Allen moon, backdrops, the chiffons and all of that staging. It was a new phenomenon for some of those 'rock 'n' roll sheds' to have a front curtain and classy production. Nelson's orchestra even had 'NR' inscribed on their music stands. Peter and our company had run rock 'n' roll differently than anyone else did. We were completely disciplined.

"We had to play every other day because Nelson would travel ahead with the rhythm section and the horns to rehearse the orchestra for three hours," Koslow explained. "Then the next day, the day of the show, we'd go in and do our sound check and rehearse with Linda and the singers for another three hours. We were one of the first to actually have a tour sponsor, which was Isuzu Motors. We had to have one because we were traveling with sets, four trucks, and a ton of people, sometimes four hundred miles a day.

"Nelson always carried his music with him. He was always hunched over, carrying that heavy bag of music. I think that's where he got his hunch from. Of course, this was a different way of touring than he had done. He loved being in front of audiences again, having his music appreciated, and getting such a positive reaction."

There is reason to believe that the seeds of the recent resurgence of swing music were sown on this tour. As Koslow pointed out, "Other than Lawrence Welk, you never saw a big band playing on television. We got young people interested and reawakened the interest of [others] who loved that kind of music. The crowd was mostly older fans. Sixty percent of the people were above the age of forty."

Looking back on the time he spent with Nelson, Koslow remarked, "He was very quiet and reserved on the outside, but he was one of the funniest men that I ever knew. You had to listen to him because he would say things under his breath or just as an aside or something that would be a comment on the situation that was amazing. He would tell the driest jokes all the time.

"He also hated to be thought of as an old man who needed to be revered. There was an incident in Australia after the soundcheck when three musicians, two women and a man, said something like, 'It's such a pleasure to be working with you.' After much groveling, Nelson started to curse at them and they walked away. I was standing in a corner and heard him. He said, 'What do they think, I'm ready for the grave or something?'

"He never complained, never asked for anything special. He was not a prima donna. I think he got $5,000 a show and all his expenses. The tour also gave Nelson a chance to have a social life."

"I can tell you that it was an unusual period because I think it possibly might have been the happiest Nelson ever was in his entire life," recalled Chauncey Welsch, in describing Nelson's feelings during the 1984 tour. "We were traveling with this nucleus of the most compatible, happy group of guys that you could ever put together. There was a really wonderful camaraderie that developed and a lot of good music. Hanging with the guys on a strictly nonbusiness level was something he probably hadn't experienced since he played in a band.

"We weren't really locked into doing things exactly the way they were on the record. We were allowed to play something different if we chose to in our solos. I always tried to keep it within a certain framework because Linda was so sensitive that I never wanted to overlap on any of her entrances."

Welsch told an amusing story about the rehearsal before the Blossom Music Center date: "We started to play the first arrangement. We got three or four bars into it. Nelson waved the orchestra down and said, 'Let's try this again.' We started up again and got maybe six bars into it before he stopped the music again and said, 'Excuse me, isn't that a bassoon part on the second chair there?' This guy was sitting there playing the passage on the baritone saxophone! The kid said, 'Well, it's written for the bassoon, but I thought it would sound better on baritone saxophone.' Nelson stared into the wild blue yonder and said, 'I'm surprised Brahms didn't think of that!'

"The guy was hired as a baritone saxophonist and told to bring along the bassoon. You know what Nelson did? Between that rehearsal and the concert he took all the difficult parts and transposed them for the baritone saxophone. The kid played the whole concert on the baritone saxophone. [Nelson figured] it was better to have a good baritone saxophonist than a bad bassoon player!

"This was something that if it had happened around here [Hollywood] Nelson would have gone ballistic. He was so comfortable and peaceful within himself that something like that was just a small obstacle."

Besides the congenial atmosphere that pervaded the entire tour, also contributing to his happiness was the fact that Laurie Brooks met him in certain cities. Brooks recalled those happy times: "Nelson was so romantic. Whenever we reached the hotel, there were always flowers in the room. We went to museums, on tours, and took boat rides in various cities. In St. Louis, we went on a riverboat. He was interested in a lot of things. We had a lot of fun together."

John Guerin remembered how sweet it was when Nelson said to him, "I've got this gal, but I'm worried that Linda's going to find out. I hate to do it, but I'm bringing her up in the service elevators in the hotels." The drummer assured him, 'Linda's been around the block. She knows about things, so please bring Laurie up in the main elevators.' He wasn't used to doing a balancing act, I'll tell you that."

According to Brooks, when they were in Atlanta, Rosemary Clooney called Nelson. "She asked him if he was happy. He said he was happy. When he hung up the phone, he looked at me and said, 'That was the songbird.' That's all he said."

In the midst of the Atlanta concert, precisely at the moment when Ronstadt sang the phrase, "When I want rain . . ." from "Guess I'll Hang My Tears out to Dry," it

Linda Ronstadt and Nelson at an ASCAP Awards dinner honoring them for their successful collaboration on *What's New*. Nelson's genuine affection for Ronstadt is apparent.

started to rain. "It was amazing," Brooks remembered.

Living in Atlanta was Don Comstock, who had been the southern regional manager at Capitol Records from 1952 to 1957. "I had attended one of the [recording] sessions for *Songs for Young Lovers*," Comstock recalled. "At the time, I was certain that Nelson was principally responsible for the new warmth and excitement in Sinatra's voice. Our friendship with Nelson grew over the years. We visited a couple of times with him and Doreen in Malibu.

"When 'Lisbon Antigua' came out, we broke it in Atlanta. Nelson came there and we had a big party for him. Many people there told me how much they liked him, not only for his talent but for his appreciative and his non-egotistical manner.

"After the Linda Ronstadt concert, we had a get-together of friends. Laurie furnished the support and companionship that he needed. Following the party, we took him to Johnnie's Hideaway where they played big band music. Nelson told me how much he enjoyed it and how good it made him feel."

Other stopovers on the road provided Nelson with the opportunity of seeing more old friends. His Ridgewood, New Jersey, boyhood friend, Dick Leonard, saw him in Milwaukee at Summerfest before the sound check. "He came walking in carrying a clean shirt under his arm. He always had a kind of a slouch. The first thing out of his mouth is, 'You never learned to stand up straight, either.'

"We spent some time together and then he started rehearsing with Linda and the orchestra. They did 'Lush Life' and then he yelled to the stage manager, 'Get Dick and Barbara out of the sun,' so they brought us up to sit on the stage.

"He asked if he could bring his girlfriend with us. Chris was playing in the band so he was with us, too. [Chris had played a solo on the "You Took Advantage of Me" track and was part of the tour.] We threw a party in a restaurant—a restaurant where Sinatra used to go when he worked in town. I was surprised Nelson didn't have any love for Sinatra. He said, 'Ya know how I get along with Frank? I have as little to do with him as I can.'"

"Funzy" Tomaino, Nelson's old musician friend from Rumson, New Jersey, drove down to Atlantic City to see him perform with Ronstadt at the Sands. He hadn't seen Nelson in more than twenty years. "He wasn't too well," Tomaino remembered. "I could tell that. His facial color was bad. He trudged into the lobby at the Sands carrying all the music in a suitcase. I took the bag from him. We walked to the dressing room, and we talked about old times. He got me a ticket for the show. Afterward, I wanted to drive him to the airport, but he said a limousine was going to take him there. That was the last time I ever saw him."

"When Naomi came around, which she would at different times on the tour, his whole attitude changed," John Guerin noticed. "He was a different guy. He just got more business-like. When she came on the buses and things like that, you knew she was in charge." Guerin's statement was echoed by several other musicians who worked for Nelson on a regular basis.

Guitarist Bob Mann relished telling the story about how Riddle exercised with Ronstadt and the traveling musician and crew. "Every morning at 9:00 A.M. on the tour we worked out. Linda had a trainer from Australia, Richard Norton, who was her bodyguard. He supervised calisthenics for about an hour. Nelson did his own version of them. His workout outfit consisted of a white T-shirt, boxer shorts, and black over the calf knee dress socks with sneakers—exactly what a man would wear with a business suit! Nobody said a word to him about it. By the end of the tour we presented him with a pair of white sweat socks. He laughed at that."

This amusing anecdote jibed perfectly with Laurie Brooks's observation, "There was a formality about him, a very nice side to him. Whether we were going out to see people or not, he was always prepared—almost like he was going to conduct the orchestra. I never saw him in a pair of jeans, for instance, or shorts or casual wear."

Saul Ilson lived in Malibu in the early 1980s. He told this story: "I was walking toward the [Malibu] Colony. I looked ahead and from quite a distance I saw the weirdest

thing: I saw a guy in a suit walking down the beach with some woman. I got closer—
'Oh, my God, it's Nelson.' He's walking with Linda Ronstadt. I said, 'One of us is over-
dressed.' He laughed and said, 'We just had a meeting, and we wanted to get away
from everybody and just kind of chat,' as if it was absolutely normal to be walking
down the beach with shoes and a gray suit and a shirt and tie. That's the picture of
Nelson that always stays in my mind. It's so out of place, and yet it seems so right."

★ ★ ★

The *Lush Life* album found Ronstadt recording first, with the rhythm section. The
orchestra was then overdubbed under Nelson's direction. Ronstadt's close friend, writer
Pete Hamill, suggested recording, "It Never Entered My Mind" and "I'm a Fool to Want
You," two songs associated with Frank Sinatra, for the album. On the November 16,
1984, release of *Lush Life,* Stephen Holden reflected in the *New York Times* on whether
lightning could strike twice. "If quality counts for anything in the pop marketplace these
days, the answer is yes." The album quickly went gold.

Holden contended that the album brought out the saucier side of Ronstadt's musical personality. He wrote that the faster tempos of three of Nelson's big band arrangements—for "You Took Advantage of Me," "Can't We Be Friends?," and "Falling in
Love Again"—allowed her to become looser and more inventive in her phrasing. The
latter tune once again illustrated Nelson's inventive musical thinking. He used a music
box introduction written in minuet tempo, which segued into a swing arrangement.

Ralph Novak of *People* also felt *Lush Life* was looser and less somber than its prede-
cessor. He singled out Ronstadt's "torchy" approach to the title song as well as Ellington's
"Sophisticated Lady," and her "tentatively swinging" approaches to "Can't We Be
Friends?," "Falling in Love Again," and "You Took Advantage of Me."

One incredulous *Lush Life* reviewer posed the question, "For this she gave up Buddy
Holly?" Ronstadt responded, "You don't give up anything. You add to [it]. I don't lose the
ability to sing anything that I've ever sung. Frankly, I think I do a much better job on
George Gershwin's songs than I ever did on a Buddy Holly song."

There was no tour scheduled in support of the *Lush Life* album. However, Linda's
appearance on *The Tonight Show* with Johnny Carson in January 1985—for which
Nelson conducted an augmented orchestra—helped the music reach a huge national
audience. To date this album has sold 1.6 million copies. It peaked at #13 and remained
on the *Billboard* pop chart for eleven weeks.

One day, in the midst of his revival, Nelson called Bill Finegan. They hadn't spoken to one another in more than a decade. There was no personal problem between
them; they were merely separated by geographical distance. "Nothing had changed. He
was still the same down kind of a guy," Finegan remembered. "He told me how he
enjoyed the experience of working with Linda Ronstadt, but he talked about how bad
his marriage was. He had that same sardonic way of looking at things that I noticed
when I first met him."

★ ★ ★

Alongside his friend, drummer John Guerin, bassist Bob Magnusson did all the touring dates after the Radio City gig in 1983 and most of the recording dates for the third Ronstadt/Riddle album, *For Sentimental Reasons,* which was recorded in 1985. Magnusson had been recommended on the basis of his work with the great jazz saxophonist Art Pepper, but nevertheless had to audition for Nelson. He played with the orchestra that was trying out Nelson's arrangements right before the *Lush Life* album was recorded.

The bespectacled bassist remembered, "Nelson was complimentary when I first got there. It was kind of 'Let's hear what you can do,' with the lowered eyebrows. He gave me some modest compliment, and I was hired on the strength of that.

Reflecting on Nelson's behavior in the studio, Magnusson said, "New York and L.A. probably have the best studio musicians in the world. . . . Nelson would get on those guys, not because they weren't great players, not because they weren't playing great, but because he thought they weren't giving 100 percent. He wanted absolutely every bit of effort from everybody all the time, which he was entitled to. I would also say he was a perfectionist.

"I remember one time when we had a cellist on one of the concerts who butchered a beautiful passage [Nelson] had written. He started singling out the cellists to play. One fellow was a nervous wreck when Nelson said it was his turn to play alone. He said something like, 'Can I play it later?' so Nelson just ate him alive!"

When I asked Magnusson to evaluate Ronstadt's ability to interpret Riddle's charts, he quickly remarked, "I think she did it very well. She's not a jazz singer. I don't think she was trying to be a jazz singer like a Sarah Vaughan [with whom Magnusson toured for several years]. She's just a good singer."

He laughed as he described Nelson's "unique" conducting style. "You could sort of decipher what Nelson was doing but it was vague. A good conductor has a beat that stops at a certain place. Well, Nelson would be different places and you wouldn't know where's the bottom. It's like an umpire in baseball—the strike zone stays the same. His strike zone was moving, so you had to deal with it as best you could.

"But his harmonies were so creative, so interesting and beautiful. He just didn't write eight bars and insert the next eight bars and the last eight bars. He was writing from a symphonic place. He was seeing it as a whole piece from A to B at the end and then he put his stamp on what he thought was musically appropriate. That's why people loved him so much."

"I'll tell you one thing, though," said John Guerin. "We would suggest certain things for the rhythm section. Nelson wouldn't change a goddamn thing. Boy, he was strict about that! I think that was from writing for big bands all those years. He left nothing to the creativity of the bass player. A lot of them felt, 'This isn't the greatest bass line in the world.' Finally, Ray Brown and I went to him and approached it in a humorous way. After that he wrote the chord changes above the staff."

Peter Asher feels that although it went gold (it never registered on the charts but wound up selling 1.1 million albums anyway), the third Ronstadt/Riddle collaboration, *For Sentimental Reasons,* was a mistake. "I recommended against doing it. I didn't think we needed it. I thought we'd sort of covered it. Linda had a very strong instinct that she wanted to do one eventually, and the time was now. And, of course, she was absolutely right because none of us knew that Nelson didn't have that long left," he recalled.

The well-known jazz drummer Louis Bellson was hired along with Ray Brown specifically to play on Nelson's up-tempo arrangements of "Am I Blue" and "Straighten Up and Fly Right" on this album. Bellson recalled, "When it came time to record 'Straighten Up and Fly Right,' Linda didn't know the tune too well. She didn't wait for those beats in between. Ray stopped and said, 'Linda, listen. . . .' and played it on the bass for her. She caught on fast. She had a very clear and good musical sound. Her intonation and her diction were very good. I had so much fun. I wish I could have done more."

Bellson remembered that when he left Duke Ellington's band in 1953 and started his own big band. "I learned years ago to try and write something that has an identifiable sound. You had to have an identifiable sound like Nelson had." (Many people fail to realize that Bellson has also been an arranger and composer for over five decades.) At that time, Bellson called Nelson, who suggested that they get together. "I went out to his house in Santa Monica," related Bellson. "He showed me how to write a certain voicing in a percussion section with a guitar. Later on, I picked up a thing called a boo-bans. Picture a xylophone or a marimba, only instead of wood they're little round tubular drums. Nelson said, 'That's a sound we can use.'

"He showed me some tricks about using a French horn, boo-bans, and guitar for melodic effect. He showed me how to use a French horn or a trombone and flugelhorns to get his identifiable sound. He was so nice about it. I remember that he spent a lot of time with me."

Terry Woodson is an arranger, orchestrator, and conductor who has been working with Frank Sinatra, Jr., for twenty-one years. In 1980, he took over as Nelson's copyist after Vern Yocum's retirement. While working together closely on the Ronstadt arrangements, he and Nelson became very friendly.

"Nelson sketched just about anything he wrote," said Woodson. "He always started with a sketch [of the arrangement] before he put it on score paper. He could orchestrate in his sleep—he could be on the phone and write an orchestration. The sheer volume of work he had done caused him to be very fast at writing orchestrations."

Speaking of the preliminary plans for *What's New,* Woodson said, "Nelson wanted to use Jimmy Rowles as the pianist on the album. Rowles was too much of a jazz player, and Linda was too much of a rock singer in [Rowles's] eyes. Then they tried Alan Broadbent for awhile. They finally settled on Don Grolnick, who came out from New York. Linda felt comfortable with him."

Woodson remembered Nelson saying to him one day over lunch, "I was fortunate to have a singer who'd give me eight or sixteen bars of my own ego. Generally you don't get that." He was speaking about Frank Sinatra. Woodson also made an extremely valid point when he said, "Nelson's compositional skills were greater in his arrangements than they were when he was actually writing compositions."

Woodson remembered how shocked Ira Koslow was when he presented him a bill for something in the $7,000–$9,000 range for copying charges to cover the cost of the arrangements for the orchestra Nelson would be conducting on the *What's New* tour. "Nelson, in a rare moment, stood up, and in a very gracious but very matter-of-fact and strong way explained to Ira that these were all negotiated agreements, and while they had been very fair with him, and he was not asking for a repayment, he felt that it was necessary that he pay the music prep and copyist.

According to Woodson, this type of behavior was unusual in Nelson. "He usually kind of let you fight your own battles. He was always thinking about something else whenever he was talking to you. You could see in his eyes that he was thinking about the next thing."

Regarding the difficulty musicians had in playing Nelson's arrangements, Woodson said, "His scores were very, very difficult for the copyist to read. You had to know his handwriting. He wrote with very little pressure because he'd been writing these things for so many years, and he used abbreviations. His pencil strokes were the least amount of lead on the paper that he could use. Some people would have big, heavy lines, and they'd have a big round notehead. He just had a dot. Consequently, you'd have to get some help sometimes, someone who was accustomed to his hand.

"On the last date he conducted for Linda, there was one mistake. It brought everything to a halt. He blew up and said, 'Terry, where are you? Take those geniuses that work for you and kick 'em in the ass right out the front door onto Gower [Street]!'"

Woodson originally began working as a bass trombonist on one of Riddle's own mid-'60s album recording dates, after having worked for Henry Mancini. He went on to play on *Tarzan, The Smothers Brothers Comedy Hour,* and *On a Clear Day* for Nelson.

"When I moved out here in '64," he recalled, "there were only about seven or eight bass trombonists in town. The music scene fell apart in 1970. There was a strike and then there was a recession. And then synthesizers came in, plus rock was so big."

He switched to the music preparation business and was on staff for several years at Universal. He saw Nelson often while he was scoring television shows there. "I remember in 1978, at a party for [trombonist] Dick Nash, Nelson looked at me—and I always quote it to this day. He said, 'You don't retire from this business. The phone just stops ringing.' That was his wit, his seriousness, and his sarcasm. But then when he started getting his strength back, Linda came into his life and gave him a rebirth."

★ ★ ★

Manuel Felix, who has been a waiter at Musso & Frank since 1974, waited on Nelson for the last eleven years of his life during his almost daily lunches there. "When you're in a public field like I am, I can predict a person's disposition the minute he opens the door. He was a fine, distinguished gentleman. He was not a person who flaunted his position. There was no pomposity in him."

Felix clearly remembered the years when Nelson was involved in the Ronstadt recordings: "When he started working for Linda, you could see new life in him. He had such enthusiasm—the way he walked—there was a spring to it. A lot of times, you know, he'd kind of stoop his shoulders. It was suddenly a different Nelson. There was a smile on his face. The wrinkles faded away—even his clothes looked ironed. They didn't look so wrinkled."

Bob Newhart also vouched for how much the success that came from working with Ronstadt did for Nelson. "My wife Ginny reminded me recently how thrilled Nelson was with the way the Linda Ronstadt records turned out—when he was appearing with her. I know he was very excited about working with Linda and [he] had great admiration for her. Standing in front of the orchestra and conducting for her was a great thrill for him.

"Ginny and I played the videotape of their HBO special and the CDs. Nelson may have given us the videotape. We flipped when every so often you got a shot of Nelson conducting in the background. After he passed on, it was one of our favorite things to do. He was still kind of with us whenever we played the tape. You know he really was one of the great arrangers of all time."

A former associate of Frank Sinatra's said that during this period, Frank was terribly envious of Nelson's success with Ronstadt. He said, "Frank thought Linda was a terrible singer. He felt that if Nelson was going to write arrangements for somebody he could have picked someone more talented." It must be noted, however, that, except for his hit "New York, New York" during the 1980s, Sinatra's name was completely absent from the *Billboard* Pop Singles and Albums charts.

There were other detractors who weren't overwhelmed by Nelson's charts for Ronstadt. Paul C. Shure of the Hollywood String Quartet, whose association with Nelson dated back to his postwar recordings with Bing Crosby, referred to them as "okay," adding, "I think Nelson was trying to find something to say that he had said long ago." Lloyd Ulyate said, "I didn't think it was Nelson's best work. To me, to play Nelson Riddle was very exciting, but this [music] didn't thrill me."

"The Ronstadt arrangements were a big hit for Linda, and I think they gained some wonderful recognition for Nelson late in his life, but I don't think they were milestones for him," added arranger and composer Artie Butler. "By the time Nelson had worked with Linda, he had already achieved his greatness and made his mark. I was happy for him because he made some bucks and maybe it was a last hurrah. I saw them perform at the Sands Hotel in Atlantic City. It was a concept. It was entertaining. It was also very musical. How bad could it be? I saw the show because it was a chance to see live music and Nelson."

Arranger Jeff Sultanof had spent time backstage with Nelson when Nelson conducted the first of four concerts in Hackensack, New Jersey—entitled "'40s in the '80s"—celebrating the fortieth anniversary of Capitol Records in 1982. The second time he met Nelson was at Warner Bros. Music, where Sultanof was working in March 1983. "Frank Military [who had become the executive vice president of Warner Bros. Music] came in with a shopping bag that contained a manuscript. He said that he got it from Jonathan Schwartz. 'Nelson Riddle has written a book on arranging. Do you think we want to do it?'

"I looked at Anthony Esposito, who was my boss, and said, 'Nobody knew he'd written a book on arranging.' [Nelson had actually started working on the book in 1971 with Irene Kahn Atkins, the daughter of the composer Gus Kahn and the wife of Lenny Atkins, the violinist who had been his friend since the Tommy Dorsey days.]

"Nelson was really in limbo then," Sultanof remarked. "I had heard that his book had been submitted to other publishers, and it had been turned down. The name identification with Sinatra had long dissipated, and the Ronstadt album hadn't come out yet. When he had finished the text, he mentioned that Linda had asked him to arrange an album for her. He had no idea that it was going to mushroom the way it did."

A month and a half later, Esposito asked Sultanof to read Riddle's book, which was then only twenty pages long. "I began reading it with the understanding that nobody can learn arranging from a book. This was a basic arranging book, but what I found invaluable about it was the fact that this was like sitting down with Nelson across the desk from you. It made me remember the conversation I had had with him earlier. It was written in such a way that it was conversational.

"I said to Tony, 'We've got to put out this book. There's no question about it.' He went to Frank Military, and then made a deal with Nelson. [I think] maybe they paid him a couple of thousand against royalties."

Sultanof's next meeting with Riddle was when he came to New York for the Radio City concerts with Ronstadt. "Nelson came up to the office, looked at me, very downbeat, very matter-of-fact. He said, 'I'm glad you guys thought that this was worth doing. I feel like I'm making a contribution by writing this book.'"

A photograph of Nelson taken by Richard Avedon graced the cover of *Arranged by Nelson Riddle*. He was smiling with a hint of a grin. Jeff Sultanof mentioned that Nelson was proud to have included in the book a photo of himself with Eleanor Roosevelt, which had been taken during a rehearsal for a 1962 Frank Sinatra TV special when Roosevelt was Sinatra's guest. Nelson called the occasion of meeting the grand former First Lady "one of the great moments of my life."

As Nelson was describing the various features of his book, Military suddenly walked into the office and said, "Nelson, it's great to see you. It's been such a long time." After a few more such pleasantries, Military remarked, "Nelson, Frank isn't happy with the arranging that's been going on with his most recent records. You guys belong together. You did a lot of good work together."

Sultanof recalled, "Nelson said, 'Frank, you know what happened with me and Sinatra.' He immediately brought up Sinatra's 'no show' incident at the Century Plaza Hotel. He made it very clear how 'that really pissed me off.' Riddle went on to mention how he had not been interested in participating in the *Trilogy* album. He concluded the conversation by saying, 'And what really bothered me even more is when somebody mentioned to Sinatra that I was upset and he said, 'Tell Nelson to get real—I'm not interested!'"

When Military left, there was decided tension in the room. According to Sultanof, "Nelson looked at Tony and me and said, 'I've got cirrhosis of the liver. I don't have to do anything I don't want to do anymore.'"

In late 1984, Nelson called Sultanof after receiving the galleys for *Arranged by Nelson Riddle*. He complimented Jeff on how beautifully he had prepared it for publication. Nelson said, "This is my big chance." "He very much wanted his book to represent who he was," Sultanof said.

Around the same time, Sue Raney, who Nelson still often used as his band singer, spotted him at Cyrano's, a restaurant in West Hollywood. "I walked in with my friend, Marilyn Jackson, and spotted him sitting there with Naomi. He looked really old and sad. Naomi was intimidating him. He was sitting there like a lost soul while Naomi said, 'He can't eat salt, he can't have this. . . .' I went away from there feeling so badly for him. I wish I would have called him the next day or done something, but I never did. His little eyes—the way they sort of looked up at you. . . . He was completely tormented. I thought to myself, 'How did he ever get to that place with her?'"

★ ★ ★

I thought that having the opportunity to interview Ronstadt in her Tucson home fourteen years after she had last recorded with Nelson might prove enlightening. I was correct. I encountered a star secure in her musical worth and unafraid of being forthcoming in admitting how much the success of her musical collaboration with Nelson Riddle was attributable to Nelson.

In the process, I also discovered an intelligent woman with a true perspective who had found a new priority in her life—her two adopted children. She had figured out, like her new friend Rosemary Clooney, that the pleasures of raising a family are ultimately more satisfying than the music business, without negating its importance in her life. Their common link, of course, was Nelson Riddle.

Ronstadt was as enthusiastic about talking about Nelson as if they were still recording together. She went into great detail about their association, saying, "I'll never forget walking into the studio the morning we cut 'My Funny Valentine,' [for the *For Sentimental Reasons* album]. I got the great arranger to write me a string quartet—stupid pop sensibility! And he did it for me. He did it for me!

"The song had been done so much. It has so much tension to it, and such a strange dark side . . .with [its] incredible passive tones. Nelson worked in all those lush colors and textures in the woodwinds. . . . There's a million subtexts chattering at every layer of the arrangement, [each one] telling a different story but weaving into the major story. I love that arrangement! I think it's one of my favorite things. Of course, what he does best is the big, full orchestra and nothing could ever take away from that—those are his, still—his legacies that he's left to us."

Turning to the subject of the Sinatra/Riddle recording combination, Ronstadt referred to their work as, "Staggeringly emotional. Nelson did such a brilliant job with his arrangements that they were almost transparent."

She described how thirty years before, J.D. Souther had impressed upon her the incisive aspect of Ray Charles's singing. "But we would always finish the evening with the same recording of *Only the Lonely*. We loved the arrangements which allowed us to simply listen to the lyrics."

She went on to relate that during the recording of the *Get Closer* album, her mother passed away. "I explained to Nelson that the Jimmy Webb song 'The Moon Is a Harsh Mistress' reminded me of my mother. He said he adapted the turmoil of his mother's death into a clarinet or bassoon passage or some little meandering line of strings going into woodwinds in *Only the Lonely*. He would share little things like that with me. I would feel so privileged."

She acknowledged that when she began working with Nelson, "I was desperate to get away from rock 'n' roll. I did my own mixes. I didn't hear that I was singing right. There were stories I had to tell. I didn't like the quality of the material I was doing.

"I'll never be able to sing standards like Rosemary [Clooney]. She was there at the time when the thing rolled out. She was on the bus with them. There's a thing that happens with that. You can't duplicate that."

Ronstadt referred to the arrangement for "Lush Life" as "the best chart that Nelson [ever] wrote for me. I was already in my thirties so I was feeling that my years were pretty advanced. I believed that I had some experience, and I also knew that some of the songs I was singing I might better understand and feel in the future."

She was never discouraged in her pursuit of working with Nelson in spite of the fact that several of her peers snickered, "Nelson Riddle—he's the guy who writes TV charts for the Smothers Brothers!" She was encouraged by the fact that he had once turned down Paul McCartney, who had sought him out to write an arrangement for one of his albums.

As Nelson told Ronstadt, "I just couldn't do it. You can't put something like that in the middle of a bunch of other things. The mood comes and then it changes. It's like putting a picture in a bad frame."

Ronstadt recalled, "I thought to myself, 'Here's a man of integrity. He knows where his music belongs.'"

The Final Chorus

At 6:30 A.M. one morning in early December 1984, the telephone rang in Nelson Riddle's bedroom at his Bel Air home. "Nelson," said the voice on the other end, "it's Frank."

Although Nelson was naturally groggy after being awakened by the unexpected early morning call, he realized that this was the modus operandi of the caller. He knew that when Frank Sinatra wanted something, the hour wasn't important to him.

When Sinatra realized why Nelson sounded so sleepy, he said, "I'm sorry. I forgot what time it was for you." In reply, Nelson used an old show business line: "That's all right, Frank. I had to get up to answer the phone, anyway." "I'll call you later at the office," Sinatra said before hanging up.

Once again Laurie Brooks was there when a fortuitous telephone call came to Nelson several hours later. "He put his hand over the phone and said with absolute shock, 'Frank wants me to work with him at the Reagan inaugural.' They spoke for awhile, and afterwards Nelson said, 'I can't believe it.' He was glad to do it, and he was delighted that the hatchet had been buried."

Twenty-four years after he had last worked for executive producer and star Frank Sinatra at a presidential inaugural gala, he again served as its musical director—this time for the January 1985 concert preceding Ronald Reagan's second inauguration. The performers, besides Sinatra, included Dean Martin, Elizabeth Taylor, Jimmy Stewart, Charlton Heston, Mikhail Baryshnikov, Ray Charles, Don Rickles, and the Beach Boys, among others. This inaugural celebration lacked the panache of the Kennedy gala; it was a gathering of stars from another era, most of whom were past their prime.

Naomi had no interest in going to Washington due to both her liberal leanings and to her aversion to Sinatra after the way he had treated Nelson. Chris Riddle, an avid Reagan admirer, took her plane ticket and played in his father's orchestra.

At the gala, Don Rickles paced the stage, delivering his familiar series of personal insults. When he saw Nelson in the orchestra pit, he remarked, "Nelson, I spoke to the

Preceding page: The last known photo of Nelson Riddle, taken in September 1985, less than a month before his death. Nelson is holding the leash of his dog, Chrissy Boy.

hospital. You died about an hour ago." It may have been just a staple of his usual shtick, but Rickles had no idea how prophetic his throwaway line really was.

After the concert, Sinatra and Riddle repaired to Sinatra's private party at the Madison Hotel. Shortly after they arrived at the gathering, Frank asked Nelson to join him in a private room,where they had a late dinner. Barbara Sinatra knocked on the door, but her husband told her he wanted to be left alone with Nelson.

Sinatra made it very clear that he felt they should put aside their most recent problems with one another and look toward working together on another album. He said he would ask Frank Military to make up a list of standards he hadn't previously recorded that Nelson could arrange for a three-CD set.

When Nelson left the private room with Sinatra, he found Chris at the party. "He was very happy and said that everything was fine again with him and Frank," Chris remembered. "He told me all about their plans to record again."

A month later, Nelson performed two concerts with the Northeastern Pennsylvania Philharmonic in Scranton and Wilkes-Barre in a program entitled *Nelson Riddle Conducts the Nelson Riddle Songbook*. After the latter concert, his old Merchant Marine friend, the now-retired trumpet player Eddie Bailey, who lived in the area, went backstage. He was appalled at Nelson's appearance. Nelson informed Bailey that he was suffering from hepatitis.

"How could that be?" Bailey exclaimed. "In the old days you never even drank!"

"Eddie, you never had to work for Frank Sinatra!" Nelson replied.

★ ★ ★

Frank Sinatra continued making concert appearances in major cities. A succession of bad films culminating in 1970 with the ridiculous MGM western satire *Dirty Dingus Magee,* coupled with his age and a face and waistline that showed the effects of years of the good life had made him unemployable in motion pictures. By 1985 his recording career was at a standstill. He had no choice but to continue touring. In the intervening decades, except for concerts in New York and Las Vegas, Sinatra had rarely been seen in performance; this had created a ready-made audience eager to see him.

During this period, my publicity office represented Woody Herman and the Thundering Herd, the George Shearing Quintet, and the Count Basie Orchestra when they appeared with Sinatra. The dates were mostly sellouts, and the audiences were universally enthusiastic. I noticed that besides lowering the keys on his arrangements, Frank had been forced to compensate for the narrowing of his upper register by making increased use of his hands and body in putting over his songs.

I still remember watching him nervously waiting to go on stage at the Boston Garden on the first date of the the Main Event tour with Woody Herman. He broke into a sweat waiting for the houselights to dim before walking out to begin his performance. After all those years, he was still faced with the dilemma every performer faces: "Will they love me tonight?"

Ron Anthony, who played rhythm guitar for the last eight years that Sinatra was on the road, delighted in playing the many Riddle and Don Costa arrangements that made up the bulk of the eternal swing band singer's concert presentation. "Thank God for those guys," he said. "I'd sit there and listen to those glorious arrangements—in some of the parts there was no guitar—and listen to Frank. In the beginning when I was working for him, he was still pretty hot, ya know! To hear some of the best musicians in the world playing those great arrangements with the most popular singer of that kind of music that you're ever going to hear in your life, the best interpreter—what could be better? And I was getting paid for it on top of it. That's pretty good!

"Frank always spoke about Nelson with the highest praise. You listen to 'Summer Wind' or 'Angel Eyes' and you ask yourself, what did Nelson have? It wasn't just the ballads, it was the swing things as well. There was a magic he had with Frank."

Replacing Irv Cottler after his death, drummer Gregg Field helped supply the rhythm underpinnings behind Frank Sinatra. He recalled, "When I started working for him, Bill Miller said to me, 'You can't play all the arrangers the same way.' It was a little intimidating because I frankly didn't know at that point what he meant. You couldn't play a Neal Hefti chart the same way you played something by Nelson. What I discovered about Nelson is that the arrangers after him always had in the back of their mind what Nelson did, the things that worked. I can hear Nelson Riddle in Don Costa.

"Nelson's arrangements allowed Frank to swing like I'd never heard him swing. That 'I've Got the World on a String' arrangement sounded as modern as anything we played. The beginning of the Frank Sinatra we all knew and loved—I think Nelson had a massive impact on that. He exploded the whole thing with his writing and then everybody followed suit. And then to hear the guy thirty years later write for Linda Ronstadt and the guy's not sounding dated at all. That's an incredible feat.

"Nelson really created a wonderful space for Frank to sing in. . . . But besides that there's always that element of knowing how to create a counterline or brass figures or reed figures that play underneath the vocal, but don't take away from it, like in his arrangement of 'All or Nothing at All.' He and Don Costa managed to weave a beautiful tapestry in between the music."

Field's rhythm section compatriot, bassist Chuck Berghoffer, once asked Sinatra, "How do you swing so hard? What do you think about?" He answered, "I just get a cuckoo rhythm section and stay out of the way." According to Field, "He only mentioned Nelson and Costa as being the arrangers who never got in his way."

★ ★ ★

The success of *What's New* and its two follow-ups had an immediate effect on the pop music marketplace. Barbra Streisand followed Ronstadt's lead by moving from *Guilty,* on which she worked with the Bee Gees, to *The Broadway Album,* which matched *What's New* in sales. Carly Simon recorded two albums of standards in a row. Michael Feinstein, Patti Austin, and George Benson did the same. And then there was Mandy

Patinkin's debut, an album by Melissa Manchester, Harry Connick, Jr.'s songs from the *When Harry Met Sally . . .* soundtrack, and Dionne Warwick's Cole Porter album. One of the bywords of American entertainment has long been "Follow the leader."

Now it was an opera singer—Kiri Te Kanawa—who wanted to record an album of standards with Nelson in London. Nelson stopped off at Kelly Travel, retired trombonist Milt Bernhart's successful travel agency, to pick up his plane tickets. He was in a wistful mood as he looked out the window and remarked, "You know, Milt, I would trade all the arrangements I've ever written for one of Hank Mancini's big copyrights." Bernhart tried to convince him otherwise, but Nelson insisted, "No, what I said is true."

Te Kanawa's repertoire for the London album, *Blue Skies,* consisted of such standards as "Speak Low," "It Might as Well Be Spring," "Here's That Rainy Day," "Yesterdays," and "The Folks Who Live on the Hill." *People* editor Eric Levin praised Te Kanawa's "slow, pearlescent 'How High the Moon' that can make the heart swoon," but Nelson's arrangements were pedestrian at best. In order to sing this kind of material, Te Kanawa attempted to eschew her operatic voice and sang with chest tones, which made for an odd presentation of her powerful voice. At times she sounded as if she were conversing rather than singing. According to Jeff Sultanof, who spoke to him in New York right after the album was completed, Nelson wasn't pleased with the results.

Arranged by Nelson Riddle was published in July 1985. To date it has sold over 14,000 copies, which, according to Sy Feldman, Senior Vice President of Warner Bros. Publications, is very good for this kind of book. The eminent jazz musician Benny Carter remarked, "I think Nelson's book was one of the best ever written on the subject. You know, there really wasn't any arrangement of Nelson's that I didn't like."

During the July 4th weekend that same year, Stephen Paley produced *A Tribute to Nelson Riddle,* a comprehensive interview with Riddle that aired on KCRW in Los Angeles. Although Paley's background was in rock 'n' roll, as an A&R man (Sly and the Family Stone, Jeff Beck, Rupert Holmes), he said, "I always admired quality, and Nelson Riddle was my idea of the best there was at what he did."

The two-hour show included perceptive comments about Nelson from Linda Ronstadt, Rosemary Clooney, Ella Fitzgerald, Peggy Lee, and Kiri Te Kanawa, along with a sampling of some of the best recordings Nelson had arranged for them. Sinatra wouldn't commit himself to appearing on the show, so Paley proceeded without him.

The tone of the show gives listeners the feeling that Nelson considered it his epitaph. Perhaps Nelson's most revealing comment was about Clooney: "I was fascinated by her voice. She was a charming lady with a wonderful sense of humor. . . . I still haven't lost the feeling for her. I've only been married twice and, please God, that's all I'll ever be married. She's very fond of me, and I'm very fond of her. I've lived two or three miles from her for decades, and I never make the trip, and I'm not about to. . . . That's all that's important. We cannot help each other at this point."

Among other topics, he also spoke about how Sy Oliver's arrangement of "Swanee

Nelson Riddle in his last years. Note his resemblance to the late Prime Minister of Israel, Yitzhak Rabin.

River" for Tommy Dorsey had greatly influenced him. "It gave a new dimension to dance band music. . . . By that time it needed it. Brass and saxes, brass and saxes, brass and saxes! Actually, dance band music dug its own grave by not having enough colors to go to."

★ ★ ★

Throughout the early 1980s, Nelson continued working casual dates, which became more numerous with his sudden resurgence. One of trumpeter Louise Baranger's first gigs working for Nelson was at the ranch of the notorious Middle Eastern arms dealer Adnan Kashoggi near Santa Barbara, where strangely enough Nelson's band outnumbered the guests. "On the bus back to L.A.," she recalled, "Nelson came walking down the aisle, took my hand, and said, 'I'd really like to thank you for playing with my band.' That absolutely blew me away because I never even dreamed I'd ever play for Nelson Riddle. He didn't see it as an honor for us to work with him. He saw that he was lucky to have those wonderful musicians working with him. I'd never had a leader do that."

But there was always Nelson's untoward behavior to deal with. At a subsequent date at Bullock's department store in Santa Barbara, Baranger saw Chris Riddle stand up in front of the band to count off the next number while Nelson was away from the bandstand. "Nelson came back and was furious. He just snapped and told Chris to 'Sit the hell down!'"

Trombonist Lloyd Ulyate, like other Riddle regulars, continued to have periodic problems with Nelson. He took over leadership of Nelson's band on several Palm Springs dates while Nelson was on the road with Ronstadt. "A couple of weeks later, I saw Nelson," Ulyate remembered. "He said, 'I guess you expect to get a big fat commission.' I didn't want anything."

★ ★ ★

Under Nelson's direction, six recording sessions with Ronstadt commenced on July 10, 1985, for their last album together, *For Sentimental Reasons. Sunday Morning,* the CBS-TV magazine show, began a piece on Nelson by shooting the July 11 session under the supervision of producer Pauline Canny.

"We had been trying to get Linda," Canny revealed, "but she wouldn't consent to an interview, so focusing on her and Nelson seemed to be the way in. I was not really familiar with his work, but after shooting two complete recording sessions I gained so much respect for him. He was very strong, in total command, and knew exactly what he wanted from the orchestra. You could see how much Linda respected him, and he was very respectful of her. She was very relaxed. She was reading *The Book of Laughter and Forgetting* (by Milan Kundera) in her recording booth while waiting to sing."

Viewing this footage, I was stunned by Nelson's severely weakened condition. His face was wan and distorted. With his hair combed straight back and his serious demeanor, I noticed how much he resembled Yitzhak Rabin, the late Prime Minister of Israel. As he walked out of the studio that day, it was obvious that this was a man who didn't have long to live.

Four weeks later, I happened to be in Los Angeles on business. On a Saturday morning I drove over to Carroll's, the Beverly Hills men's store. The moment I walked in the door, someone yelled out, "Pete!" It was Nelson, who was being fitted for a new gabardine suit. I hadn't seen him in many years. I congratulated him on his work with Linda Ronstadt. He smiled and told me how much he was enjoying working with her. I recall that he was more outgoing that day than at any other time I had been in his company. Incredibly, he looked healthy, unlike his appearance on the videotape that had been shot a month earlier.

Nelson's true feelings came out during two encounters late that summer. The first was at a dinner in Santa Monica with Naomi, Vic Lewis, and Lewis's wife, Jill. During Naomi's tirade about what he was permitted to eat, Nelson said to Jill, "The problem that has plagued me all my life is that women all seemed to fall in love with me, and I can't understand why." The second was when he said to his old friend George Duning at a memorial concert for Arthur Schwartz at the Uris Theater in New York, "I have a woman who really loves me, [Laurie Brooks] but I'm afraid to marry her. If I married her I'd be financially ruined. I'm the most unhappy man in the world."

★ ★ ★

After performing at a September 11, 1985, Hollywood Bowl concert with Ella Fitzgerald, Nelson flew to New York to conduct an orchestra at an outdoor concert at the South Street Seaport. Pauline Canny's cameraman shot the concert as part of her *Sunday Morning* story. Canny invited her good friend—my wife—*60 Minutes* producer Grace Diekhaus and me to the concert.

Just before it began, we stood on the dock with Pauline's crew as Nelson was being hoisted by two men atop a barge where his orchestra was set up to play. He looked straight at me and obviously had no idea who I was. He looked ghastly and extremely unhappy. The concert was a disaster. It was about fifty-five degrees that night, with a blustery wind blowing in off the East River, which made it doubly difficult for the musicians to play. His arrangements were not interpreted with any flavor; Sinatra was then working at Carnegie Hall and conceivably had contracted the best musicians available.

The following Monday, Nelson called Canny from Los Angeles to ask if she could wait a few weeks before coming out to interview him to complete the story. He informed her that his liver was giving him considerable trouble. Canny explained she was working on other stories and asked that he let her know when he was feeling better.

Later that month, Nelson took Ira Koslow and Gloria Boyce, Peter Asher's assistant, to lunch at Musso & Frank. "Any time any of Linda's records went gold or platinum, we went out to lunch with Nelson," Koslow recalled. "He looked terrible that day—very pale and pasty."

On September 29, Nelson checked into Cedars-Sinai Medical Center for hepatitis treatment. His son Chris and Laurie Brooks were frequent visitors. Reportedly, Naomi once again refrained from going to see her husband after he entered the hospital, restricting her contact to the telephone. She and Nelson had been living in a nearby rented house while their home was being renovated.

Earlier that month, Frank Military had completed his survey of Frank Sinatra's total recorded output. In a letter to Sinatra, he listed 260 songs "which you may have sung but I'm almost sure you never recorded," and added, "Naturally, the marriage of Sinatra and Riddle would be a dream come true for a lot of people out there."

Nelson spoke to Military from the hospital. Military then called Sinatra, who subsequently called Nelson. "It might be a few months before I'll be in any condition to record, Frank," Nelson explained. "Don't worry, Nelson," Sinatra said. "Get your strength back. I don't care how long it takes. The next album is with you." Nelson had already completed two arrangements for the proposed album before he entered Cedars.

Among other musicians, George Duning and Buddy DeFranco went to see him. DeFranco's close friendship with Nelson dated back thirty-one years, to the time when they both worked for Tommy Dorsey. The months (and often years) that musicians shared the never-ending life of long jumps in hot or cold buses, endless one-nighters, bad food, and awful accommodations helped cement relationships that were lifelong.

"He lay there totally limp," DeFranco remembered. "George and I were extremely shocked. He was fairly lucid, but certainly not close to the Nelson Riddle we knew. He didn't talk about dying. I think he expected to recover."

Chauncey Welsch and Rick Baptist visited Nelson on Friday, October 4. "I'd never seen anybody with yellow jaundice before," Baptist said. "It struck me how yellow he was. We had fun laughing a couple of times. I said to him, 'Nelson, when are we going to go back out and do the road stuff?' He replied, 'Oh, I don't know. I'm so weak right now.' We left around 9:30 that night. I said something to the nurse like, 'How's he going to do?' She just shook her head."

Suddenly, Nelson's condition worsened. His children were immediately notified. Naomi came to the hospital and signed the necessary forms to take him off life support. Nelson had agreed to a living will the year before. Rosemary Acerra and Maureen Riddle were told to come immediately from the East, and Cecily came up from Palm Desert.

Tina Bellini and her husband, Henry, had been at the hospital and had returned home to Escondido, only to receive a call concerning the gravity of her father's condition. They quickly returned to the hospital, and, on their arrival, Naomi said to Tina, "You can't go in there," which Tina vigorously protested. Tina reported that Naomi chose that moment to confront her with several department store bills, demanding to know who had been the recipient of the various items of women's clothing itemized on bills she had picked up at Nelson's post office box. Henry had to restrain his wife from physically attacking her stepmother.

On Sunday afternoon, October 6, 1985, shortly after 8:30 P.M., Nelson Riddle died in his private room at Cedars-Sinai Medical Center of cardiac and kidney failure. He was sixty-four years old. Naomi and all of his six children, as well as Tommy and Gwen Shepard, were at his bedside when he passed away. Contrary to his expressed wishes of having his ashes strewn into the sea, his remains are in a crypt at the Hollywood Forever Cemetery on Santa Monica Boulevard.

On the afternoon of October 10—the fortieth anniversary of Nelson's marriage to Doreen Moran—a memorial service was held at the chapel at the Westwood Memorial Park, the site of Marilyn Monroe's funeral, with about 150 mourners. Naomi asked Bob Bain to put together a trombone choir, which was composed of George Roberts, Tommy Shepard, Tommy Pederson, Lloyd Ulyate, Dick Noel, Chauncey Welsch, George Bohanon, and Chris Riddle, to play at the service.

Frank Sinatra called Chris the night before the service to inform him that he would not be attending. He was in New York, where he had gone to see his close friend Yul Brynner, who was dying of lung cancer. He was set to open at the Sands in Atlantic City the next night.

The morning of the service, the Riddle children met with attorney Ken Goldman to go over their father's will. According to Chris Riddle, Naomi had convinced Nelson to get rid of his previous attorney, Abe Marcus, calling him "senile." A few days later, Chris went to see Marcus, who said, "I warned your father about this woman," the implication being that Naomi had made Nelson alter the terms of the will.

Chris was inconsolable at the discovery of his father's failure to follow through with what he had told him in his last years were his intentions with his estate. It had its repercussions when George Roberts arrived from Lake Tahoe for the memorial service. When George told Chris how much his close friendship with Nelson meant to him, Chris bitterly remarked, "If he hadn't died, I probably would have killed him!"

Linda Ronstadt arrived in a limousine. When she got out of the car, she immediately saw Chauncey Welsch and threw her arms around him. She said, "Nelson and I would have done thirty-six more sides together." (Nelson and Linda had discussed collaborating on other projects—a study of Afro-Cuban music as well as an exploration of Antonio Carlos Jobim's brilliant melodies.)

Frank Sinatra, Jr., entered the chapel, but Naomi, upon seeing him, said to Bob Bain, "If his father can't attend, I don't want him here." When Frank, Jr., left in accordance with Naomi's bizarre request, he was asked by a reporter, "Does your father know about Orson Welles's death?" Show business lore is that death comes in threes, as had happened with the deaths of Riddle, Brynner, and Welles within a four-day period.

As the mourners entered the chapel, pianist Alan Broadbent played several songs Nelson had arranged for Sinatra. Bob Bain, as host, introduced Broadbent, who then delivered a plaintive version of "Spring Is Here." Nelson's daughters, Rosemary, Tina, Cecily, and Maureen, spoke, and were followed by David Rose, who gave the eulogy.

Billy May then spoke of his fondness for Nelson and saluted his extraordinary talent. During her remarks, Linda Ronstadt said, "I hope Nelson will forgive me for rock 'n' roll." (Ella Fitzgerald, sitting in the front row, said later she regretted that she wasn't asked to speak.) The trombone choir closed the service.

That night Sinatra called his son to hear about Nelson's funeral. He broke into tears when he heard of Orson Welles's death; they had been friends since Sinatra began singing with Harry James. When Frank, Jr., told his father about Naomi's directive at the funeral, the elder Sinatra referred to her as "a bad broad."

Following Nelson's death, Terry Woodson conducted the last three arrangements Nelson had written for *For Sentimental Reasons*: "But Not for Me" and the title song on November 18, 1985, and "Straighten Up and Fly Right" on December 2. On February 25, 1986, Nelson posthumously won his third Grammy for his "Lush Life" arrangement. During the summer of '86, the *For Sentimental Reasons* album was released.

Chris Riddle, ever the staunch defender of his father, was incensed that the 1991 Grammy for Best Instrumental Arrangement Accompanying Vocal(s) went to Johnny Mandel for his arrangement of "Unforgettable," the title song of Natalie Cole's extremely successful tribute album to her father's music. He claimed Mandel had merely copied Nelson's original arrangement. "They added a saxophone solo, but that essentially is the only difference," he said. Mandel contended that he completely rewrote the arrangement for "Unforgettable." "I don't really arrange like Nelson at all . . . but I loved the man. He was a dear friend of mine, and the last thing I would do is steal from him." Despite Chris's official protest, NARAS made no change in the award.

Charles Koppelman, who was running Capitol Records in the early 1990s, conceived of the idea of pairing Frank Sinatra with various pop stars (Bono of U2, Kenny G, Jimmy Buffett, Gloria Estefan, and, interestingly enough, Linda Ronstadt) and more traditional singers (Barbra Streisand, Tony Bennett, Steve Lawrence and Eydie Gorme, and Lena Horne) to record new duet versions of his biggest hits. This was accomplished through the magic of electronic overdubbing. Though *Duets* and *Duets II*, released in 1993 and 1995, were recorded at a time when Sinatra's voice was fading fast, they proved to be the most successful albums—in terms of sales—of his entire career. Not surprisingly, of the twenty-seven tracks included in the two albums, twelve were arrangements by Nelson Riddle, far more than any other arranger.

In the fall of 1996, Concord Records released Rosemary Clooney's *Dedicated to Nelson*, her testimonial to her former love. It was another of Clooney's heartfelt performances. Several of the arrangements were transcribed by John Oddo, Clooney's musical director, from her earlier albums with Nelson and her 1950s television show. On hand were such Riddle regulars as trumpeters Warren Leuning and Rick Baptist, trombonists Chauncey Welsch and George Roberts, and Sinatra's drummer, Gregg Field.

Mike Berkowitz, Nelson's one-time drummer, produced *Route 66: That Nelson Riddle Sound*, which was released in the winter of 2000 by Telarc Records. It featured

Erich Kunzel and the Cincinnati Pops "Big Band" Orchestra. Telarc's exemplary recorded sound did justice to eighteen of Nelson's best arrangements, and the 103-piece symphony orchestra actually swung on occasion—certainly no mean feat. One glaring error, however, was the omission of the well-known jazz chorus in Nelson's famous "The Lady Is a Tramp" chart. The failure to include George Roberts in the recording was another unfortunate mistake.

★ ★ ★

Naomi's continuing disdain for Nelson's children prevented them from receiving many of their father's personal possessions. A few weeks after the memorial service, Linda Ronstadt and Bob Bain separately invited Naomi out to lunch. In the course of their conversations with her, they both sought to dissuade her from her attitude toward Nelson's children. When they saw that it was of no use, they individually decided that they never wanted to see her again.

Chris wanted to continue his father's legacy by assuming the leadership of the Nelson Riddle Orchestra, but Naomi refused to give him access to Nelson's library of arrangements. Nonetheless, trumpeter George Werth had a number of Nelson's charts in his possession and was able to copy them for Chris. The first date of the Nelson Riddle Orchestra under Chris's direction was in Rochester, New York, in February 1986. Despite Naomi's hiring of a law firm, which sent Chris cease-and-desist letters, the Orchestra continues working to this day. On stage, Chris has a stage presence in front of an audience that his father never had.

In addition to community property, Nelson's royalties from his BMI account and most importantly from the Linda Ronstadt albums enabled Naomi to live quite comfortably after his death. In the next several years, she told several people how much she missed "dear Nelson." She died of emphysema in June 1998.

The terms of Naomi's will called for the University of Arizona to receive the proceeds from the sale of the Bel Air home ($1,225,000) to start the Nelson Riddle Archives and to fund scholarships in Nelson's name at the university's music department. Royalties from records and publishing continue to be paid to Naomi's estate and Nelson's estate.

On February 3, 2001, the Nelson Riddle Archives officially opened at the University of Arizona in Tucson with a gala concert of Nelson's music. Included in this concert was *Sinfonia Bravé*, Nelson's one attempt at writing a symphonic work; in reality, it was a mere eight-minute-long piece that sounded like the theme from a movie score. Riddle regular vibist/percussionist Emil Richards opened the program. Linda Ronstadt closed the concert performing eight of Nelson's arrangements backed by the university's symphony orchestra.

Those who knew Nelson best have never forgotten him. Arranger/composer Artie Butler referred to him as "the best of his era. You say Nelson Riddle, you hear the style." Louis Bellson observed, "For me, Nelson Riddle was to Sinatra, Nat Cole,

Following an August 1999 appearance at the Ventura County Fair by the Nelson Riddle Orchestra, are, left to right, trumpeter George Werth, bandleader Chris Riddle, Nelson's close friend (retired) Bob Bain, and trombonist Lloyd Ulyate.

Ella Fitzgerald, and Linda Ronstadt what Billy Strayhorn was to Duke Ellington." Linda Ronstadt said that Nelson is the person she misses more than anyone in her life who has passed away.[1] Saul Ilson remarked, "There isn't a day that goes by that I don't think of Nelson."

But saxophonist Ted Nash perhaps expressed it best when he said, "I was sixty-two when I headed for Carmel to retire. I sold all my instruments. There just wasn't the talent that we had when Nelson and all the good writers were around. As far as music was concerned, the charm was gone."

Notes

Chapter 1: The Jersey Years

1. It is important to note that the Grammys only started in 1958, making some of Nelson's finest work with Nat Cole and Frank Sinatra ineligible.

2. Riddle's dour demeanor was shared by a great many creators of significant music throughout history. From Ludwig van Beethoven and Wolfgang Amadeus Mozart in classical music to Hank Williams and Bob Dylan in modern popular music, there are countless examples of unhappy, bitter, and disillusioned personalities who only found solace and joy in the process of composing and performing their own musical creations. Rarely, if ever, was the success of their musical accomplishments reflected in their own personal happiness.

3. Nelson Riddle, *Arranged by Nelson Riddle* (Miami: Warner Bros., 1985), 193.

4. Ibid.

5. Ibid.

6. Ibid.

7. Will Friedwald, *Sinatra! The Song is You: A Singer's Art* (New York: Scribner, 1995), 209.

8. Ibid.

9. Nelson Riddle, unpublished material from *Arranged by Nelson Riddle* (Miami: Warner Bros., 1985)

10. Riddle, 193.

11. Ibid.

12. Ibid.

13. Ibid.

14. Friedwald, 377.

15. Riddle, 193.

16. Harvey Siders, "Nelson Riddle: Arranger, Composer, Conductor," *International Musician*, June 1973, 9.

Chapter 2: The Apprenticeship Continues

1. Nelson Riddle, unpublished material from *Arranged by Nelson Riddle* (Miami: Warner Bros., 1985).

2. Will Friedwald, *Sinatra! The Song is You: A Singer's Art* (New York: Scribner, 1995), 210.

3. Leonard Feather and Ira Gitler, *The Biographical Encyclopedia of Jazz* (New York: Oxford, 1999) 619.

4. Gunther Schuller, *The Swing Era* (New York: Oxford, 1989), 768.

5. Nelson Riddle, unpublished material from *Arranged by Nelson Riddle* (Miami: Warner Bros., 1985).

6. Ibid.

7. Ibid.

8. Ibid.

9. Friedwald, 211.

10. Ibid.

11. Ibid.

12. Riddle, *Arranged by Nelson Riddle* (Miami: Warner Bros., 1985), 166.

Chapter 3: The Sentimental Gentleman of Swing

1. Nelson Riddle, *Arranged by Nelson Riddle* (Miami: Warner Bros., 1985), 166.
2. Nelson Riddle, "Nelson Riddle Talking," *Crescendo International,* August 1967, 10.
3. Riddle, *Arranged by Nelson Riddle,* 166.
4. Keith Keller, *Oh, Jess! A Jazz Life* (New York: Mayan Music Corporation, 1989), 116.
5. George T. Simon, *The Big Bands* (New York: Macmillan, 1967), 328.
6. Leonard Feather and Ira Gitler, *The Biographical Encyclopedia of Jazz* (New York: Oxford, 1999), 505.
7. Esther Williams with Digby Diehl, *The Million Dollar Mermaid* (New York: Simon and Schuster, 1999), 222.
8. Riddle, *Arranged by Nelson Riddle,* 167.

9. Nelson Riddle, *Arranged by Nelson Riddle* (Miami: Warner Bros., 1985), 194.
10. Ibid., 5.
11. Ibid., 194.
12. Ibid.
13. Friedwald, 209.
14. Ibid., 214.
15. Nelson Riddle, unpublished material from *Arranged by Nelson Riddle* (Miami: Warner Bros., 1985).
16. Friedwald, 215.
17. Daniel Mark Epstein, *Nat King Cole* (New York: Farrar Straus & Giroux, 1999), 207–208.
18. Ibid., 209.
19. Leonard Feather, "The Great Performances," liner notes from *The Nat King Cole Story,* Capitol CD CDP 7 95129 2.

Chapter 4: Hollywood Calling

1. Will Friedwald, *Sinatra! The Song Is You: A Singer's Art* (New York: Scribner, 1995), 212.
2. Ibid., 213.
3. Leonard Feather and Ira Gitler, *The Biographical Encyclopedia of Jazz* (New York: Oxford, 1999), 157.
4. Ibid.
5. Peter J. Levinson, *Trumpet Blues: The Life of Harry James* (New York: Oxford, 1999), 162.
6. Carol Easton, "Jazz Orchestra in Residence 1971," in *Reading Jazz,* ed. Robert Gottlieb (New York: Pantheon, 1996), 513.
7. Charles L. Granata, *Sessions with Sinatra* (Chicago: Acappella, 1999), 83.
8. David M. Kennedy, *Freedom from Fear* (New York: Oxford, 1999), 657.

Chapter 5: Nat "King" Cole Was a Merry Old Soul

1. Leonard Feather and Ira Gitler, *The Biographical Encyclopedia of Jazz* (New York: Oxford, 1999), 139.
2. Ibid.
3. Daniel Mark Epstein, *Nat King Cole* (New York: Farrar Straus & Giroux, 1999), 255.
4. Todd S. Purdom, "Behind the Wheel and Driving the Nation's Culture," *New York Times,* 17 September 2000, sec. 4, p. 1.
5. Epstein, 223.
6. Will Friedwald and Dick Katz, liner notes for *Piano Style of Nat King Cole.*
7. Nelson Riddle, "Branching Out from the Music," *Crescendo International,* September 1967, 21.
8. Nelson Riddle, *Arranged by Nelson Riddle* (Miami: Warner Bros., 1985), 170.

9. Epstein, 288–290.

10. Michael Korda, *Another Life* (New York: Random House, 1999).

11. David Sterritt, "Alienated, Spontaneous, Non-Political: Sound Familiar?," *New York Times*, 29 August 1999, Arts & Leisure Section.

12. Riddle, *Arranged by Nelson Riddle*, 170.

13. Ibid., 68.

14. Epstein, 309.

15. Ibid.

16. Paul Grein, *Capitol Fiftieth Anniversary 1942–1992* (Hollywood: Capitol Records, 1992), 94.

17. Will Friedwald, *Sinatra! The Song Is You: A Singer's Art* (New York: Scribner, 1995), 216.

Chapter 6: "The Voice" Becomes a Cello

1. Quoted in Ezra Goodman, "The Kid from Hoboken," *Time*, 29 August 1955.

2. Frank Rose, *The Agency* (New York: Harper Business, a division of HarperCollins, 1995), 178–79.

3. Will Friedwald, *Sinatra! The Song Is You: A Singer's Art* (New York: Scribner, 1995), 216.

4. Charles L. Granata, *Sessions with Sinatra* (Chicago: Acappella, 1999), 86.

5. Kitty Kelley, *His Way: The Unauthorized Biography of Frank Sinatra* (New York: Bantam, 1986), 36.

6. Pete Hamill, *Why Sinatra Matters* (New York: Little, Brown, 1998), 71.

7. Peter J. Levinson, *Trumpet Blues: The Life of Harry James* (New York: Oxford, 1999), 68.

8. Robin Douglas-Home, *Sinatra* (New York: Michael Joseph, 1962), 25.

9. Tom Kuntz and Phil Kuntz, eds., *The Sinatra Files* (New York: Three Rivers Press, 2000), 9–10, 18–19.

10. Ezra Goodman, "The Kid from Hoboken," *Time*, 29 August 1955, 58.

11. Friedwald, 220–221.

12. Nelson Riddle, "Branching Out from the Music," *Crescendo International*, September 1967, 22.

13. John Rockwell, *Sinatra: An American Classic* (New York: Random House, 1984), 141.

14. Nelson Riddle, *Arranged by Nelson Riddle* (Miami: Warner Bros., 1985), 165.

15. Ibid.

16. Steven Petkov and Leonard Muslazza, *The Frank Sinatra Reader* (New York: Oxford, 1995), 60.

17. Riddle, "Branching Out from the Music," 20.

18. Riddle, *Arranged by Nelson Riddle*, 171.

19. Ibid., 170.

20. Douglas-Home, 34–35.

21. Granata, 100.

22. Riddle, *Arranged by Nelson Riddle*, 169.

23. Hamill, 170.

24. Granata, 121.

25. Friedwald, 236.

26. Nelson Riddle, unpublished material from *Arranged by Nelson Riddle* (Miami: Warner Bros., 1985).

27. Friedwald, 275.

28. Grein, 61.

29. Hamill, 172.

30. Kelley, 404.

31. Nelson Riddle, "Nelson Riddle and the Standards of Sinatra," *Crescendo International*, October 1981, 24.

32. Ibid.
33. Friedwald, 219.
34. Douglas-Home, 35.

Chapter 7: A Flourishing Career

1. Nelson Riddle, unpublished material from *Arranged by Nelson Riddle* (Miami: Warner Bros., 1985).
2. Gerald Clarke, *Get Happy: The Life of Judy Garland* (New York: Random House, 2000), 198.
3. Rosemary Clooney with Joan Barthel, *Girl Singer* (New York: Doubleday, 1999), 154.
4. Ibid., 184.
5. Stephen Holden, "Pop/Jazz Arrangers: What Are They?," *New York Times*, 11 October 1991.
6. Nelson Riddle, "Branching Out from the Music," *Crescendo International*, September 1967, 20.
7. Joseph F. Laredo, liner notes for *Great Ladies of Song, Spotlight on Keely Smith*, Capitol Records CDP07777 80327 2 4, 1994.
8. Online interview, MisterLUCKY.com. March 25, 2000.
9. Nelson Riddle, "Nelson Riddle Talking," *Crescendo International*, August 1967, 10.
10. Nelson Riddle, *Arranged by Nelson Riddle* (Miami: Warner Bros., 1985), 174.
11. Stuart Nicholson, *Ella Fitzgerald: A Biography of the First Lady of Jazz* (New York: Scribner, 1993), 184.
12. Ibid., 185.
13. Riddle, "Branching Out from the Music," 21.
14. Riddle, *Arranged by Nelson Riddle*, 173.
15. Clooney, 188.
16. Ibid., 189.
17. Ibid., 185.
18. Mark LeBrito, *Kubrick: A Biography* (New York: Donald J. Fine, 1997).
19. Clooney, 198.
20. Peter J. Levinson, "Oscar and Riddle: an ideal mating," *Melody Maker*, 11 January 1964.
21. Riddle, *Arranged by Nelson Riddle*, 174–175.
22. Riddle, "Branching Out from the Music," 22.

Chapter 8: The Difficult Years

1. Nelson Riddle, *Arranged by Nelson Riddle* (Miami: Warner Bros., 1985), 174.
2. Harvey Siders, "Nelson Riddle: Arranger-Composer-Conductor," *International Musician*, June 1973, page 18.
3. Ibid.
4. Ibid.
5. Ibid.
6. Irene Kahn Atkins, "Yes, Sir, That's My Gatsby," *Crescendo International*, June 1974, 16.
7. Ibid., page 18.
8. John L. Scott, "Double Yearning in Life of Riddle," *Los Angeles Times*, 29 August 1966.
9. Siders, 18.
10. Kit Snedeker, *Los Angeles Herald Examiner*, 14 September 1975, Tempo section.
11. Siders, 18.
12. Walter Arlen, "'Santa Monica' Suite Premiered," *Los Angeles Times*, 20 May 1975, sec. IV, p. 12.
13. *People* magazine file for Todd Gold, "A Riddle Named Nelson Riddle gives the Answer to Linda Ronstadt's Oldies LP, *What's New*," 17 October 1983, 59.

Chapter 9: Linda Ronstadt and the Last Hurrah

1. Nelson Riddle, *Arranged by Nelson Riddle* (Miami: Warner Bros., 1985), 134–135.

2. Les Tompkins, "Nelson Riddle Today," *Crescendo International,* August–September 1981, 21.

3. *People* magazine file for Todd Gold, "A Riddle Named Nelson Riddle gives the Answer to Linda Ronstadt's Oldies LP, *What's New,*" 17 October 1983, 59.

4. Leonard Feather, liner notes for *The Best Is Yet to Come,* Pablo Records OJCCD-889-2 (2312-138), 1982.

5. Stephen Holden, "Linda Ronstadt Celebrates the Golden Age of Pop," *New York Times,* 4 September 1983.

6. Ibid.

7. Steve Bloom, "An Intimate Conversation with Linda Ronstadt," *Down Beat,* July 1985.

8. Ibid.

9. *People* magazine file for Nov. 7, 1983 story on Nelson Riddle.

Chapter 10: The Final Chorus

1. Jonathan Schwartz, "Linda Ronstadt: Checking with the Ex-Flower Child at Home in Arizona," *US Magazine,* 18–25 December 2000, 94.

Index